DATE DUE		
MAY 1 8 1984 8 1998		
JUN 2 2 1984 AUG 1 8 2001		
OCT 1 0 1984		
MAR 8 1986		
JUL 2 6 1986		
DEC 2 0 1988		
MAR 1 5 1989		
AUG 6 1990		
AUG 2 1 1991		
MAY 1 6 1994		
JAN 1 8 1996		
MAR 1 1 1998		

Tolstoy and Gandhi, Men of Peace

Also by Martin Green

in
The Lust for Power
Trilogy

The Challenge of the Mahatmas
Dreams of Adventure, Deeds of Empire

Tolstoy and Gandhi, Men of Peace

A Biography

MARTIN GREEN

Basic Books, Inc., Publishers   New York

Library of Congress Cataloging in Publication Data

Green, Martin Burgess, 1927–
  Tolstoy and Gandhi, men of peace.

  Bibliography: p. 300
  Includes index.
  1. Tolstoy, Leo, graf, 1828–1910—Biography.
2. Gandhi, Mahatma, 1869–1948. 3. Tolstoy, Leo, graf,
1828–1910—Religion and ethics. 4. Pacifists—Soviet
Union—Biography. 5. Pacifists—India—Biography.
I. Title.
PG3385.G7   1983   327.1′72′0922 [B]   82-72397
ISBN 0–465–08631–4

To Ann Cobb, Diane Wynne,

Inga Karetknikova,

and the other friends and colleagues

who have shared my interest

in Tolstoy and Gandhi

Contents

Foreword

This is the third and final part of a trilogy, *The Lust for Power*, of which the first parts are entitled *The Challenge of the Mahatmas* and *Dreams of Adventure, Deeds of Empire*. This seemingly substantial volume is actually a pocket-sized abridgment of my *Tolstoy and Gandhi*. I have been convinced that no one wants to read my full-length treatment of the topic, and I am indeed grateful that Basic Books is willing to risk publishing this much—two thousand manuscript pages have been reduced to four hundred and fifty. I at first made two volumes of the single narrative, one telling the two life stories, the other describing the two life settings. Now I have reduced the first volume by half and left what I might call a thematic biography, meaning that some events are merely named, whereas others, intrinsically no more interesting, are treated quite expansively. The principle of selection was not the topic's importance in the life of Tolstoy or Gandhi but its importance in my argument, which means the importance in my eyes of my comments on that point. Formally, I think the result is quite interesting. Morally, I must apologize for pushing myself forward and interrupting the reader's communion with Tolstoy and Gandhi. My intention in beginning the book was precisely to give the reader a communion, contemplation, or confrontation, with two great men, but that was not to be; the law and the systematization of our intellectual life work against such intentions.

Acknowledgments

Of the institutions which have in various ways supported my work on this book, I want to acknowledge Tufts University, where I teach; Basic Books, who published the trilogy of which this is a part; the Woodrow Wilson International Center for Scholars, where I spent the year 1980–81, and the Guggenheim Foundation.

I wish to acknowledge the Navajivan Trust for permission to reprint excerpts from the *Collected Works of Mahatma Gandhi*, volumes 1 through 77. I also gratefully acknowledge George Allen & Unwin for permission to reprint excerpts from *The Final Struggle*.

Tolstoy and Gandhi, Men of Peace

clude, with varying degrees of importance, almost any kind of cultural triumphalism, or excited grandeur, or dominance and splendor in life. Only a world view that is on principle hostile to all
those can be secure against imperialism. Of course it must show
appreciation of imperialism too, to be plausible, but appreciation of
the kind that follows from renunciation. Thus, the only root of effective anti-imperialism is asceticism. And the only men who, in
their time, said no to life with real authority were Tolstoy and
Gandhi.

Of course they did not reject every kind of pleasure or every kind
of power; but of the immense range available to civilized men (that
is, to first-class citizens of great empires) they rejected so great a
quantity that there is a qualitative difference between them and
other political philosophers. It is the difference between political
radicalism and the religious radicalism that we can identify with
Tolstoy and Gandhi.

The phrase *religious radicalism*, however, brings together two powerful ideas, each of which has a number of facets, so that it could
mean many things. What I mean by religion here is in effect the
opposite of empire: that which binds people together and motivates
the group not at or from the peak of its pyramid but from its base,
not for conquest but for resistance, not in pride of greatness, but in
solidarity of faith. This definition is obviously not objective or val-
ue-free, but partisan and tendentious. I would not, in other arguments, deny the name of religion to the kind of vision that inspired
the Crusades or militant Islam, but here I mean something quite
different from that. *Empire* here means a complex of technology and
ideology (the rationalism, democracy, and economic enterprise of
the West) that often offers itself as anti-imperialist, but can be seen
by underdeveloped peoples as dominative. And so religion, as the
opposite and opponent of empire, means the resistance to all those
things.

Tolstoy and Gandhi's faith was essentially antihumanist. They
saw humanism as the self-indulgent world view of the ruling classes of great empires. They did not want wealth for everyone. In fact
they wanted poverty—not, of course, destitution—but material and
spiritual poverty. Tolstoy's religion was essentially kenotic, self-
emptying. The prayers he composed in his diary reflect this: "Help
me, O Lord, so to annihilate myself that you may live in me, pass
through me, that I may be nothing but your manifestation."[1]

Such a prayer is of course perfectly orthodox Christian devotion and would not be eccentric in Hinduism, or Buddhism, or Judaism, or Islam. But I think that most of my readers will find it eccentric, even shocking. They will guess, rightly, that Tolstoy (and Gandhi) had a martyr complex; they wanted to die for their faith.

Their religion was existential rather than theological or ecclesiastical; it was rooted in their living and dying. That is why they must be studied biographically, and not, as Gandhi was studied in the 1960s, tactically. The roots of their teaching, its structure, and its sanctions are all to be found in the detail of their behavior, private as well as public, and in their early preprophetic lives as well as in their prophetic phases. In particular, we shall look at Tolstoy's art and his cult of "domestic happiness," both in his writing and in his home, and at Gandhi's politics and his "nation building" in South Africa and India. These were the fields in which the two men rose to eminence during the years I have called "Youth," and so increased their scope during the years I have called "Manhood" that they both became world-famous. They were already great men by virtue of their achievements in these two areas, before or besides becoming men of religion; which in Tolstoy's case came later, in Gandhi's ran alongside in uneasy tandem. But their religion, their cult of peace, and their attack upon empire, all had their roots in their other experience.

Their religious prophecy was only the ultimate resource they turned to when more moderate measures failed in a long-drawn resistance movement, which included Tolstoy's art and Gandhi's nationalism. Both were resisting the same thing—the enormous and diffuse spread of the modern-world system, reaching like an octopus into Russia in the nineteenth century and into India in the twentieth, and undermining with its tentacular and electrical embrace the cultural bedrock of the lives into which Tolstoy and Gandhi were born. In the ultimate analysis—so it seems to me—both men were always reacting against that system in all their various self-manifestations, Tolstoy as officer and as novelist, Gandhi as lawyer and as reformer, and finally and above all as saint. They learned the tricks of the new culture early in their lives. In their middle years they saw, with increasing dismay, its destruction of the old, the cyclical, the continuous popular culture. In old age they threw themselves into a defense of that old culture (still established among the poor and uneducated) which was at the same time an assertion of something older and newer than all culture.

The plan of this book is to present the two lives side by side, in all their various phases, in such a way as to reveal the historical forces to which they were always responding. To do this, I have often had to use terms that may seem slightly odd, because they are the only ones that put such disparate phenomena into a single focus. The most difficult case of this, for which I wish to prepare the reader, is my use of aesthetic terms for Gandhi's politics. But I also use political terms for Tolstoy's art. This is most obtrusive in the period of *War and Peace* and *satyagraha* in South Africa.

Thus, during the period I have labeled "Manhood," Tolstoy wrote two great novels, *War and Peace* and *Anna Karenina*, and Gandhi led two great political campaigns, one in South Africa and the other in India, which humbled the rulers of the British Empire. Their achievements, disparate though they were, both defied imperialism: Gandhi's in an obvious sense, Tolstoy's by declaring a faith in private life and domestic happiness, in opposition to public and political values. *War and Peace* teaches us that it is in Natasha and Pierre that true life is to be found, not in Napoleon and his conquests.

The activities of both men, therefore, were anti-imperialist. But their opposition could not be called radical, much less religious. They were liberal and secular protests against empires. In fact, Tolstoy was still a loyal son of Russia in writing those two books (though a son of "organic" Russia rather than the state) and Gandhi was still a loyal son of the British Empire (though only as long as it lived up to its principles). But they represented the unwilling or involuntary subjects of empire, those who belonged to different races, to castes, sexes, or ages other than the rulers.

As for secularism, in Gandhi's case there was a subjective religious component to what he did, but it was separable from the political component—at least, it was separated by his followers and his enemies, and just about everyone except Gandhi himself. In Tolstoy's case, there was a religious depth and ground to his feeling for marriage and family life, for art and folk culture, but his religion was then a pantheistic reinforcement of life's ordinary pleasures, not an ascetic spirituality.

Of course Gandhi and Tolstoy were not unique in their cult of the family and of the nation. These were two of the most highly valued structures of nineteenth-century civilization. Nation building and family happiness were the two cultural activities, in the public and private spheres respectively, which were then culturally sacred—in a liberal and secular sense of sacred. (Nation building was a slogan used about Gandhi in India almost as portentously as family happiness was used by Tolstoy about his own life choices.) Not only Tolstoy, but the nineteenth-century novel in general, was dedicated to celebrating the family; and nineteenth-century politics in general was officially devoted to winning independence and self-government for national groups.

Perhaps consequently, both were to some degree cults of power and splendor, and so contained an "imperialist" tendency. When Germany finally achieved nationhood in 1870, the coping stone was placed upon the new structure by Chancellor Bismarck, who declared that Germany was again an empire. Nationalism turned out to have meant imperialism. And the power and property struggles between Tolstoy and his wife and children at Yasnaya Polyana—and those depicted in The Kreutzer Sonata and "The Death of Ivan Ilych"—show how much was at stake in the nineteenth-century home, where every man was king of his own castle, or—if his home was dedicated to life values—consort to a queen whose subjects were children and servants. If we were discussing politics in the limited sense, it would be outrageous to include these considerations in the argument, but we are discussing the roots and sources of imperialism, among which they must surely be counted.

Consequently, there were firm limits to the effectiveness of this liberal anti-imperialism. And it was only in the next period, which I have called "Old Age," that Tolstoy turned away from this social and secular faith, toward something essentially opposite. In Gandhi's case, the chronological change is not so clear-cut. From early on, Gandhi was trying with his right hand to make religious values prevail in politics, while with his left he advanced the political interests of Indians against those of competing groups. But one can say that it was in old age that he became most aware of the difference between the two activities, especially when he saw his followers take up the work of his left hand, and ignore that of his right. He himself shifted to and fro, trying to combine the two. (India was to be a great nation, but one dedicated to more than national values.)

Thus the crucial period of their lives, from this book's point of view, was their old age. As an old man, Tolstoy began to speak and to act on the same range of topics as Gandhi. His basic tone became more existential, more challenging, sometimes strident, sometimes—and this is when he was most like Gandhi—meek. You can hear this Tolstoy in his letter to the Tsar in 1881. "I, an insignificant, unqualified, weak, sinful man, am writing a letter to the Rus-

sian Emperor."² And: "Return good for evil, do not resist evil, forgive everyone. This and this alone needs to be done; this is the will
of God."³ Another mark of the general change, and one that especially reminds us of Gandhi, is Tolstoy's frequent use of Gospel passages as epigraphs, for both fiction and nonfiction.

He was now speaking not as artist but as prophet—like Gandhi.
But if we look not at his manner of speech but at his way of life, we
see much less change; and in that discrepancy lies the tragedy of
those thirty years. Tolstoy's life was still that of a nobleman and a
bookman, and the struggles he was involved in had mostly to do
with books.

It was during this time that he wrote those works, fiction and
nonfiction, which acted directly on Gandhi's imagination: notably
The Kingdom of God Is Within You (1893) but also *What Then Must We
Do?* (1886), "Why Men Stupefy Themselves" (1890), and *The First
Step* (1892).

Concomitantly, Tolstoy made changes in his lifestyle, which also
acted powerfully on Gandhi's imagination. In October 1884 he gave
up hunting; by November 1885 he had given up eating white
bread, was retiring to bed at nine, and not going out socially; by
February 1888, he had given up smoking, eating meat, and drinking
wine. He also began to do the manual labor on which his family
depended: splitting the wood they burned, and in the mornings
replenishing their stoves and bringing the water from the well. He
began to pay much more attention and give much more sympathy
to the revolutionaries, and became himself a political, though in
some sense passive, rebel.

He began to identify himself with the suffering and the humiliated. He wanted to be a *yurodivi,* one of God's fools. He develops this
idea in his diary entry for May 23, 1893: "to let oneself seem inferi-
or to what one is is the supreme attribute of virtue"; and (a little
later) "to let oneself be thought feeble and foolish." And he made
an interesting application of this idea to the art of writing. On August 29, 1889, he told himself he was wrong to worry about the
imperfections in *The Kreutzer Sonata*; artistic perfection would not
make his message more convincing, and "one must be a *yurodivi* in
one's writing too."⁴

The term is of course Russian, but the idea is Indian enough, and
it was one of Gandhi's instruments of self-definition. Going to the
Round Table Conference in London in 1931 he said: "I must go to
London with God as my only guide. One has therefore to appear

before Him in all one's weakness, empty-handed and in a spirit of full surrender. . . ."[5] While there he alarmed his industrialist friend G. D. Birla by saying that he had no idea of what he would say at the next session; he had prepared nothing and would rely on God's inspiration when the moment came. "After all, we have to talk like simple men. I have no desire to appear extra-intelligent. Like a simple villager all that I have to say is: 'We want independence.'"[6]

Similarly, religious and ascetic simplicity came to seem to Tolstoy more valuable than material or intellectual splendor. When he read Bellamy's *Looking Backward* in June 1889, for example, he noted that the one thing in it he didn't like was the Marxist-Socialist idea that in an ideal future everyone would have the luxuries now restricted to a few. We must all renounce luxury; we cannot serve God and Mammon.

By means of these changes in behavior and opinion, Tolstoy approached ideals with which he and Gandhi had long been familiar, but which had seemed hitherto to be discredited by their association with the defeated East, or the outgrown past, and destined to be confidently neglected by the triumphant modern West. Now one of the greatest intellectuals of the modern West had taken them up. During this period, moreover, Tolstoy turned to India, to China, and to the East in general, in search of truths, models, and traditions with which to replace those of his own culture. He became an Orientalist. But unlike Tagore, Arnold, Besant, or Nivedita, Tolstoy was not attracted by the colorful or splendid or mysterious aspects of the East, but by its traditions of asceticism. He was not attracted by the *rajas* but by the *sanyasis*; not by the poets but by the Buddhists; not by the great art but by the humble lives.

He became the same sort of Orientalist as Gandhi, who in 1924 wrote to an American student who had asked for a slice of Oriental wisdom: "We are taught from childhood discipline in self-restraint. Though, therefore, in the East, we ever fail to live up to it, we know that life is not for indulgence but essentially for self-denial. Would that the students of America could imbibe that one lesson."[7] Life is not for living but for service, he says elsewhere. Hinduism does not believe in men's egotism or their carnality but in their spirituality. That is to say, Hindus have no saints like the West's, "who have laid down their lives in exploring the remotest or highest regions of earth."[8]

In all this, therefore, Gandhi followed Tolstoy, in the corresponding phase of his own life. Both became manifestations of ascesis, incarnate denials of appetite, repudiations of ego, diminishments of self, limitations of consciousness. They made themselves each a multiform negative, saying no to so many things that the modern system said yes to—pleasures and powers it affirmed, urged, and propagated—that they may be said to have said no to life itself. The old negatives, religious and moral, had been very much weakened by the expansive thrust of modern culture. The Devil had died during the eighteenth century, and God was dying in the nineteenth. And many restrictions that had been built into life by poverty and material scarcity, and then had been traditionally endorsed and valued as morally right, were now done away with. And other freedoms were bestowed on man by science and technology, like birth control and medical cures. Possibilities of pleasure, invitations to appetite, opened up in every direction, accentuating the positive aspects of life. Tolstoy and Gandhi set themselves the task of creating new negatives, which derived from the traditions of the past, and which revived those traditions to some degree, but were modern in their morality and rationality, and existential in their ultimate source. These negatives were rooted in these two men's lives and deaths. Their lives were to be deaths, so that out of that brokenness new life might grow.

Both began to call themselves old men during this period, though they were only in their fifties. They were never middle-aged; they never looked physically substantial, settled, and prosperous, in the way that corresponds to financial and social substantiality, house holding, or stock holding.

They became old men because theirs was an old man's philosophy: a counsel of renunciation, a warning against appetite and enthusiasm, a serious call to a devout and earnest life, a bitter and detoxifying draught. It was not an old man's philosophy of the kind that includes and harmonizes all the previous phases of life. They did not speak out of a long experience of life's pleasures and promises, discriminating the better from the worse like epicures. What they said denied those pleasures, unmasked those promises, and was offered as the truth for young men as well as old. In fact, both thought they had only recaptured at the moment of their enlightenment a truth they had known long before, as children, and had lost as adolescents and young men.

So we may say that for them (and in them, for us) the idea of humanity, the fate of being human, is summed up in the image of the old man speaking with authority. This will help us to under-

stand some of our resistance to them, since for us being human is
summed up in the image of youth moving forward.

One might say that Tolstoy and Gandhi made it their work to
rediscover a negative vocabulary, to reintroduce *no* and *not* into our
moral syntax. Of course, people in fact are always saying no, and
often from sinister motives. But Tolstoy and Gandhi rooted their
negations in their own lives and deaths and thus completed a set of
terms for their contemporaries which could be compared with the
moral vocabulary of classical civilization.

SECTION I

The First Nineteen Years

Tolstoy 1828–1847 • Gandhi 1869–1888

The Beginnings

Lev Nikolaevich Tolstoy was born on August 28, 1828. He was the
fourth son of Count Nikolai Ilyich Tolstoy and his wife Marya, who
had been a Princess Volkonsky. The Tolstoys were quite a grand,
though not very rich or fashionable, family allied to many other
such families (some much closer to power and patronage than they
were themselves) and owning some picturesque and impressive figures in their ancestry. Perhaps they could be compared with the
Byrons as a family for a writer to be born into. And to Tolstoy as to
Byron, the fact that he was born noble was an important but enigmatic fact, especially once he decided he must be a writer.

The family home, Yasnaya Polyana, was a country house in a
large park ten miles from Tula, one of Russia's twenty largest cities,
and itself about a hundred and thirty miles south of Moscow. It had
been built, or rather begun, by Lev Nikolaevich's grandfather,
Prince Volkonsky, and completed by his father, Count Nikolai. It
was a striking, perhaps one might say an amazing building. In its
size and its newness, and above all in its overweening relation to its

setting, especially the human setting of the serfs of the vicinity, it can remind us of some of those Southern mansions—built with slave labor—that Faulkner describes.

Yasnaya Polyana remained Tolstoy's home all his life. It played an important part in his sense of himself and of the destiny he had chosen—it changed parts as that destiny changed—and it played an important part in his fiction, thinly disguised. So it is important to realize the enormous disparity between that house and the other dwellings (serfs' huts) in the village of Yasnaya Polyana. For one thing, it had forty-two rooms; and during most of Tolstoy's own married life, though he had thirteen children, he and his family lived in a somewhat expanded version of one wing. In his childhood, there were thirty servants living in the house to look after the Tolstoys. (The servants did not have rooms of their own, but slept in corners and corridors.) And for another thing, the "Italianate" style of the architecture, and the books, piano, paintings, and so on that went with it, all represented a Western European taste that was categorically foreign to the people of the village. There was an enormous disparity between the piano sonatas of John Field that Countess Marya played and the songs of the village women who heard her through the window. If Yasnaya Polyana had been an English country house, set in, say, the Brontes' Yorkshire, there would still have been disparity (think only for a moment of Heathcliff peering in at the Lintons's window), but in Russia there was the extra fact that this upper-class culture was imported. The roots of native Russian culture, however much they had been cultivated, would never have blossomed into art of this Western and aristocratic kind.

The Tolstoys were humane people, closely bound to their serfs, especially those of the village of Yasnaya Polyana. They accepted responsibility for them in many ways, and knew a great deal about their lives, things which neighbors in our society do not know about each other. But they were also set far apart from them by the difference in rank, or in caste, which brought with it such a difference in lifestyle and feeling style. Tolstoy's novels can deceive the reader about this, for the sensibility of their narrative voice—which is the standard nineteenth-century literary sensibility—is more liberal than that of his caste.

Mohandas Karamchand Gandhi was born on the second of October, 1869. He was the fourth child of Karamchand Gandhi, who was the chief minister to the ruling prince of Porbandar, a small state in

Kathiawar, which is a projecting part of the Western coast of India, north of Bombay. His mother, Putlibai, was Karamchand's fourth wife, only thirteen when she married, and of quite a low social class. Because his third wife, who had proven infertile, was still alive, he could not aspire to an equal match. In any case, the Gandhis were not a grand family like the Tolstoys, to whom one might compare, among Hindus, the Tagores of Calcutta. Nor were they a noble family; they belonged not to the Kshattriyas, India's warrior caste, but to the Banias, the commercial caste.

Nevertheless, the Gandhis were not a commercial family; their hereditary vocation was administration. The position Karamchand held, in some sense the highest in Porbandar, had been in his family for three generations. They were, therefore, closer to Brahmins in their social functions, for Brahmins have traditionally administered kingdoms on behalf of their kings. The kings belonged to the Kshattriya caste, but they left the daily work of ruling to men of the Brahmin caste, or—more often in Kathiawar—to Banias. In medieval times, English kings also employed clerics like Thomas à Becket and Cardinal Wolsey in this way. In more recent times, this custom is harder to trace, because of the disappearance of the caste system, or at least the caste vocabulary, in Western Europe. But the great bureaucratic administrators of nineteenth-century Whitehall—those hard-working Stephens and Stracheys—played essentially the same role, and were recognizable Brahmin-Banias.

Porbandar is a sea city built of limestone and is said to first appear to sailors on the Arabian sea as a bright flash of white on the horizon. It had long been full of sailors, fishermen, and travelers. But very little of this atmosphere was appropriated by Gandhi. We do not imagine him as a boy sitting at the feet of some grizzled sea dog, and feeding his soul on the tales of adventure. Almost his only reference of this sort is to Porbandar as a "village of fishermen" where he saw in their behavior the origin of the phrase "he drinks like a fish." Gandhi's Porbandar was obviously remote from theirs.

In Porbandar the Muslims were the ones who took to the seas and had the adventures. They carried the silks and cottons woven by the Hindus of Porbandar in their homes to Aden, Zanzibar, and Cape Town and sold them there. Hindus were forbidden by religion to cross the "great black waters." In Gandhi's experience (and on the whole in India) Muslims were bolder and more adventurous than Hindus. This division of roles was reflected in Gandhi's personal relations with his boyhood friend Mehtab. And the social division of Porbandar was reflected in Gandhi's unique position in Natal in the 1890s. He had been hired as legal counsel by a Muslim trader there who came from Porbandar, but he found himself also the only possible leader for thousands of Hindus brought over as indentured laborers.

The family home of the Gandhis was a three-story limestone house with walls twenty feet thick and stood about a quarter of a mile from the Arabian Ocean. (The walls were that thick to withstand siege from freebooters on that ocean.) It had been bought by Mohandas's great grandfather in 1777, just about the time Prince Volkonsky began to build Yasnaya Polyana. About twenty or twenty-five people lived in it in Mohandas's childhood. His grandfather had had six or seven sons, and all of them lived there with their families, each maintaining their own kitchen.

The house stood on three sides of an underground tank which was useful in a time of siege. There were marks in the walls made by shells fired at the house in the 1830s when Karamchand's father had offended the regent, Rupali Ba, an incident that led to the decisive intervention of the British in Porbandar affairs. In the adjoining temple was a memorial to an Arab bodyguard of Karamchand's grandfather, who had given his life to save his master. So the Gandhis were not untouched by the risks and responsibilities—and the violence—of power.

This house did not remain Gandhi's home for long or play anything like the same part in his life that Yasnaya Polyana did in Tolstoy's. Gandhi kept moving, while Tolstoy was rooted. But one can nevertheless read some parallel significances into the Gandhi house, and its difference from other houses nearby—from the king's palace not so far away, and from the miserable shacks in which the poor of Porbandar lived. The Gandhis were representatives of conscience, respectability, and responsibility; they were not rich, but they did belong to an elite. An Indian writer describes the family as "impoverished gentry."[1]

But Porbandar was a small world, left behind by world history. The British residents and political agents of Kathiawar represented the iron of modern reality, which, when it showed, made the manifold small states like Porbandar seem all crumbling stucco. Iron railways were built in Kathiawar in the 1880s, and iron bridges, iron ships, and iron machinery, were introduced all over India.

One great difference between Gandhi's starting point and Tolstoy's is that the iron in Russia was Russian iron. Yasnaya Polyana was in itself a pastoral, a dream world, but it stood only ten miles from Tula, which was the main supplier of armaments to the Russian army; and by means of that army the Russian empire was growing all through Tolstoy's lifetime, in Europe and much more in Asia. India was only a former empire now ruled by foreigners, and it crumbled geographically and morally during Gandhi's life. All that was Indian was stucco.

Thus Gandhi was to appeal to Indian national pride, while Tolstoy, in his regenerate days, abominated the Russian equivalent. But behind that difference lay a sameness. The stimulus to which both Russia and India were responding—the one with competitive expansion, the other with self-contempt and self-corruption—was the world growth of the modern system, of England and its railways and its banks and its cotton factories, and its parliament and its freedom of worship and its freedom of opportunity, and so on. All these added up to the model of success in the nineteenth century.

In 1869, the year of Gandhi's birth, Bholanauth Chunder published *Travels of a Hindu,* in two volumes, in London. This was one of the first books by a modern Hindu to be read by Englishmen. It concluded that India had never had any political life, any political science, or any political reform. It had tried nothing but crude despotism. Political life was an exclusively European phenomenon, and the British Constitution was the greatest phenomenon in world history. This was the way even non-Englishmen thought about England in those days.

What about the immediate family, the immediate environment, and the religion each was born into? Tolstoy's father was born in 1795, fought in the 1812 war against Napoleon, and died in 1837, when his son was only nine. Readers of *War and Peace* already know a partial portrait of him in Nicholas or Nikolai Rostov, the handsome young officer and then huntsman, who is loved hopelessly by his cousin Sonia but who marries the princess Bolkonsky.

To that outline we can add a few details at this point. At sixteen Count Nikolai had a child by a serf. The boy grew up to be a postillion, and after the count's death came begging from his half-brothers, who were dismayed by his close resemblance to their father. In 1812 Count Nikolai became a cornet in the Third Cossack Regiment of Irkutsk. Captured by the French, he spent two years as a prisoner of war in Paris, where he became friends with men who in 1825 were to take part in the Decembrist revolt. Both of his closest friends, Pavel Ivanovich Koloshin and Alexander Mikhailovich Islenyev, were Decembrists—as was a cousin of his wife—and the legend of that revolt of the aristocrats against the Romanov autocracy hung about the Tolstoy house and fascinated Tolstoy as a theme for fiction all his life. It was typical that Count Nikolai was involved in this political adventure only via his friends, because he had excellent taste in friends, and because, though he was not himself a liberal or an intellectual, he was, as it were, aesthetically on their side.

In 1819 he retired from the army and joined his family in Kazan, where his father was governor (the jolly and childish Count Rostov of *War and Peace*) but had got himself and the family fortunes into a mess. It was Nikolai's duty to his family to marry money. In 1821 he went to Moscow and got a bureaucratic post in the War Orphans' Service; and in 1822 he married the Princess Marya Volkonsky, five years older than himself, plain and pious and socially inept, but a considerable heiress. She brought him Yasnaya Polyana and other estates, and eight hundred serfs. In 1824 they went to live at Yasnaya Polyana, and he absorbed himself in running the estate and in living the life of a country gentleman. Lev Nikolaevich always associated his father's memory with Pushkin's description of hunting, and we may associate with him the many brilliant hunt scenes in *War and Peace*.

Lev's mother died when he was two, soon after the birth of his younger sister, Marya. He therefore never knew her, but from family tradition acquired a vivid sense of what she had been like—the sense transcribed in *War and Peace*, where Marya Bolkonsky is an unadapted portrait. The heavy tread, the plain face but spiritual eyes, the painful flush and awkward silence, the excellent intelligence and anxious spirit, all were biographical facts. Though he loved both his parents, he remained convinced that his mother was his father's superior in the spirit.

However, Tolstoy thought that *everyone* around him in his childhood had been good. "However, not only my mother, but also all those who surrounded my infancy, from my father to the coachman, appear to me as exceptionally good people."[2] He said this in his old age, but his early work, *Childhood*, is full of the same feeling.

This is a cardinal fact about Tolstoy: that he had, or believed himself to have had, an ideal childhood suffused with love. Part of its importance is that Tolstoy had an exceedingly skeptical intelligence and seemed to many people to believe in nothing, to doubt everything they told him about themselves, especially about their feelings. And yet he believed in this idyll of his childhood, a childhood that had in fact brought him, as one can see in his novel about it, his fair share of unhappiness and of treachery and falsity in others. How do we understand this? We have to conclude that he had a labile and dramatic temperament, and could and did feel very differently at different moments, which made the question of emotional truth very difficult for him, made him very skeptical. His final judgments on experience often seem to be imposed on his earlier descriptions, rather than to grow out of them. His was a temperament ideally suited to the work of a novelist, for in fiction he could distribute his different feelings among different characters; but it was a disadvantage to him as a moralist, for it made his conclusions seem harsh and arbitrary, and in his early years it made him seem—made him be—very unstable.

There is one other person who must be introduced straightaway in the parental role, and that is his aunt, Tatiana or Toinette Ergolsky. She was the cousin of his father called Sonia in *War and Peace*, who lived with the family and who, after his mother's death, acted as the boy's mother. She had always been in love with his father, but she grew to love his mother too and was fond of all the boys, but especially Lev. Aunt Toinette was very important to him in his early philosophy as a proof of the power of love, ordinary romantic sexual love, to grow until it becomes a moral virtue, transcending jealousy and possessiveness and the need for return—until it irradiates a whole personality and a whole household. In his *Reminiscences*, Tolstoy said that she taught him "the spiritual joy of loving. I could see and sense how happy she was to love, and I understood this happiness. Secondly, she taught me to appreciate a withdrawn and quiet life."[3]

Of his siblings, Nikolai, the oldest, was apparently very gifted as an intelligence and a writer, but remarkable as a personality in that he seemed to lack all egotism. Like their mother, he was modest, unassertive, and uncensorious. Turgenev once said that Nikolai Tolstoy had practiced the humility that Lev only preached. But this lack of egotism could also be described as a lack of ego. Lev said that a link was missing between his brother's kind heart and his great intellect, so that he "produced nothing." (Lev himself was determined to produce.) Nikolai was apparently his brother's model for Tushin in *War and Peace* and for Khlopov in *The Raid*. In his diaries, while he lived with his brother in the Caucasus, Lev complained of Nikolai's dirty hands, his drunkenness, and his lack of self-respect. But of course he was also acutely conscious of the contrast between Nikolai's simplicity, humility, and calm of soul, and his own restless competitive egotism.

Sergei, the third brother, was the opposite, as far as Lev was concerned, because he seemed to have a powerful but perfectly untroubled ego and could present himself to best advantage in all times and places. Lev admired Sergei's handsomeness, his singing, his ability to draw, his gaiety, his success with women, and above all his independence. He himself was always worrying about what others thought of him. In his *Recollections* he wrote, "that was probably the reason why I particularly delighted in the opposite of this in other people, namely independent egoism. . . . Dmitri [his other brother] was my comrade, Nikolai I respected, Sergei I was enraptured by his spontaneous egoism. . . . It was a human life very beautiful, but completely incomprehensible to me."[4]

As a home, Yasnaya Polyana was remote from the great world, willfully remote. Prince Volkonsky had retired angrily from the service of Catherine the Great to build this house in the country, and the Volkonsky-Tolstoys were never close to tsar or court or the central government after that. It was a gesture both historically pathetic and personally brave and privileged. Yasnaya Polyana was a pastoral idyll willed into actuality, a private domain of domestic happiness and cultured sensibility, where private life defied public. Thus what Tolstoy made of it in his fiction, and in his own married life, was a direct continuation of what his parents and grandparents had begun.

Tula, only ten miles away, can remind us of that military and technological and economic history which Yasnaya Polyana defied. A Dutchman was given the concession to establish an armaments factory there in the seventeenth century. There had been iron workings in that neighborhood from long before—near Yasnaya Polyana, for instance—and the industry grew, protected by the central government. A guidebook of 1904 described it as Russia's Birmingham and Sheffield combined.

Tolstoy said very little about the Tula arms factory, though he did visit it (he also visited the prison, the slaughterhouse, the law courts, the morgue and so on, with a journalist's eagerness to see everything for himself), and those who have written about him seem to have made even less of it. But it cannot be unimportant that such a man, with such feelings and such perceptions, lived cheek by jowl with the major symbol of industry and armaments in Rus-

sia. It may be worth noting that Nikolai Konstantinovich Mikhai-
lovsky (a left-wing intellectual who lived at the end of the century)
always used the Tula arms factory as his example of that division of
labor that he believed to be the greatest single social force in the
dehumanizing of society. Yasnaya Polyana, though itself a lovely
flowering of domestic happiness and alive with music, art, and brilliant conversation, stood next to a slag heap.

With industry came of course the ugly conditions of factory life,
which grew worse as time went by. Half way between Tula and
Yasnaya Polyana, according to the guidebook of 1904, stood "a huge
iron-works, with its unnecessary din and its belching chimneys, its
rows of little houses and its village of mud-roofed triangular dwellings." Owned by a Belgian stock company, it employed a thousand
workers seven days a week. But after you leave that behind, "the
droshky rocks for a mile across green fields" and Yasnaya Polyana
is in a different world.

The Tolstoys visited primarily with other noble families like
themselves—Turgenev at Spaskoe, sixty miles away, and the Islen-
yevs, the family Sonia Tolstoy was born into, at Pokrovskoe, only
twenty-five miles away—who lived on similar country estates. They
also spent months at a time or whole winters in Moscow, where
they again mixed with people of their own class. The only good
thing about Tula, Tolstoy once said as a young man, was that its
gipsy choir was better than Moscow's.

The religion Tolstoy was born into has to be described in paradoxical terms. Nineteenth-century Russia was in some ways still a
religious country, a religious culture, like Gandhi's India or medieval Christendom, before Western Europe was rationalized by the
modern system. There were, for instance, many holy places, and
many roads in Russia always had pilgrims on them, making quite
long journeys from one monastery to another. The main road from
Moscow to Kiev, which ran alongside one boundary of Yasnaya Polyana, had many such pilgrims, who often in Tolstoy's childhood
came to the house for a free meal. Later he visited the special inns
where they slept, in order to meet them. Moreover, Tolstoy's mother was a woman of piety who favored these pilgrims, and his aunts
Pelageya and Aline went in their old age to live in a monastery, as
indeed did his sister.

Thus striking religious practices and large religious institutions
were accessible to Lev in his childhood, in picturesque and attractive form, and his writings show that he was attentive to them.

Nevertheless, there is a sense in which religion never touched him intimately, never as for example George Eliot was touched by religion in childhood or as Gandhi was. Russian Orthodox Christianity was primarily picturesque for him and for others in his social class, primarily out of the past and primarily belonging to the uneducated peasantry. Though as a child he was certainly taught the ethic of Christianity with its prohibition of killing and its inculcation of chastity, he was also taught, and later learned predominantly or exclusively, the quite opposite ethic appropriate to a noble.

Something like this happened in every Christian country, but in Russia it was, we gather, more clear-cut. In England, for instance, the nobles and the clergy belonged to the same families, dined together, went to the same schools, and intermarried. Protestant piety was strongly echoed in secular writings like those of Carlyle and George Eliot. (Tolstoy was very struck by England's advantage in this matter.) In Russia, priests and nobles were entirely separate castes, with very different educations, houses, reading, and living habits. The Church's services were aesthetically splendid, its inmost life of prayer was impressively ascetic and mystical, but in between those two extremes, as a moral and institutional presence, it was negligible or contemptible.

We know much less about Gandhi's family and immediate environment than we do about Tolstoy's. This is because Gandhi was not a writer—much less a novelist, much less a great autobiographical novelist, like Tolstoy. Karamchand or Kaba Gandhi was the *diwan* of Porbandar. In 1841 Rupali Ba had died, and her successor invited Uttamchand, Gandhi's grandfather, back to become *diwan* again, but he recommended his son instead. Other men in the family had lesser administrative jobs; four out of five of Mohan Gandhi's paternal uncles were so employed. Kaba was *diwan* for twenty-eight years, until he quarreled with his ruling prince who imposed a punishment (on someone else) that Kaba thought unjust. Then he went to work in a similar capacity elsewhere and moved to Rajkot at the end of 1874. Rajkot was less cosmopolitan than Porbandar at that time, Ved Mehta tells us, but more important politically because the British political agent in Kathiawar made his headquarters there.

In Rajkot, Karamchand was, Prabhudas Gandhi tells us, less happy in his work and his health and his own life, a fact which "left a deep and lasting impression on his youngest son."[5] In 1882 he sided against the ruling prince in a dispute between him and a relative, and resigned. For the next three years, until his death at the end of 1885, when Mohan was sixteen, the family's income dropped from three hundred to fifty rupees a month. (In some of the major incidents of his career one can, therefore, see a kind of firmness in truth, or *satyagraha*.)

Kaba was about thirty-seven when he married Putlibai, who then was thirteen. Putlibai belonged to the Pranami sect and was therefore of a low social class. Her father was a commercial Bania who kept a village store. The Pranamis were suspected of, among other things, crypto-Muslimism. Their piety did indeed include elements of Islam, and their temple in Porbandar contained a Koran. They taught charity, chastity, temperance, and peace. Putlibai made offerings twice a day in the Vaishnava temple adjoining the Gandhi house and on holy days would visit others, including the Pranami temple about two hundred yards away.

Gandhi once told his secretary, Mahadev Desai, that his mother was more worldly than his father, and that she "had a fascination for money and for fame also." However, his basic memory of her was quite different. In *An Autobiography* he says, "the outstanding impression my mother has left in my memory is that of saintliness ... (whereas Father) to a certain extent might have been given to carnal pleasures."[6] He also described his father as being a lover of his clan, truthful, brave, generous, and short-tempered. This is something of a Kshattriya or nobleman's temperament he ascribes to his father, and the general configuration of temperaments and virtues seen in the Gandhi parents is not unlike that in the Tolstoys. Putlibai ate only from other people's leavings and fasted often. She was, like her son, very fastidious about cleanliness and purity in general. She is reported to have envied the bee, who turns all its food into fragrant honey and leaves no smelly waste behind, and she pitied the fate of the food we eat, degraded from being attractive to being repulsive. Like her son, she also suffered from constipation, a disorder we must see as at least analogous with that fastidiousness and refinement of temperament. This again can remind us of Tolstoy's mother. Though Putlibai was not an educated woman in touch with the ideas of the age, like Marya Tolstoy, who took tips on educating her children from Rousseau's *Emile*, there is a clear enough parallel between the two women. More importantly, they were remembered by their sons in the same way and with the same intensity: as saints.

In Gandhi's case, the one girl in the family (Raliyatbehn, born in

1862) was older than himself—she was the oldest child—but as was true of Tolstoy's sister, we don't know much about her or about the way the two interacted. Of his brothers, Lakshmidas, born in 1863, seems to have been a mild personality and later was described as genial, generous, and feckless. Karshandas, born in 1866, was a vigorous and willful boy, who led Mohan, three years younger, into trouble. Mohan seems to have been timid, both physically and morally, in his relations with other boys (though lively in other ways, and of course obstinate and severe when roused) and very concerned to be good.

He engaged in mild forms of rebellion, including secret smoking, and indulged in at least one session with *bhang,* the most widespread intoxicant drug among Indians. He resented the prohibitions of his elders and even agreed with some friends, who felt similarly oppressed, to commit suicide by swallowing *dhattura* leaves. Neither Gandhi nor his biographers take this episode seriously (the boys swallowed a few leaves but did themselves no harm) but it testifies surely to a significant tension. Thus the main drama of his boyhood years, as they come down to us, was the conflict between this desire to be good and the attractions of boldness and adventure, held out by his brother Karshandas.

The latter had a Muslim friend called Sheikh Mehtab, who lived close to the Gandhis in Porbandar and who played an important part in Gandhi's life. He is the one extrafamilial figure who needs to be introduced this early, like Tatiana Ergolsky in Tolstoy's case. The son of a jailer at Gondal, Mehtab represented strength, guile, and domination to Gandhi and to others. As a boy, he had many followers. He was a champion runner and jumper, and boasted that he could "hold in his hand live serpents, could defy thieves, and did not believe in ghosts." In *An Autobiography* Gandhi says, "I was dazzled, as one is always dazzled when he sees in others the qualities he lacks in himself." This was followed by a strong desire to be like him. "I myself could hardly jump or run."[7] Thus Mehtab had something of the same function in Gandhi's boyhood life as Sergei had in Tolstoy's. He was, of course, three years older.

It was Mehtab who persuaded Mohan to go to a brothel and to eat meat, in secret and expensive banquets at the Rajkot State House. And when Karshandas's debts became too high, it was Mohan who was persuaded to carve a piece out of Karshanda's gold armlet to sell for the needed amount (a crime he soon confessed in writing to his father). Mehtab stood for the opposition to piety and tradition;

he stood for boldness and freedom, innovation and rebellion, and Gandhi was attracted to those in his childhood.

But of course he was even more attracted to goodness in its traditional and pietistic form. And his India was a religious culture, in the sense defined before. There were, for example, many sects and about a hundred temples in Porbandar, which contained only 14,500 people, in 1872, when the whole state included about 72,000. The equivalent for Tula in Gandhi's life was perhaps Rajkot, with a population in 1872 of about 20,000. The similarity is that in Rajkot, where the British had set up an appeals court that settled boundary and revenue disputes between rulers and landowners, the forces of modern history could be felt. There were in effect two cities in Rajkot, one British and one Indian. The civil station of 800 acres contained 6,000 people and was kept clean and orderly; the Hindu town had only 137 acres, within the old town walls, and crammed 15,000 people into them. There Mohan saw the process of history as Lev saw it in Tula, and both were inevitably impressed by it, whatever reaction to it they then formulated. Both wanted to reform their native societies and their personal friends so that they should acquire the virtues of the English. (Tolstoy did not see the English in Tula, but he saw them "at home" in novels he read.)

In *An Autobiography*, Gandhi tells us that he lost his only other intimate friend when (and because) he took up with Mehtab, and that the whole long relationship was "a tragedy in my life. . . . I formed it in the spirit of a reformer. . . . A wave of 'reform' was sweeping across Rajkot at the time when I first came across this friend. He informed me that many of our teachers were secretly taking meat and wine."[8] Thus reform for Hindus meant essentially expanding the self and developing appetites, in imitation of the English. Gandhi regretted that this involved deceiving his parents. "But my mind was bent on the 'reform.'"[9]

As for religion, the Gandhis were devoted to Krishna, one of the twelve avatars of Vishnu, the Preserver. Vaishnavism, the cult of Vishnu, is one of the two great devotional religions of Hinduism, and the Gandhis took it seriously. Family prayers at their house lasted from 6:00 to 8:00 A.M., with a Brahmin coming for prayers at the end, and every day twenty or thirty people came for alms or a cup of whey. Kaba sat and peeled vegetables in the temple as he listened to his petitioners. Prabudas Gandhi says that "a kind of ashram had also come into being during Kaba Kaka's lifetime"[10] even in the family home. Thus we see the seeds of some of Gandhi's enterprises even in his childhood, embodied in his parents, as we see Tolstoy's idea of domestic happiness at Yasnaya Polyana embodied in his parents.

Tolstoy's Boyhood

Five was a crucial age for Tolstoy because it was then that he was moved downstairs from the nursery at Yasnaya Polyana, the world of women, nurses, nurture, love, to the boys' room where his elder brothers already lived, the world of men, horses, dogs, hunting, lessons. He says that he then first felt the sense of honor and duty, a consciousness of the cross everyone is called upon to bear. "I knew that I was irretrievably losing my innocence and happiness, and only the sense of my own dignity, the consciousness that I was doing my duty, sustained my courage."[1] His consciousness was elevated, and with that came a dangerous stress and stimulus.

It was about this time that he and Dmitri and Sergei were told by Nikolai a group of stories that stayed in Lev's mind all his life. Nikolai told them that he had discovered the secret that would make all men happy, would abolish misery, disease, and anger from the world. This secret he had written on a green stick and buried by the ravine in the Zakaz forest, part of which was in the Yasnaya Polyana estate. Lev in his old age, preparing for death, asked to be buried beside the ravine (and indeed was) partly because of his memory of that legend; for another part of Nikolai's story was the game of being the Ant Brothers—a group of men who had promised to love each other and abstain from all evil—a game which the brothers played by making a tent in the living room and sitting inside it, holding hands. This was one of the feats which they had to perform before Nikolai could lead them up the Fanfaronov Hills to happiness. At the end of his life, Tolstoy wrote, "the ideal of the Ant Brothers, clinging lovingly to one another, only not under two armchairs, curtained by shawls, but of all the people of the earth under the wide dome of heaven, has remained unaltered for me."[2] He felt he had been closer then than for a long time afterwards to understanding life rightly: "We thought of it as a game but I realize now that it is everything else in my life that has been a game."[3]

The story of the Fanfaranov Hills and the ordeals preceding their ascent are recognizably derived from the rituals of the Freemasons, according to Viktor Shklovsky. Both the boys' father and their grandfather Volkonsky were rumored to have been Masons. Many of the Decembrists had also been Masons and Russian Masonry was generally linked in rumor with revolution. But the story of the Ant Brothers derived from the stories men told about the German Protestant sect, the Moravians, the word for ant in Russian being like the word for Moravian. So we see in these stories the mummy seed of previous efforts at world salvation blown into the mind of Lev Tolstoy as a child, where they lodged as playful memories and picturesque legends until the heat of his own aspirations and the plough of his own sufferings made them germinate again.

Of his tutors, we know of a German called Rössel, and a Frenchman called Saint Thomas with whom Lev had some notable quarrels. The central scene of punishment Tolstoy describes is of the tutor having Lev locked up in a room in their Moscow house, and of the turmoil of feeling in the boy's mind as the hours passed in solitude. Though there is no need to doubt that the incident actually happened, it is notable that that scene occurs again and again in the autobiographical literature, fiction and nonfiction, of the nineteenth century. It occurs in *Jane Eyre, David Copperfield,* and Sergei Aksakov's reminiscences, for instance. That experience, when rendered into narrative and exposition, was an initiatory rite for writers. Locked up alone, the child's sensibility expanded—or seemed in recollection to expand—to the dimensions of significant imagination. It was a rite of rebellion, exploration, expansion. Gandhi had no such rite of passage.

According to some anecdotes, Lev was not considered to be as clever as his brothers. And it seems quite possible, from his own account of his childhood, that he was not then able to employ his intelligence freely, or even purposefully, on academic subjects. He was too distracted by the manifold tasks of discovering his own identity, or choosing between the many identities he was drawn to, to inhabit any one of them with enough ease and authority to be recognized by other people. He was also preoccupied by the problem of his own looks, for he knew himself not to be handsome. His eyes were small and deep-set, his eyebrows too thick, his nose broad and flat. He was very far from the Greek statue ideal, or the Romantic hero of his own day, a straight-featured, high-nosed, delicately cut face, diminishing downward from a big brow and big eyes to a small mouth and chin. Lev spent a lot of time looking at himself in the mirror and trying to change his looks by desperate measures—at one time shaving one side of his head completely— and later wondering whether one side of his moustache was thicker than the other. At twenty-four he could still write in his diary: "Aquiline noses drive me to distraction. They seem to me to possess all the strength of character and good fortune in the world."[4]

The other side to his temperament for which there is evidence is a certain hypersensitiveness. As a child he was nicknamed Leva-Reva, Leo the crybaby, because he was so easily moved to tears (though also to laughter, to awe, to ecstasy, to all sorts of extreme emotion). Even in adult life he seems to have been remarkably psychosomatic, so that his emotional upsets translated themselves into physical terms immediately. When anything went wrong for him, he had a flush of fever or stomach cramps. When his dog ran away, Tolstoy's nose started to bleed. In the Caucasus, when he couldn't find a copyist for his manuscripts, he got a migraine. These transparent symptoms—revealing a childlike egotism—made him seem very unstable, and prevented him from embodying any one of his moods or self-images with any authority, so that he often counted for very little, in his own eyes as well as in other people's. In his own, of course, he also counted for a great deal. He had a vivid sense of his own potentialities, but it was a sense that for a long time he could not trust.

His father avoided involvement with the provincial administration. Though he was no liberal, his son tells us that he, "merely as a matter of self-respect, regarded it as impossible to serve either during the latter part of Alexander's reign or during the reign of Nicholas I."[5] All his friends were to some degree opposed to Nicholas's government, and in him self-respect, a sense of style, took the place of political conviction. Even in childhood, Lev understood that his father never humbled himself or altered his tone when he met someone in power.

In the house hung the family portraits, of Tolstoys and Volkonskys, including, for instance, Count Nikolai's father, and other figures portrayed directly in *War and Peace*; which shows us another way in which his fiction was a translation of Yasnaya Polyana into literary terms. There are just two figures out of the family history which we need to make some acquaintance with at the moment. The first of these is Peter Tolstoy, in effect the first of the Tolstoys, since about those before him very little is known. Born in 1645, Peter Tolstoy was a contemporary and a favorite of Peter the Great, the modernizing Tsar.

In 1717, when Peter the Great decided to put his son, Alexei, on trial for treachery, Peter Tolstoy was appointed chief of a secret commission to collect all the evidence. (This secret commission was the origin and model of Russia's infamous secret police.) Alexei was condemned, really because he opposed his father's schemes, and took no interest in war or technology. And he had been flayed so badly in the course of his interrogation that he died before sentence could be executed.

This is of course a very lurid family drama, in which a father in effect murders his firstborn. But it is also a story about the modernization of Russia, and the absolutizing of the Russian State. Peter and Alexei stood on opposite sides on that issue, and the quarrel between them had everything to do with that. Thus the Russian State was christened in the blood of the ruler's firstborn. For Lev Tolstoy, these were living issues, and he was, if not on Alexei's side, very sharply opposed to everything Peter stood for. It must, therefore, have been an important fact to him that he was descended directly from Peter Tolstoy, the Tsar's right hand in the action.

The other person we should know something about is Lev's maternal grandfather, Prince Volkonsky, portrayed in *War and Peace* as the sardonically brilliant and harshly skeptical Prince Bolkonsky. Lev Tolstoy was said to resemble the portrait of his grandfather which hung at Yasnaya Polyana, particularly as he grew older. (We are told this by both his son Lev and his brother-in-law Stepan.) Now Prince Volkonsky's face, like his temperament, was Voltairean—little bright eyes peering suspiciously out from bunched-up little features—the very opposite of the broadly expansive, sensual, embarrassed, good-natured face Tolstoy gave himself as Pierre, and other self-portraits. If he portrayed his grandfather as a Voltaire, he portrayed himself as a Rousseau. But in his wife's diaries, and in comments by observers like Gorki, we meet Tolstoy-as-Voltaire. And since our main source for his life and persona must be his own writings, we must keep in mind this shadow self; whose existence Tolstoy himself would never have denied.

Gandhi's Boyhood

Mohandas (called Mohan or Moniya) Gandhi was, according to family tradition, a very lively baby. Certainly his sister, who looked after him as a little boy, described him as having been energetic and restless. The family was prosperous, modestly powerful, happy. Gandhi admired and revered the memory of both his father and his mother.

One of his reactions to his heritage, however, was negative. "I myself was born in a family of politicians. . . . I knew then, and know better now, that much of my father's time was taken up in mere intrigues. Discussions started early in the morning and went on till it was time to leave for the office. Everyone talked in whispers."[1] The talk was of how to get a better job, how to advance the Bania caste as against the Nagars, how to promote the Gandhi family. It sickened him of politicians. "I am atoning for their sin of clever talking by . . . the philosophy of action . . . my dislike of this [scheming] was even one of the reasons for my leaving the country."[2] In such remarks one glimpses feelings that are hidden beneath the pastoral surface of An Autobiography.

Mohan has been described as being a timid and self-occupying child, with a passion for clean clothes and for plants. In Gandhi's Truth, Erikson says that Gandhi always felt isolated in groups, and sought one-to-one relationships, or relationships in which he had the moral advantage. Thus he did not play with his schoolmates, but made peace between them when they quarreled. The peacemaking role, and the truth-telling role (both well-defined in Hindu culture) were those he preferred. Naturally, this did not make him popular. Prabhudas Gandhi tells us of a time when Mohan thus told the truth at all cost: "The incident convinced Mohan's companions that he could not be treated as one of them because of his simplicity and outspokenness. . . ."[3] If he did not like "the other boys' rough handling of one another even in play, he would stand aloof and say: 'Carry on, but I cannot join you.'"[4]

Erikson says that Gandhi could play, could be genial, only when he felt morally dominant because he was doing good to the others concerned. As a child he preferred to serve his mother rather than to play with his brothers. "Serving one's elders" is also a clearly defined activity in Hindu culture. And although Erikson's analysis

sets Gandhi in a light which must put off most Western readers
(and though there are better ways to present him) still, what Erikson says rings true to what Gandhi himself on many occasions said
about himself. In *An Autobiography* he says: "I ran home from school
so no one should speak to me."[5] He was very shy and afraid others
would make fun of him. He disliked both cricket and football, and
stood in the corner at sports time. He enjoyed going for long walks
by himself.

He told Edward Thompson that he was at his profoundest at sev-
en or eight, before education and society clipped his wings. He
wished he could have heard the boy Jesus arguing with the priests
in the temple: "then and then alone uninhibited truth must have
come out."[6] He was proud of his moral character, upset when asper-
sions were cast on it, and obedient and pious. "I was, by nature,
blind to the faults of elders."[7] And, according to Amrit Kaur, a
woman disciple, he often said he had been a dull child, shy, and
hating to be with a whole heap of other boys.[8]

Measured by ordinary Western standards, this is the self-portrait
of a prig. It is that by some Eastern standards too. Kalelkar, quite a
close disciple, once suggested to Gandhi that it was a pity his autobiography did not describe the storms of his youth, the passions he
had overcome in order to become gentle and chaste, the struggles
he had gone through to subdue his rebellious nature. His implication was that the book gave a dull if not unattractive picture of
Gandhi. Kalelkar presents *himself* as a man of ardent and sanguine
temperament, a hero Westerners could identify with, romantically
drawn to terrorism and then to anchoritism before he accepted the
discipline of Gandhi's leadership. But in reply, Gandhi professed to
have known no such *Sturm und Drang*. He had suffered certain
temptations but no enthusiasms, no inspirations or other self-swell-
ings. One could challenge that self-portrait on some points, but one
has to believe that Gandhi, looking back, saw himself in no poetic
vistas of personal beauty, power, personality. He envisaged no
greatness of force, or size of self, except spiritualized and self-
denying.

His self-image in his autobiography is like Judge Ranade's image
of himself as recorded in the remarkable biographical autobiography, *Himself: The Autobiography of a Hindu Lady*, by his widow, Rama-
bai Ranade (translated by K. van Akin Gates). These are in some
sense Brahmin self-images. Gandhi and Ranade are content to present themselves as quiet, obedient children, anxious to win their

elders' approval and merely repelled by the alternative standards represented by their peers. They wanted to be good, or at least, looking back on themselves as children, the men they became searched out the signs of goodness, not those of vitality.

This is something it is hard to imagine in a Western autobiography or biography of the same date. When books for and about children began to appear at the end of the seventeenth century in England, the image of the good child that they projected was not unlike that drawn by Gandhi and Ranade: children were praised for being prudent and pious, obedient and self-subordinating. But after 1800 the stress of admiration and approval gradually shifted to spirit and pluck and dash and guts, to manifestations of unregenerate nature. One may say that the Kshattriya virtues replaced those of the Brahmins, for children. Gandhi and Ranade are not on the side of rebellion or nature or vitality or dialectic, not on the side of the child against adults.

But Gandhi certainly knew (as "temptation") the impulse to rebellion and expansion. Thus he quotes, for instance, a quatrain by Narmadashankar, a Gujarati poet, which was popular among his boyhood friends:

> Behold the mighty Englishman
> He rules the Indian small
> Because being a meat-eater
> He is five cubits tall.[9]

This is not literally an image of adventure, but it is clearly enough an image of expansiveness, power, appetite, carnality, associated with the British. These qualities were also associated by Hindus with Muslims—who were also meat eaters and military conquerors—and embodied for Mohan in his friend Mehtab. Mehtab played his part gloriously in the system of force and violence at school. He defended Mohan, who was small and physically weak, from the bullies who oppressed him. Mohan was a year younger than the average of his class, and small and timid about many things. Thus it was natural that he should be tempted by Mehtab to eat meat (after which he heard the bleat of the goats murdered to make his food) and to go to a brothel (though he left without fornicating). Both crimes were expansions of appetite and selfhood.

The same elements of adventure might be found in the other crime into which Mehtab led Mohan (breaking Karshandas's armlet) inasmuch as it involved the theft of gold, the settlement of dis-

honorable debts, and the deception and disobedience of their father. This crime Mohan confessed to his father, and found him
"wonderfully peaceful" about it. In the crime itself Mohan was
mere cats-paw to Mehtab and Karshandas—who, one may suspect,
were deliberately implicating him—but in the confession he took
the initiative, and moved on equality with not merely older boys
but adults. That pattern was no doubt often repeated in Mohan's
life—in the realm of adventure he was only an accomplice, an ap-
prentice, but in the realm of responsibility and renunciation he was
a master—and that must have shaped his feelings about the two
realms of experience.

There is plenty of evidence that Gandhi thought of himself as
frail and feeble all through his childhood, youth, early manhood,
and even later. He also seems to have despised his body in childhood. He tells us in his autobiography that he could not, at school,
believe that gymnastics had anything to do with education. He was
ready to say "we are weak" about many groups he belonged to—
about Banias, about Kathiawaris, about Hindus as a whole, and
when he confronted individuals or groups whom he saw as powerful, his tone was playfully challenging. The Muslim politician,
Shaukat Ali, for instance, he always referred to in terms of his big-
ness, and it was a running joke in dozens of speeches and articles
that Shaukat Ali could put Gandhi in his pocket.

In a different way, Nehru, Henry Polak, Reginald Reynolds, and
other young Englishmen represented a virile vitality to Gandhi, and
his indulgent and fond relation to them reflects that. As groups, the
Zulus and the Pathans (both on the Frontier and in South Africa)
attracted Gandhi's appreciation for their size and physique, and—
more abstractly—the Muslims and the British were representatives
of power, and therefore recipients of Gandhi's challenging atten-
tions. The meek (for instance, some of the ashram women) Gandhi
treated less indulgently because he saw them as extensions of
himself.

Erikson thinks that Gandhi held his father guilty, first of involving him in sexual activity so early by arranging his marriage, and
second of marrying several times himself, thus identifying himself,
in his son's eyes, with sex.

Kaba Gandhi was also apparently short-tempered, though he did
not lay hands on his youngest son. According to the religious psy-
chology of Bania Hinduism, force and anger both were supposed to
lead the soul to identify itself with the body, to implicate and unite

those two, which it was man's duty to separate. Kings, being Kshattriyas, ate meat, drank alcohol, and smoked opium, all of which tend to mix together, to unite and homogenize, body and soul. Diwans, being Banias, did not.

If we try to place the Gandhis in their social setting, as we placed the Tolstoys in theirs, the ancestor we can put in parallel with Peter Tolstoy, *mutatis mutandis*, was Gandhi's grandfather, Uttamchand, who was the customs contractor of Porbandar, and later Diwan. He persuaded the neighboring state of Junegadh to sign over its customs rights, and also irrigated the area by building a dam, thus increasing its revenue considerably. In this way, he rescued Porbandar from serious difficulties, and set it on a firm foundation of prosperity. This performance was a considerable part of Gandhi's family heritage—as a model to aspire to imitate.

As for the English, Colonel R. H. Keatinge, who won a Victoria Cross for gallantry in the Indian Mutiny and was Political Agent in Kathiawar from 1863 to 1867, began a period of reforms there which lasted until 1882. He intervened energetically, limited the powers of the chiefs, organized police forces, and so on, but at the same time revived Rajput traditions. He gave the rajas gun salutes and built colleges to educate their sons. Thus he both reinforced and limited the powers of the native rulers. He reinvigorated them in the service of British rule. One of the new institutions was the Rajkot Rajasthanik Court, where Kaba Gandhi acted as assessor, and where, C. D. S. Devanesan suggests, Mohan may have derived his idea of law as reconciliation.

As for religion, theological and ecclesiastical forms are vague or various in Hinduism—are in some sense the individual believer's option—but the rituals are fixed and definite. Interpreted in Christian terms, therefore, it is at the farthest extreme from Protestantism. The doctrine of reincarnation and *karma*, moreover, presents individual experience on a scale of infinite time, which makes it emotionally insignificant although morally progressive. And even though Hinduism is more closely tied to philosophy than Christianity is, its thought is devotional rather than critical and is aimed at *moksha* or *samadhi*—at a state of transcendence, a freedom from knowledge and even from belief. Different beliefs may work for different people and even for the same person at different times: consistency of belief is not important.

In these ways, Hinduism is most unlike that Protestant Christianity (and Protestant philosophy) which has been one of the motors of

terms of dandy anxieties and encounters in aristocratic drawing rooms. The current of ideas (in philosophy and literature as in science) seems to have passed him by, for Tolstoy is notably unlike that "generation of the forties" which responded so enthusiastically to Schiller.

When he was sixteen, Lev's brothers took him to a brothel, where he wept on the prostitute's bed after fornicating with her. This was the beginning of many years of very active sexuality, up to the time of his marriage: with prostitutes, with serf women, with the maids of the family home, and others, all of whom he did not meet in society or fall in love with. This was an animal sexuality quite different from the poetic eroticism which surrounds the figure of Natasha in *War and Peace*. In his novels, as in most nineteenth-century novels, the focus was almost exclusively on poetic eroticism, which is one reason why Tolstoy grew dissatisfied with them, with fiction in general, and with the whole high culture which told itself fairy tales about human nature to feed its own self-love.

At this period he was erotically and poetically oriented toward other men. He was first attached, by his own account, to the Musin-Pushkin brothers, and then for some time in love with Dmitri Alexandrovich Dyakov, who was a little older than himself. He wrote in his diary in 1851: "I very often fell in love with men...."[2] But he never imagined sexual contact, he tells us, and it seems clear that in him—as so often in adolescents—the erotic and the sexual were quite distinct. "For me, the chief indication of love is the fear to offend or not to be liked by the object of my love. It is simply fear."[3]

In 1847, he had his first attack of gonorrhea, and began to keep a diary while in the hospital in Kazan. The entries are, as they would always be, concerned with his quest for self-perfection. He draws up six rules for himself, of which the first is "Read and think always aloud." What perfection means can be deduced from the marks of imperfection he is concerned to eliminate—confused, indistinct, quiet utterance. The perfect man will make himself felt, make himself count, at every moment.

While he was in the hospital he also conversed with a Tatar lama, who was there because he had been beaten up and robbed. He had, he said, suffered the attack without self-defense or attempting to escape, closing his eyes and offering up his suffering to God. Tolstoy was very struck by this. It could hardly enter into the complex of habits and values he was building up for his own use, but it stayed in his mind as a sign of the other, the non-European, the Eastern, mode of being.

As one would expect, at that period Tolstoy was attracted to a philosophy of life, of vitality, of growth, of strength.

On April 17, 1847, he writes:

If I begin to consider, looking at nature, I see that everything in her contin-ually develops, and that every constituent part of her unconsciously con-tributes to the development of other parts; man too, being another such part of nature, but gifted with consciousness, ought like the other parts, but consciously, employing his spiritual powers, to strive towards the develop-ment of everything existent.[4]

And "the reason of individual man is a part of all that exists, and a part cannot destroy the order of the whole." Immediately before, he writes that the aim of life is "to afford a maximum of help towards the universal development of everything that exists."

In the first paragraph of Youth, some of his earliest writing, he declares his youthful belief that ". . . the purpose of man is to strive towards moral perfection, and that such perfection would be easy, possible, and last for ever."[5] Such moral positiveness was of course in the air, and can be associated in particular with Rousseau. In his Discourse On Inequality he said that what distinguishes man from other species is his ability to develop or perfect his faculties.

Tolstoy read Hegel and Rousseau through the summer of 1845 at Yasnaya Polyana, and felt coursing through him "the same force of life, fresh and young, that filled Nature around me."[6] Dissatisfied by Descartes' "I think, therefore I am," he proposed beginning phi-losophy with "I want, therefore I am." This is, in somewhat carica-tural form, one of the great statements of the modern mood. It was after arriving at this formula (in 1845) that he read Rousseau's Con-fessions, about which he later reported: "I thought I was reading my own mind, and simply added a few details here and there."[7]

As well as his diary, he was keeping a Franklin journal, with dif-ferent sections allotted to different weaknesses and virtues, enter-ing his achievements and failures in each, day by day. This was one of the major forms of the spiritual disciplines of the modern system, like Robinson Crusoe's journal. (Gandhi did not keep, that we know of, a Franklin journal, but he kept a diary and pressed upon his followers the idea of keeping one, and the idea of the Franklin vir-tues, like punctuality, frugality, account keeping, and so on.)

But it was above all Rousseau who influenced Tolstoy, and among

Rousseau's works, perhaps the *Reveries Of A Solitary Walker* can best suggest why. Rousseau says, "... reverie amuses and distracts me, thought wearies and depresses me; thinking has always been for me a disagreeable and thankless occupation."[8] This distinction obviously promises some large and new ideas of human consciousness and values.

And indeed Rousseau says:

I know and feel that doing good is the truest happiness that the human heart can enjoy ... sweeter than any other ... [but he finds] ... my good deeds a burden because of the claim of duties they dragged behind them ... I always found it impossible to take any positive action against my own inclinations ... good deeds [are] irksome when they are demanded of me, even though I did them of my own accord when they were not demanded of me.[9]

What these sentences most vividly suggest is of course the uneasy alliance Rousseau (and the early Tolstoy) effected between the moral and the aesthetic feelings—an alliance that Tolstoy was to dissolve in later life, when that uneasiness became intolerable, and he returned to a harsher and unaesthetic morality. But even more interesting is the passivity recommended, the reliance upon feelings, which implies a cult of the "organic" life of the individual. Moral values are to be cultivated only as a variety of life values.

Another striking resemblance between the two men lies in their relationships with, respectively Madame de Warens and Aunt Toinette. There are, of course, large differences between those relationships, in that Rousseau's was sexual as well as sentimental, but there is also a marked resemblance, especially in the development of the two writers' sensibilities as novelists. Rousseau says:

but during those few years, loved by a gentle and indulgent woman, I did what I wanted, I was what I wanted, and by the use I made of the hours of my leisure, helped by her teaching and example, I succeeded in imparting to my still simple and naive soul the form which best suited it, and which it has retained ever since. The taste for solitude and contemplation grew up in my heart along with the expansive and tender feelings which are best able to nourish it.[10]

One need only compare that with what Tolstoy said about his Aunt Toinette—that she taught him the spiritual pleasure of loving, and the pleasures of a solitary and unhurried life. (Established at Yasnaya Polyana—which was to be his share of the heritage—Lev

summoned Aunt Toinette back to live with him.) She too was a
gentle and indulgent woman, she refused to believe in damnation,
and refused to allow savage punishments on the estate. And some
pages of Lev's letters to her read like love letters. It is a striking
coincidence that it was she who first urged him to write fiction, and
that his first novel plan was of the story of her life. The successive
muses of Tolstoy's fiction were she, his cousin Alexandrine, and his
wife Sonia. Of course there were men whose critical opinion he
valued highly when he began to write, like Turgenev. But he would
not have written at all but for those women.

Gandhi's Adolescence

In Gandhi's case, even more clearly than in Tolstoy's, this portion of
his biography must be dominated by issues of sexuality. Mohan was
betrothed to marry Kasturba at the age of seven, and she was the
third girl his parents had chosen for him. (The first two had died
before he was seven.) Kasturba was the same age as he, and lived
only a few yards from his own home in Porbandar.

Five years later, when Gandhi and Kasturba were only twelve,
they were married. Of what the experience meant to them, we
know only that Gandhi, when he spoke of such early marriages later, bitterly disapproved of them. In his articles on Hindu life for the
Vegetarian, which he wrote in London in 1890, it was on early marriage that he blamed the Indians' physical weakness compared with
the English.

Physically, by most people's accounts, Gandhi was never attractive (though photographs sometimes make him appear so), or self-
confident. He was solitary in his habits and nervous in ordinary
relationships. Kasturba, on the other hand, was strikingly good-
looking. Of her mind and nature, we know very little, except that
there was very little to know, in the ordinary sense of knowing. She
remained all her life a remarkably undeveloped personality in the
Western sense—which is not to say that she was unforceful. She
could be very obstinate and very demanding when her prerogatives
(for instance, in running of the household) were infringed. Nor was
she untouched by her husband's mission, his ideas. She took part in

the Gandhi movement. And she was, of course, his faithful companion, even in jail. But in what sense she understood it and him, how she named to herself, for instance, the difference between him and her—between him and other men—it is impossible to say because she had no gift of speech about such matters. But we are bound to assume that her understanding was intellectually primitive. She could scarcely read or write, and she had no compensatory mode of expression, yet she passed her life in a whirlwind of letters, minutes, petitions, publications, arguments, speeches, constitutions, a snowstorm of rhetoric under which she sat silent for sixty or seventy years.

We know that she refused to learn to read and write from him, often as he strove to teach her. And it seems that this was typical of a general resistance on her part. In their first years together, she refused to pledge him the fidelity which his brothers' wives pledged them. She made him jealous by running away to where he could not find her, and when he threatened punishment, she blew out the lamp and left him alone in the dark he feared. One can only assume, from his own attitude to sexuality, and from what he said about her, that she never responded to him sexually or dropped her initial reticence toward him. "There was never any want of restraint on the part of my wife. Very often she would show restraint, but she rarely resisted me although she showed disinclination very often."[1]

We seem to see in Kasturba, therefore, a shy, wild, obstinate, teasing, attractive creature, who remained in some sense deliberately a blunt and primitive mind all the time that he was developing his intellectual and spiritual gifts so extraordinarily. She was soon left far behind, intellectually, socially, spiritually, and yet she was always there, behind his shoulder, and in her primitive and perverse way, she was loyal and supportive. She could be (it seems that she often was) irritable, jealous, small-minded, resentful, but she did not betray or desert him. Lingeringly and sullenly, she always followed him, and in the long run she said yes to all the questions and all the demands he put to her.

Gandhi explained her failure to learn, his failure to teach, as the result of his sexual passion for her. He told Margaret Sanger in 1936: "I was not the ideal teacher because I was a brute. The animal passion in me was too strong and I could not become the ideal teacher."[2] He was also fairly explicit on that occasion about her sexual passivity.

Another factor in Gandhi's experience of marriage was the influence of Sheikh Mehtab, which was still powerful upon him, and which was directed, according to Gandhi, all toward arousing the young husband's suspicions of his wife, his jealousy, and his "duty" to dominate her. "The canker of suspicion was rooted out only when I understood Ahimsa in all its bearings . . . ," he says.[3] He also attributed cruelty to himself, and in the same connection: "I am filled with loathing of my folly and lustful cruelty, and I deplore my blind devotion to my friend."[4] It seems likely that all those elements—lust, suspicion, jealousy, and cruelty—were involved in his passion for Kasturba.

Some light may be thrown on Gandhi's idea of marriage by the comments of two American missionaries about the village they lived in near Agra from 1925 to 1930. In *Behind Mud Walls*, W. W. and C. V. Wiser say how struck they were by the way babies, especially boys, are deified in Hindu families, how reluctantly the mothers lose them to the world of men; and how eagerly they recapture them in adolescence, when they marry. That is, the women of the household, including the boy's mother, encourage sexual excitement and erotic dreaming. Thus they saw a mother delighted to get her son sent home from school as vaguely unwell (because his wife had gone on a visit to her parents) and his uncle trying to persuade the boy to take the rest of the year off from school. School, meaning work, was set in opposition to sex, meaning play, and the mother favoured the second.

If we transpose this to Porbandar in the 1880s, we shall find it easy to understand an extra reason why Gandhi disapproved marriage. Gandhi was taken out of school several months before the wedding, and missed a whole year of education because of it, according to Ved Mehta.[5] The institution of Hindu marriage, instead of being (like Tolstoy's marriage) a separating off from the family for two individuals, to explore each other and create a new world between them (this I take to be the ideal for modern Europeans) was a return from the exploration of the outer world, to a nursery of physical pleasures set in an inner chamber of the original family.

Kasturba was pregnant by 1885, but we don't know how Mohan felt about her condition or the approaching event. On the other hand we know from his own account that he delighted in nursing his father. To rule while serving, especially some masterful masculine spirit, some dangerous power like his father, satisfied him deeply. But on November 16, 1885, Kaba died, and Mohan was not at his bedside; he was in his own room making love to Kasturba. This coincidence was a great shock to him, re-establishing that polarity between sexual appetite and loving service, and associating Mohan himself with the evil pole. Moreover, Kasturba gave birth to a child only four days later and it soon died.[6] Thus two deaths were involved, and Mohan was doubly condemned. It seems likely that this event was so shattering for him that we cannot really know what Gandhi might have been but for it—we cannot know what other possibilities he had before contained, because we can know the Gandhi of before 1885 only through the testimony of the later Gandhi.

Stories Gandhi says he dwelt on as a child include that of Harishchandra, the Hindu Job, and Prahlad, the boy who defied his father for love of God. We in the West have, I think, almost lost the power to respond to such tales—as to our own legend of the patient Griselda—because our ideology has no use for such "negative" virtues, being built around "positive" ones like appetite and its satisfaction, bold ambition, and achieved power. But if we are to understand Gandhi we must reach across this enormous abyss—a difference which derives, in part, from the West's economy of abundance over the last couple of centuries. Stories like Harishchandra, Prahlad, and Griselda make more sense in an economy of frequent famines.

The single author who corresponds most clearly, in Gandhi's life, to Rousseau in Tolstoy's, is Tulsidas and his *Ramayana*, the title of which is more exactly translated as "The Holy Lake of the Acts of Rama," because reading the poem is like taking a purifying bath.

One of the legends about Tulsidas himself may help us to understand Gandhi, and may be taken in contrastive parallel with the stories Rousseau tells about himself in the *Confessions*. Being so passionately fond of his wife, Tulsidas followed her when she went, without his permission, to visit her parents. She reproached him, "my body is nothing but skin and bone; and if such love as you have for it had been devoted to the Lord Rama, you would have no reason to dread rebirth." Hearing this, Tulsidas at once abandoned all his ties to his home, became an ascetic votary and pilgrim, and later composed this and other poems about Rama.

There are a thousand differences between that story and Rousseau's tales of how, for instance, he stole a ribbon and put the blame on a fellow servant. But all those differences derive from the fact that Rousseau feels full of reverence for the *facts* of his experience, and wants to exalt that experience to the level of revelation—to give it transcendental significance. The story of Tulsidas, on the other hand, is clearly unrealistic—a nonempirical legend—in which the important thing is the moral lesson (which is not something revealed but something repeated for the thousandth time) that we must be ready to give up everything at a moment's notice. Rousseau's "lesson," we might say, is that it is more important to know what you have done than to do the right thing, or that we need give up nothing, because our self continues; whatever we may give or take, if we but remember it, write it down, embalm it in consciousness, it is always ours, and all other truths and duties take their places within that universe of thought. However good or bad we may be, we remain interesting.

Prabhudas Gandhi tells us that Kaba, on his death-bed, said: "Manu here will keep up my reputation. He will increase the fame of our lineage."[7] And according to Joseph Doke (who must have had it from Gandhi) the Brahmin family priest whom Mohan consulted about his career said, "if you wish to make headway in your country, and become, like your father, a man of importance, you had better relinquish the idea of graduating here. You must go to London and become a barrister."[8] It is notable that in both these anecdotes there is no hint of self-sacrifice or resignation in the motives for going, nor even that contentment with inherited station which we might expect from the devotee of Rama. When Gandhi himself was asked in London in 1891 for his motive in coming, he replied: "In a word, ambition."[9] The Brahmin had merely "fanned the fire that was burning within me."[10]

We need not interpret that word, ambition, in its narrowest sense. Mohan was, as he said about himself later, eager to see the world, and in particular to see London, the home of philosophers and poets, the very center of civilization. From Gandhi's point of view, however, that idea too could be summed up under the heading of ambition.

He had to persuade his brothers, his uncles, and his mother, to let him go. To his mother he took a vow not to touch meat, alcohol, or women while in England. He had to answer the reproaches and arguments of Kasturba and her parents. It was a three-year absence that he projected, and he was newly the father of a baby boy, called Harilal. But he had also to find somewhere in the joint family the money for the trip, which was promised him more than once and the promise broken. His friend Mehtab also interfered in this process, forging a letter in Gandhi's name to a cousin and making things more difficult. And there was the religious difficulty. A strictly orthodox Hindu was not supposed to cross the ocean. But Mohan persisted, and wore down all the resistance by meek and obstinate reasonableness. He reports himself as saying to the caste leader, "you are as an elder to me. But I am helpless in this matter. I cannot alter my resolve to go to England."[11] And he seems to have felt this situation and others later that way. Once his will was set, it was something quite independent of his consciousness or his ordinary desires.

He was going to England as a reformer, which meant, among other things, as a meat eater, though this of course was not said. In a farewell speech at his High School in Rajkot (an event which made him so nervous that his head reeled as he got up to speak) he said: "I hope that some of you will follow in my footsteps and after your return from England you will work whole-heartedly for big reforms in India."[12] It was quite clear, to him and to everyone else, that going to England was a promise to return and change things in India—to change Indian culture to make it more like English.

Interviewed in England in June 1891, just before he set off home again, he described the five months leading up to his departure as full of "terrible anxiety and torture."[13] He was hooted in Rajkot by the members of his subcaste; and in Bombay where he was to take ship, he was summoned to a large meeting, interrogated and excommunicated from his caste. (So were those members of his family who were helping him to leave, but in their case the excommunication was not persisted in.) His oldest brother, Lakshmidas, who was providing his passage money, was dismayed by the opposition, and got friends to try to persuade Mohan to change his mind even at the last minute. When that failed, Lakshmidas went back to Porbandar, and left Mohan still waiting for his ship, the money now in the trust of a friend. They then persuaded the captain to predict a rough crossing, so that Mohan was persuaded to wait for another passage. It was entirely at his own insistence, and with money from another source, that he finally got aboard another ship.

The experience must have been extremely wearing and painful for him, but to have succeeded in carrying out his own plan against almost everyone's opposition and sly interference must also have reinforced his own will to succeed and strengthened his sense of power. Talking about all this in London afterwards he freely ascribed much of the opposition to "malice"; those who opposed him were on the side of evil.

His friend Mehtab came to Bombay with him, took letters back to the family, and received money from Mohan while in London. In the 1891 interview, Gandhi described Mehtab as "very full of tricks."[14] That enigmatic relationship was still important to Gandhi. He describes an accident he fell into in those days because he was walking along abstracted by the excitement of his venture and by anxiety over a quarrel with Mehtab—with whom he was always quarreling. One is inclined to guess that one of the attractions of England was that he would be removed from a tangle of relationships (with Kasturba and Mehtab, notably) which were deeply troubling him.

So he finally sailed, on September 4, 1888, just a month short of his nineteenth birthday, going away from home at the moment when Tolstoy went back home to Yasnaya Polyana. But since Tolstoy was cutting himself free from troubling entanglements, and Gandhi too was in effect moving into solitude, the two actions were far from opposite in character. Both young men were engaged in what we later called "finding oneself."

SECTION II

Youth

Tolstoy 1847–1862 • Gandhi 1888–1906

During the period that I have labeled "Youth," Tolstoy and Gandhi found their way, after detours and defeats elsewhere, to literature and politics respectively, and rose to national eminence there. By 1862 Tolstoy was a well-known Russian writer, and by 1906 Gandhi was a well-known Indian political leader.

Within those fields, moreover, each man made his way to a particularly prestigious kind of action. Each man's achievement can be usefully associated with a phrase current at the time, as I suggested in the Introduction. In Tolstoy's case the phrase is "domestic happiness," the title he gave to one of his short novels of the period, and the ideal in the name of which he turned away from his brother Sergei and dandyism—and away from his peasant mistress and the people—to "English marriage" in life and literature. For "domestic happiness" stood for a certain kind of literature and for the quiet life an author needed, as well as for a certain kind of marriage. It even implied—in the long run—the dialectical philosophy of life-values. This philosophy expanded readers' traditional moral limits by replacing judgmental absolutes with sympathetic identification. Readers understood and judged moral situations by identifying with life-worthy characters involved in them, not by applying absolute standards. Literature expanded, displacing religion. This new scope of imagination in the modern system's art was the product of its new wealth—the imaginative counterpart of the system's practical achievements—the dividend allotted by empire to those disaffected family members who retired from the dirty work of ruling. Thus Tolstoy was implicated in the modern system even as he turned away from it to write.

In Gandhi's case, the phrase is "nation building," which was used by Gokhale, Gandhi's political guru, to define the aim of his Servants of India Society, founded in 1905. It evoked the whole world of political aspiration of the nineteenth century, not only toward the autonomy of peoples, but toward entry into the modern-world system for new national groups who had been outside it. It therefore implied specifically nineteenth-century forms of economy, industry, social organization, civilization, and consciousness. "Nation building" was the promise of a sharing out of the modern achievements of wealth and power, the promise that nonwhite and non-Christian races should join in the WASP process of success and party of self-congratulation. Within the British Empire it had a special guarantee of reward, for England was the guardian of modern-system morality; once a new nation had shown itself politically mature—through moral effort—England would reward it with independence. This meant a particularly modern, English, and prestigious kind of politics, just as "domestic happiness" meant a particularly modern, English, and prestigious kind of literature. And Gandhi chose it in preference to a legal career, just as Tolstoy chose literature and marriage in preference to dandyism. (In both cases the process of choice was gradual and for a time each man combined literature with dandyism, or politics with law. It was only at the end of the period that Tolstoy gave up his bachelor freedom and Gandhi his legal practice.)

Both men were still finding themselves and were strikingly submissive in friendships with men of their own age; in Tolstoy's case, with the philosopher, B. N. Chicherin and the poet, A. A. Fet, in Gandhi's case, with Sheikh Mehtab and Raychandbhai. But by the end of the period, it was clear to all who knew them that Tolstoy and Gandhi were, and would become more, stubbornly resistant to all influence and toughly self-original.

In public affairs a somewhat reverse pattern can be seen. Both men overtly declared their resistance to government politics, but in less obvious ways were willing to accept surprising accommoda-

tions with it. Tolstoy often spoke out, harshly, against the bureaucracy and government of Russia, and largely isolated himself in the
aristocratic freedoms of Yasnaya Polyana. And Gandhi aroused and
led his compatriots in a series of protests against the government of
South Africa. But neither one was any kind of revolutionary as yet.
Perhaps the most striking proof of that, considering their later
stance, is that both, in this period, voluntarily took part in three
imperialist wars (in Gandhi's case the third was the Great War, and
so a bit outside the period) without explicit indignation or subsequent protest. Their self-development was still far from complete.

Tolstoy 1847–1855,
Moscow and Dandyism

On April 17, 1847, Tolstoy entered into his diary a series of eleven
objectives he meant to accomplish during the next two years, which
he would spend living in the country. Only the last of these—"to
compose essays on all subjects I study"—has any literary character.[1]
Literature did not yet stand high, much less stand steady, among his
aims.

In 1850, he noted that "the position of a young man in Moscow
society partially tends to predispose him to idleness. I mean 'a
young man' who combines in himself certain qualifications, namely
education, a good name, and an income of 10,000 to 20,000."[2] He
went on to note his need of a countess, to help him get into the
right salons.

This could be Pushkin's or Lermontov's diary; it expresses the
self-consciousness of the young aristocrat in the nineteenth century,
squeezed into the role of a dandy by the pressures of bourgeois
sentiment and bourgeois politics. When such young men read Byron, they saw themselves as Childe Harold or Don Juan; when they
read about revolution, they saw themselves as ineffectual rebels,
doomed to the guillotine.

Despite his 1847 diary entry, Tolstoy spent his time during the
next two years as much in Moscow and St. Petersburg as in Yasnaya
Polyana; and he spent his energies on gambling and dissipation as

much as on those eleven objectives. He was forever in debt because of gambling. In May 1848, we find him writing to his brother Sergei that he must procure a large sum fast—before his next installment of income. He adds that he has decided to enter a Guards regiment. This plan was not carried out, anymore than several other plans to give up gambling, which embarrassed him. "Even while writing this letter I have several times got up and blushed, as you also will do on reading it—but what is to be done?"[3]

In Tolstoy's Moscow the more frivolous products of modern civilization were dispensed by French restaurants, hairdressers, glovemakers, etc., and such places are prominent in the record of his years there. He fenced and exercised with Poiret, a Frenchman who kept a gymnasium on the Petrovka; his early story, "Christmas Night," begins in Charles's glove-shop; and the hero of "The Cossacks" starts for the Caucasus from Chevalier's restaurant.

His relationship with Aunt Toinette continued to represent something different in his life. She wrote him: "When you sat beside me on the divan, I looked at you with all my soul and all my senses, I was transformed into that look, I could not utter a word; my soul was so full of you that I forgot everything else."[4] This is the sort of thing that nobody said to Gandhi—a whole world of novel reading stands behind it—and it played a big part in preparing Tolstoy for romantic marriage, and for literature. On March 17, 1850, he notes the idea of writing a novel about Aunt Toinette's life.

In his diary he reproached himself violently. But he accused himself of sin less often than of inconsistency, weakness, breaking his vows, failing his resolves. As he himself noted, he was more concerned with enforcing his will than with the moral character of his will on a particular occasion. His morality focused more on the achievement of his desires than on the dignity of those desires.

In his short novel, *Youth* the word *dandy* is often used, but even more frequent is *"comme il faut."* One whole chapter is given that title, and Tolstoy talks at length about the signs of being *comme il faut*: long nails, good French, the right way to bow, dance, and converse, and the right relation of trousers to boots. His central character is very inept at all these skills, which are nevertheless all-important to him, while his brother masters them without effort. (The same contrast was true of Tolstoy and his brother Sergei.) Tolstoy points out the immaturity, or antimaturity, of this scheme of values, which constitutes its moral pungency. Usually, he says, a man sees that he must engage in life, take part and achieve or produce. "He

chooses some kind of work and devotes himself to it; but this sel-
dom happens to one who is *comme il faut*."[5] Tolstoy was headed
towards maturity from early on, but the fascination of Sergei (and
others) made him veer off his route, and made maturity seem often
a second-best option.

In April 1851 Tolstoy set off for the Caucasus, with his brother
Nikolai. They went east to Kazan and then south by boat down the
Volga, seeing primitive tribal communities on the way. Lev went as
a private citizen, but he took part in the regiment's life, and soon
applied to join the artillery in Russia's imperialist war against the
mountain tribesmen of the Caucasus.

Tolstoy hoped to make a career in the army, which was the hereditary vocation of his caste and family. He used his aristocratic
connections to try to procure for himself the patronage of Prince
Bariatynsky, who arrived in the Caucasus about when Tolstoy did,
as commander of the left wing of the army. He did not, however,
take Lev Tolstoy under his protection, although the latter was com-
mended for gallantry by his superior officer more than once.

But the Caucasus, and the Cossacks, gave him a career in literature instead. They gave him something to write about. The Cossacks
lived in a world of license, from the civilized point of view. Drunkenness was a Cossack rite, and virtue took a different form among
the Cossacks. They on the outside of civilized society corresponded
to the military caste within it; they were hostile to bourgeois property and property owners. Thus to identify them with Nature, as
Tolstoy does in "The Cossacks," was tantamount to claiming the
same for Tolstoy's own caste, the nobles; and to excluding the mer-
cantile and the modern from that sacred association.

This was felt at the time. A review of "The Cossacks" in *Sovremennik* in 1863, spoke of the author's "downright refusal to acknowledge all that has been and still is going on in literature and life."[6]
In *Vremya*, Y. P. Polonsky criticized it as too pro-Cossack and anti-
civilized. And a woman novelist, Eugenie Tur, said: "The author is
at great pains to prove that savages are magnificent and happy, and
cultivated people are low, petty, and unhappy."[7]

Tolstoy's Caucasus letters and diaries show a continuation of his
old ambivalence. June 11, at Stari Yurt, he records having spent the
night longing for something sublime and good, in German romantic style: "I wished to blend into unity with the all-unfolding Being
. . . but not an hour had passed before I almost consciously heard
the voice of vice and vanity, and of the empty side of life."[8]

To his aunt he praised "the state of rest without worry, and with the quiet enjoyment of love and friendship, as the acme of happiness."[9] He told her that the only thing he now valued in himself was his good heart. He reassured her that he had begun to write, and that he had begun to savor the pleasures of history. But to Sergei he used a more Lermontov-like tone; on June 24, 1852, for instance, he complained about the provincialism of Tula and Piatigorsk.[10]

But by this point he had fairly regularly named these two main options of his as the good and the bad; that is, he was acknowledging what nineteenth-century society called "mature values." In August 1852, he decided to write a novel showing up the central administrative power in Russia, and after that to devote himself to organizing an elective union of Russian aristocrats which should share power with the administrative bureaucracy. This project clearly expressed the consciousness of his caste and in some sense looked backwards developmentally. But in September he contemplated writing a history of modern Europe; and not so long after, leading a reformation of Christianity. These were merely ideas which did not get far toward realization, but as ideas they were forward-looking projects of what the nineteenth century called maturity; they had no taint of aristocracy or of dandyism.

May 8–15, 1853, Tolstoy recorded getting letters from N. A. Nekrasov, his sister Masha, and his brother Sergei, all highly flattering, about *Childhood*, which he had published anonymously in Nekrasov's magazine, *Sovremennik*. His sister, moreover, had been shown the story by Turgenev, whom she had got to know, and who was himself enthusiastic about it. But perhaps the most important response was Sergei's, because from now on his tone toward his younger brother changed from condescension to respect. The balance of power between the two shifted, as it became clear that Sergei was going to live in retirement, like Nikolai and their father. His achievements were to be dandified—were to be a matter of personal style. It was to be Lev, after all, who would cut a figure on the public stage and make manifest to a larger audience the Tolstoyan gifts they shared.

His self-doubts did not, of course, disappear as soon as his literary success began. His ambitions were too extreme to be satisfied by any imaginable success. In *Youth* his hero says: "I wanted everybody to know and love me, I wanted to pronounce my name, Nikolai Irteniev, and have everybody impressed by this information and

surround me, thanking me for something."[11] Publication brought
him a taste of this, but he still hoped to meet everywhere and any-
where an appreciation which he did not find. On July 18 he wrote:
"Why does nobody love me? I am not a fool, not deformed, not a
bad man, not an ignoramus. It's incomprehensible."[12] And on July
25: "My smile is sometimes not firm, which often disconcerts me."[13]

The most characteristic and disconcerting note sounded in these
entries is still the Rousseauistic. On November 2/3 he wrote: "I
have not yet met a single man who was morally as good as I, and
who believed that I do not remember a single instance in my life
when I was not attracted by what is good and was not ready to
sacrifice everything for it."[14] He still equated a man's moral goodness with his attraction to goodness, and with the readiness to believe in someone else's attraction—his is a morality of generous imagination and sensibility, not of strenuous achievement and
consequence.

Tolstoy did not get his discharge in 1853, but did get a leave of
absence, and in January 1854 he started for home, and the four
brothers held a reunion at Yasnaya Polyana. They talked far into
the night and then made up a bed on the floor and slept together.
This kind of male comradeship, located first of all in the brothers,
was very important in his sensibility.

In February he was told, in Tula, to report to the Army of the
Danube, in Bucharest, 2,000 miles away. Russia had declared war on
Turkey, occupying Moldavia and Wallachia in July, 1853. This was
ostensibly because of the Turkish-Islamic threat to the holy places
of Christendom in Jerusalem. More really, it was another imperialist war like that in the Caucasus, but of a different kind, being between two empires, one of them outside the modern system and
decaying, the other inside the system and expanding.

Tolstoy was appointed to the staff of Lieutenant General Serzhpu-
towsky, the Commander of Artillery. He much admired his general,
and would have liked, he admitted, to become his aide-de-camp. He
was still trying to feel (and succeeding in feeling) the emotions appropriate to a soldier. He found, for instance, the spectacle of war
beautiful: "It is true, it is a curious kind of pleasure, to see people
killing each other; nevertheless every evening and every morning I
got on to my cart and remained for whole hours observing, and I
was not the only person who did. The spectacle was really fine,
especially at night."[15]

Tolstoy was soon sent to Sebastopol (where he arrived in September 1854), because England and France intervened on Turkey's side, in what became known as the Crimean War. This was the third of Tolstoy's wars, and it was imperialist in a third sense: here the Russian empire was being thrown on the defensive, being attacked by two of its cohorts in the larger system who did not want it to grow so big so fast and to upset the balance of power which they had arranged in their favor. To most Russians, including Tolstoy, this seemed a patriotic war of self-defense, like that of 1812, which he set out to celebrate in the following decade.

Tolstoy was full of patriotic excitement and proud to be in Sebastopol at such a moment, to see Russian soldiers behaving like heroes. His ambitions for a military career were revived, and he wrote various memoranda, a project for the reforming of the batteries and another for the reformation of the army. But mingled with his ambitious advice was an angry and critical satire on the Russian command, which spoiled the former's chance of success. His memoranda said things like: "We have not an army, but a crowd of oppressed, disciplined slaves, confused plunderers, and hirelings."[16] It is not surprising that Tolstoy got no encouragement to make his career in the army.

But he had by then established his character as a man of courage and had successful experience as a commander. He gambled and drank with his fellow officers, and performed feats of strength. He could lie down and lift two men, each on one of his unusually large and strong hands. Though he was still uneasy with himself in his diary, and reminded himself to accept the fact that he was different, it seems clear that he had mastered a persona which enabled him to pass in military society· he was sufficiently a manly man. But he knew that his future lay elsewhere. On September 17, 1855 he wrote that his aim in life must be literary glory, the good that he could do would be by means of his literary compositions.

However his diary for March 2–4 had said that he had an idea for a new religion: "Yesterday a conversation about divinity and faith suggested to me a great, a stupendous idea, to the realization of which I feel capable of dedicating my whole life. This is the idea— the founding of a new religion corresponding to the development of mankind: the religion of Christ but purged of all dogma and mysteriousness, a practical religion, not promising future bliss but realizing bliss on earth."[17] The idea may have owed something to Tolstoy's encounter with the English and French soldiers and his keen sense of Russia's backwardness and inferiority. For us, of course, it mainly points forward, to the Tolstoy of twenty-five years in the future, after his career in literature.

Gandhi 1888–1894,
London and Vegetarianism

Gandhi arrived in London October 28, 1888, having demonstrated on the journey—much to his own satisfaction and against the predictions of fellow passengers—that he could do without meat and alcohol even aboard ship, and even in Europe in autumn. It was a part of modern-system mythology that a cold northern climate challenged man's physiology much as free enterprise challenged his morality, so that a northerner needed more to support life; just as, of course, he made more of life.

Gandhi arrived in England a "convinced meat-eater" as he says in his autobiography, only abstaining from meat because of his vow to his mother. It was the arguments of English vegetarians (principally Henry Salt) which gave his abstention moral and ideological substance. England also forced other changes upon him which he then adopted as matters of principle. He stopped taking sweets and condiments, chutneys and chilis, at first perforce and then by design. Good food, he said later, had been his main interest in life.

Being a vegetarian and an abstainer gradually became a large part of Gandhi's identity while he was in England. It set him off immediately from most of the other Indians he met there, who followed Western ways even if that meant breaking vows. It also gave him the sort of role he enjoyed. He showed himself, while apparently meeker and less rebellious than they, to be really stronger and more defiant.

But he admired the modern system and meant to combine remaining a vegetarian with becoming an English gentleman. To compensate for the social disadvantages brought by the former, he started private lessons in elocution, in French, in dancing, and in playing the violin. He began to read newspapers—three a day—and spent ten minutes before a mirror every morning parting his hair.

(At home he saw a mirror only when the barber shaved him.) He wore elegant English clothes.

But he did not persist in these attempts at dandyism for very long. For instance, he soon discontinued his private lessons. Like Tolstoy in Moscow, Gandhi could not be successful as a dandy because his efforts in that direction were undermined by opposite drives. Of course they were profoundly different in the sense that Tolstoy's physical appetites and energies were exuberant and exorbitant, partly as a result of encouragement and policy. His caste and culture aimed at size, and his physical strength was highly developed, his bodily consciousness aroused and appetitive. Gandhi was on guard against his appetites, he aimed at diminishing his size, and his bodily consciousness was as closed, contained, and undevouring as he could contrive. He felt himself weak physically, and even weak psychologically in those powers—of authority and anger, of infectious gaiety, of voice and personality—which men associate with the body. He had no impulse to challenge other men in those ways. But we need not attribute his failure as an English gentleman merely to incapacity. Dandyism is interested in other things besides size and power, and Gandhi was sensually, intellectually, and socially very alert. He could have been a good *arbiter elegantiarum*. The basic reason he failed at dandyism was the reason Tolstoy failed—that he was called to something other and incompatible, which he found in vegetarianism.

The president of the London Vegetarian Society was A. F. Hills (1857–1927), who was the chairman of the Thames Iron Works, which built battleships. He was, therefore, a rather unusual vegetarian, socially speaking. Politically, perhaps, he was more what one might expect: he shared his profits with his workers and instituted an eight hour day, but was opposed to unions. He related vegetarianism very closely with spirituality and the Christian gospel. And interpreted this way, vegetarianism must have seemed to Gandhi very like a Hindu sect, with its diet prohibitions and its separation of its adherents from the rest of society. Mr. Hills was the sort of moral and scrupulous capitalist Gandhi liked to deal with. In India he found Ambalal Sarabhai, G. D. Birla, and Jamnalal Bajaj to be men of this type, but Western intellectuals were ceasing to believe in the existence or the virtue of such men by 1914. This was partly a result of the spread of Marxism, but partly a matter of literary sensibility. The portrait of Thomas Crich in D. H. Lawrence's *Women in*

Love is as devastating as any Marxist analysis of the inauthenticity of capitalist benevolence. This divergence of intellectual sensibility from the major images of Gandhi's crusades helps account for the intellectuals' disastrous indifference to his achievement.

Gandhi shared rooms for a time with Dr. Josiah Oldfield, the secretary of the Vegetarian Society, and wrote altogether nine articles for *The Vegetarian* in 1890. He drew a contrast between the Kshattriyas, who ate meat, drank alcohol, smoked opium, and so grew weak from debauchery, and the Shudras (whom he calls shepherds) who were strong: "Without being fierce like a tiger, he [the shepherd] is yet strong and brave, and as docile as a lamb."[1] It is lambs Gandhi likes, and as a lamb he himself speaks; which we, of course, find very disconcerting.

Being a vegetarian created various practical difficulties for Gandhi besides the quarrels with other Indians and the embarrassment of explaining and justifying himself to English landladies and colleagues. He had considerable difficulty in getting enough nourishment until he discovered the vegetarian restaurants (of which there were ten in London then) and then he began to cook for himself.

On September 19, 1890, Gandhi joined the Vegetarian Society and became a member of its executive committee. The following nine months, before he sailed for home on June 12, 1891, were the period of his greatest activity in London. On January 30, 1891, he attended the funeral of Charles Bradlaugh, who had been known for being the M.P. for India as well as for his atheism. Gandhi did not like Bradlaugh's religious position, but he did admire the way Bradlaugh had made it into a part of of his public career—had refused to hide it and had forced Parliament finally to accept it. This was an example of the Englishman's moral integrity and practical tenacity which Gandhi thought Indians badly needed to imitate—which he intended himself to imitate.

On February 20, he made a speech at the Vegetarian Society in which he defended the claims to membership of a Dr. Allinson, who advocated birth control. Gandhi disapproved of birth control but judged that the issue had as little to do with vegetarianism as Bradlaugh's atheism had to do with sitting in Parliament and, therefore, defended Allinson against the president. He was, however, still too nervous about public speaking to be able to deliver his speech himself, so he had it read out for him.

Thus his triumph was mixed with defeat and this was true of most of Gandhi's moments of success in England. On holiday on the

Isle of Wight he met Howard Williams, who invited him to speak to some vegetarians there, and again Gandhi had to ask someone else to read out what he had written. "I was ashamed of myself, and sad at heart for my incapacity."[2] On the same holiday he went out walking with a young lady who took him up a hill and then (though in high-heeled shoes) ran confidently down the slope and waited laughing while he timidly edged his way down, step by step. She shamed him, he says, "as well she might."[3]

These chapters of his autobiography are a record of constant humiliation, despite the lightness of their tone. The same is true of autobiographical passages about sex in other writings and about experiences in India and South Africa as well as England. Talking of his first visit to a brothel, with Sheikh Mehtab, he says the woman threw him out in contempt because he was trembling and could not look her in the face: "What could that smart woman do to such a fool but turn him out?"[4] And when, on one of his trips to South Africa, the ship's captain took him to a brothel, Gandhi was too embarrassed even to speak to his whore. Afterwards: "I certainly felt a little humiliated. They had seen that I was a fool in these matters. They even joked among themselves on this point. They pitied me, of course. From that day, I was enrolled among the fools of the world, as far as the captain was concerned."[5] The stress on humiliation is bound to remind us of Dostoevsky—of, for instance, *The Idiot*—but Dostoevsky's treatment of the theme is modernist, while Gandhi's will remind us more of Tolstoy in, for instance, "Alyosha the Pot."

On June 10, 1891, he was called to the Bar, on the 11th enrolled in the High Court, and on the 12th sailed for India. He still saw himself as a reformer, a Westernizer. On the way home, "as I was a reformer, I was taxing myself as to how best to begin certain reforms."[6]

His ship reached Bombay in early July and Gandhi was introduced to someone else who was to be important to him. Rajchandra (also called Raychandbhai), a Bombay jeweler, poet, and ascetic two years older than Gandhi, born in another part of Kathiawar and subjected to very similar religious influences. But Rajchandra had been a brilliant child, who had given public performances of his ability to do many different mental things at the same time. A man with this gift was called a shatavadhari—many-minded—one who concentrates on many thing simultaneously. Gandhi tested him by reciting lists of French and Latin words, which Rajchandra afterwards repeated. When he grew up, he had mystical experiences and became renowned as a *jnani;* that is a religious devotee whose devotion is intellectual rather than emotional (an emotional devotee is called a *bhakti*) or moral (a *karmayogi*, like Gandhi). He advised Gandhi to avoid pollution by politics and the outside world of social activism in general.

Gandhi found that new European tastes like tea, coffee, and shoes had been accepted in his home during his absence. He added cocoa, oatmeal, and European items of clothing. He was still a reformer. At least in his presence, his family now sat on chairs and ate from china plates instead of squatting on the ground and eating from brass plates.

In November, he applied for admission as advocate of Bombay High Court, but he was uneasy with his profession, both morally and psychologically. It involved serious collusion with the master-class and betrayal of his Indian identity—a betrayal symbolized in the wig and gown he had to wear in the Bombay court. He wanted, but did not want, to be an Englishman. He broke down when he had to cross-examine, returned his clients' fees, and despite, or because of, his nervousness, fell asleep in the courtroom. When he tried to cross-examine, and stood tongue-tied, everyone laughed, and he "hastened from the court in shame."[7]

Winding up his legal establishment in Bombay after six months, Gandhi returned to Rajkot and worked as a *vakil* with his brother Lakshmidas, drawing up petitions and memorials and making up to R300 a month. He tried to advance his own and his relatives' careers in the usual ways for instance by acquiring powerful patrons (as Tolstoy also tried).

In Bombay he had met Sir Pherozeshah Mehta, a Parsi lawyer who was known as the uncrowned king of the Presidency, the lion of Bombay, and Sir Ferocious, because of his dominant presence and domineering manner. Mehta is a good example of the kind of Indian Gandhi knew who was not weak, who admitted no connections with weakness, who embodied power, cunning, boldness, luxury, and largeness of style and appetite. In his autobiography, Gandhi remembers Mehta as always surrounded by a circle of admirers, and Gandhi "trembling with fear" while he addressed him. When Mehta encouraged him to speak louder, at a public meeting in 1896, Gandhi's voice "sank lower and lower."

There were many such figures of power among the successful lawyers of India (like Motilal Nehru), men who had mastered the rules of the modern game, great orators with booming voices, Homeric laughter, cutting techniques of cross-examination, and dramatic changes of tone. But though Gandhi wanted to escape from weakness, he didn't want to embody power. And in the end, of course, he made all that power look overblown.

He also tried to intervene on his brother's behalf with Mr. Ollivant, the British Political Agent in Porbandar. Lakshmidas was secretary and advisor to the heir to the throne, but the agent had formed a low opinion of him and was ready to extend it to Gandhi himself. "Your brother is an intriguer," he said. "If he has anything to say, let him apply through the proper channel."[8] He had Gandhi put out of his office.

Gandhi adds: "I had heard what a British officer was like, but up to now had never been face to face with one."[9] And Indian behavior pleased him no better. In Kathiawad, a brother would cut a brother's throat for a halfpenny, he said later, and "the atmosphere of intrigue in Saurashtra was choking to me." The call to go abroad again was a very happy one.

In April 1893, he sailed for Durban, in Natal, readily grasping at the opportunity to do legal work there for a merchant called Dada Abdullah, which was offered him by a merchant in Rajkot. Dada Abdullah was himself born in Porbandar and was one of those mostly Muslim merchants from West India who had followed the indentured laborers to Natal. He had built up a big business with fifteen branches and made a fortune in gold when that metal was discovered in South Africa and before its importation into India was restricted (1888–1890, the time Gandhi was in London). Now Dada Abdullah was engaged in a dispute with his cousin in Pretoria—he had advanced the latter £40,000 and wanted it back—so he needed legal advice. Gandhi left Kasturba and Harilal behind in Rajkot, intending to return in a year's time. He arrived at Port Natal about the end of May 1893, wearing frock coat, striped trousers, and black turban. He was immediately struck, before he got off the ship, by the depressed and oppressed state of the Indians there. Dada Abdullah, though himself thought so rich, was condescended to by the Europeans on the ship.

On the second or third day after arriving, Gandhi attended the Durban Court and was told to remove his turban; he might be a London barrister, but he was still, in Natal, a coolie. Refusing to do so, he left the court and wrote a letter to the press protesting the incident. This letter attracted considerable attention. Thus, Gandhi began his career in South Africa by creating a public stir, as he had never done before. The situation he had arrived in was the work of empire at its worst, a case of rank racist oppression. Natal needed laborers for its sugar plantations; in the 1850s she had applied for British convicts, had tried to employ Amatonga tribesmen, had imported Chinese and Malays from Java, and finally got the Government of India's permission to import indentured labor from there. In 1860 the first group arrived from Madras, and by 1866 there were 5,000 of these laborers in Natal. In 1869, the year of Gandhi's birth, the Indian Government renewed the contract but stipulated that after the end of their indenture the laborers should have equality of status in the country. And in 1893, the year of his arrival, Natal was granted responsible self-government, the right of the white colonists to keep down the blacks and the browns.

About a week after that first incident, Gandhi set off for Pretoria to begin negotiations with his client's cousin, Tyab Haji Khanmamud. He went by train, but at Maritzburg was told to leave the first class compartment he was sitting in because a white person wanted it. Gandhi refused on principle, was thrown out of the train, and had to spend the night in the railway waiting room. The next day he went as far as Charlestown by train and then took the stagecoach to Johannesburg. He was forced to sit outside beside the driver, and then he was ordered to change seats again. Gandhi this time refused and clung to the seat while the driver struck him and pulled him off and threw him down.

In his autobiography, Gandhi said he realized that, "the hardship to which I was subjected was superficial—only a symptom of the deep disease of colour prejudice. I should try, if possible, to root out the disease and suffer hardships in the process."[10] Natal's Law 3 of 1883 restricted the rights of Asiatics and had the approval of the Imperial Government, "in deference to European demands for the segregation of Asiatics in locations." Asiatics could not become citizens, they had to have three residence permits and licenses to trade; they could not own land, and "for sanitary purposes," they had to live on locations. This law was not enforced, but the insult cut deep. As Gandhi said, they were treated as Untouchables.

During his first week in Pretoria, Gandhi met Tyab Haji Khanmahmud and called and addressed a meeting of the Memon (Muslim) merchants there. In retrospect he called this his first public speech, and he seems to have felt none of the shyness that frustrated his speeches in England. His subject was "truth in business": "I had always heard the merchants say that truth was not possible in business. I did not think so then, nor do I now."[11] He spoke to them frankly of the things that aroused European prejudice against them (notably dishonesty and unsanitariness) and offered to help form an association to seek redress of their grievances.

He stayed a year in Pretoria and read eighty books. Many of these were about religion. With some Theosophists he read Vivekananda's *Raja Yoga* and Patanjali's *Yoga Sutras,* and learned two or three verses of *Baghavad Gita* by heart every day for a time. He read Max Müller's *India—What Can It Teach Us?* and Washington Irving's *Life of Mahomet.* But most importantly, in 1894, he read Tolstoy's *The Kingdom of God Is Within You,* which overwhelmed him, because, as he said, he was then in a crisis of religious scepticism. He also conducted an (unsuccessful) experiment in eating nothing but vital foods—uncooked grains, vegetables, and fruits.

There were regulations forbidding Indians to use the footpaths in Pretoria, and Gandhi was kicked off such a footpath near President Kruger's path; but he refused to sue his assailant, saying he would never go to law for a merely personal grievance. But he conducted a lively campaign in the press about the general issue. In September 1893, he wrote to the *Natal Advertizer* complaining about a leading article which had spoken of "the wily wretched Asian traders," as "the real canker that is eating into the very vitals of the community," and as "these parasites who live a semi-barbarous life."[12] The letter that follows is Gandhi at his most literary, his least Gandhian:

But they spend nothing, says the leading article under discussion. Don't they? I suppose they live on air or sentiments. We know that Becky lived on nothing a year in *Vanity Fair.* And here a whole class seems to have been found doing the same. It is to be presumed they have to pay nothing for shop rents, taxes, butcher's bills, grocer's bills, clerks' salaries, etc., etc. One would indeed like to belong to such a blessed class of traders, especially in the present critical condition of the trade all the world over. . . . It seems, on the whole, that their simplicity, their total abstinence from intoxicants, their peaceful and above all, their businesslike and frugal habits, which should serve as a recommendation, are really at the bottom of all this contempt and hatred of the poor Indian traders. And they are British subjects. . . . Is this Christian-like? . . . Is this civilization? I pause for a reply.[13]

In April 1894, he wound up the case with which he had been entrusted. He convinced his client of the folly of litigation, and the dispute was settled by arbitration. With that, his stay in South Africa was over, and he returned to Durban on his way home. But at a

party given to bid him farewell, he saw the announcement in the *Natal Mercury* of an impending law to disenfranchise the Indians.
The article said:

The Asiatic comes of a race impregnated with an effete civilization with not an atom of knowledge of the principles or traditions of representative government. As regards his instinct and training he is a political infant of the most backward type, from whom it is an injustice to expect that he should ... have any sympathy with our political aspirations.[14]

That no Indians had opposed the bill was urged as proof of their political unfitness, and when Dada Abdullah's attention was drawn to the article, he only said, "we are after all lame men, being unlettered. We generally take in newspapers simply to ascertain the daily market rates etc. What can we know of legislation? Our eyes and ears are the European attorneys here."[15] But Gandhi told him and the Indian merchants that they *must* resist this law, and they persuaded him to delay his departure in order to lead them in the struggle. (He refused to be paid for such work but asked them to guarantee him enough legal work to earn £300 a year: as a barrister he had to live in style—he owed that to his compatriots.) He got 400 signatures to a petition in one night, and 10,000 later. The first postponement was for only a month but it was extended, and Gandhi did not leave for India until 1914, by which time he was fully established and internationally known as a leader of political protest.

Tolstoy 1855–1862, St. Petersburg and Literature

Tolstoy reached St. Petersburg in November 1855 still officially in the army and serving as an inspector to a St. Petersburg explosives factory. He put up at first at Turgenev's and got to know a circle of Turgenev's literary friends. The moment when Tolstoy met them, the moment of the new Tsar's promise of emancipation and relaxation of censorship and so on, was very favorable to literature. Between 1845 and 1854 there were six papers and nineteen monthlies in Russia; between 1855 and 1864 there were 64 papers and 156 monthlies. And periodical literature was especially important in Russia. It was the main source of education for many groups who, in our society, go to college. Women, for instance, at least in the provinces, had to educate themselves from the periodicals, as Vera Figner points out in her autobiography.

Tolstoy himself was not a "liberal and an idealist." This was a very important fact about his relations with these new friends, but for us looking back it is not so easy to see what the crucial difference between him and them was. For liberalism meant largely a belief in the emancipation of the serfs, and idealism meant largely a belief in the spirit realizing itself through history (with a consequent self-identification on the believer's part with the process—with every new innocent, natural, or expansive growth). And both these beliefs, or tendencies of thought, were dear to Tolstoy then. And still he was not, in the sense crucial for that time and those people, a liberal or an idealist.

The source of the difference is partly Tolstoy's morally serious perversity, deriving from his search for authenticity. That irritable refusal expressed itself, when faced with his new friends' liberalism, in his declaration that he was an aristocrat, a member of the aristo-military caste. He declared himself by wearing a uniform (while they wore European civilian suits), by carousing all night, by challenging a debtor to a duel, and by returning the intellectual hospitality these friends offered him by taking them to the gypsies.

Turgenev, though an aristocrat himself and a much richer man than Tolstoy, would not assert his identity as noble against his identity as liberal. He called Tolstoy a "troglodyte" because of his "barbaric ardour and bull-headedness." Nekrasov called him a falcon or an eagle; A. V. Druzhinin, another man of letters, called him a *bashi-bazouk* (that is, a Turk) for his ignorance and forcefulness. All these epithets suggest the same idea, that Tolstoy was lacking in (was refusing) the necessary refinement and received ideas of his time, but they also implied that he had instead a valuable vigor, a special access to Nature. This was, of course, highly flattering; the record of Tolstoy's inner life in his diaries shows him torn apart by ambivalence, scrupulosity, uncertainty as to what he really felt; a monster of self-consciousness rather than of instinct. It was only now, in this society of men of letters, that Tolstoy was able to present himself and feel himself as a piece of Nature, as simpler and more forceful than those around him—as a genius. From now on, this was to be an important part of his identity. (His is one of the clearest cases of how the man of Nature forms himself with the help of a cultural idea.)

These literary men of St. Petersburg were Westernizers who believed that Russia should become as like Western Europe as she could, as quickly as she could. Turgenev wrote in 1855 that Russia's defeat at Sebastopol should serve her as Prussia's defeat at Jena had served her, as a signal to emancipate herself from "the shackles of political oppression and the debilitating burden of the lingering vestiges of the feudal system."[2] They felt great pity for the Russian peasants' suffering, but no respect for their way of life. This was another source of difference between them and Tolstoy, who believed in powers and wisdom of a non-Western sort, to be found in the individual-and-group unconscious. He might have been expected to find his fellowship among the opposite intellectual party, the Slavophiles of Moscow, but he could not sympathize with their primary enthusiasm for the Orthodox Church.

In February 1857, he arrived in Paris, where he spent a lot of time with Turgenev, who knew the city well. Their relations were again uneven. On March 10, Tolstoy wrote in his diary that he thought Turgenev "higher" than he; but on March 13 he decided that Turgenev had never loved anyone. On April 6 he attended a guillotining in Paris, which profoundly upset him, and left for Switzerland two days later. There, for the first time in a long while, he sincerely thanked God that he was alive, and, struck with the beauty of Clarens, he sat down to describe the effect it had on him in an abortive manuscript entitled "Travel Notes in Switzerland."

I wanted to love and I even felt a love for myself, I regretted the past and felt hope in the future, and life became joyful to me, I wanted to live for a long, long time, and the thought of dying gave me a child's poetic thrill of horror. Sometimes, even, sitting alone in the shady little garden and gazing and gazing at these shores and this lake, as it were with a physical sensation, I felt how the beauty flowed into my soul through my eyes.[3]

Clarens was a place he associated with Rousseau and, "as it were, with a physical sensation," that is the typically Rousseauist/Tolstoyan apprehension of the unconscious, the touching of the flow of life itself; provoked in this acuteness by the spectacle of death. Here the current of his thoughts flows back into its accustomed channels, after meeting a severe check in Paris.

He doesn't like, has never liked, strikingly beautiful views. Like Rousseau, he prefers the ordinary, the empirical:

I love nature, when it surrounds me on all sides with its warm breath, and that same breath, circling around, spreads out to an endless distance, when those same juicy blades of grass, which I flattened, sitting down on them, make up the green of endless meadows ... which, stirring in the wind, move the shadows on my face, make up the line of the distant wood, when that same breeze, ... etc.[4]

The other kind of view is for Englishmen to add to their portfolios.

Back in Russia at the end of August, he noted that he was getting on better and better with his brother Sergei. But on October 30, he remarked that his literary reputation had collapsed, or was only just alive.[5] And, in fact, between 1858 and 1860, there was no mention of Tolstoy in literary reviews and articles. He was out of sympathy with the current of literary opinion, which flowed towards political commitment.

But he was by then recognized as one of the leading writers in Russian and loved by all who were trained in the old school. He had written about his childhood and youth, about his military experience in the war and on the frontier, and about the Cossacks and the Chechen. His work had appeared in leading periodicals and was acknowledged by critical authorities like Turgenev and Druzhinin to be brilliant. These, of course, were all genres and themes tied to the aristo-military caste, and, indirectly, to dandyism. But he had also, with "Domestic Happiness," begun to write in the genre most tied, in the nineteenth century, to maturity and middle-class values. In this short novel, Tolstoy imagined a future, English–style marriage for himself, but—influenced by *Jane Eyre* in form as well as content—the story is told by his wife. He had, however, still to make himself a master in that genre, and to commit himself to those themes and values in literature meant committing himself in life also—meant marrying and making a cult of family values. Thus we can see most of his personal adventures in this period as a series of attempts at doing that.

The Death of His Brothers

During this period, two of Tolstoy's brothers died, and he became significantly alienated from his other two siblings. Taken together with his stormy relations with his new friends like Turgenev, these events left him strainfully isolated. He had chosen to put his faith in personal and family relations, but in fact his own life of that kind was unhappy.

lessly, at least in his aunt's opinion—withdrew and went to Europe.

While there he became acquainted with a very different sort of woman, his cousin Alexandra, or Alexandrine, who had passed her life at court as tutor-governess to various children of the Imperial family through four reigns. (She taught Alexander II's only daughter.) She was in Switzerland with some of her charges when Tolstoy reached there from Paris. Twelve years older than Tolstoy, she was clever, serious, socially poised, and above all charming and graceful, and with her he could play a role somewhat the opposite of that he played with Valeria. Now he was the impetuous young man, the well-meaning blunderer, the boisterous genius, and she was all understanding maturity. "A force de vouloir être vrai," she told him, "vous ne faites que des caricatures de la vérité."[7] It was a relationship well adapted to expression in letters, and Tolstoy said that his correspondence with Alexandrine (from 1857 to 1903) was his best biography.

On May, 1858, he wrote her a very important letter about his story, *Three Deaths*, which she had read. He also discussed his religious position. The three who die are a tree, a peasant, and a cultivated lady, and the deaths are increasingly painful to the reader, morally painful, because the consciousnesses are increasingly complex and intense—only pure nature accommodates death. Alexandrine had read the story as Christian in its values, and he replied that it was not. "The peasant dies peacefully just because he is not a Christian. . . . The tree dies peacefully, honestly and beautifully."[8]

Of the three women, the most interesting to us, and in some ways the most important to Tolstoy, was Aksinia Bazykin, a married serf of Yasnaya Polyana, who bore Tolstoy a son. Physically, she was handsome and robust; intellectually, and even conversationally, it seems that there was no contact between her and Tolstoy; sexually, we gather, she made herself available to other men besides her husband and him, but only to those whom she chose.

The affair between them, or at least the sexual feeling on Tolstoy's side, was powerful in the time between his two trips to Europe, in 1857 and 1861. When he came back in 1857, and was conducting his sentimental and intellectual correspondence with Alexandrine, he was sleeping with Aksinia. These two relationships could be called complementary, but that with Aksinia, though it was far from "English marriage," became obsessively important to Tolstoy. In his diary for May 10–13, 1858, he records a glimpse of

Aksinia—"very pretty"; and then, "I'm in love, as never before.... I have no other ideas. I am tortured. Tomorrow every effort."[9]

In his notebook for May 26, 1860, he records that she is not to be seen—he has been looking. His feeling for her is no longer that of a hunter for a deer but of a husband for a wife. He has tried to awaken the former feeling of satiation, but he can't. And the feeling she awakes in him is above all that of the worker's, the peasant's, "irresistible equanimity."

What Tolstoy wrote down were scattered phrases, so it is hard to be sure exactly what he meant and even harder to translate in a way that allows the reader the freedom to judge for himself. But it seems fairly clear that Tolstoy saw in Aksinia the whole peasant way of life and was attracted to that for himself. On August 23, 1860, he saw himself in a dream, dressed as a *muzhik,* and his own mother not recognizing him. And one of his students who taught in his village schools recalled later that Tolstoy often condemned civilization—the young teachers were to learn health from the peasants—and said "to marry a lady is to tie to oneself all the poisons of civilization."[10] This was while he was in love with Aksinia, and not long before he married Sonia.

At the end of his life Sonia said angrily that his love for the people was really all a taste for peasant women, and (in her autobiography) that he wanted to run away with one of them to a new life—run away, that is, from both home and civilization. And we have his own testimony. In his diary for June, 1856, he wrote: "I often dreamed about a life of farming—eternal labour, eternal Nature—and for some reason some gross voluptuousness always entered those dreams. A heavy woman with callused hands, firm breasts and bare feet always worked in front of me."[11]

Sonia was right to feel jealous. She was, after all, a reader, indeed a writer, a talker, and a listener, and therefore participated in all Tolstoy's conscious concerns. Aksinia was totally outside them, a working woman who had made love with peasants, a mother of another caste. He approached her through her and his sexuality alone, and no subsequent conversations, we gather, translated that sexuality into moral-rational-sentimental terms. By the standards of the religion of Nature, the religion of Eros, his passion for Aksinia was more authentic than his passion for his wife—as his novel *The Devil* suggests that he knew.

It is clear, moreover, that Tolstoy felt some kind of sexual obses-

sion for Aksinia which frightened him. He decided to end relations
with her, but found that he could not do it. Even after his marriage
he was not free of her. She put herself in his way and went (in early
December, 1862) with other serf women to wash the floors at Yasnaya Polyana and was pointed out to the already pregnant Sonia,
who became very jealous.

The story of this obsession Tolstoy told in his short novel *The
Devil*, which ends with the protagonist shooting to death the woman he loves. Tolstoy finished this story only in the 1890s, and it is
one of the early documents of sexual realism in European literature.
(He'd had the experience corresponding to that literary mood *before*
he wrote his marriage novels.) He had begun it in the early days of
his marriage but had given it up because Sonia did not want his
mind on Aksinia, even in that way.

However, there were another five stories he began which fea-
tured Aksinia and that were not in the harsh style of *The Devil*. They
are all openly about Yasnaya Polyana and its environs, and while
they use the names of real people and places, they are about the
peasants, not the gentry. These are, in fact, rural idylls in Berthold
Auerbach's style, peasant stories told with peasant dialogue and
plenty of folk detail, and their animating spirit is a pagan sensuality. This was another kind of literary eroticism Tolstoy turned away
from when he turned toward domestic fiction.

The Aksinia figure is sympathetically portrayed in them as the
embodiment of natural force: a merry and masterful woman. It is
particularly interesting that in one case the narrative interest lies in
discovering whom she will take as a lover, and the lucky man is a
shy boy whom she has teased. This is an erotic situation which Tolstoy does not repeat elsewhere; it is closer to the D. H. Lawrence of
The Rainbow than to the Tolstoy of *War and Peace*.

Tolstoy was thinking, dreaming, and writing about Aksinia during that summer of 1860 and spring of 1861 when he saw Auerbach,
the German writer about peasants, whose work he admired. One
must guess that he seriously thought of a common-law marriage
with her, like Sergei's with Marya Shishkin, and of writing peasant
idylls in the Auerbach manner and teaching the village children—a
whole life could have been built around that structure. But instead
he married Sonia Bers, and built the life we know, and wrote the
novels we know, about heroines like Natasha and Kitty. The only
woman in his major fiction who may have something of Aksinia is

Anna Karenina. And Aksinia's son by Tolstoy grew up in Yasnaya Polyana and was pointed out by the peasants to Tolstoy's legitimate children.

Sonia Bers

The Bers girls and their mother came on a visit to Yasnaya Polyana in 1862. Their mother, Lyubov, was an illegitimate daughter of an old-style Russian noble who had been a passionate gambler, and a desperate hunter and lover of the gypsies. This man, Islenyev, was a friend of Tolstoy's father, and lived near Yasnaya Polyana, so that Sonia spent her summers nearby as a girl. But Liubov herself at sixteen married a thirty-six-year-old German doctor. His grandfather, a Saxon, had been in the Austrian army and had come to Russia to drill the Russian cavalry. His father had married a Westphalian baroness, and he was brought up a Lutheran, so his cultural heritage and his temperament were German. He was a physician at the Kremlin, and devoted to education and culture in a modern way. He and his wife were ambitious for their five sons and three daughters, overworked to give them an education, and made them too work hard. The girls, who were older, were brought up to keep house, sew, and educate the boys. Sonia and Liza, her older sister, both had certificates to teach as tutors.

They had some, strictly controlled, contact with the students of Moscow. One of them tried to convert Sonia to materialism, lending her books by its prophets, Feuerbach and Büchner. This meant they had some contact with the world of radical ideas. Sonia also remembered hearing Turgenev's *Fathers and Sons* discussed with passionate partisanship and interesting herself in its nihilist hero, Bazarov. But their essential education was almost certainly domestic novels. Tania, at least, read nothing but novels.

Tolstoy distinguished two groups within the Bers family, the blond and the dark Bers, associating each group with one of the parents. He told Sonia, in December 1864, "the mind of the dark Bers is asleep; they can but they don't want to; hence their self-confidence, sometimes inopportune, and their tact. But their mind is asleep because they love passionately and because, moreover, the progenitor of the dark Bers, Liubov Alexandrovna, was undeveloped. The light Bers have a great attraction to intellectual interest but their mind is feeble and shallow."[12] This is, of course, in line with the standard literary ideology: the Russian had greater access to the unconscious than the German, and the aristocrat has more vitality than the bourgeois.

Tolstoy saw Sonia first when she was eleven or twelve, when his *Childhood* was already her favorite book. She waited on him at table, tied a red ribbon to his chair afterwards, and wore in her dress copied-out passages of this book, such as, "will one ever get back the freshness, the freedom from care, the desire for love, and the power of belief, which one possesses in childhood?"[13] In other words, she was carried away by the erotic influence of the arts, and of a peculiarly sentimental kind. *Childhood* is an elegy to childhood, to which she, at eleven, was already devoted.

The Bers were of decidedly lower social class than the Tolstoys. But they were related to the Tolstoy caste through illegitimacy. Dr. Bers became a collegiate assessor in 1845, and thus acquired nobility in some theoretical sense, but his wife's illegitimacy always rankled, with her and with her daughters. (Moreover, Dr. Bers had in his youth an affair with Turgenev's mother; his illegitimate daughter by her was therefore Sonia's sister as well as Turgenev's, and the latter was Tolstoy's [illegitimate] brother-in-law.)

When Sonia passed the tutors' examination, it was said that she had written the best essay of the year. She had a flair for literature and for acting and she also painted, played, and composed. She had, before Tolstoy proposed, written a piece of fiction in which he figured. She had him read that, and he had her read the diaries in which his debauches were recorded, which badly shocked her.

She was not a buoyant spirit, and envied her sister Tania in that respect. She was vivacious and attractive, but some melancholy and much anxiety lay beneath. Her father is supposed to have said: "Poor Sonia will never be completely happy." At sixteen she wrote:

Life is a hard thing, and I'm no good at guiding myself. How often have I made good and firm resolutions, yet each time my powers have failed me and I have had to abandon my intentions. But I'm becoming too pensive. I have such a queer silly temperament.[14]

Tolstoy was full of doubts about his own feelings, as he had been with Valeria. In his diary entry of August 23, 1862, he was afraid this was not love but again the desire for love, and tried to look at her weak sides.[15] But Sonia had a considerable forcefulness and vitality which Valeria seems to have lacked. On September 12 he was sure he was madly in love, and on September 23 they were married.

He would brook no delay once he had made up his mind, and the arrangements were very hurried. His diary makes it clear that he was in a very abnormal state of tension, which in his fiction is passed off as the excitement of love but which reads more like a fear of some revulsion of feeling. There was more of intention, imagination, and determination about his feelings than of anything quieter and more "natural."

Sonia soon had paths cleared on the Yasnaya Polyana estate, benches painted, and before long a tennis court and a croquet ground were created. She brought the bed linen and all the other equipment of modern culture to Yasnaya Polyana. She was the spirit of the bourgeoisie incarnate, but this did not mean only a love of money and material comforts—in the early years of their marriage it hardly meant that at all—it meant rather the love of culture, of mental adventure, of new worlds of thought and feeling. That was what Sonia had and Aksinia did not (and Kasturba did not); that was what made her a good wife for a novelist, and an inspiration for his heroines.

Gandhi 1894–1906, Johannesburg and Politics

When it was settled that he was to stay on in Natal, Gandhi rented a villa on the beach in the most fashionable part of European Durban. He was next door to the attorney general, Harry Escombe, who was later the prime minister. This was a highly Westernized period of his life. He set up what he later referred to as a gymnasium in his house—we know of swings and parallel bars in the backyard. This means a Western-style cult of the body and is as near as he ever got to the style of the unregenerate Tolstoy.

His house was a lodging place and home to several of his clerks and colleagues, though his family was still in India. Most strikingly, he sent to Porbandar, inviting over, not Kasturba but Sheikh Mehtab, who came and acted as a sort of major domo to the household. But he apparently used the house, when Gandhi was out of it, for disreputable purposes (whether out of mere slyness or with the intention to desecrate, we cannot now say). Gandhi seems to have disregarded warnings or at least hints as to what was going on: "I had disregarded the warnings of kind friends. Infatuation had completely blinded me. . . . I had known that the companion was a bad character, and yet I believed in his faithfulness to me."[1]

Finally, one morning in 1896, one of his servants came to the office and brought Gandhi back to the house, where he found Sheikh Mehtab with a prostitute. When he demanded that Mehtab leave, the latter threatened to expose him. It is not clear what he thought he could expose—perhaps he meant ridicule—but it seems he felt he had some hold over his old friend. But Gandhi sent for the police, and that was the final end of their long relationship. Mehtab stayed on in Durban, attaching himself to an Indian merchant there and making a reputation as a reciter of romantic Urdu poetry. He was a master of the revels, an enhancer of life's pleasures. But later his wife and daughter became *satyagrahis*, and "He worshipped me from afar," according to Gandhi.

The big puzzle of the friendship is of course, what held Gandhi so long attached to, infatuated by, the other man. He calls him an "evil genius" in *An Autobiography*, and all his language about him suggests that he had size in Gandhi's eyes, and that Gandhi had persuaded himself that, though evil, Sheikh Mehtab was faithful to *him*. One of Faust's self-deceptions was that Mephistopheles would do *him* no harm. (In the Gujarati version of the autobiography, Gandhi says his friend caused him *moha*, enthusiasm, intoxication, and would have prevented his spiritual advance.)[2] One can only suppose that Gandhi was trying to subdue, attach, and redeem all that force of nature which was not his, in the person of his boyhood hero.

Politically, he was immediately immersed in action over the Franchise Law Amendment Act. On June 27th, 1894, he sent telegrams asking that it not be considered by the legislative assembly until the Indian petition was presented, and he was granted two days' grace. On the 28th he submitted a petition, signed by five hundred people, asking for a commission of enquiry. On the 29th he led a deputation to the premier asking for a week's delay in order to present their case more exhaustively. On July 1, he addressed a meeting of Indians. On the 3rd he led another deputation, to the governor. And so on. From now on, this was to be Gandhi's life, what he called "public work." The amazing thing is that he engaged in it so totally and so immediately.

The issue was broader than mere politics; it might have been called historical. In the pamphlet, "Indian Franchise: an Appeal to every Briton in South Africa" (December 16, 1895), Gandhi cited the Indian Immigrants Commission Report, which had said that white men would not settle in South Africa to become hewers of wood and drawers of water. Every Englishman now identified himself, outside the British Isles, as upper caste—even as aristo-military. Lord Selborne, who succeeded to Sir Alfred Milner as high commissioner in 1905, said:

What is wanted more than anything else in these two colonies are British subjects, who, if need be, can fight, which is the same thing as saying white British subjects. For in these colonies a white man must always be a fighter, whereas this is the one thing the Asiatic can never be, both owing to the peculiar circumstances of the country and to the fact that the Asiatics who come here are not of any martial race ... but as trader the white British subject is hopelessly beaten out of the field by the Asiatic.[3]

A good deal of Gandhi's defence of the Indians in South Africa amounts to an argument that they have more of the spirit of *Robinson Crusoe* than the South African English do, and so better deserve to belong to the modern system.

On the other hand, Gandhi was asking for a limited position for the Indians in South Africa, a Bania position. He explicitly and repeatedly renounced all political ambition on their behalf, saying that the property qualification would prevent their theoretical franchise from counting politically, and that no Indian would object to the imposition of an even larger qualification of that kind, or an educational qualification. He kept himself off the voters' lists. What he objected to in the franchise bill was the cultural insult; it was the honor of India he was concerned to preserve, not any political right.

On June 5, 1896, Gandhi left for India. He had decided to bring back his family (Sheikh Mehtab having been finally dismissed), but was also commissioned to represent South African Indians in India for six months. On the journey he wrote a pamphlet with the title: "The Grievances of British Indians in South Africa." Again his complaint was that the law treated them as barbarians. "There is a very good reason for requiring registration of a native, in that he is yet being taught the dignity and necessity of labor. The Indian knows it and he is imported because he knows it."[4] This was, of course, crucially important; a large part of what both Gandhi and the whites meant by civilization was aptitude for work. But the whites themselves were now too "civilized" to work.

His time in India was a series of journeys and speeches. In September, he spoke at meetings in Bombay on the South African situation. Being back in India, his voice failed him again, and someone read his speech out. On October 12, he spent the day in Poona, and met the famous leaders Tilak, Gokhale, and Bhandarkar. In Calcutta he briefly, and humbly, met the leaders of Bengal. In Rajkot he taught the schoolchildren the National Anthem for the Queen's Jubilee of 1897. But on November 12, he got a wire from Durban, asking him to return because the *Transvaal Volksraad* had recommended that Indians be confined to "locations."

Gandhi left Bombay for Durban with his wife and two sons and his sister's son Gokuldas on November 30, 1896. Four days before that there had been a mass meeting of whites in Durban which had set up a Colonial Patriotic Union and had hissed Gandhi's name. Gandhi's pamphlet on Indian grievances had been published in Rajkot and its contents had been reported rather exaggeratedly by Reuters, so that white opinion was inflamed against him.

His ship reached Durban on December 18, but on the 19th the Natal government declared Bombay an infected port and put ships coming from there under a five-day quarantine, which was extended again and again until January 11. The "men of Durban" lined the quay in military ranks to prevent his disembarkation.

Gandhi landed secretly, but was recognized, mobbed, and assaulted—his turban torn off, his ear and eye struck, and he might have been seriously injured or killed but for the intervention of a brave Englishwoman. He was saved by the protection of her parasol, which must have satisfied the sense of the "men of Durban" that they had destroyed him. He would not have his persecutors prosecuted, but he sent copies of his Memorial to Joseph Chamberlain to public men in London because there was to be a Colonial Premiers conference there that year.

The *Johannesburg Star*'s comment on the incident was that: "The whole country is still in its boyhood, and there is nothing a boy loves more than to refer his disputes to the gory arbitrament of physical force. Looked at in that way, this week's doings in Durban may be excused with an indulgent smile."[5] This reflects the son-versus-father structure of sentiments, the sentiments that structure Kipling's work, and it would be easy to point to the Kipling short stories built around an incident like this—bringing out the men, quarantining the ship, and then mobbing the agitator till he hides behind a woman's parasol.

Of course, when even South African newspapers were being serious, they could only deplore such conduct. The *Natal Mercury* said (January 19, 1897): "Mr. Gandhi is endeavoring to perform for his compatriots similar services to those which Englishmen have always been ready to perform."[6] But the colonists, being young, allowed themselves to act humorously—that is, nonseriously, out of the part of themselves people are officially ashamed of but profoundly fond of. This is very important in judging the plausibility of Gandhi's politics, since he appealed so exclusively to the best and most serious part of his audience.

Eighteen ninety-eight was the year of a crisis in Gandhi's relations with his wife. He had a number of his colleagues and employees staying in his house from time to time, and one of them was an Indian Christian clerk whom he liked. Most Indian Christians had been of very low caste—pariahs—and, of course, by renouncing Hinduism they lost caste anyway. Kasturba refused to clean out the chamber pot used by this man in his bedroom. We must remember, in order to grasp the full implications of this, that the caste structure, and Hinduism in general, is based very largely on rituals of purification, and that human excreta are the very apotheosis of filth. Morris Carstairs speaks of Hindus' "preoccupation with the noxious properties of human faeces, the arch contaminant, which was associated with personal and social degradation."[7]

Another, and substantial, cause for Kasturba's discontent was the disappointment her sons felt, and especially Harilal, that he was not being prepared for one of the professions as his father had been. Gandhi had ceased to believe in those professions and in Western education altogether, and, as time went by, his lack of belief hardened into disbelief. Moreover, at this time, he could find no Gujarati tutors for his sons, and they had no teaching at all except what he could give them as they trotted along beside him as he went to his office. They felt themselves (again, it was Harilal, above all, of whom this was true) made light of. He and Gokuldas went back to India to school, but it was not many months before Gandhi sent for them to come back again.

In 1899, the Boer War broke out, one of the official British grievances being the Boers' treatment of British Indians. The troops that fought for Britain came from all over the Empire, and 10,000 Indians came to defend Natal, even though, as Gandhi pointed out, Natal was refusing to give shelter to Indian refugees who had fled the Transvaal. But Gandhi rallied the Indian community to the British cause. "We once again feel that, though in Natal, yet we are British subjects, and that in time of danger the enchanting phrase has not after all lost any of its charm."[8]

Gandhi urged the Indians to fight for the Empire, saying: "Our existence in South Africa is only in our capacity as British subjects. . . . It must largely be conceded that justice is on the side of the Boers. But every single subject of a state must not hope to enforce his private opinion in all cases. . . . If we think the government's action immoral, we have to argue against it first, which we haven't done, and this is not that kind of moral crisis."[9]

On October 19, a hundred Indians volunteered, at Gandhi's suggestion, to serve with the British army without pay even though they could not handle arms. The Indians were on the battlefield only to bind up wounds; the British did all the fighting. As one might expect, the ordinary British soldiers' attitude to their Indian ambulance-men was condescending. But Gandhi claimed that the Indians overcame that.

As soon as the war was over, Gandhi began noticing signs that the wartime promises of imperial statesmen would not be kept. He wrote Dadabhai Naoroji in London that Mr. Chamberlain was:

. . . anxious to go any length to respect the wishes of the self-governing colonies. . . . The India Office, on the other hand, appears to be terribly inactive. . . . The activity of the Cape Colony seems to show that the services rendered by India . . . will be entirely forgotten, and the Indian treated, if they had it all their own way, as a social leper.[10]

On April 20, 1901, he noted that Chamberlain had recently announced that all the old legislation of the Transvaal and the Orange Free State would be respected by the new rulers insofar as possible. This, of course, included the anti-Asiatic laws, and in fact those laws were now enforced more severely than under the Boers. Before the war, Chamberlain had said that he was powerless to intervene but sympathetic to the Indians' position. After the war, he was powerful, and yet things got worse. The King's speech from the throne referred to the ideal of equality for "all white races south of the Zambesi," though the old phrase had been "all civilized races."

Nevertheless, Gandhi felt that *his* task in South Africa was completed. In October 1901, Gandhi and his family sailed back to India, having promised to return within a year if the community needed him. The Indian community made them gifts of jewelry (two gold chains, a fifty guinea necklace, a diamond ring and pin, a purse with seven gold coins), but Gandhi insisted on putting all these into a safety deposit as a reserve source of funds for the community cause. This occasioned another bitter quarrel between him and Kasturba. From her point of view, such jewels were family property and would be needed when her sons got married. When the latter joined the argument on their father's side, she accused him of trying to make *saddhus* of the boys. But to Gandhi the jewels were the marks of a family-scale imperialism, as repugnant as the national kind.

After a visit to Congress, the annual convention of Indian nationalists, and a short tour, Gandhi set up legal practice in Rajkot but again had no great success and moved to Bombay in July, where too he was not successful. In a letter of August 6, 1902 he said he was now "free to lounge about the High Court letting the Solicitors know of an addition to the ranks of the briefless ones . . . ."[11] This is a very uncharacteristic note of irony, directed against himself and the world in general, which he soon retrieved: "But I do not despair. I rather appreciate the regular life and the struggle that Bombay imposes on one."[12] He must, however, have felt a great difference between this life and his busyness, his neededness, and his importance in South Africa.

In November he was summoned back to Natal, and after some reluctance (he cited ill-health in himself and in his children), he sailed back. On December 28, he led a deputation of Natal Indians to see Chamberlain, who was visiting South Africa, and prepared a memorial for Transvaal Indians to present in January. He found the officers in charge of the new Asiatic Department in Pretoria to be "adventurers who had accompanied the army from India to South Africa during the war and had settled there in order to try their luck."[13] About fifty Pathans had also arrived there in the same way. Both of these were groups Gandhi was going to have to confront, and both were particularly difficult for him to deal with. He explains the Pathans thus: "To kill and get killed is an ordinary thing in their eyes, and if they are angry with anyone, they will thrash him and sometimes even kill him. . . . A Pathan's anger becomes particularly uncontrollable when he has to deal with anyone whom he takes to be a traitor. When he seeks justice he seeks it only through personal violence."[14] This is very much what Kipling might have said, and in this next phase of his life Gandhi moved

even further into Kipling country and confronted its inhabitants
and ran into its incidents. But he also moved into another world,
much more like that of the modern intellectual.

He was an attorney of the Supreme Court in Johannesburg,
where he had a large practice. One of his firm's letter books, covering a three month period, included a thousand letters. He earned
£5000 a year—his share of the gold boom. And Johannesburg was
often called Jo'burg, and sometimes Jewburg, because of the number of Jews living there. (Anti-Semitism developed in conjunction
with other aspects of white racism. In London in 1906 one of Gandhi's sponsors was Sir Lepel Griffin, a retired Indian official, who
blamed the plight of the Indians in the Transvaal on the Jews
there—"the offscourings of the international sewers of Europe.")
And it was among the intellectual Jews that Gandhi found his circle
of friends.

Two of them who became important friends were Henry Polak
and Hermann Kallenbach. Through Kallenbach, to whom her mother entrusted her, Gandhi hired a new secretary, Sonja Schlesin, a
seventeen-year-old girl of Russian Jewish descent and strong opinions and high ideals, who soon became a trusted collaborator. She
was, in effect, the executive director of the whole movement at
times when Gandhi was in jail, but she refused a raise in salary
because it would "betray the principle which had attracted her to
him." She competed with him, morally, but asserting a different
morality; and he enjoyed the frank challenge, which he did not get
from his Indian disciples. He also always enjoyed establishing a
friendship with someone of opposite type.

Besides these close friends, there were Gabriel Isaacs, a vegetarian
and jeweler who lived with Gandhi at his Phoenix settlement, Louis
Ritch, the Theosophist, who also did a lot of legal work for the
Indian cause, Morris Philipson, a Jewish member of the South African Parliament who represented their interests there, and others.
These men were not religiously orthodox, but from them Gandhi
got glimpses of Jewish tradition and of the modern-intellectual temperament which few Indian politicians had.

On May 9, 1903, there was a public meeting of Indians and a
resolution protesting the anti-Indian laws. But still, in a petition to
the Transvaal government (June 8, 1903), Gandhi said that British
Indians "ask for no political power. They admit the British race
should be the dominant race in South Africa."[15] All they asked for

was freedom from restrictions on trade, movement, or property, and no legislation directed against brown skins.

In June of that year, he began to publish *Indian Opinion.* At first it was published in four languages, English, Gujarati, Hindi, and Tamil, and the bulk of it was written by him. (The Gujarati articles tend to be more factual, detailed, and down to earth than the English.) Its principal function was to give information about the fortunes of the Indian cause and to shape Indian response, in the course of which Gandhi introduced quite a few Indian fables, proverbs, and so on. But there were also articles of a wider and less direct interest, articles on other Eastern countries, like Japan, then rising to prominence through her successful self-modernization, and on leaders of other oppressed races, like Booker T. Washington, and on April 23 and 30, there were, for instance, extracts from Tolstoy's essays on science. Perhaps just as interesting is what was not in *Indian Opinion.* Gandhi said writing for it must be an exercise in self-discipline, and he was very much on guard against rumor, paranoia, exaggeration, and falsification. He also eschewed, on principle, all bitter and biting rhetoric: he told Henry Polak to imitate the London *Times* in his articles. *Indian Opinion* is an exercise in clarity, sobriety, and plain speaking.

He finally took over complete financial responsibility for the paper (which amounted to £3,500) in October, and in January 1905 told Gokhale that his legal office was being run in the paper's interest. Albert West, an English immigrant who had volunteered to work with Gandhi, found the paper's financial condition to be so bad that Gandhi set off from Johannesburg to Durban to investigate. Reading John Ruskin's *Unto This Last* on the journey, he became enthusiastic about the idea of founding a Ruskinian settlement, and the next day set about buying a hundred acres at Phoenix, fourteen miles from Durban, where the paper could be produced (when somewhat reduced in size) and agriculture could be practiced, and the simple life followed. Twelve compositors worked on the press, which Gandhi called a village industry. The Phoenix Settlement came into existence that November and December, and it marks an important stage in Gandhi's progressive self-disentanglement from city life and from the ordinary circumstances of secular modern life.

In February 1904, he visited the Indian location of Johannesburg, which was in an unsanitary area, and on the 15th warned the medi-

cal officer of health about it, repeating the warning on the 20th—
again in vain. On March 1, he wrote to say that the plague had
broken out there, and during the month, with minimal help from
the city, he organized a hospital and a quarantine. It was his work
against the plague which won him the friendship of Albert West
and Henry Polak, and it was Polak, already a vegetarian, a Tolstoy
reader, and a critic of technology, who gave him the copy of *Unto
This Last*.

Gandhi commented on the Immigration Restriction Act: "The colonies have become very powerful, and are becoming more and
more so day by day. The Indian subjects of the King-Emperor therefore, have to patiently and quietly submit."[16] But in other articles
(and indeed implicitly here) his language grew more prophetic, de-
nunciatory, and inflammatory. In *Indian Opinion* for the 8th of October, 1903, under the heading "Mockery of God in the Orange River
Colony," he said that the State's Day of Humiliation had been pro-
claimed without the proclamation giving any hint of sacrifice or
repentance, and he called the colony's color prejudice a national sin
before God.

Even then, however, his aggression was tempered by other tones;
he called the Orange proclamation "in itself a sign of a godly
heart." We are a long way from Marx or Lenin's tone about their
enemies. It is perhaps worth reflecting on the use Marx would have
made of Johannesburg in his writings had he lived there, in the
central sin spot of civilization, as it was called. All Gandhi will say
is: "Things are done post haste here in the Transvaal. The million-
aires want to extract their gold in a few years."[17] And he commented on the labor commission's report: "If the country is to be boomed
and exploited for the benefit of the capitalist and only for the present generation, there is no doubt that the Majority Report is perfectly sound, but if it is to be gradually developed, there cannot be
the slightest doubt that it must rest content with what labor may be
available in the colony."[18] Gandhi saw as clearly as Marx what was
at stake, and the disaster that was impending, but his tone remained
studiously—though not exclusively—moderate.

The enemies of the Indians were organizing themselves into
white leagues and vigilants' committees. The Johannesburg White
League was formed in 1902, because the city was being "flooded
with undesirables." Gandhi could, of course, prove that the number
of Indians was very small and could suggest that the European population itself was not very desirable. But he knew that such argu-

ments had no effect, and by 1905 (on the 28th of June), he was speaking of a life-and-death struggle that lay ahead for British Indians in South Africa.

These were years in which world events had a big impact on the self-image of Indians. First of all came the Russo-Japanese War of 1904–1905, in which, for the first time, a nation of the East defeated a nation of the West. There was also a dramatic difference between the two countries in geographical area, in size of population, and in length of participation in the modern system. Japan seemed a boyish David against the Goliath, the colossus, of Russia. But it was, above all, the spectacle of yellow-skinned men handling the weapons of modern war and turning them against whites successfully which excited other Oriental nations.

And then came the Partition of Bengal by Lord Curzon in 1905—or more exactly, the large-scale and prolonged agitation in Bengal against that partition. This was the first large political action against the British in Indian history, and it brought to the fore names that were to be very important throughout Gandhi's life time, like Arabindo and Tagore, as well as others already famous, like Surendranath Banerjee and Bipin Chandra Pal. It also employed methods of agitation that Gandhi was to use, notably the support of *swadeshi* and the boycott and burning of foreign cloth. All these things Gandhi commented on with Indian patriotism in *Indian Opinion*.

During the Bambata Rebellion, which led to the Zulu War, Gandhi again raised an Indian Ambulance Corps and served in it with the rank of sergeant major. The rebellion broke out when a chief killed a tax collector with an assegai, and it was quelled by means of floggings and hangings. In New York the *Gaelic American* called Gandhi's cooperation with the English army "contemptible beyond expression," and in London the *Indian Sociologist* called it "disgusting." Polak and Doke say that Gandhi would never talk about the experience of serving on that campaign, and Erikson suggests that the spectacle of the bodies of blacks killed and wounded by whites—and killed by machine guns against which they stood no chance—may have reinforced his revulsion against white, male, sadistic civilization, and his self-identification with opposite forces, with women and passivity and suffering.

During the marches of the Ambulance Corps during the Zulu War, Gandhi came to the decision that a public worker should be a *vanaprasthi*, that is, one who has renounced the cares and responsibilities of marriage and a family. And in 1906, he took the vow of

brahmacharya, or abstinence in thought and deed from sexual pleasure. "Procreation and the consequent care of children are inconsistent with public service."[19]

In natural parallel, Gandhi's sense of his own vocation grew more
religious. On May 27, he replied to an angry letter from his brother
Lakshmidas, nine years his elder, who had become treasurer of Porbandar. (Gandhi later said Lakshmidas sent him curses by registered
post for fourteen years.)[20] Gandhi declared that he had not given up
all family responsibilities, and that he would look after Lakshmidas's children and widow if that became necessary. But he could not
be primarily a family man, and he would not devote himself to
making money.

Thus, if Tolstoy married at thirty-four and entered into domesticity as a career and a faith as well as a personal relationship, Gandhi
at thirty-seven withdrew from marriage, at least sexually, and to
some degree from domesticity. He was henceforth engaged not in
public work but in a political crusade. Over this period of his youth,
he had gradually committed his life to political activism, as completely as Tolstoy had committed his to the art of writing; but from
now on, Gandhi's politics would be boldly nationalist.

INTERLUDE

The New Life, 1894–1910

The Encounter Between Them

We turn now, though briefly, from collocation to confrontation. It was in 1909/1910 that Gandhi and Tolstoy thought about each other. Of course, Gandhi knew of Tolstoy long before that and thought about him long after. But the two were chronologically out of each other's sight most of the time, though sailing towards the same destination; it was only then that they passed close enough for Tolstoy personally to pass on to Gandhi the relay torch.

The story begins in 1894, when a friend sent Gandhi a copy of A. Delano's English translation of *The Kingdom of God is Within You*, which had been published in Russia in 1893. He had certainly heard of Tolstoy before then, but it seems that he had not before read any large work, or received any intense impression. But one cannot be sure, especially about knowledge of Tolstoy's life. In 1887, the year before Gandhi reached London, George Kennan wrote an article about Tolstoy for *Century* magazine, which made him well-known—made Ruskin call Tolstoy's the noblest life story

he had ever read. In the same year, Madame Blavatsky wrote enthusiastically about Tolstoy in her Theosophical magazine, *Lucifer*, re-
viewing his book *On Life*.

The subtitle of *The Kingdom of God is Within You* is *Christianity not
as a Mystical Teaching but as a New Concept of Life*. Historically, the
newness in question refers to the way Christianity differed from
the Roman imperial culture in the midst of which it developed, but
ultimately it points to the incompatibility between Christian con-
cepts and the Russian empire of the nineteenth century and modern
Western civilization in general. It denounces that civilization and
prophesies its doom, on the authority of true Christianity.

Tolstoy began by referring to the Quakers as his spiritual ancestors, citing Tom Paine as well as George Fox, and then to the American abolitionists, quoting from Garrison's 1838 "Declaration of Sentiments." He described the Quakers' repudiation of patriotism and
politics and the courts, and contrasted with them what he called the
jacobins or terrorists: "The spirit of jacobinism is the spirit of retali-
ation, violence, and murder."[1] Then he expounded the lost truths
taught, in his *Catechism of Christian Non-Resistance*, by Adin Ballou
(who founded a nonviolent community in Massachusetts in the
1840s), truths which had been known and lost before, having been
taught by the fifteenth-century Bohemian Chalicky in his *Drawnet
of Faith*.

Tolstoy was not interested in the supernatural part of religion, or
life after death. But to humanize religion is also to destroy it. To try
to love humanity as a whole in a sentimental or romantic way is
merely to extend and dilute personal and social love. (This is what
Tolstoy himself had understood by Christianity in the 1850s.) Humanity as a whole cannot be loved in that way, and such love is a
fiction. Christian love is really love of self—love of the God within
us. But it is not selfish, in any ordinary sense. To be Christian is to
deny your ordinary ego and to change your life completely. Perhaps the most notable such change is that Christ imposes on us the
law of nonresistance. Since men can never agree on what is evil,
they must never resist evil with force. Christians thus become force-
less, feeble, by the standards of the world. This remains true even
though (as Gandhi even more than Tolstoy was to show) they may
resist evil and may exert force of another kind.

And now (in the 1890s) it is time for society as a whole to change
its life; because material conditions now make that possible, and
because the contradiction between Christian ideals and social facts,

above all those of war, is now so great. There is a contrast between our consciousness and our life, and the latter needs to catch up. Consciousness means more or less public opinion—what might be expressed in some ideal (uncensored and conscientious) range of newspapers.

This is one of the ways Gandhi carried out what Tolstoy suggested, carried on where Tolstoy left off, for Gandhi was an ideal journalist in this sense as much as he was anything. He worked with public opinion, "consciousness," as perhaps no one else ever has.

But our consciousness is not fully expressed (in the 1890s). We see this even in literature, which now has at its disposal an unprecedented wealth of ideas, forms, colors, and yet retreats to pagan and even animal values, fearing the loftiness of those new values and aspirations—such as universal brotherhood and eternal peace— which everyone knows have replaced the old creeds and prohibitions. Indeed, novelists seem to fear every definiteness of thought and of expression. There are no novels, that is, expressly condemning war. "The indefiniteness, if not the insincerity, of the relation of the cultured men of our times to this phenomenon [war and conscription] is striking."[2]

Tolstoy's enthusiasm for definiteness and clarity is reflected in his own style and structure, which tend toward the effect of a geometrical theorem. "We must take the Sermon on the Mount to be as much a law as the theorem of Pythagoras." This comes as a surprise and an unpleasant shock to any reader expecting nonprofessional philosophy, and especially to any devoted reader of Tolstoy's novels. His new way of dealing with life and consciousness seems crude and stark, and many readers have accused him of willfulness. But from our point of view, this difference from his fictional manner is simply a return from reverie to thought, to use Rousseau's terms, and reverie is simply the imaginative equivalent of the dialectical consciousness, to use Hegel's terms.

When Tolstoy turned to religion he turned away from dialectical consciousness. Indeed he had never been completely committed to it, and readers of *War and Peace* have always complained about the harsh character of the sections on Napoleon and war and history, which was harsh just because in those sections Tolstoy had given up reverie for thought. Particularly interesting for us in connection with this is Gandhi's Euclidean simplicity of proposition and diction, and his love of arithmetical or geometrical analogies (which can be found also in his greatest intellectual disciple, Vinoba

Bhave). Though distrustful, and indeed scornful, of modern science, Tolstoy and Gandhi wanted both to "experiment with truth" and to prove their ideas "scientifically." And in fact people of scientific training find them (at least, their style and manner) more accessible than do people in the arts and humanities. To the latter, the men in this intellectual tradition seem not to be intellectuals at all, seem to be in some disqualifying sense simple-minded, because they refuse the complexity and the flexibility of the dialectical consciousness and the reverie. Tolstoy's case is especially interesting because he had shown himself a great master of these modes before.

But to return to *The Kingdom of God is Within You*, a Christian need not, must not, pass judgment on a government, but he must, for himself, refuse to support it. "Christianity in its true meaning destroys the state." That is why Christ was crucified. But such resistance—for instance, refusal of military service—must be individual.

Our action has to be turned inward, in self-purification. Socialists and liberals deny this, thinking that *they* stand outside this system of privilege and guilt. They think they will be able to adjust the external structure of the state, and, without altering the old mode of consciousness, all the valuable features of the old culture will develop and increase and distribute themselves better than before, bringing the clever more and more pleasures of the old kind. "The metaphysics of hypocrisy," as Tolstoy calls it, persuades them that *they* will need not to change *their* lives. But that is wrong.

Such is the message of the book Gandhi read in 1894. As we shall see, it was (in the words of the official Soviet edition) the completion of Tolstoy's publicist work of the 1880s, and the climax of all those searchings begun by him as early as the 1860s. It was praised by Lenin as posing concrete questions of democracy and socialism and expressing a sincere protest against class domination.

But what did it mean to Gandhi? We may note, first of all, that it did not have the effect which this summary might suggest—it did not turn him away from war and everything military, or from politics and government. In the years immediately after reading it, he volunteered for service in three imperialist wars and immersed himself in legal/political activity. What Gandhi said was that it saved his religious faith, that when he arrived in South Africa he was in a crisis of scepticism, especially about soul-force, and that Tolstoy saved him from it. "I was at that time a believer in violence. Reading it cured me of my scepticism and made me a firm believer in Ahimsa." (Said on the occasion of the century of Tolstoy's birth, in 1928.)

Now there is very little theology in the book and that little is of the negative kind that disproves the need for theology. But it is a kind of theodicy, and even a handbook of piety. We must remember that Truth is God, and Ahimsa is Christ, or Rama. To love God is to love oneself, for God is Truth. Those two religious puns, as E. M. Forster might have called them, were mines of meaning to Gandhi and Tolstoy, however obscurely transparent they may be to others.

However, it is most likely that the book made its impact by the way that *many* of its features, Tolstoy's face as a whole, met the corresponding features of Gandhi's mind and sensibility (he read "Ivan Ilych," which also moved him deeply, at the same time), both sets of features being animated by an intensity of earnestness hardly to be met with in any other men among the millions who stood between Yasnaya Polyana and Pretoria.

In India this was the time of Arabindo's return from England to take up first education and then revolutionary work, and of Annie Besant's arrival, where she extended her influence out from theosophy to cultural revival and overt politics. This was also the time of Vivekananda's visit to the United States, which meant the beginning of the Vedanta Mission's work to bring Western virtues to India and Eastern virtues to the West. Gandhi himself was just becoming a political reformer along the same lines as those three and in implicit rivalry with them. They were all harnessing the Hindu religion to the cause of nation building in India. Insofar as Gandhi was a partner of theirs in 1894, he was not a suitable recipient for Tolstoy's message. But because he was many other things besides a political reformer, he did respond to it very strongly; though it seems likely that the figure and influence of Tolstoy did not become dominant in his mind for another decade or more.

When he started going to prison as part of *satyagraha* after 1906, he read *The Kingdom of God is Within You* again. It is one of the books we hear of him carrying with him in court and from one prison to another. He had by then met other Tolstoyans like Henry Polak. He had also read, by 1909, *On Life, My Confession,* "The First Step," *What is Art?,* "The Slavery of Our Times," and "How Shall We Escape?," since he recommended them in the appendix to *Hind Swaraj.* At some point when he was in South Africa, he read *What Then Must We Do?,* where he found: "There was good reason why Christ died

on the Cross, and good reason why the sacrifice of suffering conquers everything," which is perhaps the religious truth that charac-
terizes his and Tolstoy's sensibility most profoundly.

He did not read, so far as we know, *War and Peace* or *Anna Karenina*; and if he had, he would surely have had to reject them in be-
wilderment, since they carried a quite opposite message to that of
the late books. They were not written by his Tolstoy. In 1912, John
Middleton Murry compared the English translation of Dostoevsky's
The Brothers Karamazov with North's translations of Plutarch, which
had such an inspiring effect upon Elizabethan English writers, including Shakespeare. And a reviewer in *The Spectator* said that Russian novels in general held for Englishmen the vast and potent inspiration of the Renaissance.[3] Tolstoy as novelist was a part of this.
But Gandhi did not receive that inspiration.

In 1909 Gandhi went to London, but what he saw there and what
he read drove him even further from modern ideology and brought
him even closer to Tolstoy. London no longer exerted any charm
over him. In an article for *Indian Opinion* in October, entitled "This
Crazy Civilization," he wrote:

London has gone mad over Mr. Blériot [the pioneer aviator]...We have
trains running underground; there are telegraphic wires already hanging
over us; and outside, on the roads, there is the deafening noise of trains. If
you now have planes flying in the air, take it that people will be done to
death. Looking at this land, I at any rate have grown disillusioned with
Western civilization.[4]

As he said in a letter to Polak: "Every time I get into a railway car,
use a motor bus, I know that I am doing violence to my sense of
what is right."[5] On this visit, we may say, Gandhi saw London the
way the early Christians saw Rome, or the Jews Babylon—the way
the Expressionists were to see the Metropolis. Turning away from
Westminster, he went into the Cotswolds to see the Tolstoy colony
at Whiteway, and bought more Tolstoy books for Phoenix and read
with growing enthusiasm Tolstoy's "Letter to a Hindu."

In 1908, when Tolstoy was eighty, he had received greetings from
Gandhi among many other people, some more and some less eminent. That year, moreover, he got a letter about nonviolence from
an Indian revolutionary called Taraknath Das, his reply to which
turned out to be in effect addressed to Gandhi—his "Letter to a
Hindu." Its literal addressee was an exile living in Vancouver, Can-
ada and editing an insurrectionary magazine called *Free Hindustan,*

which carried the slogan: "Resistance to tyranny is obedience to God," and which had on its cover quotations from Herbert Spencer, then the intellectual hero of political iconoclasts. (Spencer was the very opposite of Tolstoy and Gandhi, for he defined civilization as ever-increasing complexity, and valued it therefore.) Das had sent two copies of his magazine and asked for an article, but protested to Tolstoy that nonviolence was self-defeating and contradicted altruism as well as egotism. Tolstoy sat down to write a reply on June 7, the day he got Das's letter, but it took him 413 manuscript pages and six months before he completed it, having discarded twenty-eight tentative versions.

What Tolstoy said was that Hindus must resist England nonviolently, because to resist it violently would be to yield to its ideology. Only thus could they retrieve an integrity they had already lost, for the East India company could never have enslaved two hundred million people if the latter had not accepted its values, its vision, its sense of the possible. Only by their own inherited nonviolence could Hindus defeat "the deeply immoral forms of social order in which the English and other pseudo-moral Christian nations live today."[6]

Mankind must move to a new level of consciousness, and the law of love must rule instead of the law of violence. But this will happen only if men free themselves from belief in "all kinds of Ormuzds, Brahman, Sabaoth, and their incarnations as Krishnas and Christs, as well as from belief in science." Hindus must give up Hinduism as they have known it. The old religions were no longer true. Like "the futile exercises of mind and memory called the sciences" (in which Tolstoy included law, history, anthropology) they obscure "the simple clear law of love, accessible to everybody and solving all problems and all perplexities."[7]

Gandhi read this letter-essay in 1909. He could not accept Tolstoy's brusque way with Indian religions, for his mind was always more pious. There was a Voltairean and even a Nietzschean style to Tolstoy's performance in the world of ideas. (In *What is Art?*, for instance, one recognizes his Prince Bolkonsky side.) Gandhi did not approve of using that style on any subject, but least of all on religion. But the main message of the "Letter to a Hindu" is exactly what Gandhi himself might have written, and on the subject dearest to his heart. It is from the moment he read the Letter that one can detect, as one would expect, a fairly constant scrutiny fixed by Gandhi on Tolstoy, even in the midst of his other occupations.

On October 1, 1909, Gandhi wrote to Tolstoy, asking him to confirm that he had written "Letter to a Hindu," which Gandhi had just read reproduced in some unofficial form (it had not been published, for Taraknath Das did not like it) asking if he could put it into print, and also asking if Tolstoy would give publicity to the nonviolent resistance to the state being mounted by the Indians in the Transvaal. Tolstoy replied immediately (he wrote on October 7) giving that confirmation and saying that Gandhi need pay no royalties if he used the Letter. Gandhi made some unsuccessful attempts, with the cooperation of Tolstoy's English disciple, Aylmer Maude, to get English newspapers to reproduce the Letter (he tried the *Daily News* and the *Manchester Guardian*) but then resigned himself to distributing it as a separate pamphlet himself. With financial help from a friend, he got 20,000 copies printed. He wrote again to Tolstoy, on October 11, giving some details of his work in South Africa, and in November sent Joseph Doke's biography of himself, which was just off the press.

Tolstoy read this book and made notes in the margin. He may well have brooded over two sentences in the accompanying letter: "I may add that my son has joined me in the struggle and is now undergoing imprisonment with hard labour for six months. This is his fourth imprisonment in the course of the struggle."

The reason Tolstoy may have found that postscript very painful is that none of his sons were joining him in his struggle; they were, in various ways, notably indifferent to, scornful of, or resentful of his public work, and had on various occasions declared him to be a public and private nuisance. Though there were exceptions, it is by and large true to say that his family hated him and that he lived in a domestic hell.

There was that difference between the two life stories. One would not say that Gandhi lived in a domestic hell, but the difference was only that in Gandhi's case the domestic tragedy was muted. For the ultimate irony of that postscript rebounded on Gandhi, and whether or not be believed it when he wrote, that Harilal was now his comrade in the cause, he had already behind him a painful history of disappointment and mutual reproach. Indeed, in the years to come, Harilal destroyed himself, and Gandhi's other sons diminished themselves because of their father, as Tolstoy's sons already had; partly in hopeless awe, partly by trying to diminish him, having first failed to rival him, challenge him, destroy him.

In April 1910, Gandhi sent Tolstoy a copy of *Hind Swaraj* (Indian

Home Rule), which is his major work in the world of ideas. It is a discussion of the right kind, and the wrong kind, of home rule for India to work for. In its appendix he listed as recommended reading six books by Tolstoy, two each by Ruskin and Thoreau, and one each by Socrates, Mazzini, R. C. Dutt, Henry Maine, and Edward Carpenter. The book is a Socratic dialogue between an Editor who represents Gandhi (the whole thing was written for the magazine he edited, *Indian Opinion*) and a Reader, whose opinions are a composite portrait of the Indian extremists Gandhi had been meeting in London, but whose submissive and respectful manner of arguing is more that of his South African readers and clients. (He said later that this Reader was his old friend, Dr. Pranjivan Mehta.)

The manuscript was written on *The Kildonan Castle*, between December 11 and 18, while Gandhi was returning to South Africa. He also then translated "Letter to a Hindu" into Gujarati and wrote a preface in which he said that its central principle was exactly his own. The translation of Tolstoy and his own essay were written in tandem.

Introducing *Hind Swaraj*, Gandhi said: "These views are mine, and yet not mine. They are mine because I hope to act according to them. They are almost a part of my being. But, yet, they are not mine, because I lay no claim to originality. They have been formed after reading several books."[8] He added that these views were also held by thousands of advanced Europeans (the Tolstoyans and so on) and by millions of Indians (those untouched by "civilization"). They represented a return to tradition.

The Reader says that young Indians are angry with their leaders and have turned away from Congress, for instance, considering it an instrument of the perpetuation of British rule. The Editor defends Congress, and even more the man associated with it, Gokhale. The Reader is perceptibly an adherent of Tilak and so an enemy of Gohkale. But, the Editor too is no constitutionalist. He says he finds parliaments and newspapers too merely expedient and insufficiently moral. He is disillusioned with modern civilization in general, and attacks law courts, medicine, hospitals, railways, and textile factories. The whole modern system is an Upas tree, its root immorality, its branches the parasitic professions.[9] Lawyers have enslaved India to English law and English eloquence. Doctors induce us to sin, because they eliminate the punitive effect of self-indulgence.

Gandhi deplores the whole quality of modern life; people in modern civilization keep up their energy by using intoxicants and are unhappy when they are alone. The English, at least, have lost all interest in the God of Christianity and worship money; and the Indians, in their turn, are losing faith in the Religion which underlies all religions.

Indian civilization is the best because it lasted, while the Greeks and the Romans destroyed themselves. That is, village India lasted, largely indifferent to the cities, the palaces, the dynasties, the conquests that rolled over it. The focus of Indian culture and even the tendency of Indian civilization is to elevate the moral being, because their forms are based on a belief in God, while modern civilization is essentially materialist and appetitive. Our ancestors wisely set a limit to our indulgences, intellectual as well as sensual, for (as a result) Indians have had no life-corroding competition. Our ancestors saw that the mind is a restless bird, and their social institutions caged it for its own good. (On other occasions Gandhi calls it a drunken monkey.) But modern civilization is a mere congregation of chattering birds and monkeys, since the need for limits has been forgotten.

However, the Indians' quarrel is not with the English, who are themselves suffering as a result of that civilization. He, the Editor, has no more against the king-emperor than against Indian princes, and if the English could recapture their old nature they could be accommodated in India. They could even rule the country (through its Kshattriya, its princely caste) if they would respect the culture.

The real evil is embedded deep in modern industry and the modern economy. "Machinery is the chief symbol of modern civilization; it represents a great sin . . . a snake-hole which may contain from one to a hundred snakes."[10] But those whom the Reader represents are eager to introduce all it involves into India. They think they are revolutionaries, but: "You want the Englishman's rule without the Englishman; the tiger's nature but not the tiger; you would make India English."[11]

He is perfectly aware that he is "going against history." But he repudiates history as a criterion of wisdom. "To believe that what has not occurred in history will not occur at all is to argue disbelief in the dignity of man."[12] Besides which, "history, as we know it, is a record of the wars of the world. . . . How kings played, how they became enemies of one another, how they murdered one another . . . if this were all that had happened in the world, it would have ended long ago."[13] And by the same token, it is only in *their* history that organized violence is natural and inevitable. "Kings will always use their kingly weapons . . . [and] England is, I believe, easily influenced by the use of gunpowder. . . . But the fact is that India will not adopt arms, and it is well that it does not."[14]

Political progress of the kind that the modern system holds up to admiration—nation building—is a fraud. It does not build the kind of nations we want. Italy has won for itself the kind of freedom which suited Cavour and Garibaldi, but not the kind Mazzini dreamed of—freedom for all the people of the land.[15]

Violence cannot ever bring about true freedom. The Reader proposes to murder a few English by assassination and then raise an army to fight a war of liberation, admitting that perhaps a quarter of a million Indians might die in the course of it. The Editor, on the other hand, declares that India did not gain by, for instance, the murder of Sir Curzon Wyllie. And, of course, his objection is based on feelings more profound than the calculus of profit. He quotes the Tulsidas line: "Pity is the root of religion, as egotism is the root of the body," and says that he believes this to be a scientific truth; and that that nation is great which rests its head upon death as upon a pillow. His politics, like his ethics, are based upon sacrifice.

Hind Swaraj, therefore, does not make sense of a modern politics kind, and Nehru and most of Gandhi's political allies in the years to come ignored it. In effect, Gandhi himself ignored it insofar as he was politically active. We can understand its relation to his public career only by remembering that ideological or vertical split in Gandhi, corresponding to the chronological or horizontal split in Tolstoy, which separated his religious self from his political self. The left hand did not know what the right hand was doing; Gandhi was aiming towards religious results via political activities. But the passage from one to the other could not be smooth and continuous. The road runs over the edge of a cliff, and he who follows Gandhi politically has to climb down hand over fist till he stands on solid ground again, in *Hind Swaraj*.

This is Gandhi's major statement of his beliefs. It was issued in South Africa as a pamphlet in Gujarati in January 1910, but its distribution in India was proscribed by the Government of Bombay (which ruled the Gujarati-speaking areas), on March 24. An English translation, with a foreword, was published by Gandhi's International Printing Press on March 30, and that was the version sent to Tolstoy. No Indian edition was published until 1919. Along with *Hind Swaraj*, *Sarvodaya* (Gandhi's Gujarati version of Ruskin's *Unto This Last*), and *The Story of a True Warrior* (his life of Socrates, also derived in fact from Tolstoy) were also prohibited by the Bombay government. And the magazine *Gujarat* had also been prosecuted for printing his translation of the "Letter to a Hindu."

Having read *Hind Swaraj*, Tolstoy noted in his diary that Gandhi is "very close to us, to me," and wrote him a short letter on April 25. (In his diary for April 20, he had noted: "In the evening read Gandhi about civilization; very good"; and on April 21: "Read book about Gandhi. Very important. I must write to him.") To this Gandhi replied on August 15, describing his settlement, called Tolstoy Farm, where the families of *satyagrahis* were supported and trained. And on September 7, Tolstoy wrote at some length, saying: "The more I live—and especially now that I am approaching death...." the more the eternal enmity between love and violence struck him as a fundamental truth.[16] This enmity was between more than feelings, being between two structures of ideas and indeed of behavior. (He had just developed the same idea in the long essay, "The Law of Love and the Law of Violence.") The whole of Christian civilization, so brilliant outwardly, has grown up on the self-evident and blatant misunderstanding that the two can be reconciled and combined—a self-contradiction sometimes conscious and cynical but mostly unconscious and sentimental. He could see that Gandhi, if no one else, had grasped the danger of that lie. Thus, "... your work in the Transvaal ... [is] ... most fundamental and important ... [and] most weighty practical proof...."[17] This was Tolstoy's last long letter, and it is appropriate and moving that it should have been addressed to Gandhi.

His only reservation was on the question of patriotism. Gandhi was alert to the dangers of Western-style nationalism, but he wanted Indians to go through a phase of patriotic virtue as a moral discipline, while Tolstoy was a fierce denouncer of all nationalism. He would have had no truck with Gandhi's seventeenth-century British and nineteenth-century American heroes of national freedom. It is more than a mere coincidence that Aylmer Maude should have cited Pym and Hampden when he argued against Tolstoy that he failed to do justice to modern civilization. (He also cited Washington and Lincoln.) Tolstoy would certainly never have cited those examples to inspire his followers—and Gandhi was soon to cease to do so. Pym and Hampden were names representing a WASP complacency about WASP politics, which led Maude to say in 1918, again arguing against Tolstoy: "I have tried to suggest reasons for believing that, however urgently the building may need repair, the foun-

Kenworthy was also a member of the Land Colonization Society, which encouraged and helped people to escape from the city to the country, in settlements like Gandhi's Tolstoy Farm. (Gandhi described his Ashram's aim as "to implant the spirit of Tolstoy, and then a knowledge of country life, and of the way to make the best use of it.") Ebenezer Howard, the founder of Welwyn Garden City, was a member of the fellowship, and many other members went to live there or in other garden suburbs. Raymond Unwin, a friend of Carpenter's, was a garden-city architect, and Carpenter himself took up the cause of Small Holdings. The famous school, Abbotsholme, was founded by him and Cecil Reddie as a fellowship school. In the world of journalism, there were the magazines *New Age, Commonwealth,* and *Daily Chronicle,* and the famous journalists H. W. Massingham and W. T. Stead (who prayed publicly for Britain's defeat in the Boer War) were Tolstoyans for a time. The *New Age* began in 1898, and *New Order* in 1899, to give accounts of experimental communities, and the same function was performed by Joseph Edwards' *Labour Annual,* a publication Tolstoy read and prized. Thus there was a lot of New Life begun in the late 1890s, in various areas of the British scene, much of which had considerable effect later, in devious ways. Education, town planning, journalism, and politics all bore the marks of this period of idealism. Gandhi was in touch with all this on his visits to London in 1906 and 1909. The New Life was the general crop that grew up after Tolstoy's sowing, and Gandhism was the orient and immortal wheat he had intended.

Their Enemies—
The Men of Violent Revolution

There is also a certain connection between Tolstoy's and Gandhi's enemies. The opposite group to the one just discussed, the group that included Gandhi's bitterest enemies, were those Indian extremists in London who were represented by the Reader in *Hind Swaraj.* They were modeling themselves upon those Russian revolutionaries who were Tolstoy's bitterest ideological enemies in Russia. From the Tolstoy-Gandhi point of view, they wanted not the New Life,

dations are as firm today as when they were first laid."[18] Gandhi soon after that came to agree with Tolstoy in finding those foundations shaky.

In November, 1910, Tolstoy died, and on November 26 Gandhi wrote an obituary in *Indian Opinion,* saying: "He was for us more than one of the greatest men of his age. We have endeavored, as far as possible, and as far as we understood it, to follow his teaching."[19]

Thus the character of the transaction between the two is tolerably clear. Though each had reservations about the other's work—Gandhi thinking Tolstoy was too rationalist in his approach to traditional religion, and Tolstoy saying that Gandhi's Hindu nationalism "spoiled everything"—still both asserted that they were in accord about the most important things and that something had passed from one to the other—something that no one else could give Gandhi and that no one else could take from Tolstoy.

Their Friends—
The Movement They Belonged To

But besides the direct transaction of their letters and books (those "general letters," or letters to the world, as Tolstoy called them) there were indirect transactions via other people and via the atmosphere which Gandhi knew in England and English publications. We might perhaps call this the London of the New Life, people who were experimenting with new diet, new political parties, new religions, new sexual ideas, people whom Kipling satirized, for instance, in "My Son's Wife," people whose spokesmen were G. B. Shaw, William Morris, Annie Besant, Madame Blavatsky, and so on. Edward Carpenter represented them, in his *My Days and Dreams,* with a long list of such names.

We might say that this London came into existence in the 1880s. It was during that decade that Herbert Mayers Hyndman founded his Democratic Federation, Edmund Gurney his Society for Psychical Research, Helena Petrovna Blavatsky her Theosophical Society; in 1889, while Gandhi was in London, the original *Fabian Essays* was published, and in 1893 the Independent Labour Party was formed;

vegetarian and antivivisection societies were set up as well as Thoreau and Whitman groups, the Socialist League, and the Fellowship of the New Life. This last may be taken to be emblematic of the rest, for its name and for the number of Tolstoyans it contained.

This fellowship had been founded in 1882 by, among others, Havelock Ellis and James Joynes. Ellis was very close to Olive Schreiner, whom Gandhi knew in South Africa, and Joynes was friend and brother-in-law to Henry Salt, the vegetarian and humanitarian Gandhi knew. Ramsay MacDonald, later prime minister, was its secretary until 1892, and many socialists were involved. This was the parent organization from which the Fabian Society split off. In 1889, it began to bring out a quarterly called *The Sower* (later called *Seed Time*.) Tolstoy was its great prophet. Gandhi is not recorded to have known anything of the fellowship during his first stay in London, but he did cite Tolstoy in some of his writing for *The Vegetarian*, and the vegetarian world overlapped with the fellowship at several points.

Tolstoy was in touch with all this activity—was himself a member of the movement. In a list of the magazines he read, drawn up on March 15, 1890, he put down a Swedenborgian journal called *New Christianity*, the American *World's Advance Thought*, the *Religio-Philosophical Journal*, the Orientalist *Open Court*, the Theosophical *Lucifer*, *Theosophical Siftings*, and the Brotherhood Church's *Dawn Sower*. That is a very representative list of New Life publications, and shows Tolstoy as receiving as well as giving its doctrines.

Thus, it is very appropriate that the first issue of *The Vegetarian* appeared in January, 1888, the year Gandhi arrived in England. And that, the year before, the Sheffield Socialist Group was founded by H. M. Hyndman the Marxist and Pyotr Kropotkin the anarchist, Annie Besant the theosophist, and Edward Carpenter the prophet of the simple life. All four of these people, and the ideas they represent, were significantly related to Gandhi; but let us restrict our attention to the last. Carpenter's *Civilization: Its Cause and Cure* was a very important book to Gandhi in 1909 when he was composing *Hind Swaraj*.

The book was published in 1888, the year of Gandhi's arrival, but he was then less ready to accept its sweeping condemnation of the West and its call to simplify individual as well as social lifestyles. It was reviewed by H. S. Salt in *The Vegetarian* on September 29 of that year. So it is quite likely that Gandhi was at least familiar with its main ideas even then. But at that time he may have—like the Fabi-

ans, to whom the ideas were delivered as lectures—found it me embarrassing. Over the next thirty years, Carpenter's ideas spr In *My Days and Dreams*, he says that even Sydney Webb and G. Shaw, the Fabians who had most attacked him for that book, h themselves ceased to use civilization in its "old optimistic and mi Victorian sense."[20] Above all, Carpenter was, in the 1880s and 1890: the greatest teacher of "simplification" in England.

Carpenter was also interested in the East—as a counterbalance to the West—as were many people then. Theosophy was a major, perhaps the major, example of the orientalizing mood which Gandhi met in London. It was a new religion, founded in New York in 1875, by Madame Blavatsky and Colonel Olcott. It derived from combining all the old religions and extracting the essence of each, but also from appealing to certain ancient, esoteric doctrines and powers handed down secretly through the ages from master to disciple and particularly associated with India and Tibet. Thus, if one face was close to Unitarianism, the other face was close to magic, alchemy, and witchcraft. Blavatsky and Olcott went to India in 1879, and by 1885 Theosophy had a hundred branches there, where it was practically a revival cult of Hinduism. In England, it amounted to a readiness to turn away from positivism and patriotism, masculinism and WASP imperialism, toward spiritual values, and especially those values associated with India. Carpenter was one of Theosophy's speakers.

We, however, can concentrate on Tolstoy and Tolstoyans as sponsors of the New Life in England. We might take, as a first new example, John C. Kenworthy, whose book, *A Pilgrimage to Tolstoy*, was published in 1896 by the Brotherhood Publishing company and written in the form of letters home from Russia to the magazine *The New Age*.

Kenworthy had founded the Brotherhood Publishing Company together with Chertkov, Tolstoy's leading disciple who was exiled from Russia and living in England, where he published a good deal by Tolstoy himself which had not appeared in Russia. Gandhi corresponded with Chertkov and the latter's friend Isabel Mayo and read the publications of the Brotherhood Press.

It was in 1894 that Kenworthy had come to be the pastor of the Brotherhood Church in Croydon, which was closely linked to the Fellowship of the New Age. In 1893 he both joined the committee and published his *Anatomy of Misery*, which Tolstoy read and admired.

but the old life rearranged, with more of the same material goods, more of the same political powers, and all of the old pleasures in hotter and stronger draughts.

This group's social center in London was India House, supported financially and directed by Shyamji Krishnavarma, the publisher of *The Indian Sociologist*. He provided scholarships for potential political leaders of India to spend time in London and be exposed to revolutionary ideas. They had to swear not to serve the government. One of those scholarships was held, during Gandhi's time in London, by Vinayak Rao Savarkar, who was the dominant personality in the group. Born in 1883, he was a revolutionary at school and college in Maharashtra, and after getting his degree he traveled through the villages singing patriotic ballads and giving revolutionary talks. In England he studied law and wrote a history of the Mutiny as a war of Indian independence. He had been the inspirer of the assassination of Sir Curzon Wyllie by Madanlal Dinghra, which occurred just a week before Gandhi arrived in 1909; and he was to inspire (however little he was involved in the detailed planning of the event) the assassination of Gandhi himself in 1948.

Gandhi wrote: "Mr. Dinghra's defence is inadmissible. In my view, he has acted like a coward. All the same, one can only pity the man. He was egged on to do this act by ill-digested reading of worthless writings . . . . It is those who incited him to do this who deserve to be punished."[21] This is directed against Savarkar. And he remarked that a new magazine had begun to appear in Switzerland, called *Bande Mataram*, which advocated violence, made a hero of Dinghra, and attacked Gokhale for his moderation. "This is madness," Gandhi said.

Bande Mataram was in fact edited by Har Dayal, another of Savarkar's friends and disciples, who had come to England in 1905 at the age of twenty-one. A disciple of Bakunin, the anarchist of violence, Har Dayal represents another intellectual strain of Russian revolutionism. He was soon to go to America, where he would become friend and ally to Taraknath Das, and to M. N. Roy, who, as leader of the Indian Communist Party, was to be another of Gandhi's major enemies. During the war they founded the Ghadar (Revolution) Party in America, which inspired thousands of Punjabis to return to India, armed, to fight against the British. (Some of them became Gandhi's friends in the 1920s and 1930s.)

Nevertheless, Gandhi sought out Savarkar and the others like him in 1909, and took every chance to exchange ideas with them.

One occasion we know about was a dinner given on October 24 to celebrate the Hindu festival of Dussehra, or Vijaya Dashami, at which he was invited to speak. (Vijaya Dashami, the Triumph of Rama, is celebrated on almost the same day as Dussehra.) It was arranged by what Gandhi called the Extremist committee, and was attended by about seventy Indians. The practical arrangements of the dinner were inefficient, and it was very late starting, so Gandhi, in his usual style, worked anonymously at cutting up the vegetables. His speech was introduced by Bipin Chandra Pal, in a stentorian voice and oratorical manner. Gandhi's talk, unimpressively delivered in a flat, quiet voice, dwelled on the theme, taken from the *Ramayana*, that before Rama achieved the happiness celebrated at Vijaya Dashami, before he "qualified as a public servant," he and Sita and Lakshman had spent twelve years in exile in the forest and had voluntarily undergone many kinds of suffering and sleeplessness and celibacy. His remarks were received with polite but damp applause, and he then introduced Savarkar as the speaker of the evening. Savarkar, who had known what Gandhi was going to say, made a fiery speech in return, pointing out that before Vijaya Dashami came Navrati, a nine-day period dedicated to Kali-Durga, the bloodthirsty ten-armed Mother-Goddess of Calcutta and the object of Savarkar's personal cult.

This is an important image of Gandhi for us to dwell on, sandwiched as he is there between the old and the new, Pal's nineteenth-century parliamentary style and Savarkar's twentieth-century conspiratorial one. He was ineffectual and insignificant in the company of both politicians and revolutionaries. He belonged—as he may well have been saying to himself, considering the date—at Yasnaya Polyana. It was Tolstoy's blessing that hung over his chair at that banquet. But the only effect that it had on the others present was to mark Gandhi out as an enemy and prospective victim—an occasion for the exercise of revolutionary ruthlessness.

Who then was Savarkar, in 1909? He was a young man of twenty-six, with a face marked by broad cheekbones and an ivory pallor. In India an activist in Tilak's movement (he lit a bonfire of foreign cloth there, long before Gandhi's more famous bonfires), in England he ran the boarding house for Indian students in Highgate. (Krishnavarma sought the greater security of Europe in 1907.) He seems to have exerted an almost hypnotic influence over these young men—for instance, over Madanlal Dinghra, whom he trained for heroism and martyrdom by driving a needle into the palm of his hand, among other things. On the morning of Gandhi's assassination, Savarkar is supposed to have presented Dhingra with the revolver and said: "Don't show your face here if you fail this time."[22] (To his biographer, Dhananjay Keer, Savarkar claimed full responsibility for the Wyllie murder.)[23] While in prison, Dinghra wrote a proclamation—or some suppose Savarkar wrote it for him—which sealed his fate when published in the papers. "The only lesson required for India at present is to learn how to die, and the only way to teach it is by dying ourselves."[24] (It is no accident that this should have the ring of Sasha Ulyanov's speech from the dock and all those other Russian orations.)

Savarkar was another Chitpavan Brahmin, like Tilak, and had long been committed to conspiracy, militancy, and terrorism. But of especial interest to us is that this political alternative too can be so often connected with Russia, and therefore indirectly linked to Tolstoy. These Indian terrorists looked to the Russian terrorists as their predecessors and models. (And the Russian revolutionaries looked to Tolstoy as their major opponent on the left.) In 1908, Tilak accused the British of employing a Russian repressiveness and threatened them with a Russian terrorism in response. Savarkar sent two disciples to Paris to learn bomb making from Russian refugees. And the *Indian Sociologist* referred often to "the Russian method," meaning above all assassination by dynamite bomb.

The same analogy between India and Russia was employed by Secretary Morley to Viceroy Minto in January, 1910, arguing against the recourse to repressive methods: "That's the Russian argument: by packing off train-loads of suspects to Siberia, we'll terrify the anarchists out of their wits, and all will come out right. That policy did not work brilliantly in Russia, and did not save the life of the Trepoffs, nor did it save Russia from a Duma...."[25]

Russia was for every other country the home of the bomb and the assassin. In India, for instance, Sir Samuel Hoare's book about Boris Savinkov, *The Fourth Seal*, was much studied. In fact, dynamite had come to Russia from the West. Invented in 1867, its possibilities had come to the attention of the revolutionaries when there were reports of how it had been used to destroy buildings and claim insurance on them. Joseph Kablitz went abroad to study its terrorist potential in the 1870s, and brought some back to Russia from England.[26] From there it spread to India and Indian exiles. Taraknath Das distributed a bomb manual in North America, and an Urdu pamphlet "Shabah!", published for the Ghadar movement, had three sections: the Philosophy of the Bomb, the Bomb, a Useful Weapon, and the Praise of the Bomb. The last section ended: "Worship it, sing its praises, bow to it. Bande Mataram."[27]

Gandhi, like Tolstoy, stood for the very opposite teaching. In *Darkness at Noon*, Arthur Koestler's fictional analysis of Bolshevism, the new-model communist says:

The greatest criminals in history are not the type of Nero or Fouché, but of the type of Gandhi and Tolstoy. Gandhi's inner voice has done more to prevent the liberation of India than the British guns. . . . To want to conduct history according to the maxims of the Sunday school means to leave everything as it is.[28]

SECTION III

Manhood

Tolstoy 1862–1881 • Gandhi 1906–1921

This is the period of great achievements for both men. They had become eminent in the earlier period I have labeled "Youth," but there were limitations to their scope then. Tolstoy had not yet written a full-length novel, which was the greatest artistic form of his period, and he had not married, which was the period's major mode of eroticism, the major compensation it offered for the discontents of civilization. Gandhi's activity had been confined to a minority of the population of the least of the great provinces of the British Empire. And he had had no chance to lead a movement of millions, to revive Hindu culture as a whole, or to build a new nation in India.

This scope and size of achievement, palpably denied them in their youth, was to be granted in their manhood. Both were to defy empires, the Russian and the British; at least they were to deny some imperial achievements and repudiate the energies manifested in them, Gandhi in an obvious sense, Tolstoy by his attack on the winners of wars and the makers of history and by his exaltation of private life over public. But both were, as yet, still ready to endorse the best parts of imperial culture and considerably to reinforce it by their activities. Their radical attack was only to come in the succeeding period of their old age.

What unites the two men, or creates the parallel between them in this period as in others, is their reaction against contemporary empire—empire as modern system—against something perceived by them at this time as an excess or corruption of the true imperial idea. Tolstoy attacked this by his depiction of Napoleon in *War and Peace* and by his projected novel about Peter the Great. Both those men were incarnations of the modern system, the modernizing process, from Tolstoy's point of view. Their enemies are therefore his friends. His depiction in *War and Peace* of the hereditary and traditional Tsar, Alexander I, is patriotically Russian; and in general his attitude to Russian imperialism in the narrow sense was ambivalent and hesitant. What was decisive was his turning away from politics and public life as a whole, his self-burial in domestic eroticism and life-values aestheticism.

The two parts of each Tolstoy subsection here detail these two absorbing interests, but they should be read with an eye also to what Tolstoy was turning his back on. For instance, subsection A covers the 1860s, one of the most sharply and singly characterized decades in all Russian history, when everyone was talking about certain political subjects, about reform, reaction, revolution. This was the decade of the emancipation of the serfs, and of sweeping reforms in law and local administration. It was the decade of Nechaev's murder of Ivanov, of Karakozov's attempt on the Tsar, of the secret society called Organization, with its terrorist branch called Hell. It was the decade when Russian radicals rejected the leadership of Herzen, with whom Tolstoy, as another repentant noble, always sympathized, and followed that of Chernyshevsky, with whom Tolstoy was very unsympathetic. The superfluous men of the 1840s and 1850s were replaced by the bilious men of the 1860s.

Tolstoy and Sonia, it appears, did not discuss these topics at all. Both said so, very definitely, at the time and later, looking back; they knew and cared nothing about what was going on in Russia at large. They absorbed themselves in the domestic life of Yasnaya Polyana and in the writing of *War and Peace*. One must believe them, but one must also ask the meaning of so striking a gap, a silence, a discontinuity. A statement was surely being made about the unimportance of public affairs. Their absorption in each other and in art and in family surely carried a message against politics. As the contemporary reviews make clear, to publish a novel like *War and Peace* at the end of the 1860s was a gesture as provocative as it would have been to publish *Lolita* at the end of the 1960s; and in fact Tolstoy was the Nabokov of the 1860s from the point of view of the politically serious.

In Gandhi's case, the reaction against the British Empire on behalf of the Indians in South Africa is obvious enough. What one needs to remind oneself is that Gandhi believed in some of the ideals (not the behavior) of the British Empire and in those of an imperialist culture. If *Hind Swaraj* showed his scepticism about modern politics as a whole, he was, by the same token, no revolutionary. He was willing to work with British ideas, like the self-governing dominion, when they brought what he wanted for India. As antiimperialism, his doctrine had a character as indecisive as Tolstoy's; he was much less principled about "dominion status" than, say, Nehru was to be. And if he sent back his government medals to the viceroy in 1921, and declared himself disaffected as a citizen of the empire, he maintained his faith in the greatness of India and in Hindu culture, even though that culture was clearly the humanist flowering of the old Hindu empire. (He of course fought Untouchability, but he did not fight the caste system.) There is a similar contrast in Tolstoy: If in *Anna Karenina* he criticized the Balkan War of 1878 and the feverish patriotism it aroused in Russia, he also in the same book declared his faith in the manifest destiny of the Russian people to occupy and cultivate new lands.

But in both there was the comparatively hidden, or temporarily ignored, strain of thought which became so prominent in the next period, the religious ascetic, the truly antiimperialist. In the first part of this period it was Gandhi of whom it was especially true that his religion claimed quantities of energy which do not appear on the balance sheets of his political career. And besides the hours of prayer, private and public, his fasting and diet experiments, his nursing and doctoring, his teaching of children and guidance of the ashram, were all in part religious activities which absorbed some of the best of his energies. This strain of thought became increasingly powerful in both Tolstoy and Gandhi during this period and provided the ultimate resource and bedrock for their antiimperialism in the next.

Tolstoy 1862–1870, *War and Peace*

Tolstoy was married on the 23rd of September, and already on October 1 he noted in his diary that by his marriage he had distanced himself from both the students (the teachers in his village schools) and the people. He wrote in a letter the same day that he was weary of his educational work and was drawn to writing a novel of some length.

To marry Sonia Bers was to locate one's work in the world of art and family, though Tolstoy did not resign himself to that fate without some protests. On November 23, Sonia wrote:

He disgusts me with his people. I feel he ought to choose between me, i.e. the representative of the family, and his beloved People. This is egoism, I know, but let it be. I have given my life to him, I live *through him*, and I expect him to do the same.[1]

She cites a certain lack of understanding in him, and explains it, ". . . but then he has never had a family and can never understand it."[2] This last announces a theme—her superior claim to know about and understand "family"—which was to run through her diary and her life. In 1890 she wrote: "He never knew how to love—it is something he never *learned* in his youth.[3] . . . He had no family when he was young, and this lack of a *family* sense has lasted all through his life."[4] "Family" meant to her what it had been in her own home: a structure, an activity, a cult, built around a wife and mother, to whom a man played consort.

Tolstoy seems to have tacitly conceded her claim, and that was an important concession since their relationship and their life at Yasnaya Polyana was all built on the importance of "family." That was what they were *doing* there. On December 6, she felt herself insignificant, a worm, "some day I shall kill myself with jealousy"—she had found out about Aksinia—but resolved that she would create a family for herself. In December 1864 Tolstoy himself wrote her: "What my writing is to me, your children will have to be to you." And on May 19, 1863, she had consoled herself: "Mother said that she felt life much more cheerful as she grew older; and it was only when the children arrived that she found something to take up her mind."[5]

It seems clear that until and unless she had "family," she felt her very existence threatened by him. On December 6 of that first year:

"His past is great, rich and varied, and, even if he died now, his life would still have been a full one."[6] And "if I could kill him and then make another man exactly like him, I should do it joyfully."[7] She knew what she was saying: we find on November 13: "In a few years I shall have created a *woman's* world for myself, which I shall love even more because it will contain my husband and children."[8]

Their relationship was in part a competitive struggle that put their identities at risk. On the second of January, 1865, she wrote "I am so terribly afraid of being ugly, morally as well as physically,"[9] and in March 1865 "I can feel that he is strength and life itself, while I'm only a worm crawling and feeding on him. I'm afraid of being weak."[10] Finally on October 26 of that year: "I am afraid of everything and feel unfriendly towards the whole world. It's a strange desire for power, for being above everybody else. It's hard even for me to understand, and yet it is true."[11]

Sonia's ideology of family quite overrode facts. "He had never had a real family—neither father or nor mother; he was brought up without them."[12] This was of course not true. He had a father till he was nine, Aunt Toinette after that, three brothers and a sister. He had Yasnaya Polyana, which was a family in itself. She said this partly because she thought of marriage in its nineteenth-century "nuclear" form, carrying with it a whole range of modern cultural implications. Talking of the aristocrats' predatory attitude to the peasant women in the villages around Yasnaya Polyana, she said: "The life of landowners in those days was still full of the old serf-owning spirit,"[13]—which was, she might as well have added, to be displaced by the new house-holding spirit. Tolstoy's relation to Aksinia was to be displaced by his relation to *her*.

Sonia arrived at Yasnaya Polyana like the spirit of Christmas to Come, with the last chapter of every Dickens novel as her script. Her children's memoirs are full of the family romance she created for them. Describing the family parties in the summers, when Tanya Kuzminskaya also brought her family to Yasnaya Polyana, Alexandra Tolstoy exults: "Sometimes the whole horde, eight or twelve of them, drove off in the long katki . . . to bathe in the Voronka River, and the mothers had to watch to see that no one fell under the horses' hoofs, or choked in the water or caught cold."[14] This is the maternality Tolstoy celebrated in *Anna Karenina*, as embodied in Dolly. But he came to have mixed feelings about it as embodied in Sonia.

She seems to have identified herself with her mother in her own (projected) career as a wife and mother. She noted a likeness between them in her diary, especially in that she, like her mother, felt herself to be "a good woman" and as such to *deserve* that all her failings should be forgiven her. This is an important statement about Sonia, but let us concentrate on Liubov. In other words, the mother was a forceful personality, sure of her own (amoral) righteousness. She certainly impressed herself upon her daughters. (One may note that Tania Bers married a man who had been devoted to her mother, and that Tolstoy himself was suspected, early in his courtship of Sonia, of being in love with Liubov.) And Tolstoy endorsed the idea that she and Tania were like their mother and not their father. It is therefore of interest that, according to Tania Bers, Liubov remained always "patronizing" towards Tolstoy. She presumably saw him as unstable, a poor provider and unreliable support for a wife-mother; a weak consort for a house queen; and she was not—being "undeveloped intellectually"—impressed by his artistic and intellectual gifts. Dr. Bers was, but he did not count for so much in the family, at least with the daughters.

Since Tolstoy as well as Sonia subscribed to the matriarchal maternalism that Liubov triumphantly represented, he was always somewhat guilty before his wife and her mother. He had chosen those values to believe in, but he was not committed to them past question and past choice, as she was. He was a valued but distrusted convert, like Newman in the Catholic Church. While after 1881, when he renounced belief in that religion, he became of course a major criminal in their eyes and other people's.

Sonia brought with her many family traditions, known collectively as Anke pie because of a crumbly cake with jam inside and almonds outside that was always made on special occasions and named after Dr. Anke, a friend of Dr. Bers. But these traditions covered much more than food. They went all the way from jokes to religious pilgrimages, and they entangled and circumscribed all these things in the matrix of family life, in the placenta of domesticity.

These traditions, and the gift for spinning more of the same all the time, were Sonia's dowry—her enablement to be a Wife and Mother and to create a Family and a Home. Tolstoy himself contributed a great many jokes and sayings to the family store and was the hero of dozens of the family anecdotes and activities; for instance, the charge of the Numidian cavalry, when he would lead the children in a gallop around the house when boring visitors had finally

left. But when family traditions were instituted and consecrated all
over the estate and throughout the calendar, he found that family
life had become reified and materialized. Tolstoy wrote his sister-
in-law Tania, on October 19, 1884: "I live only in the assurance that
Anke pie is not eternal, but that man's reason is eternal."[15] Bourgeois domesticity was only a passing phase. (After the revolution,
his son Sergei wrote that Anke pie had indeed been driven out of
Russia, as Tolstoy wanted.) At their silver wedding in 1887 he observed that it was not his marriage that was being commemorated
but the triumph of Anke pie.

But originally domesticity and literature were mutually supportive. Marital relations improved as soon as Tolstoy engaged himself
in *War and Peace* and Sonia was able to play a large (supportive) role
in the writing, as well as being mother and housekeeper. He wrote
to his cousin in October 1863: "The [village] children come to me in
the evenings and bring with them memories for me of the teacher
that used to be in me and is there no longer. Now I am a writer
with *all* the strength of my soul, and I write and I think as I have
never thought or written before. I am a happy and tranquil husband and father who has no secrets from anyone, and no desires
except that everything should go on as before."[16] Now he can pity
the people but cannot love them. On October 17, 1863 he says in his
diary that everything is fine. "I don't want to die, I want and I love
immortality. There is no need to choose. The choice is already
made. Literature, art, pedagogy, and the family."[17] Their marriage
was very happy in those years. July 31, 1868, Sonia noted: "And yet
I still love him in the same restless, passionate, jealous and poetic
way."[18] In 1913, after Tolstoy's death, Professor Vengerov wrote
her, commissioning her autobiography, and suggested that literature had been sacrificed to family life at Yasnaya Polyana. She denied that and pointed to the difference between Tolstoy "whose
family life was completely reflected in his novels," and Gogol, Turgenev, Goncharov, and Lermontov, bachelors without families. She
was surely right about the content of Tolstoy's two great novels,
about the relation between his living and his writing in those years,
and about the differences between kinds of writers.

Sonia was indeed a gifted amateur of literature, and, as their acquaintance remarked, the perfect wife for a man of letters. She rejoiced in the development of the Russian novel in the nineteenth
century; this was her empire, and she participated in its triumphant
expansion. "I was fascinated and surprised that the Russian tongue

should have developed out of its feeble beginnings in monastic writings into the language of Pushkin. It was like the growth of a living creature."[19] To her nineteenth-century sensibility, monastic manifestations of life all seemed feeble—or gross or monstrous. Sonia was in many ways the perfect reader for *War and Peace*, and she loved the work she did for it—work so extensive and intensive that it deserves to be called participation in the novel's creation. "I desired nothing else but to live with the characters of *War and Peace*; I loved them and watched the life of each of them develop as though they were living beings. It was a full life and an unusually happy one. . . . "[20]

The characters were alive, and she was alive in "loving and watching" them. Life is the key word, the original entity, and the source of this life is Tolstoy's loving and watching of her and himself, and further out, of her and his sisters and brothers, and by extension, out on the fringe, of all history. The personal relations between the characters in *War and Peace* are those of the Bers and the Tolstoys in fancy dress, and that which is not familial is represented above all by Napoleon, a cardboard monster. Thus *War and Peace* was in some sense written for Sonia.

In one sense, the violence of their individual egotism and mutual reproach in their diary entries is not to be taken seriously. They wrote in their diaries on impulse, but they were in some sense showing off their impulsiveness; their complaints were an implicit boast that these were feelings which other happily married people felt but did not dare acknowledge—an implicit promise that this was just the rough underside of their love—rougher than usual only because the embroidery on the other side was bolder and more brilliant. But, as the subsequent development of their relationship showed (just because they were so brave) their feelings were not merely subordinate parts of love; they could not be restricted to their assigned function; they acted also as the seeds of established irritation, alienation, and hate.

Meanwhile, the themes of "life"—the themes of conflict and reconciliation between bourgeois domesticity and an older aristocratic lifestyle—were being replayed in a louder and brassier orchestration. The romance between Lev and Sonia was being repeated between Lev's older brother, Sergei, and Sonia's younger sister, Tania, across greater gaps of difference. He was twenty-two years older than she, and she was only sixteen when they got engaged. And if Lev had had a diary full of records of his sexual past, Sergei had a common-law wife, Marya, whom he had lived with for sixteen years, and several children by her. Tania, the Natasha of *War and Peace*, was the purest and brightest of nineteenth-century novel heroines, the most authentic manifestation of the domestic idyll, and Sergei could not bring himself to tell her of Marya's existence. When Tania found out, in 1865, she broke off the relationship, but was brokenhearted and her health went into a decline.

In the Tolstoy children's memoirs, we hear that Sergei was always handsome and distinguished in manner and never engaged in arguments. He loved his brother's novels and hated his later books. He loved Russian music and often assembled a choir, listened to them for hours, and paid them in vodka. In general, he reembodied the old aristocratic idea. He treated both muzhiks and bureaucrats as thieves and rascals, and when he left his estate in his four-wheeled carriage, all the peasants in view had to take off their hats. He was also deeply melancholy. According to Lev Tolstoy the younger, he would stay whole months in his rooms reading or writing reports on his property and weeping, sometimes so loudly that he could be heard throughout the house.

His handsomeness, his talents, his perversity, his mysterious melancholy, his romantic seclusion, all this adds up to the hero of a dozen brilliant domestic novels, from the early Rochester and Heathcliff to the late Grandcourt (in *Daniel Deronda*) and Osmond (in *Portrait of a Lady*), to restrict ourselves to English fiction. In such novels, which everyone was reading, the girl represented the triumphant and innocent energies of the rising bourgeoisie, and the man the distinguished and sophisticated intelligence of the defeated aristocracy. Tolstoy altered the pattern of the relationship, superficially, but he put part of the story of Tania and Sergei into *War and Peace* as Natasha and Andrei; another part of the story—the uglier side—is told by George Eliot in *Daniel Deronda*. Sonia was for a time very angry with Sergei, and one effect must surely have been to make Tolstoy guilty before her, as the sexually wicked aristocrat was always guilty before the pure young bourgeois girl.

After other tentative affairs (one with Tolstoy's old friend, Dyakov), in 1867—still of course very young—Tania married a childhood sweetheart, a lawyer called Kuzminsky. She was the most gifted and original of the Bers and seems to have had in real life the same life-enhancing qualities as Tolstoy portrays in Natasha. There can be no doubt that Tolstoy was very attracted to her, in every sense. He has a diary note of December 30, 1862: "Tania is sensual-

ity."[21] According to her, he tried to persuade her not to marry anyone. She remained very vividly related to him, though that relationship was half antagonistic after 1880. She was in some ways a more
outright asserter of domestic values against religious ones than Sonia, and the chief champion of Anke pie. It seems clear that Tolstoy
was more important to her than Kuzminsky in many ways, and that
he could relate to her more freely and gaily than he could to Sonia.
(We have a splendid reply by her to his attempt—much later—to
remind her that she too must die one day. "Me? Die? Oh, Lev, another of your silly jokes!")[22] She, Sonia, and Tolstoy were very close
to each other; he added a postscript to his wife's first letter to her
sister after the wedding: "I love you very much, Tania. I know that
you, like Sonia, love to be loved. That is why I write."[23] One cannot
be sure how much he means by "why I write," but it would be true
to say that *his* whole career as an artist sprang from *his* love of being
loved, and that in this postscript he acknowledged his kinship with
Tania and Sonia.

It is remarkable that Sonia, jealous by nature, seems rarely to have
been jealous of Tania, and was on the contrary very close to her and
dependent on her always. We must suppose that in the Bers family
structure Tania was so central that Sonia felt her to be part of herself, which is to say that in that family there was a feeling-structure
and a centripetal action so strong that it was something like a religion. But then we have to add the Tolstoys to the Bers pattern, because of the curious way Lev and Sergei replaced each other with
Tania. There seems to have been a remarkable sliding of individuals
into and out of the key roles of these erotic relationships. Perhaps
that has to do with a remarkable self-consciousness of these
relations.

Both Lev and Sonia appealed to Tania to appreciate every turn in
their relations, from the beginning. On September 25, 1862, Tolstoy
added a postscript to another letter of Sonia's to Tania: "If you ever
lose this letter, charming Tanichka, I shan't forgive you for a lifetime. Do me a favour. Read this letter and send it back to me. Do
you feel how wonderful and touching it all is—the thoughts about
the future, and the powder?"[24] A little later Sonia read Tolstoy's
letters to Valeria and commented in her diary: "What a charming
man." They appreciated each other like theatre performers. That
they insisted nevertheless that this was *real life* produced a curious
blending, a mutual reinforcement of aestheticism and vitalism.

Tania's autobiography expresses the cult of family even more viv-

idly than Sonia's. Her husband, as well as Sonia's, was to be pitied
for his lack of family. Kuzminsky, she says, was brought up largely
by an uncle. "He was deprived of family life with its habits of trust
and candour. He was strongly attracted to our household and loved
my mother very much."[25] It was a feature of this cult that other
men, not formally part of the family, should revolve around the
mother, and sometimes these were men with families of their own.
In Sonia's case, Urusov, the vice-governor of Tula, hung around
her. "How he spoiled me, with his unending sympathy and his belief that I was worthy of everything good—that I could do whatever
I wanted, and that everything I did was right."[26]

In many ways, Tolstoy took over the Bers' values, or allowed their
energy to reinforce his own convictions. He judged other people by
their power to be intimate. In October 1863 he wrote his cousin,
Alexandrine, reproaching her for keeping him at arm's length. "In
our relation you always only gave me the general view (you will
understand me) of your mind and your heart; never did you talk to
me about the details of your life—the simple, tangible, private parts
of it. . . . I do not even know what is dearest to you, the most pre-
cious in your life, etc. As soon as I come in contact with you, I put
on white gloves and evening dress, a moral dress-coat. . . ."[27] (Personal relations in the domestic idyll of the nineteenth century were
conducted in morning wrappers, not evening dress.) This is the
kind of reproach that Kitty addresses to the religious Varenka in
Anna Karenina and is usually attributed to the "simple, tangible, private parts" of life (the domestic empirical) and the only true transcendental is that which manifests itself through those parts.

And in another letter to Alexandrine later in the same month, he
describes Ivan Aksakov blushing when he came upon Tolstoy together with his sisters-in-law. "I was very glad about that. A man
who blushes can love, and a man who can love can do anything."[28]
Blushing (and stammering) are key attributes of Tolstoy's heroes because they are the signs of organic life, of the sap within the plant,
of the coming and going of feeling—of the dialectic. They are morality itself: "To make a mistake and blush in front of a child is
much better educationally than to make *it* blush."

Of course Tolstoy did not succeed in insulating himself entirely
from the political, religious, and existential problems that had tormented him before. In 1869 occurred what is known as the Arzamas
episode. On his way to inspect a piece of property he might buy,
Tolstoy, together with a servant, spent the night in an inn in a town

called Arzamas, and was struck down, psychologically, with a horror of death. This is the episode he described in "Confessions of a Madman," 1884. It was especially horrifying to him because it showed how ill his philosophy of nature and life values served him, how totally exposed it left him. But he was still not ready to change that philosophy. In 1865 he wrote Boborykin: "If I were told I might write a book in which I should demonstrate beyond a doubt the correctness of my opinions on every social problem, I should not waste two hours at it; but if I were told that what I wrote would be read twenty years from now by people who are children today, and that they would weep and laugh over my book and love life more because of it, then I should devote all my life and strength to such a work."[29] And that is in fact what he did. He abandoned the people for the reading public, but for them he created a book they still weep and laugh over and love life more for.

The Writing

In the first years of his married life, Tolstoy's writing was in the service of his marriage—in celebration of "domestic happiness" and in defense of the old institutions—but it was, in order to be effective, more than merely defensive. *War and Peace* is a synthetic achievement from many points of view. For instance, the method and point of view of writing which we have labeled reverie and associated with Rousseau is to be found in the character of Pierre and nearly everything to do with him, in the character of Natasha and the Rostovs, in Kutuzov and the historical themes connected with him, and in Karataev and all he stands for. But there are other themes that are treated in the mode of thought we have associated with Voltaire—more exactly, scenes and characters are treated in the mode of satire and analysis. Perhaps most notably the figure of Napoleon and the themes of war and history, but also the figure of Prince Andre and the Bolkonsky men in general—cold, sharp people, offended by life. Satire is also the mode of the high society scenes like the one with which the novel opens, and of characters like Julie Karagin, and of passages like the depiction of an opera through Natasha's eyes—where Tolstoy withholds all sympathy from the thing described. (Intuitive identification is of the essence of reverie, but Tolstoy refuses that as strikingly in some chapters as he gives it in others.) What is most Tolstoyan is still the intuitive reverie, but in this novel Tolstoy had extended his purview out beyond the subject matter to which reverie is suited (personal relations, domestic happiness, nature, agriculture) to cover war, armies, politics, and councils of military strategy, and he had therefore to devise new techniques and to call into action hitherto hidden powers of his mind. There would now be guilty men in his fiction. Positions would be taken.

Tolstoy's most striking declaration of political position was omitted from the final drafts, an omission typical of much that happened in the rewriting. This is to be found in a chapter called "Princes and Ministers," written in 1864:

I am not a bourgeois, as Pushkin boldly said, and I boldly say that I am an aristocrat by birth, by habits, and by position. I am an aristocrat because I am not only not ashamed, but positively glad to remember my ancestors— fathers, grandfathers, and great grandfathers. I am an aristocrat because I was brought up from childhood in love and respect for the highest orders of society and in love for the refined as expressed not only in Homer, Bach, and Raphael but also in all the small things of life. . . . I am an aristocrat because I cannot believe in the high intellect, the refined taste, or the absolute honesty of a man who picks his nose as his soul converses with God.[30]

It is clear there how consciously Tolstoy is defying the liberal consensus of literature, not to mention the radical consensus of political youth. Dostoevsky and Leskov and the *raznochintsy* writers were presenting characters who picked their noses while their souls conversed with God. Similar remarks are also to be found in "A Few Words About War and Peace," and in one of his drafts for an introduction. "The life of clerks, merchants, seminarists and peasants is uninteresting and half unintelligible to me; the life of the aristocracy of that time, thanks to the documents of that period and for other reasons, is intelligible, interesting and clear to me."[31]

This political position is most interesting where it is allied with the life-values philosophy and expresses itself in caste feeling. One of the most vivid cases is in the treatment of two of the book's "guilty men," Napoleon and Speransky. These two have very little to do with each other as far as the plot goes, but they both represent history, and perhaps more vividly than any other characters, since they represent historical change—the reorganization of society— and they are associated with each other in Tolstoy's sensibility by a series of hints. For instance, Tolstoy insists that both have plump white hands; it is something he mentions almost every time he presents either one of them. Speaking from the point of view of politics, Shklovsky says that those hands tell us that both characters are *raznochintsy*, men of mixed caste, which is to say no caste. From the point of view of life values, the hands tell us that these men have no contact with the sun and the wind and the soil, they do not make things, shape things, cultivate things, they only manipulate symbols. They are bureaucrats, agents of civilization, far from life itself. They are men of theory, incapable of experience. Their plump white hands represent the plump grey lobes of their over-developed brains. It is the caste feeling of the Russian nobleman against the bureaucrat which Tolstoy evokes in the reader by his portrait.

And in close alliance with this caste feeling goes patriotism, which is expressed not only in the portraits of Kutuzov and Karataev but in that of the Tsar and the heroes' feeling for him. "Nicholas, seeing Alexander's handsome and happy face, experienced a feeling of tenderness and ecstasy such as he had never before known. Every trait and every movement of the Tsar's seemed to him enchanting. . . ." and every man felt "self-forgetfulness, and proud consciousness of might, and passionate devotion"[32] as the Tsar approached.

But the novel clearly subordinates such aristo-military values to those of marriage. For instance, dandyism, though sympathetically presented, is condemned. It is indulged by the author as an episode valuable in the formation of a man. At Voronezh, we see Nicholas playing the dandy: "Jauntily shifting the position of his legs in their tight riding breeches, diffusing an odor of perfume, and admiring his partner, himself, and the fine outline of his legs in their well-fitting Hessian boots, Nicholas told the blonde lady that he wished to run away with a certain blonde lady in Voronezh."[33] But a few pages later Nicholas sees the Princess Marya, and becomes a different person, a prospective husband.

When Natasha, who above all others represents marriage values, comes up against the dandy Anatole, all our sympathies are with her. Her readiness to run away with him, and her sullenness with those who prevent her, evokes our admiration not our condemnation, because it is the proof of her passionate sexual susceptibility— her capacity for being carried away by forces which are in her nature but outside her ego. When she comes up against Denisov, though she is a half-grown girl and he a full-grown man of war, we see that she is the strong one of the two. Even Dolokhov, the really challenging embodiment of the dandy idea, is subdued by Sonia.

In an early draft, Tolstoy said he would write about "people who do not have the faults which one must have in order to leave traces on the pages of historical chronicles."[34] And the central point in the complex structure of his values in *War and Peace* is shown in passages like this, where "life" is quite clearly identified with the Rostovs.

Meanwhile life—actual everyday life with its everyday concerns of health and sickness, work and recreation, and its intellectual preoccupations with philosophy, poetry, science, music, love, friendship, hatred, passion—ran its regular course, independent and heedless of political alliance or enmity with Napoleon Bonaparte and all potential reforms.[35]

This passage is closely followed by Andrei's vision of the oak tree in winter,[36] his hearing Natasha talking in the moonlight,[37] and his sight of the oak stirring to life again;[38] a prime example of the reverie method, and of the empirico-transcendental philosophy. The oak "spread out a canopy of dark, sappy green, and seemed to swoon and sway in the rays of the evening sun. . . . 'No, life is not over at thirty-one,' Prince Andrei decided."[39]

Life worthiness is of course the property of all the Rostovs (except the unworthy Vera) although only Natasha raises it to a high power:

Never had love been so much in the air, and never had the amorous atmosphere made itself so strongly felt in the Rostovs' house, as at this holiday time. "Seize the moments of happiness, love and be loved! That is the only reality in the world, all else is folly. It is the one thing we are interested in here," said the spirit of the place.[40]

What makes Tolstoy a distinguished novelist is that we can react to that phrasing with some alarm or dislike at the same moment as we yield to it with delight. Tolstoy always draws our attention to Natasha's egotism: "Natasha was also happy because she had someone to adore her; the adoration of others was a lubricant the wheels of her machine needed to make them run freely. . . ."[41] and later, "That morning she had returned to her favorite mood, of liking and being ecstatic over herself."

These life values triumph over those of religion, as well as over those of politics and war. Both Princess Marya and Natasha have a religious vocation, but turn away from it to marriage. Natasha mourns for Andrei so passionately that she turns away from worldly and carnal life completely, but as soon as Pierre comes to call, she becomes again essentially nubile, as if that other self had never been. When Marya, who has lived her life practically as a nun, thinks of marrying Nicholas and entering the world of activity, "completely opposed to the spiritual world she had lived in,"[42] she chooses marriage in an unhesitating way that seems (inside the novel) inevitable. Pierre too has something of a vocation; he has found the "peace and inner harmony" he had sought, "simply through the horrors of death, through privation, and through what he had seen in Karataev."[43] He has realized that Russia and Napoleon were "no business of his"; that he needs no object in life now that he has faith in the God in Karataev.[44] But almost as soon as he finds Natasha, he proposes to her, and that is the climax of the novel, of his and the reader's spiritual development.

The marriage values are also wildness-and-animal values. Natasha is described as a Cossack[45] and as a Tartar[46] and the quality of excessiveness in her is stressed. Her voice is too shrill, her vivacity exceeds decent bounds. She does not belong in society, because she is Nature incarnate. She dislikes Dolokhov because she sees that "everything he does is thought out beforehand."[47] But her main mode of action is not to be critical of others but to be creative of herself, unconsciously self-creative. "Her voice had a virginal purity, an unconsciousness of its own powers, an unforced velvety tone, which so combined with its lack of knowledge of the art of singing that it seemed as though nothing in that voice could be altered without spoiling it."

But this is not just to be found in Natasha. Animal metaphors and physical images are the dominant way in which people are presented to the reader. Sonia is a kitten, the little Princess is a squirrel and then a dog, and the former's heavy plait of hair and the latter's lifted lip and Natasha's thin arms, are inseparable from what Tolstoy wants to say about them. Heart is a key word, with its suggestions of root; Pierre has an excellent heart, Nicholas has so much candor and heart, Vera has no heart.

These terms act directly upon the reader to instruct him in how he should be, in order to enter the community of the novel; not to mention living the rest of his life; he should be naive, open to life, constantly in growth. In the 1865 letter to Boborykin quoted before, Tolstoy said, "the goal of an artist is not to solve a question irrefutably, but to force people to love life in all its innumerable, inexhaustible manifestations. . . ." That expresses both the opposition of reverie to thought, and the alliance of art and "life."

The intellectual function of reverie is to bring into consciousness that which is not ordinarily there—in fact, what resists consciousness and can be but glimmeringly apprehended. Tolstoy's attempt to present this fictionally has obvious analogies to his preference for men and societies whose forces are not clearly organized and fully at their own disposal, for men and societies (the family, the cossacks, guerilla bands, the people) whose forces are evoked and aroused only exceptionally by something outside acting on them. This accounts for Pierre's reverence for Karataev, and for the alignment of him with Natasha, even though in terms of ego he is Natasha's opposite. "Karataev had no attachments, friendships, or love, as Pierre understood them, but loved and lived affectionately with everything life brought him in contact with. . . . " His talk was all folk-sayings, barely conscious, unintentional, transparent. And Kutuzov scorned intellect and wisdom. His weapons were patience and time; when in doubt, do nothing.

Above all, the people embody these values. "To be a soldier, an ordinary soldier," thought Pierre, as he dropped off to sleep. . . . But how? . . . Singleheartedness consists in submission to the will of God; there is no escaping Him. And *they* are single-hearted. They do not talk, they act."

Out of this comes Tolstoy's theory of the swarm-life of man in history; the self-important plans of generals and emperors (most notably Napoleon) are in fact ineffective epiphenomena upon the surface of events; and the latter move according to deep-lying laws of their own which *cannot* be known.

One of the most obvious and advantageous departures from the so-called laws of war is the action of scattered groups against men pressed together in a mass. . . . This was done by the guerillas in Spain, by the mountain tribes in the Caucasus, and by the Russians in 1812. . . . Guerrilla war (always successful, as history shows) directly infringes that rule.[48]

Napoleon is the villain of the novel because he is an entirely "produced" personality, entirely conscious of his own effects, all intention, calculation, rhetoric, theater, and vanity. We hear him telling himself: "I shall speak to them as I always do: clearly, impressively, and magnanimously." He has no hidden sources, no unknown self, no fertile darkness or hinterland. This wrongness in him coincides with his role as national enemy (the French being less natural than the Russians) and with his role as representative of the revolution; which is not just the French event of the 1790s but the potential Russian revolution of the 1860s, which also seemed to Tolstoy rhetorical, ideological, theoretical, and theatrical.

It is worth noting that all three of the novel's heroes are deeply drawn to Napoleon at the beginning of the action. Andrei quotes him by heart, Pierre praises him in the first scene, and in an early note for the book, all three are said to be "ambitious à la Napoleon." Andrei is looking for his own Toulon, and Pierre had longed with all his heart to establish a republic in Russia, and then himself to be Napoleon.

Thus *War and Peace* pays enthusiastic attention, gives ardent sympathy and sensibility to, adventure, war, history; and yet finally turns away, subordinates all that quite firmly to "family happiness."

Gandhi 1906–1915,
Satyagraha in South Africa

People and Events

Gandhi and his Muslim colleague, H. O. Ally, arrived at Southampton on October 20, 1906, to represent the Transvaal Indians in England. Gandhi carried the burden of the deputation's work (to get the British government to disapprove the Transvaal Asiatic Ordinance.) This included writing 5,000 letters in forty days, addressing a meeting of a hundred Liberal M.P.s, meeting Campbell-Bannerman, the prime minister, Lord Elgin, the colonial secretary (who had been viceroy 1895–1899), John Morley, the secretary for India, and Curzon Wyllie, the latter's political secretary. He also met Savarkar at India House, and Winston Churchill, then Under Secretary for the Colonies, whose hostility was to confront Gandhi as persistently as Savarkar's. Churchill and Savarkar were both great orators; in fact, Savarkar was later known as the Churchill of Maharashtra. And though different in most other ways, both represented a revived but unregenerate nationalism, one in England, the other in India, which Gandhi called on people to transcend.

His mission was superficially successful. Gandhi left London on

December 1, and on December 3 Churchill announced in the House of Commons that the government would not approve the Transvaal Ordinance. But only three days later, on December 6, the Transvaal and Orange River colonies were granted self-government, and so could make their own laws, which would certainly be racist. Thus, British imperialism proved morally ineffective; it could not enforce its will upon the colonies, when the latter were set upon injustice. The empire was an ineffective political conscience, a superego that the tough colonial ego acknowledged only sentimentally. Gandhi's work was to be to create a new political conscience, which would work at first on behalf of the empire and then against it.

In 1909, as we have noted, Gandhi saw London as Babylon or Metropolis, a great and wicked city. This was a big change from the way he had seen it in his years as a student. And he now saw England as Empire in the wicked sense, not as the virtuous enemy of empires, a young David against those old Goliaths. This change had been fermenting for some time, and the culture of the ferment was his experience in South Africa. Gandhi had become a colonial, a frontiersman.

As early as 1897 (in his Christmas dinner speech aboard the "Courland"), he had begun to name the West as Empire—as a social system based on force. Implicitly, thereby, he named the East as the opposite of Empire. But there was very little in the Mogul or the Hindu regimes in India to inspire such a view; those too were elaborative and exploitative systems, socially and culturally. Seeing the West as Metropolis, Gandhi was taking the point of view of the frontier. He had not of course been the frontiersman fully; he was not a man of violence, and he was not of the ruling race; but he had had the other, more exhilarating, half of the frontier experience— he had simplified his life, he had liberated himself from old social forms, he had practiced self-help. Within the next twelve months, on Tolstoy Farm, he was to push that experience much further; he made himself his own farmer, carpenter, cook, laundryman, doctor, sandalmaker, just like Robinson Crusoe; and for the rest of his life he was to refer back to that time on Tolstoy Farm as his moment of greatest faith. His faith was a spiritualized and ascetic version of frontier self help.

But we must turn back to an earlier point in the story, to describe an important new thread in the tangle of Gandhi's family relations. In 1907 Gandhi's oldest son, Harilal, returned from India, bringing a wife with him. He had married the year before, without his father's consent, and indeed quite against his father's wishes. He joined Gandhi's political work in South Africa, and went to jail more than once, but from this time on there was growing difficulty and strain between them. In August, 1908, Gandhi wrote proudly to *Indian Opinion* that "it was part of Harilal's education to go to gaol for the sake of the country."[1] But this pride had something to do with Gandhi's conviction that modern education was "a thorough fraud,"[2] which Harilal did not—at least steadily—share. He was, Gandhi said, ambitious.

Then twenty, Harilal is described by Robert Payne as being tall, lean, and better-looking than the other Gandhi boys. He was proud of his hair, which he wore long, and parted in the middle. He was also serious, sympathetic to all suffering things, and popular. But though ambitious, it seems that he needed to be looked after and to be reassured. It seems appropriate that he should have fallen ill while living in India and been nursed back to health by his host, and then married his nurse's daughter. (The most nearly comparable Tolstoy son, Lev, married the daughter of his doctor.) He had very little power of resistance to his father but considerable power of resentment.

He was arrested four times in the *Satyagraha* cause, as Gandhi boasted to Tolstoy; and in jail railed to his friend Pragji Desai, saying that Gandhi wanted him to be nothing but a pliant tool in his hands.[3] He made himself the official defender of his mother's rights in the household, and plaintiff on her behalf. Perhaps this was in the beginning agreeable to Kasturba, though it ceased to be.

In the *Autobiography* Gandhi explains Harilal's rebellion by saying that he was affected by Gandhi's own state of mind—his "half-baked knowledge and indulgence"—during his school years. Harilal still (in 1925) thinks those were Gandhi's best years. In the Gujarati version, Gandhi says: "Why should he not think that at that time I trod the royal road followed by the whole world and was, therefore, safe, whereas the changes effected later were signs of refined egotism and ignorance in me?"[4]

There developed thus something of an alliance between Harilal and his mother, against Gandhi and those they thought he favored, like his nephews, Maganlal and Chaganlal. Harilal, and later his brothers Manilal and Ramdas, said that their father was hard on them, which in some senses of the phrase can hardly be denied; and that he treated them badly, which seems likely to mean that he did not give them special favors as his sons.

Gandhi was trying to turn his domestic ties into something like ideological links and to form a party out of his family; Maganlal and Chaganlal were devoted disciples and workers for his causes, and were therefore closer to Gandhi than his sons. Gandhi's effort was quite the opposite of the marriage idea, or marriage religion, that Tolstoy was beginning to practice in the corresponding period of his life. While Tolstoy was bonding the strongest possible erotic relationships with his wife, with her sister, with his children, with his garden, his estate, his dogs, his peasants—making them his own, identifying himself with them—Gandhi was loosening all those bonds. In a letter to his cousins, who had reminded him to get his sons married, he said that would only make them sensual, "and thus the tree of lust flourishes. I do not think this is religion, whatever others may say."[5] As for property, the satyagrahis lived communally, at Phoenix and later at Tolstoy Farm, owning nothing individually. Gandhi was fond of individuals and places, and glad to be fond of them, but there were clear limits to his attachment. Eros, that drive to possess whatever pleases one, and to take pleasure in whatever one possesses, was not his god.

The strain this put on family life can be glimpsed and guessed in a few external facts. On January 5, 1909, Harilal and others were remanded at Volksrust. On January 10, Kasturba, who had been seriously ill for three months, was operated on in Durban. Gandhi looked after her, but on January 16, he himself was arrested and deported; he returned immediately and was rearrested. On February 4, he brought Kasturba, still convalescent, to Phoenix. On the 10th Harilal and others got sentences of from three-to-six months. When Gandhi himself was taken from jail to court in handcuffs as a witness on March 10, passive resisters congratulated Kasturba on his third imprisonment. The next day, she sent a message to a meeting of Indian women in Johannesburg to say that had she wings she would fly to them.

It is clear that family comfort and prosperity were sacrificed to the cause, and one is bound to suppose, furthermore, that the family members found themselves engaged in exciting acts, and using excited language, which they knew when they asked themselves all derived from Gandhi.

Family relations did not break down completely. In 1911, Gandhi wrote to Harilal that he didn't like his views, but had no suspicions of his character, and therefore felt no anxieties about him.[6] But in the spring of 1911, Harilal left his home in anger, saying in a letter that he was breaking all his family ties. His letter, which imitated one in a Gujarati novel about a man who ran away from his family, made his friends fear suicide, and they openly blamed and reproached Gandhi. Harilal had in fact disappeared to Delagoa Bay where Kallenbach had to follow him to persuade him to come home. Even after long discussions with his father, he remained unreconciled and went back alone to India to begin a formal education at the age of twenty-three.

In his letters, Gandhi appears most often understanding and compassionate. He told Maganlal[7] that the fault in the parting was not Harilal's but his, Gandhi's; Harilal was not to blame. And to Harilal's wife he wrote on February 18, 1912: "I can well understand your natural desire to be with Chi Harilal. I do not at all wish to come in your way in this. Live, both of you, as you wish and do what you like. I can have but one wish: that you should be happy and remain so,"[8] and he said he knew that Harilal would not do anything wrong.

This has seemed to some people too cool and mild a response. Indeed, it is not often that Gandhi directly expressed grief or self-dissatisfaction within a concrete and personal context; he was not an expressive personality even in the sense that Nehru was, he had too strong a sense of decorum. But he felt things deeply; there is a letter of April 22, 1914, written after the discovery of sin at Phoenix (boys had been sodomizing) and during the fourteen-day fast he imposed on himself:

> Never perhaps have I spent such days of agony as I am doing now. I can do no writing whatever. The heart seems to have gone dry. The agony I am going through is unspeakable. . . . I have often wanted to take out the knife from my pocket and put it through my stomach. . . . I have a strain of cruelty in me, as others say, such that people force themselves to do things, even to attempt impossible things, in order to please me. . . . Even Gokhale used to tell me that I was so harsh that people are terrified of me.[9]

But if his relations with his immediate family were strained (though not unmixedly black), Gandhi found ardent disciples among his nephews, Chaganlal, Maganlal, and Jamnadas, the sons of his cousin Khushalal. He also found stimulus, support, and consolation in English friends, like Henry Polak, Albert West, Louis Ritch, and Sonja Schlesin.

He also formed a happy relationship with a man he surely felt to be as close to him, Joseph Doke, the Baptist minister. Only eight years older, Doke was a man of delicate health and little schooling who had come to South Africa in 1881 and had also taught Chinese immigrants in New Zealand. One can guess at some similarities of temperament linking him and Gandhi. In Doke's obituary, in *Indian Opinion* August 23, 1913, Gandhi praised him warmly. His was not, Gandhi said, "a modernized or civilized Christianity. He practised the original."[10]

Doke's place in Gandhi's life was immediately taken by C. F. Andrews, who was for the next sixteen years a close friend, an advisor, and a representative and right hand man, especially in causes involving Indians in South Africa, in Fiji, in South America, and elsewhere. Andrews arrived in South Africa only five weeks after Doke died, January 1, 1914. He had been working with Tagore at Shantiniketan, but had volunteered to come and help in the struggle in Africa. When he stepped ashore, he asked which of those who greeted him was Gandhi, and bent down and took the dust from his feet. This was a dramatic gesture, especially performed as it was in the presence of a superior church dignitary, Archdeacon Gregson, and it gave great offence. Andrews was a somewhat effusive personality, but the gesture fitted both his sense that he was in the presence of a saint, and the historical importance of what they were doing. In Andrew's person the Church of England, the religious cult of the Empire, abased itself before one of its subject races, did penance, paid homage, acknowledged a Christlikeness greater than its own.

Soon after he met Gandhi, Andrews was to give up his priesthood, but his sensibility may be said to have remained "high church." Writing about Gandhi, he pointed to St. Francis of Assisi as a Christian parallel to Gandhi's "amazing sweetness and childlike innocence. . . . When I read the Little Flowers of St. Francis, with its medieval setting, I say to myself . . . 'how like Gandhi.'"[11] This comparison, and the idea behind it, was taken up by two more representatives of High Anglican enthusiasm, Verrier Elwin and Jack Winslow, in their *Gandhi: The Dawn of Indian Freedom*:

> He is in no sense a Puritan: he is an ascetic, but an ascetic of the Catholic type. He can combine the romance of life with its renunciation. . . . Child of the seashore and of desert, there is a strong vein of poetry and romance in his soul. He has a deep love of natural beauty. . . . Music also sings in his heart . . . the half-forsaken ideals of Catholic Christendom.[12]

These are the rather sentimental terms in which High Anglicans grasped Gandhi. Doke's more Protestant approach seems intellectually preferable, if only because closer to Gandhi's own way of thinking. Doke stressed Gandhi's Bunyanism and his experimental adventurism. He wanted to call his biography "The Pathfinder" or "The Jungle-Breaker."

It was during this period of his life that Gandhi began to develop his interest in diet and health. He wrote a long series of essays for *Indian Opinion*, later published as a book, on "General Knowledge About Health." He recommends vegetarianism, restraint of appetite, scrupulous cleanliness, nature-cure with earth and water. Perhaps the most striking essay is the seventeenth, which appeared on March 19, 1913, and declared *brahmacharya* the most important of all rules of health. Sexual activity fritters away our energies, our integrity, our health. "He who has conserved his generative fluid is known as *virayan*, a man of strength."[13] We should, he suggests, store within our body the mysterious power which Nature has bestowed upon us. Men and women are blinded by sexual passion; Gandhi himself on occasion had lost all sense under that influence. All the other passions derive from violations of chastity.[14]

In saying this, Gandhi is tracing out, in another field, the consequences of his great principle of conservation, concentration, contraction, self-restraint, the opposite of the modern world's principle of expansion, exfoliation, self-multiplication. It is the doctrine Tolstoy teaches in *The Kreutzer Sonata*.

"Our diet, our way of life, our talk, our sights which surround us, are all such as to excite our lust."[15] That quotation is from Gandhi, as is the next, but both could perfectly well be by Tolstoy. "People of the West have broken all bounds in this matter. They adopt various techniques so that they may have pleasure without being burdened with children."[16] Not that large families are good. In India, children have children, and the country is as swarmed over with worthless creatures as it is with ants. The good is restraint, diminishment, singularity, sublimation.

His ideas about health were closely connected to Tolstoy Farm and his experiences there, and to Tolstoy himself. On December 10, 1910, *Indian Opinion* included an extract from Tolstoy on Bondarev and the idea of bread labor. And Tolstoy's influence was strong in many matters. Gandhi sent Maganlal, as "invaluable," Tolstoy's pamphlet, "The Relations Between the Sexes," and wanted everyone at Phoenix to read Tolstoy. Even such surprising items as

signed by both Gandhi and Smuts, which exchanged a promise of repeal of the Registration Act for a promise of voluntary registration. On the 30th, Gandhi was taken out of jail and brought secretly to a confrontation and conference with Smuts in Pretoria. Gandhi was immediately freed and addressed a midnight meeting of Indians a thousand strong. The next day, all the *satyagrahis* were released from jail.

But there were soon disquieting reports of Smuts' understanding of what he had agreed to, as expressed in his comments to his party. It seemed doubtful that he would keep his promise, and many Indians felt betrayed. Moreover, Gandhi himself had involved their cause with subtleties. He had to explain to the suspicious Pathans an apparent change of position, or at least of tactic. To register in obedience to the Black Act, he had insisted, would be a sin; but now he said that voluntarily to give their fingerprints would be the hallmark of a gentleman. They were not convinced.

On February 10, voluntary registration began, and Gandhi meant to be the first to offer his fingerprints, but on the way to give them he was struck from behind with a cudgel by a Pathan, Mir Alam Khan, in the company of other Pathans. Mir Alam was, Gandhi tells us, fully six feet tall and of powerful build. Gandhi fainted, with "He Ram" (O God) on his lips. Taken to Mr. Doke's house to recover, he asked that no vengeance should be taken against his assailants. Mr. Chamney, the registrar of Asiatics, came to the house eager to assure Gandhi of legal redress, but Gandhi insisted instead that he be registered—he had promised to be the first to do so, and wired the attorney general to discharge Mir Alam. (Europeans prosecuted him, however, and he was jailed for three months.)

By February 29, 3,400 Indians had registered. On March 5, however, there was another attempt on Gandhi's life at a meeting in Durban (the lights were put out, and a Pathan with a big stick rushed the platform) and the next day when he had a meeting with the community leaders of the Durban Pathans, they told him he had betrayed them. The rumor was that he had taken £15,000 to sell them out.

These events followed a very Kipling-like story pattern. The Pathans, a martial people, were a group the English liked to deal with, and they had been induced to put their faith in a *babu*, an educated, nonmartial, clever-talking Indian, who promised to lead them in a nonviolent revolution against the English masters. He turned out to be a man of words who did not keep his promises, and they were betrayed, so they took their revenge with murderous violence and turned back to their hard but just English masters.

It was in terms of such legends that the English understood India, the empire in general, and their role as its rulers. Lord Milner actually referred to Gandhi as "some clever *babu*"; a term which Anglo-Indians said had "a slight flavor of disparagement, as characterizing a superficially cultivated, but too often effeminate Bengali."[26] And many facts of Indian life did fit those Kipling patterns, as this whole story would have done if Gandhi had run away or fallen silent. But on August 16, when he began a new phase of the campaign, Mir Alam and other Pathans admitted their error, burned their registration cards, and resolved to fight with him to the end. What we see here is Gandhi breaking the pattern of expectation in both English and Indian minds by the strength of his resolve and the clarity of his mind.

By May 9, 8,700 applications for registration had been received, and 6,000 accepted. Soon after, however, Smuts made it clear that Asiatics who had lived in the country would have to register when they reentered, which was against the compromise agreement as Gandhi understood it. On May 16, Gandhi accused Smuts of foul play. The next day, Pathans assaulted the chairman of the British Indian Association. On May 26, the British Indian Association told the colonial secretary that they were withdrawing their voluntary registrations, and on May 30, Gandhi announced that *satyagraha* would begin again.

This campaign, he announced on July 2, would be on behalf of people not yet in South Africa—of the Indians who were prohibited from immigrating, and he suggested that everyone who had registered ceremonially burn their certificates if the voluntary applications were not returned. One of the three prohibited categories was "educated Indians," and Smuts offered a compromise by which the other two would be accepted if Gandhi would agree to the exclusion of the educated—the clever-talking, middle-class *babus*. Gandhi of course refused, seeing it as an attempt to exclude Indian culture and to admit Indians to South Africa only as laborers, as plantation fodder. So on July 16, hawking without licenses was begun. On July 27, Harilal Gandhi was arrested. And on August 16 and 23, citing the example of Thoreau, 3,000 certificates were ceremonially burned.

On January 16, 1909, Gandhi was arrested at Volksrust. Escorted to the border, he immediately returned and was rearrested, and on the 20th wrote to the press that the struggle had entered its third and final phase. On January 28, the Indian merchants of Johannesburg decided to operate without licenses and court arrest. Cachalia, Naidoo, and others were sentenced to three months each on the 30th.

However, in June of that year Gandhi left for London with Hajee Habib to represent the Indians to Whitehall. General Smuts was also in London, to discuss the act creating the new dominion, the Union of South Africa, a major event in the development of the British Empire: an event which the Indians knew would worsen their position because it would make the colonists more independent of England. The secretary of state for India, John Morley, told Gandhi that the Imperial Government could exercise little control over self-governing dominions; the tie between mother country and colonies was made of silk, and would snap at any tension. Smuts left London on August 29, confident that the Indians in the Transvaal were "sick to death" of the agitation. And back in South Africa he made the treatment of passive resisters harder, deported some to India, and imposed the law upon women and children as well as upon grown men.

On June 1, 1910, the Union of South Africa was born; and on the same day Sorabji, one of the most peristent *satyagrahis*, was arrested for the seventh time. On June 30 another of the *satyagrahis*, Sammy Nagappen, was released from Johannesburg Jail in a dying condition, and died on July 6, martyr to the cause. It was also in June that Kallenbach gave his 1,100 acre farm in Lawley for the accommodation of *satyagrahi* families; there were from sixteen to sixty people there at one time or another.

In 1911, things got better. In January, India prohibited indentures to Natal; in April, to all South Africa. The South African government presented a new Immigrants Restriction Bill, which the Indians protested against in March. But in April, Gandhi agreed to suspend *satyagraha*, even without the amended bill being passed, in response to Smuts' desire for peace in South Africa during the coronation of George V and in exchange for certain promises. Smuts promised that existing rights would be maintained, that former *satyagrahis* would be allowed to register, and that five or six educated Indians would be allowed to enter as settlers each year. A provisional settlement on these terms was agreed on in May.

In April 1912, a new phase of the campaign began, involving women, provoked by the government's ruling that Indians *prove* themselves legally married. Kasturba decided to join in the resistance activity herself. She was incensed by the thought that she and those like her were not wives in the eyes of the law, but concubines. Sonja Schlesin, as secretary of the Transvaal Indian Women's Association, announced that it would offer *satyagraha*. The police wanted no martyrs and refused to arrest the first group of women. On September 16, Kasturba and fourteen others from Phoenix, who had kept their expedition secret and refused to give their names, *were* arrested, and she was given three months hard labor.

That was the day after *satyagraha* was revived. On October 2, Kallenbach and twelve women also "offered themselves." The enthusiasm was widespread; the Zoroastrian and Islamic Anjumans supported the Hindu movement. Gandhi had declared in *Indian Opinion* on May 3 that this impending third campaign would be the last, the purest, and the most brilliant of all. He wrote to Harilal in India that he and his wife should return and take part.

The first group of women, being left free, had returned to Natal and made their way to the Newcastle coalfields where they urged the coal miners to strike. The response was much greater than Gandhi had expected; he had in fact neither the money nor the workers to deal with a mass movement.

But on October 17, he himself went to Newcastle, and urged the indentured Indians working there to strike until the £3 tax was repealed. Seventy-eight did so, and four were arrested and given two weeks imprisonment; and as a result 3,000 more decided to strike on October 20. These mineworkers lived in houses owned by the mine owners and used water and electricity supplied by them. The workers were thus wholly dependent on their employers, so Gandhi decided they could not stay home to strike, but must "fare forth like pilgrims," selling what they could of their possessions, and abandoning the rest, bringing with them only blankets.[27] On October 28 he led them on a march from Newcastle to Charlestown, the Natal border village, where two hundred arrived on the 30th.

On November 6, he led 2,200 out of Charlestown and crossed the border to Volksrust. On November 11, Gandhi was sentenced to nine months imprisonment, to which another three were added. All the miners were sent back to their mines, now as state prisoners. All Indian labor in Durban struck, and the plantation labor, and there were mass meetings everywhere. Soon there were 60,000 men on strike besides the *satyagrahis* in jail.

On December 11, the South African government appointed the

Solomon Commission to investigate the situation, and on the 18th
Gandhi and Kallenbach and Polak were released. He decided to
boycott the commission. He did so against the advice of Gokhale,
the viceroy, and Lord Ampthill, but he carried mass meetings of
South African Indians with him. Meanwhile, the movement had
more martyrs. An old man, Hurbatsingh, died in jail at the age of
seventy on January 5, 1913; a girl Valliamma died of an illness contracted there at the age of seventeen on February 22. Gandhi had
already taken to wearing the costume of the indentured, out of
mourning for previous martyrs to passive resistance, and he regularly reminded audiences of those who had given their lives for the
cause.

Finally, in January, 1914, a settlement was reached; the £3 tax was
abolished and monogamous Indian marriages were recognized as
valid. Gandhi was free to return to India at last. He was by now a
great political and religious hero. At a farewell banquet in Johannesburg on July 14, a man presented Gandhi with his four sons, so
that he should train them for national service.

If we now put this campaign next to *War and Peace*, how can we
compare the two? First of all, both were manifestos and manifestations of resistance. (*War and Peace* was more of a manifesto, *satyagraha* more of a manifestation, but we can see both the novel and the
political movement in roughly similar terms.) They were resisting
the evils of imperialist government; in one case the Russian Empire,
in the other the British; but at the same time both maintained their
loyalty to the good of empire, the protection it offered to real values, real life. Real life lay with the Rostovs' domesticity, said Tolstoy; Napoleon, and even the Russian court, represented unreal life.
For Gandhi, true wealth lay not in the diamond mines of the Rand,
but in the sufferings of the *satyagrahis*. True splendor was not to be
seen in Rhodes and the millionaire capitalists, but in the martyrs of
his campaign. They were the true heirs of Hampden, Bunyan, and
Pym, the heroes of liberty. What Napoleon was to Tolstoy, the Boer
Generals were to Gandhi. Smuts, Hertzog, Botha, were seen as heroes of militarism and emblems of oppression.

Gandhi's campaign was an attempt to build a nation, or rather
national pride and national consciousness; the Indians' circumstances in South Africa gave no scope for full-scale nation building.
Tolstoy, on the other hand, had built up family pride and family
consciousness. He had showed the superiority of that institution
(the incubator of "life itself") over government and politics. And

Gandhi, though overtly so political, did the same. Gandhi's politics were markedly cultural, or religious, even later on, in India; and in South Africa, where the Indians were political bystanders, as far as the main conflicts went, this was even more clear-cut. He himself declined to vote in elections, and did not seek the vote for his compatriots. What stirred him to organized action were insults to Indian national pride and consciousness, like the registration act and the marriage regulations. His nationalism was to some degree an alternative to politics. Thus both men were creating worlds of feeling and action that could be, for others as well as themselves, refuges from the political pressures to rule or be ruled.

The great difference between the two was that at this point Tolstoy was offering those who followed him an expansion of the self, parallel though opposite to the expansion of self promised by empire. Through his heroine, Natasha, he called on his readers to awaken new appetites, arouse new senses, assert new desires they could find in themselves. Gandhi called for a contraction of the self, a diminishment of appetite, a denial of desire; the expansion he promised would be purely of the spirit, the soul.

Thus the dominant images of the campaign are of suffering and simplification; going to jail and being locked up, faring forth with a staff as a pilgrim, wearing the costume of the indentured laborers, falling sick and dying; and the burning of the registration certifications is an image of destruction. The dominant images of the novel are hunting and dancing and singing, the trees growing, the rivers flowing, the stars shining. At the same time, *War and Peace* also includes prison, the march of the prisoners of war, and Platon Karataev. The latter are charismatic Gandhian images, and they foreshadow Tolstoy's future development. While Tolstoy Farm and Gandhi's exaltation of the outdoors life and his nature cures could be called Tolstoyan images within Gandhi's work.

The scope of both efforts, of mind and will, is enormous and in that sense comparable in the two cases. One may point to the number of years, and of hours per day, which the two men put into their work. Moreover, when Gandhi spoke of his third campaign as the last, the purest, and the most brilliant, he imposed a sense of form on the whole quite comparable to a novelist's; and when he spoke of his "experiments with truth," he was seeing his life in terms which Tolstoy might have employed. And if Tolstoy extended the scope of fiction, in *War and Peace*, by including war, and historical figures, and military and political strategy, Gandhi extended the scope of politics by including religious morality, and women and children, and voluntary suffering.

Finally, one must speak of success in each respective enterprise, and achievement. These are two great successes, judged by the criteria appropriate in the two cases. The greatness is in part a matter of their having modified those criteria, and so it was possible to condemn this or that aspect of their work as literature or politics. But by most of the criteria it is reasonable to apply to those fields, *War and Peace* and *satyagraha* in South Africa were brilliant successes, and Tolstoy and Gandhi are great men by virtue of these achievements alone, without counting all that was to come.

Tolstoy 1870–1881, *Anna Karenina*

The Main Events

Tolstoy's first thought of the narrative that came to be called *Anna Karenina* is recorded on February 23, 1870, but the actual writing began much later, and was much interrupted. Tolstoy had various fictional subjects on his mind, and the first two or three years of this decade were devoted mostly to a novel about Peter the Great.

Moreover, he had many other nonfictional projects. On December 3 he began to learn Greek and poured all his energy into that for a time. Soon he was reading Xenophon and Homer in the original, with wild excitement. On February 6, he told Fet that he was living in Athens and was talking Greek in his sleep. With his gift of self-dramatization and self-intensification (one of the things he shared with the Bers sisters), this may well have been true. When he went to Moscow he showed off his mastery of the language to a professor of Greek, and on the tenth of June, 1871, his friend S. S. Urusov wrote to Sonia that the whole city was talking of how Tolstoy had learned Greek in three months.

Reading Greek literature affected his sense of what was beautiful. He felt he must write something as free from everything superfluous as Greek sculpture, architecture, and poetry are. The difficult thing in art, he decided, is the leaving out. This idea took him back to folk tales, not to the modern novel or the epic history. He demonstrated what he meant in tales like "God Sees the Truth But Waits" (1872) rather than in *Anna Karenina*. Such work derived from the oral literature of the Russian people and from collections of legends and saints' lives, like the *Cheti Minei*, in which, he told Sonia in March 1871, the authentic poetry of Russia was to be found. As early as 1851 he had remarked on the paradox that "writers" wrote for other writers, and not for plain readers. As he wrote *Anna Karenina*, he knew he was betraying his vocation to write for the people.[1]

On March 3, 1872, he wrote to Strakhov that in their time artistic creativity of every kind—music, painting, and poetry—was declining, while there was a proportionate access of zeal in the study of Russian folk life—music, painting, and verse. "It seems to me that this is not just a decline, but a death, with the pledge of a rebirth in folk life [*narodnost'*]. The last poetic wave—a parabola—occurred with Pushkin at the highest point, then Lermontov, Gogol, we sinners, and the line went under ground."[2] And in a letter of March 25, he added that he now found even Pushkin ridiculous: "while the language the people speak and in which there are sounds for the expression of everything a poet could wish to say—this language is dear to me. . . . Should you wish to say something superfluous, bombastic, morbid—the folk language does not permit it, but our literary tongue wags on. . . . I simply love the definite, the clear and beautiful and temperate, and I find all this in folk poetry and language and life—and the opposite in ours."[3] Our language has no skeleton; one can pull it in any direction one wants; everything is literature—nothing is established truth. (Tolstoy was seeing the other side of that dialectic of consciousness which had given him such scope and power as a novelist.)

He also associated the Greeks he was reading with the Bashkir tribesmen of Samara, among whom he went to live in the summer of 1871 and whom he visited most summers of this decade. He wrote from there to Sonia, on June 23, 1871, that he felt himself becoming a Scythian such as Herodotus described ("Herodotus' pages smell of the Bashkirs") and everything had again become new and interesting to him. He told Fet on the sixteenth of July that year that Herodotus had described the Bashkirs exactly, and that everything in Samara was virgin and unspoiled. The country was just losing its virginity. In 1875 he told Fet: "You must see the struggle which occurs under one's eyes here, the encampment of the nomads (there are millions of them on an immense space) against primitive agriculture."[4] He was revitalized, we can see, because he felt himself at the roots and source of societal life. (The use of "smell" above signifies, in vitalist terms, the excitement of the origin.) On about the twenty-fifth of August, he went to Moscow to buy land in Samara; he paid R20,000 for 2,500 desyatinas (nearly seven-thousand acres). He was moving to the frontiers of the empire (the socio-cultural frontier), becoming a summer frontiersman; like Burton and Kipling in England, or Parkman and Roosevelt in America, he was renewing the vitality of empire by participating in adventure. He was recharging the energies of the metropolis while seeming to repudiate it in the name of the frontier.

In the summer of 1873, the whole Tolstoy family spent the summer in Samara. There was a famine there that year, and Tolstoy conducted a survey of the village near him and sent a description of the distress to the Moscow *Vedomosti*. He described the poor harvest of 1871 and 1872, classified the peasants, and cited the prices of foodstuffs. He itemized twenty-three households (every tenth house in the village) giving the inhabitants' ages, incomes, expenses, stock, and so on. He pointed out that peasants, being peasants, were not ready or able to look after themselves in such an emergency; they were able only to suffer and die. He suggested two subscription lists, one for outright gifts, the other for two-year loans. His appeal attracted a lot of attention. The empress made the first contribution, and altogether R1,887,000 and 21,000 pounds of corn were given, which, during the summer of 1874, Tolstoy distributed. Thus, he was able on occasion to use the techniques of social science and to take social action.

Another major interest during this period was education. From January to April 1872, there was again a school at Yasnaya Polyana, in which he and his wife and their elder children taught. Tolstoy was also at work writing schoolbooks, usually called his *Azbuka*, his ABC. On January 12, 1873 he told his cousin Alexandrine how much he hoped from this. His life ambition was that two generations of Russian children, from the imperial family to the peasants, should be formed by, and get their first poetic impressions from, this book; then he would die happy. The *Azbuka* was in fact a failure, and sold only four-hundred copies. But in October 1874, a committee of the Ministry of Education recommended the reading books that went with the ABC proper, and these sold in very large numbers throughout the rest of Tolstoy's lifetime. (In 1909 the twenty-fifth edition came out; each edition after the nineteenth was of 100,000 copies.) Part of the teaching in these books was of elementary mathematics, physics, and chemistry, so Tolstoy was brought into contact with the hard sciences as well as the social sciences and the humanities.

In the early years of this period, there are no clear signs of the religious conversion to come, but Tolstoy reacted violently against the society of Moscow and the bureaucratic state whenever he came in contact with them. On February 20, 1872, he wrote Alexandrine that he had been disgusted with Moscow on his recent visit, with its idleness, luxury, and depravity, on every level of society; he could never go there again. He refused jury duty and was fined for doing so in both 1872 and 1873. In April 1872, he told her that he had not read a newspaper in three years. And in September, when he was confined to his local district, because of a court case, he reacted with great indignation. "It is intolerable to live in Russia—intolerable to a man like me, with grey hair and six children. . . . I have decided to go to England once and for all, or at least until a period that shall see everyone's freedom and dignity assured over here."[5] This seems rather childish petulance, until one realizes that one element in it is Tolstoy's dangerous reliance on being allowed a private life. If he could not live privately, if he had to come in contact with the state, and live politically, he would have to take up radical protest activity, and renounce a "normal" balance of pleasures and participation. The precariousness of that reliance, a moral as well as a pragmatic precariousness, made him irritable and petulant.

The mention of six children can remind us that the major activity of the Tolstoy household during this period, along with his attempts to write, was the bearing and raising of children. There were to be thirteen altogether, of whom eight grew to maturity, and they were educated at home, by tutors who lived in during this period. In October 1872, Tolstoy went to Moscow to meet an English girl who was to help look after them, and in 1877, V. I. Alekseev came to be tutor, the first and perhaps the most radical of the series.

Sergei Tolstoy tells us, in Tolstoy Remembered by His Son, that he was very influenced by his tutor Alekseev and by the latter's friend Bibikov, who became bailiff on the Tolstoys' Samara estate in March 1878. Alekseev was twenty-nine in 1877 and one of the eight children of a Pskov landowner-officer and a peasant woman. During his education at St. Petersburg University, he read Mill and Lewes and became a narodnik (a Populist) and made propaganda among workers. He joined a famous revolutionary circle headed by Nikolai

Chaikovski (1850-1925). After graduation he fell under the influence of A. K. Malikov (1839–1904), a former revolutionary who preached a new, mystical-social, nonviolent religion that he based on a doctrine of God-manhood. He had come to believe that revolution must begin inside each individual. And when Nikolai Chaikovsky declared that he needed to find absolute Goodness and absolute Truth, Malikov convinced him that he must find God in man, which meant renouncing all revolutionary violence—a man cannot hate his sore arm, however diseased it may be, because it is a part of himself. (This idea is obviously like some of Tolstoy's and the two men did meet, through Alekseev; V. G. Korolenko believed that Tolstoy's thought derived from Malikov, but there seems no reason to suppose any large-scale debt.)

Alekseev joined Malikov's group, which decided to found an agricultural collective, and with money provided by one of the female members they bought a farm in Kansas. Fifteen of them, including Alekseev and his brother, went there in 1875 and persisted in the venture for two years.

Alekseev returned the husband of Malikov's wife and father to his children, so his household represented the revolutionary movement in its various phases quite vividly. He was very poor, but when he took the post of mathematics tutor at Yasnaya Polyana, he insisted on living in the village rather than in the big house, because there dinner was served by footmen wearing white gloves. He was a tall, thin, narrow-shouldered man, with a scanty red beard and no hair on his cheeks, according to Sergei, not strong physically or passionate emotionally. Tolstoy admired his passionlessness and wanted to imitate it. (Some of Gandhi's most trusted followers and helpers were of this type). Alekseev tried to live by his own labor and to follow the Golden Rule, but to solve social problems by the help of science. Sergei says that he, too, soon grew greatly attached to Alekseev, who sowed good seeds in his heart—"He is not to blame if they did not all bear fruit."[6]

That last sentence is an allusion to Sergei's personal pathos, at having come to nothing. But it could also point to the pathos of his father's fate, for the worldly forces that stifled the seeds Alekseev sowed in Sergei—forces represented in the family by Sonia—were those Tolstoy too had to fight. Sergei called Alekseev the first Tolstoyan and one could put the proposition the other way round. Alekseev could be said to have preceded Tolstoy himself in reli-

gious radicalism. They had many arguments about religion and Tolstoy at first defended Orthodoxy, but he was always uncomfortable
in that position and soon argued himself out of it.

It was Alekseev who took down in writing Tolstoy's expurgated
and demythologized version of the Gospels, which became the most
widely known of his religious works during his lifetime. Alekseev
was his confidant and consultant in composing his letter of protest
to the new Tsar in 1881, against the execution of the assassins of
Alexander II. A little later Tolstoy wrote him, after some disagree-
ment had arisen:

> We have the air of having forgotten that we love each other. As far as I
> am concerned, that is not true. I don't want to forget that I owe you much
> of the calmness and clarity in my present conception of the world. You are
> the first educated man I met professing not only in words but in your heart
> the religion which has become pure light to me. That is why you will al-
> ways be dear to me.[7]

We may say that the great change in Tolstoy was symbolized by
Alekseev replacing the worldly Fet as his main confidant. When
troubled by sexual attraction to the woman who did the cooking at
Yasnaya Polyana, Tolstoy confided in Alekseev, and asked him to
stay near him and be his conscience.

Despite his temperamental meekness, Alekseev had been in the
center of radical activity. He had belonged to the most famous radical group of the early 1860s. And among those who went to America with Chaikovsky and Alekseev, at least Malikov, V. F. Orlov, and
Bibikov had been among the 193 arrested after the 1866 attempt on
the Tsar's life by Karakozov. These three all came to know Tolstoy
later. Thus, Tolstoy was brought face to face in his own home with
the radical movement in Russia, from 1877 on. He told Strakhov on
January 3, 1878 that he had met three of the best representatives of
the socialist extremists through Alekseev; and he found in its representatives a much more sympathetic response to his concern with
salvation than he did in his own family. For example, when Sonia
overheard Tolstoy and Alekseev discussing his letter to the tsar, she
burst in upon them in a fury, reproached Alekseev with endanger-
ing the family, and insisted upon his being discharged. He went
with Bibikov to the Samara estate.

Meanwhile, in Russia at large, the fervor of the revolutionaries
mounted, and the sympathy of society at large with the revolutionaries increased. In 1878, at the trial of the Fifty, the spectators open-

ly described those in the dock as saints and martyrs. And in 1878, when Vera Zasulich was put on trial for her attempt to assassinate General Trepov, it was said that it was Trepov who was on trial with the spectators and even with the jurors, while she was compared with Charlotte Corday and William Tell—the heroes of modern freedom. Eighteen seventy-eight was the year of the split within the main revolutionary organization, Zemlya u Volya, which led to the development of terrorism by one side of the split.

Thus, the tutors at Yasnaya Polyana represented a lot that was very challenging in the outside world, and Tolstoy encountered a good deal of revolutionary theory and revolutionary experience in his own home in the late 1870s. The pastoral haven, the liberal-bourgeois idyll, was betrayed from within. It is from 1878 on that his letters to Strakhov become testy, his letters to Fet infrequent.

No doubt it was partly for that reason that Tolstoy soon came to have doubts about the fiction he was writing. As early as February, 1873, he wrote to Alexandrine that *War and Peace* was now disgusting to him. Having to look through it again (because a new, corrected, edition was called for) he had felt repentance and shame, as at traces of some orgy he had taken part in. This repudiation of what he had just done, so typical of Tolstoy, no doubt represents a weakness of his temperament, but we must remember that it was in fact only by means of "orgies" of imaginative activity that he was able to do his work. That is, he had to become each character in turn and go through each action—seduction, murder, battle; the toll on his nerves, in headaches and sleeplessness, is recorded in his diary. It was all done, finally, for fame, admiration, applause; and for several years *War and Peace* rapt him away from the place and time in which he was actually living. When Tolstoy went to write in his study, he closed and locked doors between him and the rest of the family.

His feelings about *Anna Karenina* went bad soon after he began it. On March 18, 1873, he noted a story-beginning in Pushkin which he could emulate, and on May 11 he wrote to Strakhov that he was now writing not about Peter the Great (the last reference to that subject comes on March 17) but, for the first time in his life, a real novel. "It came to me involuntarily, and thanks to the divine Pushkin, whom I picked up by chance, and read right through in ecstasy."[8] It was a great release for him to find a subject he could write about, but the consciously pagan and aesthetic language of that sentence signals the conflict he would soon feel.

There were a number of deaths in Tolstoy's immediate circle in 1873 and 1874, beginning with his baby son, Peter, who died on November 9, 1873. His aunt Toinette died June 20, 1874, and in 1875 another son, Nikolai, died on February 20. Sonia suffered a premature birth on October 30, and Aunt Pelageya died December 22. Tolstoy wrote his brother on August 25, 1874, that it was time for *him* to die and there are other signs of such feelings in his letters to his brother, to Fet, and to Strakhov. But it was not terror of death that preoccupied him, rather attraction, and it was not physical dying so much as the renunciation of life. When in 1875 Strakhov sent him an autobiographical story expressing self-disgust, Tolstoy said that such feelings of being essentially superfluous were nothing to be ashamed of. They were evidence of a great new movement of mind, incomprehensible in Europe, but which would be easily understood in India. The reference (perhaps via Schopenhauer) implicitly recommends a Buddha-like retreat from all life involvement.

It is no wonder that he started referring to *Anna Karenina* as "disgusting" as early as 1874, and called it "boring and vulgar" in 1875, while longing for someone else to finish it for him. He did not want his mind so choked and charged with empirical detail—and detail all oriented, like magnetized filings, toward "life," which is to say toward Eros.

It was religion, though as yet the church religion of Orthodoxy, that was absorbing him more and more. It was not faith in Christianity he felt—rather doubt—but he struggled as best he could to believe in what the church taught. On April 14, 1876, he wrote Bobrinsky that to live without faith, as he had done hitherto, now seemed a frightful torture; and on March 3, 1877 Sonia recorded his saying that he hoped soon to become a completely religious man— that he could not live much longer in the religious uncertainty of the preceding two years. In June, he and Strakhov went on a pilgrimage to Optina Pustyn. He wrote Strakhov afterwards that he himself would never become a monk; to be a fool in Christ (a *saddhu* or a *sanyasi*, in Indian terms), was the only thing that made sense. In August, Sonia said that he was praying every day, going to mass every holy day, and was obsessed with the idea of humility.

But in that year he finished writing *Anna Karenina*, and had his idea for a next novel—that should deal with the power of conquest of the Russian people, manifested in their migrations. Thus, his lit-

erary imagination was still nationalist, and indeed imperialist. Sonia recorded this on the same day as she recorded his hopes of becoming completely religious. And of course Dostoevsky was then
reconciling to his own satisfaction his Slavic imperialism with his
Orthodox spirituality.

But in Tolstoy's case the scene was set for conflict. His son Ilya's
Reminiscences gives a feeling of the struggle in the family as early as
1878:

> As a boy of 12, I felt that my father was getting more and more estranged
> from us . . . gloomy and irritable . . . a stern and censorious propagandist.
> We still had the same Nikolai the cook, the same Anke pie, imported from
> the Bers family and deeply rooted in the life of Yasnaya Polyana, the same
> tutors and governesses, the same lessons, the same succession of babies that
> my mother still nursed at her breast; all those foundations on which the
> life of our ant-heap rested were as unshaken as ever and as necessary for
> our selfish enjoyment. . . . The conflict of ideas with traditions, of 'life ac-
> cording to God' with "Anke Pie," resulted as such conflicts in human life
> always do. . . . What hope was there of reconciling 'life according to God'
> with the invariable duty of taking soup and cutlets at dinner, of talking
> French and English, of preparing for the Gymnasium and the University, of
> learning one's part for theatricals? And we children often felt that it was
> not we . . . but he who had ceased to understand us, because he was occu-
> pied with 'some ideas of his own'. . . we all found him tiresome and
> uninteresting.[9]

On March 1, Alexander II was assassinated. With Alekseev's help,
Tolstoy composed a letter to the new tsar, begging him to forgive
those responsible. The letter, which speaks a new, Gandhian language of meekness and humility, was sent to Strakhov to give to
Pobedonostsev, the new procurator of the Holy Synod, to give to
the Tsar. (Sonia added a note to Strakhov, not to pass it on if it
would endanger the family.) Pobedonostsev wrote back on June 17,
telling Tolstoy: "Your faith is not my faith, your Christ not mine;
yours is sickly and ailing, mine is a figure of power."[10]

Pobedonostsev was more than once compared with the historical
Grand Inquisitors of Spain by his contemporaries, and he can be
identified for us with Dostoevski's Grand Inquisitor in the *Brothers
Karamazov* fable. The Grand Inquisitor reproaches Christ, when he
meets him reincarnated in sixteenth-century Spain, with having refused to use the only three powers which could bind men to do
their religious duty—mystery, miracle, and authority. What could

better define Tolstoy's version of Christianity? And who but Pobedonostsev could condemn that creed?

Such was the public dimension of Tolstoy's new life. Privately,
the assassination and his letter about it intensified the conflicts between him and his wife and other people. Sonia told her sister on
April 22, 1881, that because of their quarrels she had often wanted
to leave him. When his Slavophile friend, Samarin, came to stay,
and said that revolutionaries must be hung, Tolstoy quarreled with
him bitterly. On May 18, he made his first diary note on how isolated he felt from everyone around him. And on May 28, he wrote to
Strakhov, attacking both Orthodoxy and Autocracy, two of the pil-
lars of Strakhov's faith.

He drew up a plan of how the family could all live at Yasnaya
Polyana, giving away the income from their Samara property and
restricting themselves to necessities. All they would need would be
one room for all the men, one for the women, one for a library, one
for physical work. They would learn from the servants how to look
after themselves. They would change their dress and food for something much simpler, and on Sundays prepare a dinner for poor people. They would concern themselves with science and art only insofar as those can be shared with all.[11] Needless to say, this plan did
not recommend itself to his family.

In September 1881 Sergei entered Moscow University and the
Tolstoys moved there for the winter. This was to be the pattern of
their lives from then on, much against Tolstoy's will. Their son Lev
says: "In 1881, however, my mother took a decision—the first of her
life, perhaps, in which she overcame my father's wishes. She decided that from this time forward it was necessary the whole family
should pass the winter in Moscow."[12] They became henceforth a
Moscow family who spent their summers in the country. And as a
Moscow family they were involved in luxuries and festivities and
depravities they had not known before. On October 5, Tolstoy noted that the preceding month had been the worst of his life.

On March 20, 1873 Sonia wrote her sister that Lev had decided to
write a novel about private life in contemporary times. She added
that she was glad of the change and expected that Tania would be
too. This story gradually became *Anna Karenina*.

In *Anna Karenina*, as Tolstoy said, the main "idea" is the family.
The hero becomes himself, saves himself from tormenting problems, by marrying, and marriage attracts him because it means
family:

Strange as it may seem, Konstantin Levin was definitely in love with the whole family, and especially the feminine half of it. Levin himself did not remember his mother, and his only sister was older than himself, so that in the home of the Shcherbatskys he found himself for the first time in the environment of a cultured and honorable old aristocratic family, of which he had been deprived by the death of his own father and mother.[13]

Levin's own house (recognizably Yasnaya Polyana) was a whole world to him. "It was the world in which his father and mother had lived and died. They had lived the sort of life which seemed to Levin the ideal of perfection, and which he had dreamed of restoring with a wife and family of his own."[14] These passages are obviously autobiographical. They also ally marriage and family to tradition and the aristocratic caste, and so defy the most powerful current of opinion in Russia when Tolstoy was writing. *Anna Karenina* celebrated the family in defiance of radicals, revolutionaries, and nihilists.

The story of Levin and Kitty carries this theme; and contrastive but consonant in the meaning is the story of unmarried love, embodied in Anna and Vronsky. This is the material which was new, both new because it was not to be found in *War and Peace*, and generically "modern" in that the story involves modern social features like divorce, birth control, contemporary fashions; and new in the sense that it resembled European modern novels, especially French ones. This meant, for instance, an exploration of the ways hatred can be involved with love, desire with repulsion, as it is between Anna and Vronsky at the end, and the ways the body itself speaks against the mind and the soul—forbidding Anna, for instance, to feel anything but hatred for her husband even when he is being generous.

It is then primarily an erotic novel. There are other elements, but they are subordinate. And seen as an erotic novel, the two poles of its emotional current are pride and humiliation. Certain qualities— calm, pride, gaiety, strength, beauty, goodness, love—are stressed and interlinked as values. Kitty early thinks of Vronsky's "strong manly face, his great calm, and his goodness that came out in everything he did."[15] These are all different aspects of manly vitality, the animating energy of life values. Correspondingly, Vronsky noted Anna's animation, ". . . which seemed to flutter between her brilliant eyes and the barely perceptible smile that curved her red lips. It was as though her entire being were brimming over with something that against her will expressed itself now in the sparkle of her

eyes, now in her smile."[16] At the opposite pole to that are the images of humiliation, of suicide, shame, deceit, jealousy, hatred, of
something broken and hanging down, as in Levin's feeling when
his proposal is rejected, or Kitty's reaction when she realizes that
Vronsky is in love with Anna and is overcome with terror and
despair.

On the whole, the images of pride are associated primarily with
the illicit lovers, and humiliation with those who seek marriage.
But there is a dialectic of progression, for if the former association
makes a clear pattern at the beginning of the book, by the end it is
Kitty who is proud, calm, happy, strong, and so on, and Anna who
is broken and humiliated in every way.

However, there is a third set of images, associated with other
characters in the book, which are described in terms like flat, thin,
dry, clumsy, cold. The most obvious case of a personality summed
up in those terms is Karenin, and they clearly convey his failure in
eroticism. Eros can find no lodging within him, cannot inhabit and
animate his body; this Rhadamanthine truth is embodied in his
ears, fingers, voice, thighs,—things he cannot change—as well as in
the behavior he is morally responsible for. But the same terms are
applied to another character who is yet ranked as being somehow
on the side of life—Dolly, Anna's sister-in-law. Eros, or Venus, has
had but a brief lodging in her and will never return; that is what
her thin hair and wrinkles tell us, but Magna Mater (motherhood)
has replaced Eros. Dolly does not, like Karenin, lack all grace and
warmth in personal relations. She in fact, visiting Anna in the
country, comes off best in the contrast. Another pair characterized
by the same polar terms, though less completely contrasted, are
Levin's brother Sergei, whose mind is completely rational; and Kitty's friend Varenka, who is religious. There is the same contrast; in
the woman's case the condemnation by Eros is softened or blurred
by a suggestion that she may have gained more than she lost by
becoming the temple of agape instead. The characterization of the
man, on the other hand, suggests that Eros is an all-dominant deity,
and his is the final judgment.

This conflict of values is not resolved within the novel, no doubt
because it was far from resolved within the writer. The novel's
dominant scheme of meaning is erotic, and all of the four characters
just discussed are harshly treated at one point or another, while the
four main and dominant characters are all characterized by their
eroticism, Kitty and Levin as much as Anna and Vronsky. We are

told that Varenka is good-looking but not attractive to men. "She
was like a beautiful flower which, though its petals had not yet
begun to droop, was already faded and without fragrance. Besides,
she could not be attractive to men because she lacked that which
Kitty had too much of—the suppressed fire of life and the consciousness of her own attractiveness."[17] In that "too much," brushed
aside in a first reading as a mere intensifier, lies the seed of Tolstoy's later judgments. Levin says that his brother "can't come to
terms with reality, and Varenka is after all a reality."[18] This is very
like the harsher judgment on Karenin: "Karenin was face to face
with life. . . . And every time he had come up against life itself, he
had kept aloof from it."[19] Thus Koznishev and Varenka do not marry, and Kitty explains why to her husband in the metaphor of two
kinds of kissing:

'This is what I mean,' she said, taking her husband's hand, raising it to
her mouth and just touching it with closed lips. 'The way one kisses a
bishop's hand.' 'Who isn't biting?' he said, laughing. 'Neither. This is
how it should have been. . . .' 'Some peasants are coming. . . .' 'They didn't
see. . . .'[20]

This is one of the moments the later Tolstoy must have considered
vulgar, both in its elliptical and suggestive technique, and in its
triumphal preference for the appetitive.

The world of the novel is erotic, and while within it the reader is
bound to sympathize with Anna when he reads:

'He's in the right! In the right!' she said. 'Of course, he's always in the
right! He's a Christian! He's magnanimous! Yes, the mean disgusting man!
And no-one understands it except me. . . . They don't know how for eight
years he has crushed my life, crushed everything alive in me, that he has
never once thought that I was a live woman in need of love. . . . But the
time came when I realized that I couldn't deceive myself any longer, that I
was alive, that I couldn't be blamed if God had made me so, that I have to
love and live.'[21]

And this is exactly what Kitty says to Varenka: "'I can't live except
as my heart dictated, but you live according to rules. I have grown
fond of you just because I felt like it, but I expect you did so only in
order to save me, to teach me.'"[22] Kitty and Anna are sure they are
right, because their drives come from the unconscious.

The treatment of the religious life, as embodied in Madame Stahl
and Lidia Ivanova, is cruelly satirical and hostile; it is erotic values

that are accepted and the rest of life is seen from that point of view. Of course eroticism extends to more than sensuality—Eros is the son of Magna Mater, the goddess of fertility and the love of children. Dolly is glad that Levin could see her with her children—"in all her glory. No-one could appreciate her splendour better than Levin."[23] This is the imperialism of the world of women. Eros also implies the glorification of the body, as a way of knowing as well as a thing known. Levin is like Anna and Stiva (and Kitty) in forwarding his physical sensations. His brother is sitting indoors when Levin bursts in, "his matted hair clinging to his perspiring forehead and his back and chest black with moisture. 'We've mown the whole meadow!' he cried joyfully. 'Oh, I feel so good, so wonderful! And how did you spend your time?' he inquired, completely forgetting their unpleasant conversation of the previous day."[24] He imposes his physical sensations upon his brother as a charter to his personality and to the life he will share with him. He brings his sensations to the other person as wealth, as achievement. Similarly, Stiva had "a physical impact that cheers people up," and the old prince, Kitty's father, "communicates his high spirits to everyone."

These sensations derive their value from their freshness, from their recent emergence from the unconscious. During the mowing we are told that:

... more and more often now came those moments of insensibility when it was possible not to think about what one was doing. The scythe cut of itself. Those were happy moments ... it was not that his arms swung the scythe, but that the scythe itself made his whole body, full of life and conscious of itself, move after it, and as though by magic the work did itself, of its own accord and without a thought being given to it, with the utmost precision and regularity. Those were the most blessed moments.[25]

A natural extension of this is the character of Levin's sincerity, which rejects all conscious system and stability, whether in the world or in a man's beliefs. "'Well, you see,' said Oblonsky, 'You are a thoroughly earnest and sincere man. This is your strength and your limitation ... you want life to be earnest and sincere too, but it never is."[26] Thus, Levin always reacts against established truths, and is a negative and critical mind despite his naiveté. This is what we might call his authenticity—he is like Rousseau or Alceste—and it depends on his staying dissatisfied. His search for values delights us as readers, like the instinctive behavior of an animal, for example, Keats's stoat. But a rational, and even an irrational, philosophy, when completely worked out, is bound to seem inferior, as it does in figures like Koznyshev. The reader contemplates the characters from the heights of Olympus (as Keats suggests) and he/she is bored or offended by men who are not "graceful and instinctive" like the stoat, but dead certain. The reader is both naive and dialectical. He knows that indirect evocation and even inarticulacy are better than analysis and rhetoric. (Readers who have been taught this are proportionately disappointed by Tolstoy's religious writings after 1881.)

This dominant scheme of values is all a defense and glorification of the marriage and family scene at Yasnaya Polyana. But there are manifestations of other feelings, rebellions against that scheme. The most important occur in the treatment of Karenin's repentance, and his humiliation, and self-sacrifice. Karenin's tragedy is summed up in terms of two laws. "He felt that in addition to the beneficent spiritual force that governed his heart, there was another force, harsh and powerful, if not indeed more powerful, which governed his life, and that this force would not let him have the humble peace he longed for."[27] This force emanates, of course, from institutionalized Eros—that socially though tacitly prescribed animality which drives the social world, and on whose behalf that world was punishing Karenin. "Never before had the impossibility of his position in the eyes of the world, and his wife's hatred of him, and altogether that harsh mysterious force which, contrary to his inner mood, governed his life and demanded fulfillment of its decrees and a change in his attitude to his wife, appeared as evident as it did now."[28]

It is of course possible for the reader to leave that problem, that conflict of laws, merely as "tragedy"; or to regard the novel's motto ("Vengeance is mine, sayeth the Lord") and the sinister glow of love happiness on Anna's face ("the terrible glow of a fire on a dark night,")[29] as merely marking unmarried love off from married. But the distinction between the two is not an important one within the scheme of erotic values, and so to build large emotions upon it seems intellectually external here, and morally vulgar. The novel is saved from that reproach only when one realizes that Tolstoy was deeply ambivalent about this question and was in fact half ready to reject Anna and prefer Karenin.

The novel is in fact conservative in its technique and erotic philosophy, and allied to this is Tolstoy's conservative feeling about the peasants and about history. Levin believes that:

Russia's poverty was not only caused by a wrong distribution of land and a false agricultural policy, but that of late years it was fostered by an alien civilization artificially grafted on Russia, particularly by the means of communication, that is, the railways . . . [which] had come prematurely, and instead of promoting agriculture, as had been expected, had outstripped it, and by stimulating the development of industry and credit facilities had arrested its progress. . . .[30]

This is in line with the Gandhi criticism of capitalist development, of course. But it was as yet allied to quite imperialist ideas about the expanding power of the Russian people:

In his opinion, the Russian people, whose destiny it was to populate and cultivate enormous unoccupied tracts of land consciously, till all those lands had been occupied, kept to the methods best suited for that purpose, and those methods were not by any means as bad as was generally thought.[31]

Of course, this was not state or government imperialism, and Tolstoy took a different view of that. In the final chapters, he satirized the contemporary Russian enthusiasm for a war against Turkey in the Balkans, to liberate fellow Slavs and create a new sphere of influence for Russia. His attitude was so "unpatriotic," so anti-imperialist, that Katkov refused to publish those chapters as part of the novel (which was being serialized in his magazine). But the grounds of Tolstoy's opposition to the war were not radical but conservative, not passionate but skeptical.

This skeptical conservatism is embodied in the figure of the old prince Shcherbatsky, Kitty's father, a minor character but important in the value structure of the novel. Dostoevsky pointed out the unacceptable moral prominence of this figure, to whom Tolstoy ascribes importance on the grounds of hearty healthiness (that is, a determination to be ordinary) and a shrewd though limited judgment (a shrewd insistence on accepting ordinary limits). On these scanty grounds, Tolstoy asks us to accept the old prince's judgments on war and politics, on Madame Stahl and Varenka, on intellectuals, and history. He associates Kitty with her father, in the scene where she condemns Koznishev and Varenka as unerotic, as a way to endorse the former pair. The prince's is the voice of a seasoned eroticism on public matters. This aspect of the novel is indeed vulgar.

In *A Confession* (written 1879–1880, immediately after the novel) Tolstoy explained why he turned away from the kind of art that

Anna Karenina represented: "It was plain to me that art is an adorn-
ment to life, an allurement to life. But life had lost attraction for
me—so how could I attract others."[32] "The power which drew me
away from life was stronger, fuller, and more widespread than any
mere wish. It was a force similar to the former striving to live, only
in a contrary direction. All my strength drew me away from life."[33]

Gandhi 1915–1921,
The Mahatma of India

During this period, Gandhi's major achievement, corresponding to
Tolstoy's writing of *Anna Karenina*, was his capturing of the national
leadership. Without denying the obvious differences between the
two achievers, it is possible to see some likeness. Like Tolstoy, Gandhi had to identify the national problems that seemed to him crucial, and to present solutions, or at least appraisals, that could convince a huge audience. He had to devise a discourse that would
challenge, enchant, arrest, convince that audience, saying something about religion, something about politics, about love and marriage, the nation's past and future, and its rulers and its serfs. He
had to weave into his own schemes and subdue to his own temperament such various types as Nehru, Jinnah, Rajendra Prasad, G. D.
Birla, Vinoba Bhave, J. B. Kripalani, and C. V. Rajagopalachari. This
was an operation not totally unlike that by which the novelist
weaved Vronsky, Koznyshev, Oblonsky, Anna, Kitty, and the in-
sights and interests they severally represented, into his primary
scheme. These fictional characters were all based on people and
ideas Tolstoy had met and wrestled with; making them part of his
book meant knowing them and mastering them, sympathetically
but also synthetically. And if Gandhi had to challenge and in some
sense silence rival leaders and rival ideologies, like Tilak and Annie
Besant, Tolstoy had had to deal with the sort of religion represented
by Lidia Ivanovna and the sort of politics represented by Karenin.

In any case, Gandhi's scope was immensely expanded. The scene
of his actions was now transferred from South Africa, only one of

the components of the British Commonwealth, to India, a subcontinent of 300 million people. And in India Gandhi was to lead not a minority that was almost a bystander in the conflict between black and white, but the majority group, the Hindus; and was to lead them into outright defiance of the whole modern system.

When Gandhi arrived in Bombay in January 1915, though he was a famous name he was essentially nobody in the world of Indian politics. He had no important constituency and only one powerful alliance (with Gokhale), in which he was the minor partner, and his style was unimpressive by comparison with most political leaders. Several of the young men who went to meet him then said later how disappointed they had been by his lack of fire and flair. Neither in position, personality, nor oratory was he comparable with Tilak, or Annie Besant, or Pherozeshah Mehta, and if he was comparable in personality—though less impressive intellectually—with Gokhale, he was the other's *chela*. Indeed, a dozen lesser figures stood between him and that highest level of national leadership; figures like Lala Lajpat Rai, Bipin Chandra Pal, C. R. Das, and in somewhat different fields, Pandit Malaviya, Rabindranath Tagore, and Srinivasa Shastri. Because of his ignorance of the scene, he had promised Gokhale to make no public pronouncements for the first twelve months after his return. And yet by the end of 1921, after a year of national nonviolent noncooperation, it was clear that none of these other figures could challenge Gandhi for the leadership of the nation.

One of the things Gandhi did was to introduce Western styles of action and Western traits of character into Indian politics. He was not the first or only politician to do this—one could point both to the parliamentarians like Bipin Chandra Pal, and to the revolutionaries like the Indian Communist Party. But the traits Gandhi embodied were peculiarly proper to and co-original with, modern-system ideology. Lloyd and Suzanne Rudolph have pointed out in their book, *The Modernity of Tradition*, how much of Benjamin Franklin's morality is reflected in Gandhi's. Gandhi brought to India the work ethic and the interest in economy of time and effort. Like Franklin, he went over his accounts daily and was determined that nothing should be thrown away.

Cleanliness was another modern value as important to Gandhi as to Westerners, and with the same resonance. In his writings, he associates the need to cleanse particularly with temples, and their combination of gold (and jewels) with filth (and blood). He hated all confusions of the spiritual with the animal, the sacred with the sacrilegious—everything Tantric. His cleanliness symbolized a zeal to keep those things separate, to exalt the one and repress the other. Most modern enthusiasts for the East serve exactly the opposite zeal.

But of course Gandhi's modernism of morality was combined with a traditionalism of general philosophy—a readiness for self-sacrifice and a strong drive towards *moksha*. His political leadership was also religious. As he rose up toward eminence and leadership, he sank down toward simplicity and poverty. As far as eating was concerned, he took a vow in April 1915 to limit the number of food-stuffs he would eat in any one day to five and to eat nothing after sundown. In 1921, he began to observe total silence on the Monday of every week, sitting at his wheel or his prayers, working alone or writing notes to those who came to see him, enclosed within a transparent shell of isolation. And as far as clothes were concerned, by the end of 1921 he had reduced himself to a loincloth and shawl. He had shaved off his moustache and refused to replace the teeth he had lost. He had discarded the apparatus and prostheses of modern civilization and was an Indian villager. He was also, by the same token, man naked, unadorned, and unprotected. He was a living manifesto against Western, and indeed any other, high civilization.

He had long before (we might say, in 1906) reached the point that Tolstoy reached in 1881. His path had been easier, though not easy, as far as domestic obstacles went. We might contrast with Tolstoy's agonized note of 1881 about his sense of isolation—his horror at the way his family lived in Moscow, and his terrible quarrels with his wife which drove both to wish for death—Gandhi's passing observation to his secretary, of August 13, 1921: "Ba [Kasturba] and I do not have the same temperament. Ba does not understand me."[1] We must of course take into account Gandhi's inexpressiveness, and note that the worst of his griefs over Harilal were to occur during this period. But the scope of all these concerns was more limited in his life than in Tolstoy's. The bulk of his energies had long gone into public life where he was now moving from loyally supporting though resisting the empire to denouncing it as satanic, and where he was engaged in projects as ambitious, as troubling, as full of triumph and failure, as *Anna Karenina*.

Main Events and Concerns

For the first twelve months Gandhi traveled and observed and reflected. The India he in some sense explored and appropriated lay midway between British officialdom and the revolutionaries. He sought out those who were reconstructing Indian culture. Soon after landing, he went to see Gokhale in Poona, and to the Arya Samaj school at Hardwar, and then to Tagore's school at Shantiniketan, where the other people from the Phoenix Settlement were staying. While he was there, Gokhale died, February 20, 1915, and it soon became apparent that Gandhi would not be chosen as his successor at the Servants of Indian Society. He had to start on his own, and in May he founded an ashram at Kochrab, outside Ahmedabad. He took into it a family of Untouchables, a move which outraged Kasturba and many of his supporters.

Gandhi thought a lot about caste in these first months back in India and about the position of Untouchables in Hinduism. On May 1, he said he was beginning to study his religion, and if he found untouchability to be an essential part of it he would give up his allegiance to it.[2] (It was at just the corresponding period of Tolstoy's life—in the late 1870s—that he began to study his religion, and with similar anxiety.) On the other hand, Gandhi decided that the discipline of *varna* had on the whole benefited his country. "Our society was organized according to *varnavyavastha* (division by vocation) for the purpose of self-control, that is for self-denial. It is a vain effort to replace this structure by a single community."[3]

He declared his loyalty to the British Empire in a speech on April 24, but he based that loyalty on the fact that it was "that government which governs least." His was the politics of a nonpolitical man. He wanted to arouse the Indians to pride and independence of the government.

At the same time, Gandhi often warned students against terrorism. He advised them to terrorize themselves instead. There was thus an ambivalence to the message which young people and others took from him. The most striking case of this was his speech at the opening of the Benares Hindu University, which he gave on February 6, 1916. This university was Mrs. Besant's creation, and she presided over a platform crowded with princes and rajahs who glittered with jewels and satins. The university was to revive and reincarnate the glorious heritage of Indian high culture, reuniting princes and poets. That was not of course the India Gandhi wanted to revive, nor were elaborate ceremonies of any kind to his taste. (He was a private man, and also irritable and impatient; it is notable how often, at the innumerable events held to honor him, he began by scolding his hosts.)

When Gandhi got up to speak at the opening ceremony, there had already been two days of speeches, and he was, under the surface, exasperated. He had been complaining for some time of too much feasting and speechifying at Indian events, and of their too elaborate politeness. In this speech, he complained of the speakers' use of English, of the dirt around the famous temples of Benares, of the vulgar luxury of the rajahs in their satin pajamas, and of the detectives guarding the viceroy. The speech was a praise of the new university and a warning against terrorism and anarchism, addressed to the students in the audience, but what came across also was the undercurrent of bitter resentment. That came across inspiringly to some of the students in the audience—one of whom was Vinoba Bhave, who there heard the call to follow Gandhi—but ungraciously to the people on the platform; Mrs. Besant interrupted him and prompted the princes to walk out.

In that incident, we see in epitome Gandhi's complex personality and challenge to his rivals and followers. He called for Hindu tradition—but not the current tradition; for peace—but not the peace of the status quo; for humility—but equally for pride. To those who had ears to hear, like Vinoba, it was all consistent in its complexity. But to the princes, and Mrs. Besant, and the terrorists, and the communalists, like Tilak, it was a bewildering mishmash, intellectually confused and morally distasteful for its religiosity.

Another major cause was *swadeshi*, which for most Indians meant the use of Indian cloth, not foreign, but which Gandhi defined on February 14, 1916, as self-restriction to the use and service of one's immediate heritage; one's indigenous political institutions, one's ancestral religion, and the goods produced in one's own country and region. But *swadeshi* also implied the propagation of Hindi as a national language which all Indians should learn. Gandhi devoted a lot of time to this cause in this period. In January 1917, he drew up his Prospectus for a National Gujarat School, in which no English would be taught for the first three years. He thought that the learning of English as a national language not only wasted six years of the student's life, but left him nervous, insecure, afraid of examinations, afraid to make a mistake, an imitator.

Gandhi's immediate family was split up in this period. After a brief reunion in early 1915, Harilal again parted from his father in anger. Ba stayed with her husband, even accompanying him on tours, as in Champaran, but the old jealousies persisted. Gandhi asked her to be a mother to Maganlal, now the manager of the ashram, who "has parted from his parents and made my work his own . . . who has so trained himself that he can carry on my work after me."[4] But she still resented the usurpers who had displaced her sons.

Gandhi had hoped his widowed sister, Raliyatbehn, would join him at the ashram and become a mother to the many children there. That would be true *Vaishnava dharma*, he told her reproachfully, not the conventional pieties she practiced, and seeing her he would have some reminders of their mother constantly about him. But in her eyes Gandhi was still an outcast because of his trip to England. "The world does not regard me as defiled. I am so to you, however," he wrote.[5]

But the great tragedy of his family relations continued to be those with Harilal, who was from every point of view degenerating. In 1918, he wrote to tell his father that he had been accused of losing (embezzling) R30,000 of his Madras employer's money. On May 1 Gandhi wrote back: "I got your letter in Delhi. What shall I write to you? Everyone acts according to his nature."[6]

On March 30, 1918, he gave a talk on Indian civilization at Indore, which expressed an idea that preoccupied him at this time; of the unique character of India's vocation:

India alone is the land of karma, the rest is the land of bhoga [enjoyment]. I feel that India's mission is different from that of other countries. India is fitted for the religious supremacy of the world . . . India can conquer all by soul-force.[7]

Later in the year, he came to doubt that. He wrote to Andrews on July 6, full of perplexity, saying that the ancient Indians did *not* repudiate war, as one sees in the *Mahabharata* and the *Ramayana;* and later: "The Hindus were not less eager than the Mahommedans to fight." They were simply disorganized, physically weakened, and torn by internal dissensions.[8] But by May 1919 he was asserting the simple faith again, perhaps relying on practice to solve his problems with the theory, or else allowing his long physical illness to obliterate the mental struggle he had been involved in. Again we read that India is unlike other countries, "she deliberately abandoned the universal use of brute force."[9] But what did Gandhi think as he inserted the word "universal"? He saved his sentence from refutation but sacrificed its force of meaning.

His campaigns in Champaran in 1917, and in Ahmedabad and Kheda in early 1918, had all been successful, but each had been on a small scale and not of central national interest. His next effort was to recruit volunteers for the British army, and this he found exhausting. His fatigue was caused by the physical strain of the speeches, and the disappointing results (some days he walked twenty miles, and found no one who listened to him at the end of them), but perhaps even more because of the moral perplexities just mentioned which it evoked in him. He fell seriously ill, and remained so throughout the rest of 1918. On October 1 he was at death's door, and in January had to submit to an operation, and then to the ultimate humiliation, the breaking of his vow against drinking milk. The doctor told him he needed milk, and since he had been thinking of cow's milk at the time he took the vow, he agreed to goat's. He knew it was a compromise, and felt he had "lost lustre." He wanted to live, as he admitted.

And then suddenly a national cause arose, and his response to it made him the nation's leader. It was provoked by the Rowlatt Bills, which the government introduced to give itself emergency powers to deal with insurrection, conspiracy, and revolution, including powers to investigate revolutionary movements. Indignation against them was rife in India, and a general need was felt to give it expression. On February 9, 1919, Gandhi wrote: "The Rowlatt Bills have agitated me very much. It seems I shall have to fight the greatest battle of my life."[10] And soon he was writing letters to the Press, explaining *satyagraha* and distinguishing it from methods like boycott.

The Rowlatt Bills, aimed at suppressing protest, provoked much more, in large groups and small, and those responsible for maintaining order grew very uneasy, especially in the Punjab. Thus when in Amritsar, the holy city of the Sikhs, on April 13, 1919, thousands of people gathered in the Jallianwala Bagh, the British General Dyer, giving no order to disperse, opened fire upon them. There were about six-thousand people in an area the size of Trafalgar Square, and 1,650 rounds were fired (the aim shifting to where the crowd was thickest); 1,516 casualties resulted, 379 were killed, and more than a thousand injured.

Gandhi drew up the Congress Report on the Punjab Disorders— their answer to the Government Report—and he drew a brilliant portrait of O'Dwyer simply by quoting him. Chapter two of Gandhi's report is entitled "Sir Michael O'Dwyer's Administration" and presents him dismissing the educated Indians' protests and appealing over their heads to the peasants—and to all the martial races—as confidently as any Kipling hero: "I found I could meet the Punjabi, whatever his class or condition, as man to man, without suspicion or mistrust. I found him, in the mass, loyal but not subservient, brave but not boastful, enterprising but not visionary, progressive but not pursuing false ideals, or mistaking the shadow for the substance."[11] The educated Indians were leading the Punjabi peasants to disaster. "The British Government, which has crushed foreign foes and quelled internal rebellion, could afford to despise . . . a handful of noisy agitators . . ."[12] but it felt a duty to protest its loyal and simple-hearted subjects.

"The recent puerile demonstrations against the Rowlatt Act," he found, "ludicrous" and he spoke of ". . . ignorant and creduous people (not one in a thousand knows anything of the measure). "This was his appraisal of the Gandhi movement.

He held it undesirable to allow trials to such revolutionaries "or other sedition mongers":[13]

In these days when we are in danger of being deafened by political harangues and of being blinded by the shower of political manifestos, it is well occasionally to return to mother earth to clear up our minds of shams and illusions, and to ask ourselves what will all this noise and talk do for the man of the soil, the man behind the plough, the man whose life is a long-drawn question between a crop and a crop.[14]

Such are the "loyal and sturdy men of the martial races of the Punjab,"[15] "the great martial races of the Punjab who differ but are united to each other and the Government by two bonds of steel, loyalty and valour."[16] They have, he continues, been insulted by those who have no martial spirit themselves and no appreciation of the valor and loyalty of those who defended *their* hearths and homes, those who were "true to their salt."

O'Dwyer thus appealed to the martial Indians in the name of the martial English, and there is no reason to doubt his sincerity in this. The English had become a martial race—at least the aristo-military caste which ruled the empire had—and they did have a link with the corresponding groups in India, both warriors and peasants, which Gandhi lacked.

He was clearly aware of this and puzzled over the problem it brought him in 1918. But in the second half of 1919, he was mostly concerned with the tragedy at Amritsar and with the way the Government had handled it and its aftermath. He spent a lot of energy investigating the cases presented against Indian "revolutionaries," and protesting against their sentences. It was also at this point that spinning became of prime importance in his program. In an interview in *Hindu* (1918–1919) he said: "I want every man, woman, and child to learn hand-spinning and weaving. . . . Even a few decades back, every village had its hand-looms and the people were wearing only clothes woven therefrom." On October 5, 1919, his Gujarat paper, *Navajivan*, announced a R5000 prize for a portable wheel, made of indigenous components, which could take on ten spindles simultaneously.

This was also the period of Gandhi's relationship with Saraladevi Chaudhrani, the wife of Pandit Rambhuj Dutt Chaudhuri, one of the nationalist leaders of the Punjab. Her father was a founder of Congress and her mother a writer, so she was born into cultural reform. Three years younger than Gandhi, she was also the grand-niece of Rabindranath Tagore and herself a poet, a singer, and a pianist. The couple lived in Lahore in 1919, but had known Gandhi in 1910, and now became Gandhians, sending their son to be educated at his ashram. The Pandit invited Gandhi to Lahore, but was himself in jail by the time he got there, on October 17, 1919. Gandhi and his entourage stayed with Saraladevi, and she traveled with them. She took up the cause of *swadeshi*, giving song recitals, making speeches, and later opening a shop for *khadi*.

Her relationship with Gandhi is worth remarking because it was personal in a way unlike his other relationships. It was erotic. Writing to her in spring, 1920, he more than once says he has dreamed of her, calls her the greatest Shakti [female power] in India, says, had she been there, she would have dragged him from his bed to watch the sunrise, and so on. He dreams of her leaving her husband and coming to him. (Later she did, in fact, separate from the Pandit because of his opposition to Gandhi's nonviolence.) And whether or not sexual pleasure was consciously in question (later he said it was, for him) the relationship was erotic because she invited him to explore her personality.

On August 23, 1920, he wrote: "Your letters have your usual self. Some of them decidedly despondent and skeptical and suspicious." She complained about his companions (Narahari Parikh and Maganlal are mentioned) because they criticised Gandhi's intimacy

with her. He replied that they were his superiors, because they
were so jealous of his character, which was their ideal. "I would
surrender all the world to deserve a love so pure and unselfish. . . .
You should be proud of their jealousy and watchfulness. . . . You
asked for a reward of your great surrender. Well, it is its own reward. With deep love. Your L.G."[17] The initials stood for law giver.
In an earlier letter, he had said she must enslave India by becoming
India's slave in thought, word, and deed; she must get rid of her
inertia and give her music to the nation.[18]

To his old friend Kallenbach he wrote on the tenth of August:

I have come in closest touch with a lady who often travels with me. Our
relationship is indefinable. I call her my spiritual wife. . . . It was under her
roof that I passed several months at Lahore in the Punjab.[19]

To her, on August 24:

Your letters have caused me distress. You do not like my sermons. And yet
so long as you remain a schoolgirl, what should I do except give you sermons? . . . What is the reward of your having given years to acquiring perfection in piano playing? You give all for the cause you represent because
you cannot do otherwise. . . ."[20]

He asked her to do household work in the Ashram—to become a
complete woman. After that there is a gap until December, when he
wrote, on the eleventh:

I have certainly not betrayed any annoyance over your complex nature, but
I have remarked on it . . . I refuse to call an indefinable complexity a piece
of art. All art yields to patient analysis and shows a unity of design behind
the diversity on the canvas. You are hugging your defects even when they
are pointed out by a friend in a friendly manner. I do not feel vexed but it
makes my task of helping difficult. What art can there be in moods, in fits
and starts?[21]

Simple natures are called so only because they are understandable
and yield to treatment. And again, more yieldingly, and with a kind
of metaphysical wit: "I love you more for loving me less for any
hate you may see in me."[22]

Finally, on December 17 he wrote again in this new voice, as new
for him as the humble voice in which Tolstoy wrote to the Tsar in
1881. But this letter is in effect a farewell, a breaking off of their

relationship. Gandhi did not want to develop that new voice. A
door had opened before him but he closed it again:

> I have been analysing my love for you. I have reached a definition of
> spiritual wife. It is a partnership between two persons of the opposite sex
> where the physical is wholly absent. It is therefore possible between broth-
> er and sister, father and daughter. It is possible only between two brahma-
> charis in thought, word and deed. . . . For this special partnership to subsist,
> there must be complete coincidence, not from faith, but from knowledge. It
> is a meeting between two kindred spirits.[23]

Such people can never be physically wedded:

> Are you spiritual wife to me of that description? Have we that exquisite
> purity, that perfect coincidence, that perfect merging, that identity of
> ideals, that self-forgetfulness, that fixity of purpose, that trustfulness? For
> me I can answer plainly that it is only an aspiration. I am unworthy to have
> that companionship with you. I require in me an infinitely higher purity
> than I possess in thought. I am too physically attached to you to be worthy
> of enjoying that sacred association with you. By physical attachment, I here
> mean I am too much affected by your weaknesses.[24]

They have sharp differences, and must accept a brother-sister relationship. "This is the big letter I promised. With dearest love I still
subscribe myself, Your L. G."[25]

Gandhi often referred back to this relationship in a veiled way. In
1936, when discussing birth control and marital experiment with
Margaret Sanger, he said: "This is the argument I had with a woman with whom I almost fell. It is so personal I did not put it into my
autobiography. We had considered if there can be this spiritual
companionship. . . . I came in contact with an illiterate woman.
[That is, he married Kasturba.] Then I meet a woman with a broad,
cultural education. Could we not develop a close contact, I said to
myself? This was a plausible argument, and I nearly slipped. But I
was saved, I awoke from my trance. I don't know how. For a time it
seemed I had lost my anchor. I was saved by youngsters who
warned me. I saw that if I was doomed, they also were doomed."[26]
In other places, he makes it clear that the "youngsters" included his
son, Devdas, and his secretary, Mahadev Desai.

In these letters, we see Gandhi moving in an area otherwise
closed to him; the area in which Tolstoy's relations with his wife
inscribed themselves, in which so many major novelists have writ-

ten. Saraladevi, at least as she is reflected in Gandhi's letters to her, is a familiar figure to readers of Turgenev, Goncharov, Chekhov, or the Shaw of *Heartbreak House*.

Russian novels (but also French and German and English) were in the later nineteenth century full of ladies who rise gracefully from the piano and cross to a window, where they lean their brows upon the cold glass and sigh—and later laugh and dash off some brilliant *ballade*. They emanate fascination, and one may say that the novels, as novels, belong to them. If the central character, or some harsher hero like Turgenev's Bazarov, breaks free from their spell, he by that action passes out of the novelist's and reader's ken. It is no accident that these figures are so frequently seen at the piano—a central organ of civilization and its discontents—and it is very appropriate (not to be counted on, since she was Hindu) that Saraladevi should have been a pianist. It is also very appropriate that she should have been a Tagore, one of that dynasty of singers, dancers, painters, poets, actors, who made a palace of art out of their various homes. Gandhi described her and Tagore as two of the most artistic people in India.[27] Saraladevi should be counted among the multiple transactions between Gandhi and Rabindranath.

Tolstoy's novels are *not* built around such figures, except for *The Kreutzer Sonata*, which is a violent reaction against all they represent. His erotic taste was too vigorous, his erotic knowledge too authentic, to express itself through these conventions. But his wife Sonia, his sister Masha, his daughter Tania, and Valeria Arseneva and Tania Kuzminskaya, all in varying but important ways got trapped in the miasma of music, lured into that erotic-melancholic marshland, and much of the animus of *What is Art?* derives from his experience of that.

Gandhi broke free, and though letters to Saraladevi and allusions to her recur as late as the 1940s, she seems to have played no significant part in his life after 1920. His was the briefest of stays in the land of eros. But one is bound to suppose that its coincidence with his acquisition of the national leadership was more than accidental. This was also the time of his approach to an approval of violence. Gandhi suddenly found himself an embodiment of power; eroticism and a general expansion of the self was an inevitable temptation.

But Gandhi refused to be distracted from his purposes, to be entangled in that thicket of lilacs, nightingales, and moonlight. He turned his attention to, among other things, Congress. On his recommendation, the membership dues were reduced to four annas, to

make membership economically feasible to almost anyone. And at
the Ahmedabad session in 1921, an Indian cultural style was introduced in clothes and seating. Much to the discomfort and disgrun-
tlement of many, congressmen squatted on the ground in *dhotis*—
Gandhi had stolen their chairs and their trousers.

At the Amritsar Congress, Tilak and C. R. Das had argued for
rejecting the Montagu-Chelmsford reforms, but Gandhi led a movement to accept them which Jinnah and Malaviya supported, and a
compromise resulted. This put him on a level with the leaders, and
after that he was taken into their intimate counsels. There, and in
meetings about Khilafat, he had disagreed with the big men, and
succeeded.

By 1921 Tilak was dead, Mrs. Besant was publicly hissed when
she disagreed with Gandhi, Jinnah was no longer at home in Congress or in the Home Rule League as Gandhi had remodeled them,
and so on. India had chosen a new leader—as yet we can speak of
India, Muslims as well as Hindus—and it was Gandhi.

The Great Campaigns

Gandhi had, then, an ashram. He ran newspapers, he went on
tours, speaking in support of national revival. But besides all this,
he engaged in intensive campaigns on particular issues. These were
the large-scale achievements that in some sense crystallized the values and tendencies more fluidly active in the rest of his life; these
were the equivalent for Tolstoy's major fiction. We cannot discuss
here his variously triumphant campaigns in Champaran, Ahmedabad, and Kheda, but must pass to the more troubled record—impressive just because so troubled—of his recruiting for the British
Army in 1918.

Gandhi asked the Government to make him its chief recruiting
agent on the thirtieth of April. He hoped to get twenty men from
each of the six hundred villages of Kheda. This was work which no
nationalist leader had touched, and for which there was no national
constituency. There were 800,000 Indians in the army, but they
came from areas and groups which had nothing to do with Congress. It was work always done by British agents, and among the
martial races. Gandhi had to say the things Sir Michael O'Dwyer
said—to complain, for instance, that 400,000 men from the Punjab
joined the army during the war but only 70 of them came from
among the 10,000 university students. He had to praise martial loy-

alty and valor and to blame the educated middle class that refused to defend its country or to respect those who did. And the work involved him in endless explanations of how he reconciled this work with his opposition to violence. No wonder he wrote to his friend Dr. Mehta on July 2: "You must be watching my work of recruitment. Of all my activities, I regard this as the most difficult and the most important. If I succeed in it, genuine *swaraj* is assured."[28]

One of his arguments was partnership: if Indians want to have the benefits of being treated as equals in the empire, they must take a part in its defense comparable with the part the English took. He himself had twice volunteered for service in this war, in France and in Mesopotamia, because he had convinced himself that he was accepting the military protection of the empire. He also said, as in Nadiad on June 17, that *swaraj* without military power would be useless, and joining the army was the way to acquire military power.[29]

Another way in which Gandhi defended his consistency was by saying that military training was intended for those who did not believe in *satyagraha*. "That the whole of India will ever accept *satyagraha* is beyond my imagination."[30] Thus, he had one message for one section of his audience, another for another. This was politically realistic but morally confusing, for it left his listeners free to assign themselves to a section, or to invent a new one.

It is one of Gandhi's most striking characteristics that, while identifying himself as a man of a special type, an abnormal and extreme phenomenon, he addressed the whole range of human types and invoked the criteria of cultural normality, of reason and tradition and culture. Most importantly, he was concerned about men of violence, and their place in society, and their virtues: "There can be no partnership between the cat and the mouse, between the ant and the elephant."[31] He had a strong sense that he himself, and the group he belonged to, *were* mice and ants.

> Any stout fellow can successfully intimidate us. If a Pathan were to come here and start hitting out with the lathi, we would all run away. An overbearing Kabuli, entering a compartment already crowded, will get the people to vacate the seats . . . and occupy the room for four.[32]

He often said in this period that he was ceasing to be a Bania and becoming a Kshattriya. "Satyagraha is a soldierly instinct, and Banias are largely associated with money-making rather than with fighting for a cause. Hence, I have the fewest co-workers from among fellow-Banias.[33] His movement's prime aim is self-purification, or the revival of the Kshattriya spirit. And perhaps his most striking formulation of the idea occurs in a letter to Andrews: "You cannot teach *ahimsa* to a man who cannot kill."[34]

This idea involved him in debate and doubt of himself, much more than did his ideas of sex, for on this issue he was strongly drawn in opposite directions. In *Young India* on October 20, 1921 we find:

> ... the sooner we are left free to fight, the better for our manhood, our respective religions, and our country. It will not be a new phenomenon if we fought ourselves into sanity. The English carried on internecine warfare for 21 years before they settled down to peaceful work. The French fought among themselves with a savage ferocity hardly excelled during modern times. The Americans did nothing better before they evolved their commonwealth. Let us not hug our unmanliness for fear of fighting among ourselves.[35]

This is an example of Gandhi citing the lessons of history, which he usually repudiated. It is also an example of why he had finally to repudiate them. The lessons of history are not in accord with the gospel of peace.

He had a clear enough formula, that a man must be capable of violent resistance before he was capable of nonviolence. But it involved him in many difficult questions of application which tormented him in the summer of 1918:

> It is clear that, before I can give a child an idea of moksha, I must let it grow into full manhood. I must allow it to a certain extent to be even attached to the body.... What is the meaning of having a vigorous body? How far should India have to go in for a training in arms-bearing?[36]

On the seventeenth of July he wrote to Hanumantrao at the ashram:

> I do believe that we shall have to teach our children the art of self-defense. I see more and more clearly that we shall be unfit for swaraj for generations to come if we do not regain the power of self-defense. This means for me a rearrangement of so many ideas about self-development and India's development.[37]

Twelve days later he wrote to Mashruwala:

In what manner should the children learn to use their strength? It is a
difficult thing to teach them to defend themselves and yet not be overbear-
ing. Till now, we used to teach them not to fight back if anyone beat them.
Can we go on doing so now? What will be the effect of such teaching on a
child? Will he, in his youth, be a forgiving or a timid man? My powers of
thinking fail me. Use yours.[38]

On the same day he wrote to Andrews:

I must indulge myself again. I begin to perceive a deep meaning behind
the Japanese reluctance to listen to the message of a Prophet from a defeated nation. [Tagore had gone to Japan, preaching pacifism, and had been
coolly received.] War will always be with us. There seems to be no possibility of the whole human nature becoming transformed. Moksha and ahimsa
are for individuals to attain. Full practise of ahimsa is inconsistent with
possession of wealth, land or rearing of children.[39]

Rajendra Prasad tells us in his *Autobiography* that Gandhi was full
of indecision and self-doubt after his recruiting campaign, and often wept and said: "I do not know what God's will is."[40] It does not
seem, moreover, that Gandhi ever resolved the problem. His activity, from then on, had an insecure foundation.

But in some ways this internal debate shows us Gandhi at his
most impressive, and also his most like Tolstoy. It shows his imaginative flexibility and willingness to imagine points of view and
modes of being quite unlike his own, something comparable to the
novelist's ability to lose himself in characters who manifest themselves upon his page in seeming contradiction of his own sympathies and judgments. It shows his experimental interest in ventur-
ing out into behavior that may get him into trouble and may puzzle
and annoy his natural allies, the interest a novelist can express in
plot. And it shows that sometimes this flexibility and experimental-
ism led Gandhi, as they led Tolstoy, into irreconcilable self-con-
flicts. As he wrote *Anna Karenina*, Tolstoy was irresistibly drawn
both to the erotic values of which Anna was the tragic heroine, and
to those opposite values of renunciation and spirituality represented by Varenka and by Karenin in his crisis. Tolstoy came down on
the side of the first, but the strain and conflict can be felt both by
the reader of the novel, and by the student of his life, in which,
indeed, the next big development was the renunciation of erotic
values. As Gandhi took over the leadership of the nationalist movement in India, he was drawn both to the nonviolent values he had
learned from Tolstoy and to values that answer to and express the

whole range of kinds of human strength, including the soldier's kind. He came down on the side of the first, but it seems to have been by virtue of a dangerous illness and a recoil from a tangle of feelings to which there was no solution.

As a last example of his power of imaginative projection at this time, we might take a letter of July 28 to Maganlal:

> I have come to see, what I did not so clearly before, that there is non-violence in violence. This is the big change which has come about. *Brahmachyra* consists in refraining from sexual indulgence, but we do not bring up our children to be impotent.[41]

And Gandhi would not be impotent. He overcame his indecisions—by an act of will. For, however doubtful the connection one thinks one sees between that indecision and the major illness which ended it, there is no doubt that his recovery from that illness was an act of will, and one taken against conscience. In order to recover, he allowed himself to be given goat's milk, breaking his vow against milk, on the consciously sophistical grounds that he had been thinking only of cow's milk. He did this, he tells us, because he wanted to live. He wanted to act. And with the strength the milk gave him, he seized power in India. He led a great national movement which was nonviolent and so in some sense nonpowerful. He had resolved, in practice, the dilemma of violence and nonviolence.

Part of the attraction of nonviolent noncooperation for Gandhi was that this would create his kind of anarchy in India, which was not disorder but culture without civilization, government without a government. But he was ready to risk disorder. In November 1920, he had said:

> Yes, if I can carry the country with me, I think it is quite possible to run all the present institutions without any Government aid. . . .[42] For I do really believe that anarchy will be preferable to a continuance of the orderly humiliation and emasculation of a whole nation.[43]

In December, he rerecommended *Hind Swaraj*, (though he added that he was now working only for parliamentary *swaraj*, because India was not yet ripe for the fuller freedom.) "All we need is the courage to live without councils, law courts and schools provided by government."[44] This was exactly the teaching of Tolstoy in his old age.

SECTION IV

Old Age

Tolstoy 1881–1910 • Gandhi 1921–1948

Introductory

Within this section the divisions are determined by political dates; in Tolstoy's case, 1881 was when Alexander II was assassinated, 1894 when Nicholas II came to the throne, and 1905 when the revolution broke out. This sort of division seems appropriate because in this period of his life Tolstoy lost his privacy and refuge. Deprived of the social screens that had protected his idyll, he had to turn around to face the bitter winds of revolutionary protest and government repression. In Gandhi's case, 1921 was when he became undisputed leader of the Indian freedom movement, 1931 was when he attended the Round Table Conference in London, and 1942 was the year of his Quit India Campaign and his imprisonment.

But the theme that overrides all these divisions is aging; a man's conscious and cooperative aging, in which he practices the arts of asceticism in the contemplation of death. One might say that Tolstoy and Gandhi rooted in aging and death a mode of authority equal but opposite to that authority most of us acknowledge in youth and life. Our imaginative culture is built on our cult of youth and life. Tolstoy and Gandhi offer us the possibility of a cult of age and death.

Tolstoy was only fifty-three in 1881 and Gandhi was only fifty-two in 1921—both younger than lots of men who call themselves middle-aged—and yet both of them were old men, in their own view and others'. But being old did not mean to them accepting defeat or diminishment. Tolstoy thought about this a good deal, feeling isolated by his belief in the ripening power of age. In his diary for August 15, 1900, he noted that old age was no longer recognized as the source of wisdom it is. He set out to win recognition for that truth again.

In "Religion and Morality" (1894), he defined the Christian religious idea as "doing the will of Him Who sent me," and said that every old man involuntarily felt the truth of this idea. He added that, in his opinion, this truth was now being realized by humanity as a whole, as well as individuals.[1] On September 2, 1900, he wrote in his diary that men have a critical period of spiritual development, at about fifty, just as they have a critical period of sexual development much earlier.

He pursued the same line of thought in his anthologies. In *The Pathway of Life*, we read: "It is generally thought that the life of the very aged is of no consequence, that they are merely winding up their days. This is untrue . . . the value of life is in inverse ratio to the square of the distance from death."[2] And in *The Circle of Reading* for March 3, we read: "The older a man is, the more he sees the foundation of the world to be spiritual,"[3] and on May 12: "The worst mistake is to forget Death."[4] Chekhov called Tolstoy's an old man's philosophy, and he was right, but he said that (in 1897) as a way to free himself from Tolstoy's influence. We don't have to accept the disparaging intention; the description can be taken as enhancing.

Gandhi's was also an old man's philosophy, from the beginning. Many of the traditional traits of youth—self-expansive youth—were never his: He never, for instance, played games. In the 1930s, he wrote to a correspondent that he did not know what hockey was: "I have never to my recollection, watched any game, either in England, South Africa, or in India. I have never attended cricket matches, and only once took a bat and cricket ball in my hands, and that was under compulsion from the headmaster of the High School where I was studying, and this was forty-five years ago."[5]

Tolstoy was of course of a different temperament. He had engaged himself in youth as energetically as anyone ever did. But his experience was not entirely unlike Gandhi's. In "Memoirs of a Madman," (1884) he says he had premonitions in childhood that life was unlivable when he saw his nurse and the housekeeper quarreling, when he heard the story of the crucifixion of Christ, and when he saw a serf boy beaten. On those occasions: "I sobbed and sobbed and began knocking my head against the wall."[6] Then in youth he forgot these things, corrupted by pleasure; and then, in Arzamas, the premonition of death "brought his madness back."

Gandhi never had the unregenerate young man's courage, vitality, or optimism: "As a coward, which I was for years, I harboured violence," he said, in 1924.[7] By and large he withdrew from boyhood and youth, waiting for age. "And now I feel as though I was naturally built for silence. I was silent at school, and in my London days I was taken for a silent drone by my friends."[8] His own version of qualities like courage and optimism are quite different, because twice born. "On the horizon I see nothing but impenetrable darkness. God's ways are inscrutable. I am an optimist. There is nothing to warrant hope, but still I do not lose hope."[9]

He hated noise, crowds, explosions, exuberance. "I went to a place where everybody was busy shouting "Mahatma Gandhi Kijai" and everybody was trying to fall at my feet but no one was willing to listen to me."[10] And in an article he wrote about himself in the third person: "Crowds pressed in upon the rickshaw from all sides. The din and the dust and the shower of flowers choked him. This went on for nearly an hour. He sat dazed and dejected in the rickshaw feeling perfectly hopeless."[11]

Reginald Reynolds, who went to India full of expansive youthfulness, in 1929, says that when he met Gandhi, he was struck by how old he looked, and he noted in his journal that he understood Gandhi the way he would a great Catholic (medieval) saint. One might contrast with his account of Gandhi, Reynolds' description of the English pacifist he knew, Jack Hoyland, as a "big, handsome, virile, jolly Quaker."[12] Hoyland had been a young man—in the crucial sense, he remained so—and so he was closer to Reynolds than Gandhi could be.

We can trace this denial of youth and life in their costume and lifestyle, as well as in their words. Gandhi's costume, in this period of old age, is well known: the sandals, the loin cloth, the shawl, the toothless grin, and skinny nakedness. Tolstoy wore Russian blouses, one made out of linen in summer, and one made out of wool in winter, plus a sheepskin *shuba* and a kaftan. Aylmer Maude says his blouses were made longer than usual, out of modesty. He wanted the erogenous zones of buttocks and genitals fully and loosely covered. Gandhi (and other Indians) found even nineteenth-century European dress immodest because it so tightly outlined those zones.

Someone speaks of "the prophet's brow, the patriarch's beard, the peasant's blouse" in Tolstoy, and that neatly sums up the impression most people got from pictures of him in old age. To go into more detail, the painter Repin described his looks in 1884 thus: "Hewn with dashing strokes of an axe, he is modelled so interestingly that after his, at first glance, coarse and plain features all others seem dull." He talks at length about Tolstoy's hands:

> The large working hands, despite their long fingers, are "motor" hands with unusually developed joints—a peasant trait: the joints of aristocrats' fingers are *slimmer* than the phalanx . . . the colour of the thick skin is terracotta, the transparency of aristocratic skin, whiteness and bluish veins—all these tokens of pure aristocracy are absent.[13]

Sergeenko says that when irritated, Tolstoy's features had a harsh and bristling quality which reminded him of Prince Bolkonsky in *War and Peace*. But in moments of illumination his harsh features beamed, he listened patiently and talked calmly, with his head bowed and hands clasped; when the other man was at a loss for a word, Tolstoy put his hand on his shoulder or knee.[14] Andreev also speaks of an extraordinary softness of manner and personality, and Makovitsky says he never frowned or gesticulated as he talked.

Two more traits that will remind us of Gandhi are noted by Sergeenko; his repugnance for things finely finished, and his dislike of public acclaim and public occasions. Both men were too susceptible to the intoxication of applause to develop a normal tolerance, and both were in love with work and with products which bore the marks of workmanship.

Repin's attitudes are ambivalent. He says that he was made to feel Tolstoy's superiority in physical and mental exuberance, as horseman, driver, and so on, when they were out together in a snowstorm. It is clear that Tolstoy did challenge other men in those ways (he repents it in his diaries); but it is also clear that these famous artists and writers who have left descriptions of him came ready to measure themselves against him.

S. T. Elpatevsky, a Yalta doctor who knew him, 1901–1902, seems free from this stress of mutual challenge. He describes Tolstoy's stern and severe face, broad, stooping shoulders, and big long hands, as looking powerful, and as a typical White-Russian peasant's face. He also spoke of Tolstoy's hunger for muscular work, and his attitude to medicine, as a peasant's—he despised "mixtures" and believed only in "serious remedies" like compresses, and "serious" measurements, as of temperature and weight loss. In this and other of these descriptions, as in the judgments of Russian politicians, the determining question is: "Was Tolstoy a peasant or an aristocrat?" Which caste did he belong to? Different witnesses give different answers, but all seem to have asked the same question.

The equivalent question behind descriptions of Gandhi was perhaps: "Was he feeble and sickly or was he strong and healthy? Had he succeeded in terms of physical life?" The government Englishmen tended to see him as feeble and sickly, the Gandhians and the American journalists as the reverse. Viceroy Irwin described Gandhi to the King thus: "Small, wizened, rather emaciated, no front teeth, it is a personality very poorly endowed with this world's trimmings. And yet you cannot help feeling the force of character behind the sharp little eyes and immensely active and acutely working mind." Irwin had more sympathy with Gandhi than the other viceroys he dealt with, but he never spoke of him except as "little" and "strange." Louis Fischer, on the other hand, says that his body did not give the impression of age; his skin was soft and smooth with a healthy glow, and his beautiful hands (big and expressive, with well-formed fingers) did not shake like an old man's.[15] Ved Mehta quotes Woodrow Wyatt as saying that Gandhi looked like a polished nut, all bright and shiny, with no spare flesh. "He gleamed, you know. His chocolate-colored skin was smooth, healthy, and young-looking, and shone all over."[16]

Francis Watson gives us a vivid description of Gandhi in 1939 ". . . shining with that look of coppery well-being . . . the bat-like ears, the flitting smile, the coiled energy in the angular body, the snowy scrap of clothing."[17] He had just dethroned Bose and was going on to the Tripuri Congress after his Rajkot fast. Watson asked Gandhi how Europe's rush to Armageddon could be stopped: "With a smile as wan as the solution he answered: 'Give up your ill-gotten gains.'"[18]

The objective facts about Gandhi's looks are clear enough. He was five feet five inches tall; the veins in his temples protruded, his fat nose pointed downward, and his lower lip pushed up to meet it.

And the semiobjective fact is that he and Tolstoy were ugly. This is not to say that it is or was unpleasant to look at them. In fact, the late images of both are most often impressive and moving. But Tolstoy and Gandhi were never beautiful young men, and their later selves show that.

That marks them off from men like Edward Carpenter, Havelock Ellis, and Walt Whitman, also heroes of the New Life, whose complacently cultivated old-manly beauty goes with a certain complacency and limitedness in their thinking. Tolstoy's form, and Gandhi's form, was never beautiful like theirs; our men's circumscriptive line never completed itself. They never fully realized a natural self, at least in youth, and that was both cause and consequence of the way they reached out unrestingly to the reality beyond.

In Tolstoy's old age Yasnaya Polyana was still a beautiful country estate and center of gracious living. Although far from luxurious by English standards, the gap between it and the peasants' homes nearby was at least as great as it had been when Tolstoy was born. But there were now quite large factories less than ten miles away, and the railway line passed so close to the house that passengers could see much of the estate, and the Tolstoys heard the trains and saw the smoke. And the guards Sonia had hired lounged in the hallway. They were concealed behind a partition, but the smell of the cheap tobacco they smoked betrayed their presence.

And the homes of the peasants were still primitive, the chimneys just a tin pipe poking through a straw roof. Repin wrote to Chertkov in August 1887: "At the sight of the inhabitants of Yasnaya Polyana in dark greasy huts with cockroaches, without any light, vegetating in the evenings by the kerosene lamp, which gives out only black and greasy soot, I felt ill, and I don't believe in the possibility of a free or joyful mood in that Dantean hell."[19]

As for Tolstoy's own feelings about this background to his life, we can take two comments from 1893. In his diary for May 4, he notes: "The battle between Christianity and paganism here is escalating. Lev has returned from St. Petersburg; the two boys [Andrei and Misha] are alienated and sullen."[20] And in June to Biriukov: "The starving stand outside, and the footman runs to us with pies, and I, who preach simplicity to others, am a participant."[21]

Gandhi's main home, in the beginning of this period, was his ashram at Sabarmati, described by Verrier Elwin:

On the further bank I could see in panorama many of the forces against which Gandhi was in revolt. There were the tall chimneys of the factories which were helping to destroy the hand-spinning industry. There was the palace of the Collector, symbol of a foreign domination which had done so much to ruin the quiet peasant life of the villages. Opposite were the low roofs of the simple dwellings of the ashram. The forces of the world and the forces of the spirit were here in vivid symbol arrayed, against one another—machine-force against soul-force, force of arms against love-force.[22]

Gandhi's second Indian ashram was at Sevagram, near Wardha, in the center of India. It was in a village inhabited largely by Untouchables and riddled by disease, where, it was said, even the children lacked the energy to brush away the flies that settled on them. The ashramites planted sugar cane and vegetables and showed the villagers how to improve their lives. But there was an element of economic artificiality to the ashram, as there was to Tolstoy's manual work at Yasnaya Polyana. It was supported financially by G. D. Birla, and cost him $17,000 a year. Tolstoy and Gandhi inevitably inhabited enclaves within the prevailing economic order.

Ved Mehta's picture of Gandhi stresses a harshness, in his temperament and lifestyle, in reaction against the legendary, or saint's life, effect of the Gandhians' portraits. Edward Crankshaw's picture of Tolstoy, and that of most of those who wrote in sympathy with Sonia, does the same. We can assume, I think, that the two men, like other prophets, were both gentle and harsh. Their unregenerate natures were ambitious, their perceptions were all-piercing, and the strain of differing from the whole world and resisting the pressures on them to conform to custom made them harsher. And we must also take into account the fact that those who describe them are men of letters who have a vested interest in humanism which is endangered by radical religion. The harshness occurs between Tolstoy or Gandhi and them, and expresses the incompatibility of those two textures and temperaments.

There is another kind of tendentiousness in these interpretations, which is not caused by simple enthusiasm for or against the subject, but which is worth quarreling with. In Tolstoy's case, it is a stress on his power. In Gandhi's case, a stress on his gaiety. Both those who like Tolstoy and those who don't, both those who see him as an aristocrat and those who see him as a peasant, see him as powerful, formidable, semidivine. But in fact the record of his last thirty years show him as weak and ineffectual, at least in his home, the arena where he was in conflict every day.

His daughter, Tania, writes: "It was not in my father's nature to dig in his heels over such things."[23] She is referring to a barouche which Sonia wanted while he wanted a Russian conveyance: and Sonia got her way "over such things". But Tania says the same was true of moral matters. "I would like to stress this trait in my father's character; not only did he never preach or moralize to people, even within his family, he even refrained from ever giving them advice. He talked to us very rarely about his beliefs. His inner struggle was something he pursued alone."[24] His family openly flouted his beliefs, defied his "power."

In portraits of Gandhi, there is a comparable stress on his youthfulness and gaiety, his jokes and his laughter. Of course there is some truth to this, but it was a secondary truth, and what was primary was almost the opposite. Annie Besant said in 1918: "Gandhi believes in suffering and he is not happy if he achieves his object through normal evolutionary methods. He wants to build character through suffering. That is not my way. He is the martyr type and believes more in suffering than in achievement."[25] Mrs. Besant was hostile to Gandhi, but Rajaji, who was his disciple, confirms her insight, and Hanse Mehta says he was cheerful on occasions of gloom, but: "I was moved to tears and could hardly speak or reply to questions he was asking. There must have been something terribly pathetic about him, for I always felt deeply moved in his presence."[26] And Nehru said his eyes were often full of laughter "and yet were deep pools of sadness."[27]

Both began early to look like old men in at least some ways, and perhaps the most striking of those ways were voluntary. In Tolstoy's case, one can point to the ordinary physiological signs of greyness, wrinkled skin, falling hair, rotting teeth, but the look of age in his photographs is also a matter of his growing a long beard, refusing to replace lost teeth, refusing to smile at the camera, and adopting peasant dress and posture—his head lowered and his thumbs thrust through his belt. He became a manifesto of the eternal, of the ancient in that sense rather than in the sense of personal aging.

In Gandhi's case, the physiological signs are more ambivalent as far as age goes, for in this period he revealed a body which by its slenderness, lightness, and quickness announced itself as youthful—almost as adolescent. (Of course, we face a problem of translation here. That is what Gandhi's body announces in *our* language, dominated by images of beaches, discotheques, and sun-oil advertisements. Gandhi did not speak that language, and when we listen to him properly, we get a different message from his body.) Even so, from certain angles, and at certain times (for instance, when he had been fasting), that youthful body disconcerts us by becoming skeletonic, and the face looks shriveled up and fallen in and flesh-less. And again it was above all the postures and gestures, the delib-erate toothlessness, the sitting cross legged at the wheel or sunk in prayer, which announced the ancient past.

But a certain kind of gaiety both men did have. Nehru said Gan-dhi radiated light-heartedness. "There is something child-like about him, which is full of charm. When he enters a room he brings a breath of fresh air with him which lightens the atmosphere."[28] What kind of light-heartedness this was is perhaps best explained by Vinoba in *The Third Power*, when he says: "I laugh a good deal nowadays, partly because although there is plenty to weep about nothing is gained by weeping. I laugh also because I have discov-ered a way to make all India happy, if only people will accept it, and I think of the happy future. And I laugh also because this world does not appear to me to have much reality."[29] We must not, of course, take such laughter to be bitter or ironic. The discovery of the world's unreality temporarily liberates Vinoba (and Gandhi) from the death-dealing pressures of grief and disgust. Such laughter is not hedonistic. In *The Steadfast Wisdom* Vinoba says: "it is wise to restrain the heart when pleasure comes,"[30] and "take pleasure in happiness by all means but do not clap your hands and shout aloud." So light-heartedness is not pursued or cultivated. But to dis-cover that the world is not fully real, that the injustice, the ugliness, the malevolence, the imperialist aggression and the wars, are all the misbehavior of trivial personalities who have never found out what they want or who they are—to rediscover this, at recurrent mo-ments in the long anxiety or anguish of involuntary involvement—can be an alleviation and a breathing space. Such lightness is a good in itself.

And Tolstoy felt something of the same. In his diary for June 21, 1905, he writes that having listened to a political argument, he went into a room where there was singing, and "I was clearly aware of the sacredness of gaiety—gaiety, joy—that is all one of the fulfil-ments of God's law."[31] His daughter, Alexandra Tolstoy, adds that when he watched her skating she was aware that he admired her for her gaiety. And Goldenveizer tells us that soon after they met (in 1896), he and Tolstoy went on a bus together, and Tolstoy made a cockerel (which fluttered its wings when you pulled its tail) out of his bus ticket. When the inspector came for the ticket, Tolstoy made the cockerel perform, but the inspector sternly unfolded it, checked it, and tore it up.[32] It seems that Tolstoy was ready for foolishness. When he worried in his diary over the time he was putting into cycling, he consoled himself with the thought that this was nature's form of *yurodivnost.*

Such lightness obviously has to do with a kind of self-denial, the refusal to take oneself seriously. On January 14, 1907, he wrote in his diary: "To lead a peaceful life, you need a low opinion of yourself, as St. Francis said."[33] He escaped from his own self as much as he could, finding reality outside himself. This lightness went with a confidence in the sole reality of moral power, which is manifested solely in individuals. Institutions are not fully real. In the extreme case this personalism meant, as Gandhi taught, that one man could defeat an empire—that soul-force was indeed a force.

This is a paradox, for soul-force is not the same kind of thing as brute force. But occasionally history make a pun, as when we have to say that Gandhi defeated the British Empire. Political scientists and historians always pull a long lip at such propositions, and in a way they are right. There were many forces at work in that political situation that were much more reasonably to be credited with the withdrawal of the British than he. But if the historians put all their belief into those reasonable arguments and reduce Gandhi to a mirage, to an epiphenomenon of one or more of those sanctioned and accredited mechanisms, then they will have deceived themselves. Gandhi did make a difference, and Gandhi was soul-force. History did make a pun; then and on other occasions, lightness breathed through history itself.

But such lightness of heart is unprocurable except by means of the acceptance of death. In the old days, Tolstoy avoided that. He wanted to live and to live abundantly. On June 23, 1874, he admitted to his cousin Alexandrine that for the last two or three years of his Aunt Toinette's life, when she was obviously failing, he had avoided her company; contact with death was a desecration of his commitment to life. And in December of that year he wrote Alexandrine: "You say we are like squirrels in a cage. That is very true. But you must never think it or say it. I, at least, whatever I do, always feel convinced that forty centuries look down upon me from the heights of those pyramids, and that the world will perish if I ever stand still."[34]

Suddenly, however, in 1881, Tolstoy began calling himself an old man and living toward death. He often wished he was dead already and took pleasure in the thought that his death might come soon. To him, this attitude felt like a new love of truth and was accompanied by a distaste for art. He told Fet; "Art is a beautiful lie, and I can no longer lie."[35] And to Sergeenko, Chertkov's secretary, he declared; "When you write fiction you feel ashamed—why invent lies—write about what happened."[36] In this opinion he agreed with Gandhi in the latter's advice to Mulk Raj Anand, and in his speech to K. M. Munshi's Literary Conference—"The less we reveal in the realms of fiction, the better it will be for us."[37]

For Tolstoy, art and sexuality went together, and finding truth in death meant finding lies in eroticism. Thus in the second supplement to the *Kreutzer Sonata*, Tolstoy wrote that sex was natural only during the child-bearing phase of life, and that it was debilitating and exhausting. Couples, he wrote, should live like brother sister, suppressing instead of arousing all sexual excitement. We must—to use Tolstoy's image—try to suppress sexual excitement in the same way a valve on a steam engine suppresses the pressure of the steam. Gandhi's doctrine was the same. The natural relation between men and women, he insisted, was asexual. As for child bearing and the survival of the human race, both men agreed that since it is true life and love we care about, it doesn't matter that brute life might become extinct.

Art and eroticism sustain and intensify the divinity of life and induce men to worship it by the cult of their self-perfection. In his diary, Tolstoy wrote. "Who-ever sees the meaning of life in perfection, cannot believe in death—in the breaking off of that perfection."[38] In Gandhi, we find the same distrust of the arts, eroticism, the pleasures of life, and the pleasures of the mind. All these must first be given up if their inner truth is finally to be imbibed.

Gandhi's favorite Hindu scripture was the beginning of the *Isopanishad*. "That is full; this is full. The full comes out of the full. Taking the full from the full, the full itself remains. Om, shantih, shantih, shantih. All this that changes in the changing world, is encompassed by the lord. You may enjoy it by renouncing it. Envy no man the possession." We frustrate eros by teaching every movement of desire to turn back upon itself and leave the object as it was, separate. This, as Tolstoy would have agreed, is that fundamental denial of "life" which affirms and opens true life to the denier.

Tolstoy 1881–1894,
Renunciation of Rank and Wealth

Main Events and Ideas

This period of Tolstoy's life begins with the assassination of Tsar Alexander II in March 1881, or, more exactly, with the condemnation of the assassins. When, a quarter of a century later, Biriukov asked Tolstoy what he had felt about the murder of the Tsar, he couldn't remember, but he knew how upset he had been about the execution of the murderers. He had dreamed that he was one of the victims, and when he awoke from the dream in great distress, he composed an appeal to the Tsar—which was, he said, much better and stronger than the one he finally sent.

Already, in 1878, Tolstoy had told his family of accidentally meeting the Tsar in a photographer's shop in St. Petersburg and finding that he had eyes "like a tracked beast." He could see that the Tsar thought Tolstoy, "a man he knew nothing about, was going to kill him."[1] To receive such an impression was likely to give an imaginative man like Tolstoy a foretaste of identification with the assassins. And then the event dramatized long-familiar issues, aroused long-quiescent passions, in everyone. Eighty thousand people watched the executions on Semyonovsky Square, and all Russia was aware of them. The Tolstoys were still safely at Yasnaya Polyana, but they were planning their move to Moscow. Henceforth they would be in the center of events, and the events would be more and more dramatic. After 1881 the radicals turned from populism to terrorism decisively (not finally), and at the same time Tolstoy turned from literature to religion.

But he still had to live out the issues of this new life in the domestic arena and had to fight out the issues of his change. For him the danger and the struggle were not with the Tsar and Pobedonostsev when they got his letter about the assassination, but with Sonia, who burst into the room where he sat with Alekseev, composing the letter. It was she who exiled his friend to Samara and who denounced Tolstoy himself as traitor to his children. He was, according to her, a subversive, or at least irresponsible. She was, in that house—as much as Pobedonostsev in politics—the embodiment of responsibility; for the great cause, in terms of which all these questions of virtue were measured, was the family. From the point

of view of Yasnaya Polyana, the state, religion, and everything else
was a mirage, only unclearly to be seen, shimmering in the waves
of heat emanating from the domestic center.

In April and May of 1882 Tolstoy bought the family a house in
Moscow (their previous lodgings had proved unsatisfactory) and
had an addition built to it and furnished it himself. As in other
unhappy families, the husband's and wife's roles in this move were
in discord with their deeper feelings. Tolstoy, who did not want to
live in Moscow, took on the task of moving the family there; Sonia,
who did, didn't want him to buy the house or furnish it. (This work
with furnishings and ornaments is perhaps recalled in "The Death
of Ivan Ilych," where the hero's fatal bruise is acquired by falling
while decorating his house.)

Tolstoy himself had two small rooms in the house, with a pail
and washstand, an iron foot for cobbling, complete with a hammer,
rasp and cobbler's nails, and a kerosene stove on which he cooked
his oatmeal. (Gandhi also cooked his own oatmeal in London.) The
house was an old one and had a large (two hectares) garden, with
lilac trees, limes, elms, maples, and birches. Everyone who saw it
said it was not like a town house, but a country estate in Moscow.
But there were carpets on the floors, and the menservants who
served the meals wore dress coats, white ties, and white gloves.
And the "country estate" stood among a number of small factories
that made stockings, silk, cosmetics, and beer. Their whistles went
off at 5:00 A.M. for the day's work to begin, at 8:00 A.M. for a thirty-
minute break, at 12:00 N. for a lunch hour, and at 8:00 P.M. again for
dismissal. As Shklovsky says, instead of roosters crowing in the
morning, Tolstoy then heard factory whistles, and it was not long
before he knew he must find out what they meant.

So just as he had absorbed himself in house buying and furnish-
ing, property and prices, and all the other details he hated, so he
absorbed himself in the misery of proletarian and industrial Moscow. In December 1881 he visited the Liapinski House, where dere-
licts could get a free night's lodging (what he saw and felt is described in *What Then Must We Do?*), and in January 1881 he took
part, as one of the eighty organizers, in the Census of Moscow, asking to be assigned to one of the worse districts. He and the young
students who volunteered to work with him (in response to his letter to the papers, on January 20) began with the intention of helping those whom they found in such bad conditions. But they came

to realize that the problem was too large to be solved by such small-scale measures, and also that they had no moral right to intervene; since they profited by the arrangements which were based on this degradation, they were guilty before these people.

Tolstoy's religious activity began to draw the attention of the authorities. In September the Minister for Internal Affairs (another Tolstoy, also descended from Peter the Great's favorite) directed the attention of the authorities to his dangerous relations with sectarians. The police began to keep a secret watch on his house. On December 26, Pobedonostsev wrote the minister a protest against Tolstoy's being chosen to be marshal of the nobility in his district. Pobedonostsev said that Tolstoy had now succumbed to religious mania. On February 1, 1883 a pamphlet appeared in Geneva entitled, "Tolstoy-Christ and Tolstoy-Caiaphas," which contrasted the two Tolstoys in terms of the crucifixion story. But it was Pobedonostsev who was more fully characterized by the role of the condemning high priest.

In February 1884, *What I Believe In* was suppressed by the police after it was printed. The copies were not burned, in fact all of them were distributed among officials concerned with the case, or among their families or friends: Pobedonostsev got two, so that even a suppressed book by Tolstoy had a wide circulation in the highest circles.

He was in touch with many revolutionaries; Aleksei Sergeevich Buturlin (1845–1916) for instance, who had known Bakunin in Switzerland and had been named by Nechaev to one of his "groups of five." On April 10, 1884, Tolstoy noted that the revolutionaries' activity with books and proclamations was quite lawful. It was only when "they" forbade that activity that the bombs appeared: "We have grown so stupid that this expression of our own thoughts seems to us a crime." And a week later he noted having been moved to tears by the poems of a woman revolutionary.

In November, he brought into existence a new publishing firm, called *Posrednik,* or Intermediary, that was to publish books for the people, the peasants, the uneducated, which would be easy for them to understand and yet have some moral and imaginative dignity. The main editorial work was done by Tolstoy's disciples, notably Chertkov, but he himself wrote for the firm, found books for himself and others to adapt, and wrote to other Russian writers to persuade them to contribute to it. Several did—notably Leskov, Ostrovsky, Saltykov-Shchedrin—and 20 million volumes were sold in six years. In April 1886, the police were watching the Tolstoy house in the belief that a press was hidden there.

Theirs was a model for other attempts at a cheap library of the classics in other countries. In 1888, the English journalist and man of letters, W. P. Stead, came to Yasnaya Polyana and discussed how to set up a Penny Universal Library in England. Such projects were a part of the New Life—an attempt to redeem the masses from the diet and the stigma of stupidity which the old culture assigned them. Stead's assistant, Grant Richards, later brought out the famous World's Classics Series, which was taken over by the Oxford University Press, and became a staple literary diet for middle-and-lower-middle-class English children. In India, Gandhi's version of Posrednik, the Navajivan Karyalaya, run by Swami Ananananda, brought to the Gujarati reading public "the purest gems of Gujarati literature understandable by the masses."[2] And later some of his followers, like C. Rajagopalachari and K. M. Munshi, brought out a popular edition of Indian classics.

On December 9, 1887, Tolstoy founded the Society Against Drunkenness, which by 1890 had 741 members. He passed out pamphlets in the street for it, for instance in March 1889. He was still trying to give up smoking. In January, 1888, having heard that a student called Novoselov had been arrested for having copies of Tolstoy's story "Nikolai Palkin," Tolstoy wrote to the head of the Moscow Police that he was the one who should be arrested. Minister for Internal Affairs D. A. Tolstoy wrote to the Tsar that the novelist should be asked to explain himself. He was summoned to appear before the governor general of Moscow, but refused to go. On the 25th, the Church censors condemned his book, *On Life.*

A telling description of Tolstoy's mode of participation in the family summers in the late eighties is given by Stepan Bers. Tolstoy was generally calm but sad. His former merriment was now fragmented and distributed among the others: "Unconstrained by his presence, they freely indulge in their romps and mirth . . . he listens to the conversation going on around him, but does not, after his old fashion, take part in it. . . . [He] preserves an all but absolute silence."[3] When he did speak, Bers said, he was sarcastic rather than humorous, especially with Tania Kuzminskaya, and he betrayed irritation with Sonia.

In June 1891 we find Tolstoy's first diary entry about the famine that had broken out in Russia. He says how disgusting he found the protestation by the rich of pity for the poor and of a desire to help. All this is vanity and fear, he says, not goodness: "the hypocritical pretence of the privileged minority to save the majority which it has deprived of everything."[4] In September, he wrote a letter to the press about the famine, which drew attacks on him from all sides. On the 17th he decided that, illegitimate as he felt philanthropic activity to be, he had to do something. Sonia had said she would have gone to work in the famine, but for duty to the younger children. On November 3, *her* letter to the press appeared and provoked a flood of contributions. He and his older children worked on setting up dining rooms in famished villages. Their activity was attacked in *Moscow Vedomosti* in November, and he was reviled as the Antichrist in some villages. On December 18, he told Nikolai Ge, the painter, that his famine work, bad as it was in itself, had united him with Sonia as never before. (In February 1892, he consoled himself for the uneasiness he felt at giving this "charity" by the thought that he was redeeming the sins of his father and brothers.)

By July 1892, he had set up 246 kitchens, which fed 13,000 people every day, and had collected R141,000. Like Gandhi, Tolstoy was scrupulous about receipts and statistics and about notes of expenditures. He was careful not to exaggerate or to believe exaggerations. Also like Gandhi, he insisted on arousing the initiative of the starving and on finding them work, which he regarded as being just as important as food. He wanted them given flax so they could spin, and bast so they could weave. He wanted the average and rich peasants helped as well as the poor, because it was the agricultural economy as a whole that was in peril.

But of course Tolstoy felt that the root problem was the relation of the rich townsmen like himself and his readers to the poor peasants. They are hungry *because* we are well-fed. We constitute separate castes within the Russian nation. We must *go to them*, in repentance, meekness, and love. We must do what we have to do, for *our* salvation, not decide what is best for them.[5] This is the characteristic, existentially moral, stress of Tolstoy and Gandhi.

In 1892, he made over his estate to Sonia and the children, divided into ten shares (the nine children and Sonia) each of which seems to have amounted to R55,000. Masha refused her share, though Tania and her brother Lev told her she had no moral right to do so. (Tolstoy overheard this and was much upset.) Sonia held the money in trust for her, sure she would change her mind one day (as in fact she did).

We may pick out three main themes of Tolstoy's experience during these thirteen years. The first two were increasing conflict with his family and increasing conflict with the government (there was some coincidence between these two—Sonia refused to copy some of those manuscripts which attacked the church and state). The third was increasing sympathy with, even partial alliance with, young rebels. But this last change of feeling did not include approval of the terrorists, or even of the revolutionaries as a whole. Tolstoy never thought that they were right, but he came to feel that the government was more wrong. This was a great change and it came about only gradually. Even in 1881 he had written, "Revolutionaries are specialists. They exercise a profession like any other, like the military profession for example (the analogy is perfect). It is a mistake to believe their profession nobler than any other."[6] (We will find Gandhi, too, half-inclined to treat Indian revolutionaries as being like professional soldiers—as a recrudescence in modern terms of Kshattriya legends.) But on April 17, 1886, he noted that the revolutionaries he was reading about had only been playing at revolution and had been taken too literally by the authorities and by society in general.

Sonia was jealous of the new friends who claimed Tolstoy from her. At the very end of this period, when V. G. Chertkov had persuaded Tolstoy to have his photograph taken together with some of his other disciples, Sonia went to the photographer and demanded the negative, from which she cut out the image of Tolstoy and destroyed the rest. Before then, she had resolutely refused to let Biriukov marry her second daughter, Masha. And later her hatred of Chertkov reached such a pitch that she went around accusing him and Tolstoy (then in his late seventies) of homosexual relations.

Tolstoy wanted to leave her and his family, to start life anew. On July 26, 1882, she recorded in her diary his outcry that the one thing he wanted in life was to get away from them: "As long as I live, I shall remember the sincerity of that cry which broke my heart. I yearn for death with all my strength, for I cannot live without his love. . . . My love weighs me down, but it only irritates him. He is filled with his Christian ideas of self-perfection. I am jealous of him."[7] And we have to remember the special sanctity attached to "family" by the Bers to realize how profoundly wounded she must have been. To Sonia, for a father-husband to leave his family in anger seemed an ultimate evil, and she worked to prevent it by every means at her disposal, finally in effect hanging round his neck like a dead weight. She threatened to commit suicide and did in fact halfheartedly attempt it more than once, and deliberately degenerated into hysteria and semimadness. If he left her, he would have to step over a corpse, or a madwoman, or at least a pitiful wreck of what she had been.

Even in her despair, however, Sonia extended the range of her activities and acquaintances, becoming busier than ever and ever more triumphant in every other relationship. She took over all his property, and, still herself a young and attractive woman, went out into Moscow high society—to balls and theaters and receptions—as the chaperone of her oldest daughter. She also made herself Tolstoy's publisher (editing, buying paper, supervising printing, selling), and she brought out the fifth and all subsequent editions of his works. She consulted Anna Dostoevsky about this venture, and set up her office in an upstairs room in the Moscow house. It is said that Tolstoy instinctively frowned whenever his eye fell on the publishers' sign outside that door. He thought her terms too harsh on booksellers and felt embarrassed when he met them on their way to protest or bargain with her.

These two activities, the commercial and the social, both of which were the opposite of everything Tolstoy wanted, may be said to coincide and culminate in her interview with the tsar in 1891, when she persuaded him to allow the publication of a volume of Tolstoy's *Collected Works* which had been forbidden by the censors.

This was Volume 13, which included *The Kreutzer Sonata*, to which Pobedonostsev and others objected. When she actually saw the Tsar, she told him that Tolstoy had been exasperated by the interference of the censorship but was ready to go back to literature and to give up his radical religion. To which the Tsar replied. "What a blessing that would be! Such a wonderful, wonderful writer!" She asked him to make himself Tolstoy's personal censor, and the Tsar agreed. "Just send his works straight to me."[8] (Quite apart from the obvious objections to this, it had the grimmest of echoes in Russian literary history; Tsar Nicholas I had made himself Pushkin's personal censor and then had helped hound Pushkin to his death.) Then he and she chatted together about their respective children.

Beforehand, on February 15, she told her diary she was dreading the interview. "I seem to have lost that personal power with people, which, not so long ago, I could feel so strongly."[9] Afterwards, she felt triumphant. "I can't help feeling rather proud about it; for I, a woman, have dealt directly with the Emperor, and have got from him what no one else was able to obtain. And there is no doubt that my personality did it. I told everybody that if only I could feel sufficiently inspired, even for a moment, to influence the Emperor as a man, I should be successful; and indeed this inspiration came, and I persuaded him. . . ."[10] And on June 1 she returned to the topic, saying she had been determined to show people she could act for herself—that she was not merely the helpless victim of her husband's caprices, as most people thought. "I was certain of my success with the Emperor. I haven't yet lost the capacity to impress myself on people, and I certainly impressed him with my personality and my way of talking."[11] The Emperor had commented afterwards on how young and handsome she was. "All this tickles my female vanity, and I feel revenged for the way my husband has always treated me; for not only did he never try to raise me socially, but, on the contrary, always did his best to lower me."[12]

Tolstoy's general feelings were expressed in, for instance, a letter to V. G. Chertkov, written December 9–15, 1885, which begins. "I am sorely heavy at heart. . . . I'm living what may be the last hours of my life and living them badly, in despair and in anger with those around me. . . ."[13] He felt himself "pushed to one side" by his family, "like maggots in beehives which the bees can't kill and so smear with honey so that they shouldn't be in the way. . . ."[14] He hated the way they lived. "I never see anybody who isn't always rushing off somewhere and isn't to some extent angry as a result of this rushing about and, moreover, convinced that this rushing about is not only necessary but also as natural as breathing. And if you begin to speak, then the person . . . looks at his watch and at the door. . . ."[15] This bustling style was above all Sonia's. Her body movements were full of self-conscious energy, according to Repin, and her tongue was unresting. A family joke was that she had told her whole life story to a shopkeeper in the process of buying a length of cotton. And this bustle was a declaration of faith in "life"—in all that Tolstoy was denying.

In December 1884 she had written to him. "If you leave, since I cannot live without you, I shall kill myself. As for changing the way we live, it is beyond me. And I cannot understand why it is necessary to destroy an existence that is happy in every way just for the sake of heaven knows what wild ideas."[16] And on January 26, 1891, she recorded in her diary a discussion between them in which he grew irritable. "I quietly pointed this out to him and left him, feeling rather bitter. There is so little genuine warmth and kindness about him; his kindness does not come from the *heart*, but merely from his *principles*."[17] This phrasing cannot but remind us of Anna Karenina's complaint against her husband, and it was Sonia's frequent tactic to turn Tolstoy's ideas and written work against him.

Some of her resentment was expressed in terms of bourgeois delicacy. "To wash is quite an event for him. He told me that his feet perspired so much that they got sore between the toes. He nearly made me quite sick...."[18] This fastidiousness is clearly related to her enthusiasm for the life of the arts, the intellect, and the imagination. On February 4 of that year, she wrote that her favorite son, Lev, was having a story published.

It made me quite happy to think that this intellectual and artistic atmosphere, to which I have been used all my life, would not end with Lyova [her husband], but that should I survive him, my son would continue the tradition which has made my life so happy and interesting. I will be able to devote myself to him and, through him, love my own life and his father.[19]

On November 20, 1890, she wrote. "I feel like killing myself or running away, or falling in love with someone—anything to escape from a man whom, in spite of everything, for some unknown reason, I have loved all my life, although I now see clearly that I idealized him without realizing that there was nothing in him but sensuality.... He never knew how to love."[20]

On May 16, 1884, Tolstoy wrote: "O Lord, save me from this hateful life which is crushing and destroying me. The one good thing is, I long to die. Better to die than to live like this."[21] And on May 29, he says that the most terrible thing is that he is responsible for all the evil—for the luxury and decadence in which they live.[22] It was not only Sonia he quarrelled with. On June 4, his oldest son, Sergei, told him that he only talked about his beliefs and never acted on them. Tolstoy was deeply wounded and wrote in his diary that Sergei was just like his mother—evil and unfeeling.[23] And on July 15, he told Sergei that he was tired of his bourgeois malice and stupidity, whereupon Sergei wept, and when Tolstoy later apologized, Sergei begged his forgiveness.[24]

It is legitimate to guess that the children's resistance was encouraged or inspired by Sonia. Whatever she may have said explicitly would be less important than the example she gave, of a continual denial of Tolstoy's beliefs, and an irritable and sometimes hysterical ridicule. The moral triviality, the inconsistency and brute egotism of much of her behavior may well have made it more infectious. An

infection is what we seem to see—and what Sergei and Sonia afterwards admitted and repented, exclaiming: "How could we have
done that?" In Gandhi's case, though resistance certainly spread
from one son to another, the idea of an infection seems less appropriate; perhaps because the Gandhi household was so soon split up;
the Tolstoys, on the other hand, were all too united a family, right
up to 1910.

Of course Sonia was not always unfeeling or uncomprehending.
She wrote to her sister:

> He is a man ahead of his time, he marches in front of the crowd and
> shows the way it must follow. And I am one of the crowd, I live with it
> and, with it, I see the light in the men ahead of their time, like Leo, and I
> say yes, that is the light, but I cannot walk any faster than the crowd to
> which I am bound; I am held back by my environment, by my habits.[25]

This is in some sense generous in its appraisal of their relationship
and situation, but it is also notably detached, "philosophical," outside the realm of behavior.

What she wanted of him in a positive way was very simple—that
he should again become a great artist. When he told her of an idea
he had for an imaginative work she replied:

> You have sensed what I have long waited for and desired. In that is
> salvation, happiness; in that, which gives you solace, and brightens your
> life, we will again be united. This is the real kind of work for which you
> were created and outside of this sphere there is no peace in your soul.[26]

And proofreading *Childhood, Boyhood, Youth* in 1883 (for a new edition), she wept, remembering her former tears when she first read it
when she was eleven, and said "I love the same things in you today. But certain other things which have been added to them and
are crystallizing I do not love. They are excrescences. Oh! scrape
them away and what will be left will be pure gold."[27]

The strain told on her psychologically. In October, 1885, she described going to a market, then a bookstore, then another market,
and suddenly realizing she had gone to and fro three times for no
reason:

> I had completely forgotten where I was. I was afraid that I was losing my
> mind; in order to check myself, I began a conversation with a peddler.
> Then I took a trolley and returned home as fast as I could. Later I came to

realize that I had been wandering around, preoccupied, imagining that *I was doing some thing.* But there was nothing that needed to be done.[28]

She became a hysteric, a *klikusha*, as Shklovsky says, the kind of woman who cried out in church in lamentation: "I just now gave the table a little push and Lev's portrait fell to the floor. In the same way I am using this diary to push him off the pedestal which he has all his life been busily erecting for himself."[29]

In this period Tolstoy's private and unprinted thoughts also became institutionalized, twice, under two different auspices. His wife began copying out his old diaries to preserve them for posterity; and at Chertkov's suggestion, his daughter Masha began (August 13, 1894) copying out all his current letters. This prefigured the later painful struggle over the later diaries, which both Sonia and Chertkov wanted to have in his/her possession, and over his papers generally. (In Sonia's case, she felt an extra anxiety about the way she was presented to the world in the diaries. She wanted to censor them; and the disciples wanted Tolstoy's imprisonment in the family to be revealed.) Even at this early stage, Tolstoy found it all very painful. He did not want to be reminded of the person he had been, in, for instance, his days in the Caucasus. And he did not want to feel self-conscious about the letters he was currently writing.

Tolstoy often asked Sonia not to copy out those early diaries, and it seems clear that there was conscious malice (though also other motives) behind her doing so. On January 18, 1891, she writes: "I copy his diaries with the zest of a drunkard; the drunkenness consists in working myself up into a state of jealousy over the women he describes. . . ."[30] On February 12, she reports that he has often protested against the copying and has just made a scene. She told him he couldn't be as badly hurt as she had been by his last book, *The Kreutzer Sonata;* he had hurt her so badly before the whole world that they would never be even. He is angry because these diaries drag him down from his pedestal into the mud. On February 15 she says he has forbidden her to copy any more, but she continues in secret: "I decided long ago that I *must* do it."[31]

The Writings

Tolstoy's writings in the period 1881–1894 can be said to fall into roughly three categories (though his plays fall a little outside any of

them): polemical pamphlets and books, some long and learned; stories written for the people, mostly short and simple; and a few
works of fiction—notably "The Death of Ivan Ilych"—which are
recognizably the work of the great novelist of *War and Peace*,
though that novelist's values have clearly undergone a complete
reversal.

Even in 1881–1882 Tolstoy was writing his *Critique of Dogmatic
Theology*, in which he rendered judgment on the Orthodox Church's
Symbol of the Faith, on Filerat's "Catechism," on the "Epistle of the
Eastern Patriarchate," and on Makari's (new) *Dogmatic Theology*, a
selection of the state church's most important documents. His judgment was that these works were more blasphemous and faithless
than Voltaire and Hume, because they adapted the Gospel message
to quite opposite meanings and perverted it morally and intellectually. Dogmata, such as God is both three and one, meant nothing
to Tolstoy. He dismissed the sacraments as "savage customs," suited
to an earlier phase of civilization. Reading these books of theology
would have made him an atheist had he not independently found
his faith in Christ's actual message: "I had intended to go to God,
and I found my way into a stinking bog, which evokes in me only
those feelings of which I am most afraid; disgust, malice, and indignation."[32] Despite himself, Tolstoy's Voltairean self stirred to life; or
rather—since it had always been alive—to public expression.

As for his political views, in a short pamphlet of 1882, entitled
"Church and State," he declared the phrase *Christian State* to be as
paradoxical and nonsensical as *hot ice*; either such a state is no state,
or more likely its Christianity is no Christianity. Kings, after all, are
simply anointed robbers. Christ's teaching is hostile to the state,
and Christians, though not called on to destroy the state, are called
on not to support it or to comply with many of its demands.

In 1884 he finished *My Religion*, in which he described himself as
having behind him five years of faith in Christ and thirty-five years
of nihilism (faith in nothing). He presented himself to the reader as
one of the robbers on the cross, come down to preach.[33] His conversion had occurred when he realized that "Resist not Evil" (Matt.
5:39) meant what it said. This was a revelation to him because he
had always been taught that Christ's laws were not practical, and so
must be interpreted—in effect, circumvented. What he had been
taught that was practical was quite opposite in tendency: "I was
taught to judge and punish. Then I was taught to make war, that is,
to resist evil men with murder, and the military caste, of which I

was a member, was called the Christ-loving military, and their activity was sanctified by a Christian blessing."[34] He was involved in this contradiction very early because he was born noble, but nowadays, when military service and jury duty have been made universal, all men are involved in it.

What Then Must We Do?, which was finished in 1886, described the Tolstoys' move to Moscow and his horror at urban poverty. (In the country the little good he did "created around me an atmosphere of love and union with these people"[35] in which he could calm his guilt.) He described the Khitrov dosshouses he visited, and the five course dinner and the white-gloved servants in the house he came home to. And when he spoke to friends of what he had seen, they assured him that it was his extraordinary goodness which made it disturbing to him, thus corrupting his feelings about the problem.

If we turn now to the popular tales Tolstoy wrote during this period, we find a similar didacticism. Their scope is much narrower than that of his earlier fiction, and among what is omitted is the whole realm of eroticism. In a diary entry for June 11, 1884, he says that he has discovered why he found it impossible to write the novel he projected about migrant peasants; it is because a novel must have love as its center, and peasants do not know love of that desirous kind. So he could not write novels for them any more than about them. They needed a different style. In 1886, Tolstoy told a young man who wanted to write for *Posrednik* to eschew all fine writing, and to keep his eye on the *simple* reader. Old men, women, and children should be able to follow what he wrote and feel better as a result. (It is clear this was not merely prudential or tactical advice—that Tolstoy himself found simple writing more beautiful.) They needed new, or rather old, forms. In his introduction to a collection of pieces for popular reading written in 1886, he stressed the difference between literal and moral truth. Literature is good and necessary only when it shows what should have happened, not what did: "The world lies in evil and temptation. If you describe many lies, your own work will not be true. . . . For instance, if a story shows a greedy man ending his life up happy, it tells a lie."[36] Didactic legend is, therefore, better art than realistic fiction.

His major literary productions of this period were fiction again, but very different in form, tone, and values from the great novels. He now wrote against, not for, domestic happiness, eroticism, and life values. So what he wrote was not, in the old sense, literature. At the end of June, 1883, on his deathbed, Turgenev wrote him a "last sincere request," in a letter he never finished. "My friend, return to literary activity. After all, that is the gift out of which everything else came to you. Oh, how happy I would be if I could think that my plea would take effect on you. . . . My friend, great writer of the Russian soil, pay heed to my plea."[37] We may hear the expression of all Russia's writers' and readers' feelings there, but it is only the more lyrical expression of what we hear—mixed with more rage and malice—in Sonia's voice. It was their own settlement of life's claims that he endangered.

Tolstoy, of course, still valued folk art and all art of the narrow scope. He still also took a lively interest in the more elaborate kinds. He was not denying the fact of pleasure in art, but following out its developing laws. An indication of the change in Tolstoy's sensibility can be found in his essay on de Maupassant. At first sight, Tolstoy's enthusiasm for the French writer is surprising, not only because of the latter's narrow compass and cynical sensuality, but because he describes the working class "not merely with indifference, but with contempt," as Tolstoy says. And disapproval Tolstoy certainly did feel. In his essay, he condemns French aestheticism and eroticism. "And in the circle in which Maupassant moved, the beauty which should be served by art was, and is, chiefly woman—young, pretty, and for the most part naked."[38] To explain that circle, Tolstoy quoted Renan on female beauty and on Christianity's failure to appreciate it: "So that . . . only now have Paris milliners and coiffeurs corrected the mistake committed by Christianity and re-established beauty."[39] Nevertheless, Tolstoy very much admired de Maupassant, and as truth teller as well as craftsman. Why?

We should remind ourselves that Tolstoy's early life situation had been closer to de Maupassant's than to writers about "domestic happiness" like George Eliot. If he accused his earliest pieces of a "democratic" insincerity, he might have found his major novels erotically insincere. There is discernible, in Tolstoy's attitude even to Natasha and Kitty, what one might call the guards officer's sensibility to women, which one finds also in de Maupassant.

Though combined with other things in Tolstoy, this feeling focuses on the ballet dancer image of woman—the thin shoulders, the gauze dress, the fragility, the graceful posture, and the "poetry." De Maupassant liked that, but "disbelieved" in it, and by 1894 Tolstoy disbelieved in it too, seeing sexual appetite as too gross to be made poetical, except lyingly. (It was a bourgeois erotic image that corresponded to Sonia and Tania, not to Aksinia.) So he praises de Maupassant for his truthfulness and strength: "An artist is an artist because he sees things not as he wishes to see them but as they really are. . . ."[40] He now found the French eroticism, of illicit love, more authentic than the English—because it was more unpleasant.

The greatest of his works in this disillusioned mode is certainly "The Death of Ivan Ilych," which he finished in 1886, a story Gandhi found deeply moving. This is a notably factual piece of writing: the story line, the event-content, is very "realistic"—that is, carrying grim conviction because it is accompanied by the grimly challenging implication: Isn't this true? Isn't this the way funerals are, men die, wives talk to husbands? Isn't this all there is to, for instance, marriage? This is true of other works of this period—it is what we feel, in "Master and Man," about Brekhunov's relations with other people and his general consciousness. And a further grimness is evoked by the gradual emergence of death out of a pleasantly worldly life-horizon. We first see that horizon as very limited and condescend toward the character, but are persuaded to accept it as representative—to agree, with some uneasiness, that our own is no broader. Then on that horizon emerges a point, which grows larger and larger until it overwhelms everything, and it is death. We see the central character ignore it because he is obsessed with, for instance, buying some property or making his career; and we, as spectators of the drama, are even more existentially involved.

It is, of course, Everyman art, or, as people said at the time, Biblical art. It allows none of the exhilaration of the early Tolstoy. It has no special people, like Natasha Rostov, whose powers of life enhancement and whose priviledged fate suggest to us that we too may be exempted from limitations if we can adopt her mode of being, identify ourselves with her. "The Death of Ivan Ilych" shows us the underside of the Tolstoyan embroidery of life. It is about newspaper events, not flashes of the transcendental in the empirical. It is about the city, not Yasnaya Polyana. It is not a drama of consciousness. And it is about merchants, the middle class, and so on, the people Tolstoy refused to write about before.

The one note of hope or rather consolation is embodied in Gerasim, the servant, the one person whose presence is a help and not a torment to the dying man. He lifts Ivan Ilych's legs up and puts the feet on his own shoulders. This is an intimate gesture which yet means nothing in ordinary life—it is part of no vocabulary of postures, and just so Gerasim and Ivan Ilych are intimate in a way for which there are no words. What does Gerasim do for his master? We can say that he does not deny death, as the dying man's family does—they follow the decorum that educated people observe about it. But we cannot say that Ivan Ilych wants death asserted; and we are not told of anything positive in Gerasim's attitude, any significant pity or love for his master. He is full of physical vitality, that is positive, but in itself vitality might well be the worst irritant to a dying man. In fact it is not, but that is because Gerasim's physique is not possessed by or intensified by an ego. It is unconscious; he has no consciousness, no self. He is a consolation not an irritation to his master because he does not involve him in all those mutually reflective modes of consciousness which belong to "life." He knows how to die and how to help others die because he knows nothing. But it is not ignorance which is in question, but unconsciousness. He is ontologically simple, because his being has not been teased into personality.

In 1889 Tolstoy finished *The Kreutzer Sonata*, which, like several of the fictions of this period, had epigraphs from the Gospels. In his letters, Tolstoy was soon dismissive of this work, saying that it was the product of two incompatible devices and of bad motives. And it is indeed clear that the basic artistic plan is artificial—is Dostoevskian rather than Tolstoyan. It is a murderer's dramatic monologue, and was in fact suggested to Tolstoy by an actor who had had great successes reading Marmeladov's monologues from *Crime and Punishment*. And as for bad feelings, the murder is disturbingly suggestive of a fantasy revenge on Sonia.

But the novel does have a certain artistic interest as an attempt at writing antierotic fiction. In the broader sense of "erotic"—eros being the appetite for life—the same could be said of "The Death of Ivan Ilych." Here, however, the challenge is sharper because the novel is all about love, although it sets out to disinfect rather than infect the reader with erotic emotions. This is done partly by a distasteful stress on intramarital hatred, on sex during pregnancy, on birth control, on cosmetic and costume methods of enhancing sex appeal, and so on. But there is also a less direct attack on the passions even in their purity, on the world of women insofar as that is always associated with eroticism, on sexuality itself, on art, and even on music. Tolstoy treats the Beethoven sonata named in the title as a high-culture muzak, a soothing and lubricating background for the business of shopping in the world supermarket, a subliminal suggestion which persuades the shopper to open his/her purse easily.

Gandhi 1921–1931,
Politics Left and Returned To

If we look at this period of Gandhi's life in conjunction with the corresponding phase of Tolstoy's, we are struck by the way that the former withdrew from political action while the latter entered upon it. As Judith M. Brown says in *Gandhi and Civil Disobedience*, in the 1920s Gandhi seemed a spent force politically, and he seemed to turn inward, referring increasingly often to his "inner voice," and fasting more often. This is not, of course, true of 1929–1931, when he resumed national leadership, but the decade began with the dramatic reversal after Chauri Chaura, when Gandhi canceled the civil resistance movement and continued with the handing over of Congress to his Swarajist opponents. He called on his followers to accept political impotence, to devote themselves to spinning and other "constructive work," and he himself retired to the ashram. He repeatedly named the latter as his "best creation." "It is my best and only creation. The world will judge me by its result."[1]

This corresponds exactly to the time when Tolstoy was making ineffectual efforts to leave *his* ashram, Yasnaya Polyana; but to say that reminds one of how different the two places were, and how completely the two life courses diverged. Both places were opposites to the city, and in some sense ideal villages, but the one was an aristocrat's estate, the other an idealistic commune, a secular monastery. And even in the late 1920s, Gandhi's life was embroiled in the issues of Indian national politics as Tolstoy's never was in Russian politics. As Erikson says, comparing Gandhi's truth with Freud's, it is the Westerner of these contrastive pairs who turns out to be the inward-turner, the Easterner who is the activist. But if we look at the two lives from inside, each was undergoing a change of direction in this period which brought them closer to each other.

Both were involved in a striking ineffectuality. As Tolstoy was enchained within his family situation and condemned to seem to enjoy it—to seem a sniveling hypocrite about his professed beliefs—so Gandhi was removed from leadership of a national movement which seemed within a hair's breadth of defeating the Empire, and relegated to pacifying the squabbles of the women of the ashram. Nor did he have any unmixed success there; the Sabarmati ashram was generally acknowledged to be less well run than Vinoba Bhave's ashram at Wardha. Even when he did return to national leadership, Gandhi found himself involved in uncongenial top-level negotiations, trapped in the spotlights and the headlines with the viceroy and later at the Round Table Conference in London. This was not where Gandhi felt at home, and the only great example of Gandhi's kind of politics in this decade was the Salt March to Dandi in 1930.

And just as the readers of Russia—led by his wife—surrounded Tolstoy with pleas that he should write them another *Anna Karenina*, so did the nationalists of India surround Gandhi with demands for more *satyagraha*. What Tolstoy did write in the 1880s, quite apart from its not getting into print, seemed to most readers and writers no compensation for the missing sequels to *War and Peace*. And the politicians of Congress groaned over the *khadi dhotis* they had to wear and the yarn they laboriously span at their wheels when they might have been dominating or subverting the legislative councils.

The two men themselves, of course, embraced the ineffectuality and redeemed it into renunciation. Tolstoy chose to stay with his family, chose to make that his martyrdom. For Gandhi, the issue was less dramatic, because he had always intended his politics to be subordinate and functional. In 1924 he wrote: "My national service is part of my training for freeing my soul from the bondage of flesh. Thus considered, my service may be regarded as purely selfish. . . . Politics bereft of religion are a death trap because they kill the soul."[2] And in 1925 he defined his goal as "to see God face to face, to attain *moksha*. I live and move and have my being in pursuit of this goal. All that I do by way of speaking or writing, and all my ventures in the political field, are directed to this same end."[3] But that is not to say that Gandhi did not suffer a painful sense of defeat. In 1927, he was not expecting to live beyond Amritsar Day, 1928, and this was a psychological rather than a medical prediction. ("I have nothing further to say or give.") Gandhi's fluctuations of effort and direction in this period show a complexity and a flexibility in him which were not so apparent before and which reminds us of Tolstoy.

And finally one might say that for both men the issue of representation became more acute and difficult in these comparable periods of their lives. They were challenged repeatedly to justify their claims to speak for others, their claims to speak for the "dumb millions" to the literate and literary minority, to represent within consciousness the cultural unconscious, to represent the past, and the poor, and the soil; a claim which was in both cases intuitive or existential, undemonstrable and, therefore, in some sense, arrogant. There was an absoluteness and uniqueness to their vocation, to their sense of their constituency, and in Gandhi's case to his conscience. The term "dictatorship" was often used (for instance by Nehru) for Gandhi's control of the civil-disobedience movement. Of course, that was before Hitler and Mussolini had given "dictator" the unequivocally evil ring the word got in the 1930s, but even in 1921 it attracted the righteous indignation of democrats. (By 1930, when it was applied to those in charge of local *satyagrahas*, Gandhi said the word should be changed to "First Servant.") In Tolstoy's case the charge of dictatorship did not arise (it was Chertkov who was accused of being authoritarian) but he certainly seemed, to his family and his former friends, obstinate and obsessive in his preoccupation with the peasants, in his claim to represent their interest, and in his demand that people like his audience should dispossess themselves, reduce and abase themselves before "the people."

For Gandhi the most striking case came at the Round Table Conference at the end of this period. He had persuaded the Congress to name him its sole representative, but in London he insisted that he represented all India. Courteously, as always, but ruthlessly, he denied the authority of the princes and the authenticity of the other (Government chosen) "representatives" of all the myriad social groups in India. Such denials, based ultimately on a moral or religious criterion (of personal seriousness) with which most politicians were uncomfortable, aroused great anger against Gandhi among rival "representatives."

The same was true of both the literary and the political opposition to Tolstoy. Both the belles-lettres writers of Russia and the professional politicians—and even more the revolutionaries—objected to his claim to speak for the dumb millions of the peasantry. (They objected so strenuously because this claim implied his refusal to be a writer or a politician himself, and named them as special interest groups.) In both countries the opposition insisted that Tolstoy and Gandhi spoke only for themselves, and their selves were sick; spoke only out of their imaginations, and their imaginations were sick; they were subverters of manhood, hysterical life haters and life spoilers, haloed harpies who poisoned for others the banquet they could not enjoy for themselves.

The Main Events

At the beginning of this period, the wave of noncooperation which Gandhi directed was cresting throughout India. The British government leaders afterwards admitted that they had felt themselves within a hair's breadth of defeat, and historians have agreed with them. They think the moderates would have allied themselves with the extremists under Gandhi's leadership if he had not sounded the retreat. But Gandhi's feelings about what was happening were never as exultant as other nationalist leaders', because for him the nonviolent character of civil disobedience was always of first importance, and he was not secure about that. Afterwards he said he had been praying for defeat because of the violence he felt in the air. There had been so much violence that "I was actually and literally praying for a disastrous defeat."[4]

However, there was more to the nationalist movement than civil disobedience, and 1921 was *annus mirabilis* of the spread of spinning and *khadi* and the theory of nonviolence. Lala Lajpat Rai and C. R. Das became converts to these doctrines and practices at the time, and Motilal Nehru and Abul Kalam Azad. Though Gandhi wrote consistently in warning against anarchy and destruction, it is easy to detect a note of exhilaration in his comments on what was happening, like this of December. "Freedom is to be wooed only inside prison walls and sometimes on the gallows, never in the council chambers, courts, or the schoolroom . . . she builds her temples in jails or on inaccessible heights."[5] He says he would have loved to see Motilal and Jawaharlal Nehru handcuffed together and made to walk to prison. (His "loved to" expresses not malicious glee but idealistic enthusiasm; the conflict between Gandhi's usage and ours is typical of many other differences.) The Congress pandal that year was made of *khadi* and decorated by artists from Shantiniketan. On January 26, 1922, Gandhi wrote. "India is slowly getting to be a holy land, aye, a purified country."[6] And in later years, for instance, early 1927, he looked back to 1921 as a period of enthusiasm when everyone was eager for sacrifice and miracles were happening—"the heroic days when people were excited about khadi." He planned a *satyagraha* campaign in Bardoli.

But on February 4, 1922, a procession of civil resisters at Chauri Chaura (in Gorakhpur, in the United Provinces, 800 miles from Bardoli), after conflict with the authorities, surrounded a police station, killed twenty-one policemen, and set fire to their bodies. They had been chanting Gandhi's name as a slogan, and Gandhi felt responsibility for what they did. His teaching aroused the people, excited them to public emotion, incited them to public action, and so he was responsible for what they did, even when that went against his explicit instructions.

On February 8, he wrote that "for the third time" he had received a shock on the very eve of mass civil disobedience, and he canceled the campaign, to the dismay of his allies and followers. They said that this retreat would disgrace India before the world.[7] But Gandhi wrote to Nehru on February 19:

I assure you that if the thing had not been suspended, we would have been leading not a nonviolent struggle, but essentially a violent struggle. It is undoubtedly true that nonviolence is spreading like the scent of the otto of roses throughout the length and breadth of the land, but the foetid smell of violence is still powerful, and it would be unwise to ignore or underrate it. The cause will prosper by the retreat.[8]

He obviously wanted to escape from the position which made him responsible, in the future as well as the past, for the killing of others, and he had to find a median between that desire and his contrary vocation and ambition. On March 2, he declared that he hated his command of a huge majority (which was what brought him his leadership). He would feel safer (morally) without it.

I have always been in a minority. . . . I have begun to wonder if I am not unconsciously allowing myself to be 'exploited.' I confess that I have a dread of it as I never had before. My only safety lies in my shamelessness. I have warned my friends of the committee [the All-India Congress Committee] that I am incorrigible. I shall continue to confess blunders each time that the people commit them.[9]

Two of the people he had to explain himself to were the Nehrus. To Jawaharlal he wrote: "I see that all of you are terribly cut up over the resolution of the Working Committee [to cancel the cam-

paign]. I sympathize with you, and my heart goes out to Father."[10]
As usual, Gandhi treated his own decisions, and even his emotions,
as given facts and looked sympathetically to the problems they created for others—whose decisions and emotions were *not* given facts
but struggling, fluctuating, tendencies.

"Above all, whatever you do, don't be disgusted with the spinning wheel," he continued to Nehru.

You and I might have reason to get disgusted with ourselves for having
done many things and having believed many things, but we shall never
have the slightest cause for regret that we have pinned our faith to the
spinning wheel or that we have spun so much good yarn per day in the
name of the motherland.[11]

It was a general habit with Nehru's friends to address him as being
only reluctantly, or only half, a politician. When they said "You and
I" most of them allied themselves with him as men of sensibility, of
soul, of poetry. Gandhi named him a spinner, and it seems likely
that the spinning wheel was—in these early years—the key to, the
sign of, the hope for, a Gandhian Nehru. Not many politicians did
like to spin—certainly not Motilal Nehru—and that rather "feminine" aptitude in Jawaharlal was the key to Gandhi's influence over
him and ultimately to Gandhi's nomination of him as his heir. (In
fact, of course, Jawaharlal became his father's heir after all, but that
was not predetermined in 1922.)

On March 10, 1922, Gandhi was arrested and was charged the
next day with writing three inflammatory and disaffected articles in
Young India. A week later he was tried and, though treated very
courteously by the judge, committed to six years in jail. His speech
in his own defense remarkably combined—along the same lines as
his earlier articles—his two main statements about his political leadership. He acknowledged guilt:

Thinking over these deeply and sleeping over them night after night, it is
impossible to dissociate myself from the diabolical crimes of Chauri
Chaura, or the mad outrages in Bombay and Madras. . . . I knew that I was
playing with fire. . . .

But on the other hand:

I would still do the same. . . . I had either to submit to a system which I
considered had done an irreparable harm to my country, or incur the risk
of the mad fury of my people bursting forth when they understood the

truth from my lips. . . . I am, therefore, here to submit not to a light penalty but to the highest penalty. I do not ask for mercy. . . . To preach disaffection towards the existing system of Government has become almost a passion with me . . . by the time I have finished my statement, you will, perhaps, have a glimpse of what is raging within my breast to run this maddest risk a sane man can run.[12]

And besides the Government, he had the revolutionaries to explain himself to. Gandhi had been opposed by "working class militants" ever since 1921, according to Manmathnath Gupta. Sachindranath Sanyal, who had been released in 1918 after confinement for his part in a Bengal conspiracy, wrote to Gandhi, and Gandhi published the letter and his reply in *Young India* on February 12, 1925.

Sanyal described Gandhi's ideal as:

. . . an imperfect physical mixture of Tolstoyism and Buddhism and not a chemical mixture of East and West. You adopted the Western method of Congress and Conferences and tried to persuade the whole nation to accept the spirit of ahimsa, irrespective of desh, dal, and patra (place, time, and recipient) like Tolstoy, but which was a matter of individual sadhana with Indians.[13]

Thus what the revolutionary points to as Western and Tolstoyan in Gandhi's doctrine is its universal applicability, its overriding of the Hindu patterns of thought, which allot different *dharmas* to different groups. (The same point was to be made about the Tolstoy-Gandhi doctrine of bread labor later.) This Western universalism can be seen, from a Hindu point of view, as a kind of religious radicalism, an insistence on "one thing needful," which overrides, for instance, the *varnashrama* doctrine that at different stages of a man's life different duties impinge upon him. From a Western point of view, of course, this moral radicalism is merely natural. It belongs to conservatives as much as to radicals, and the difference between them is all in the way they apply it. But in world-historical perspective, we can see that the Western view is typical of the modern-world system, which is built, comparatively speaking, on a sort of existentialism—the assertion of self-determination or self-creation—the assertion therefore of permanent change, the constant social evolution which alone makes possible self-determination.

But some young men, Sanyal's letter continues, dare to go against your wishes:

... these are the Indian revolutionaries. They have now decided to remain silent no more and therefore they request you to retire from the political field or else to direct the political movement in a way so that it may be a help and not a hindrance to the revolutionary movement.[14]

It claimed that the revolutionaries had saved Indians from their fear of death.

Gandhi replied that if he were convinced that India wanted a bloody revolution he would indeed retire, for he would have no part in that.[15] Later he said that the revolutionaries' sacrifice, nobility, and love were not only a waste of effort, but, "do and have done more harm to the country than any other activity."[16] They were ruining India's tradition. India had had armies and warfare, but militarism was never the normal course of Indian life. "The masses, unlike those of Europe, were untouched by the warlike spirits."[17]

In another letter the revolutionary denied this, saying that his comrades:

... are entering villages, and have been successful everywhere. Can you not believe that they, the sons of Shivaji, Pratap, and Ranjit, can appreciate our sentiments with more readiness and depth than anything else? Don't you think that armed and conspired resistance against something satanic and ignoble is infinitely more befitting. . . . [to Indians]?[18]

In reply, Gandhi relies in effect on the doctrine of castes again: "Are we all descendants of these heroes [Shivaji, Pratap, Ranjit] in the sense in which the writer understands it? We are their countrymen, but their descendants are the military classes."[19]

It is clear that Gandhi was uneasy in this area of the argument. How then, if his heritage was so different, could he speak for and about the "military classes"? He was soon frank, as always. Sanyal asked what Gandhi thought about Washington, Garibaldi, Lenin, Kemal Pasha, and de Valera, the past heroes of national revolution: "This is a hard or rather awkward question . . . it is highly likely that, had I lived as their contemporary and in the respective countries, I would have called every one of them a misguided patriot. . . ."[20] He took refuge, like Tolstoy, in a denial of historicism. Even if Indians always had been warlike, that was no reason why they should go on being so: "I positively refuse to judge men from the scanty material furnished to us by history."[21] More fully, he said:

As it is, I must not judge them. I disbelieve history so far as details of acts of heroes are concerned. I accept broad facts of history and draw my own lessons for my conduct. I do not want to repeat it insofar as the broad facts contradict the highest laws of life.[22]

Tacitly, he accepted the claim that the revolutionaries were the kshattriyas of the modern age.

In response to the question "Will your swarajya government keep armies?," he replied:

Alas, in my swaraj of today there is room for soldiers. . . . I have not the capacity for preaching universal nonviolence to the country. I preach there-fore nonviolence restricted strictly to the purpose of winning our freedom.[23]

He suffers this incapacity because: "I have yet anger within me, I have yet the divait bhava (duality) in me."[24]

It is also worth noting that on March 1, 1927, Gandhi went to call on V. D. Savarkar, the nationalist revolutionary, who was in exile at Ratnagiri. He said his visit expressed his regard for Savarkar as a man who loved the truth and would lay down his life for it. Gandhi offered to find two or three days to come again so that they could discuss national issues together, but Savarkar declined, saying that they could correspond. In fact Savarkar attacked Gandhi severely in print (in *Shraddhanand*) from the Hindu nationalist point of view. This meeting occurred just about half way between their first meet-ing in 1906 and Gandhi's assassination in 1948.

Gandhi was therefore as engaged in encounters with revolution-aries as Tolstoy was in the equivalent phase of his life, but in his case he was the embodiment and director of an organized national movement and they were asking him to step down or join them. In Russia the revolutionaries were the embodiment of a movement, and Tolstoy was the newcomer to the political scene. But both men combined admiration for the revolutionaries with steadfast opposition.

On January 3, 1926, Gandhi announced that he was retiring from public life for a year to concentrate upon the ashram. He suffered a breakdown from strain that March, and in the second half of the year wrote:

I still have enough strength to be left alone to think and do my work, but the ability to talk to a group, to guide and to explain things to a succession of people coming to me, to humour them, to get angry with them and get work out of them, has all but left me.[25]

But in the second half of 1928, Gandhi gradually emerged from his political retirement. He had watched with scepticism the efforts of various nationalist leaders to unite in their response to the government's Statutory Commission, but he himself participated—from the ashram—in the Bardoli *satyagraha*, which was directed by Patel. This ended successfully in August, and Gandhi said the success had been made possible by the ashram's training of the participants: "the way to constitutional swaraj may lie through Lucknow [the scene of the nationalist leaders' meeting]," said Gandhi. "The way to organic swaraj (self-rule), which is synonymous with Ramarajya (Rama's-rule—the golden age), lies through Bardoli."[26] And he wrote to Andrews: "Bardoli victory . . . has almost restored the shattered faith in nonviolence on the political field."[27] That restoration may have happened to his own faith, for the Salt March was a kind of extension of the Bardoli *satyagraha*, covering the same territory and similarly relying on Patel's organization in Gujarat and on the ashram members.

At the Lahore Congress in December 1929, he resumed national leadership, identifying himself with radical youth and sponsoring the resolution demanding "complete independence."[28] This was, he said, a matter of honor: "Organizations like men . . . must have a sense of honour and fulfil their promises."[29] "The nation wants to feel its power even more than to have independence. Possession of such power *is* independence."[30] In such apostrophes of honor and power, Gandhi was of course far from Tolstoy, who recoiled from patriotic politics and its chivalric language. Gandhi's language about Nehru was in fact in the most literal sense chivalric, for he spoke of him as "a knight sans peur et sans reproche," as being pure as a crystal, the jewel of India, truthful beyond suspicion, and so on.[31]

The viceroy, Lord Irwin, had announced that a Round Table Conference would be held in London to discuss India's future. Gandhi cautiously welcomed the announcement (to Nehru's displeasure) but saw Irwin on December 23 to ask for some guarantee that such a conference would accept as a starting point the idea of Dominion Status. The viceroy could give no such guarantee and so, at the congress meeting immediately after, independence was made India's goal.

This led to the great Salt March of 1930 that aroused all India, and for which Gandhi was again imprisoned. Released for talks with the viceroy, he agreed, though with misgivings, to attend the Round Table Conference in London. His misgivings were justified, and the nationalists were outmaneuvered, through Gandhi had a personal success with the English press.

When the conference ended, he visited France, Switzerland, and Italy on his way home. He went to France and Switzerland primarily to meet his old admirer and fellow Tolstoyan, Romain Rolland, with whom he spent five days. And in Rome, where he had an interview with Mussolini, he also met Tolstoy's oldest daughter, Tania. During a visit to the Vatican, he was profoundly moved by the sign of a crucifix: "It was not without a wrench that I could tear myself away from that scene of living tragedy. I saw there at once that nations like individuals could only be made through the agony of the Cross and in no other way."[32] This we may see as implying a theory of nationalism opposite in emotional character to the exhilarated rhetoric about Nehru as a knight of chivalry, a jewel of India, a hero of youth, and so on. In this affirmation that the Cross is at the heart of all life, including politics, he rejoined Tolstoy.

Writings and Political Action

Ordinarily, in the Gandhi sections that correspond to the Tolstoy sections on his writing, we concentrate on Gandhi's larger campaigns. But it happens that this ten-year period he spent largely in political retirement, and that he then produced his two largest books, the Autobiography, and Satyagraha in South Africa, so it seems appropriate at this time to consider these works and Gandhi's literary activity in general. (Gandhi was of course very much a writer; he left behind him about ten million words, which means he wrote an average of 500 words a day for fifty years.) The Autobiography appeared in Navajivan from November 29, 1925 until February 3, 1929, and was translated in Young India in the corresponding issues, a week later.

As for Satyagraha in South Africa, the book is eminently instructive and "relevant." In the introduction, Gandhi says:

But our present fight is epic in character. . . . The reader will note South African parallels for all our experiences in the present struggle to date. . . . I have neither the time nor the inclination to write a regular detailed history.

My only object in writing this book is that it may be helpful in our present struggle....[33]

Obviously his two books are not to be considered achievements of the same order as *War and Peace* and *Anna Karenina*. Gandhi invested in his writing nothing like the intensities of mind and will that Tolstoy put into his. They are essentially transparent records of the events they recount—it is those events, those actions of Gandhi in the past, that are the feats of mind and will—and the writing attempts merely to make them clear to the reader. There is nothing in the books' consciousness to dazzle or impress, to arouse and combine similar forces in the reader's mind—no magic of memory and imagination, no sleight of hand in narrative or rhetoric, no ecstatic flights of vision or melting sinkings of sentiment. We might cite Tolstoy's chapters of autobiography as examples of *that* sort of writing, though they were written as late as 1892 and in their own way they are artless and innocent—comparatively speaking. But "their own way" led on to Proust and Nabokov, and no doubt that is why Tolstoy left them uncompleted. This is polychromatic or polyphonal writing, while Gandhi's is black and white, or melodic.

Gandhi's writing is nevertheless remarkable from a literary point of view, because of the range of tones, of humor, reasonableness, solemnity, and tenderness which he can coax out of his limited instrument, but also because of the purity of effect which is given by that very limitation. (This was the aesthetic charm of the folk tale for Tolstoy, and the aesthetic reason he took up that form.) There is no self behind this writing and so no echoes, no intimations of caverns the writer and the reader may yet explore together. The soul has no romantic caverns, just bottomless pits into which writer and reader disappear, when writing and reading cease to make sense. To change the metaphor, the other voice in the dialectic mode of consciousness just isn't there, and so neither are the complex harmonies of autobiography.

Gandhi says at the beginning of his *Autobiography* that a friend had protested to him that autobiography was a form peculiar to the West, that had never been written in the East except by those under Western influence. Gandhi's reply was that his was not a real autobiography, only the story of his "experiments with truth" (which was the book's title in Gujarati) and that the experiments were in the spiritual field. In effect he is saying that it is a book about a soul, not about a self. (The same could be said about preliterary autobiographies in the West, like that of St. Teresa of Avila.) One sign of that is how rarely Gandhi evokes the feel of his day-to-day living, of the empirical flow of his experience; his closest approach to that is his narrative of his first few days in South Africa, when crucial events followed so fast upon each other that the reader has a sense of complete knowledge. But that is not only fortuitous, but also not really empirical, since the events were categorically political and announced the significance as they occurred. They did not need to be transformed from above by the transcendent, or from below by intuition.

Gandhi did a lot of writing in this period besides his two major narratives. He wrote quite a long series of essays which could be put together as a book, on his "Jail Experiences." This represented an extension of his readers' consciousness (in a simple, nontranscendent sense) for Gandhi wanted to familiarize them with life in jail as part of training their imaginations for political action and cultural regeneration. He wanted them to be ready for hardships, for social ignominy, ready to identify themselves with "the insulted and injured." But if one compares his essay with Dostoevsky's *House of the Dead*, one sees how little Gandhi gives us of the rawer facts and rawer feelings of the experience. When, for instance, he lets the reader know that incidents of homosexual rape occurred where he was imprisoned, the fact is signaled (not described) by the phrase "unnatural vice." Gandhi treated literature as one of the habits of polite culture, which should represent only a polite selection from the range of experience. Modernism from Dostoevsky on has included more and more impolite material, extending its harmonic range by including the shrieks and groans of the reader's (and the writer's) consciousness and sense of taste as they struggle against so much that challenges and offends.

Perhaps the most striking aspect of Gandhi's literary work is something which can be conjoined directly with Tolstoy's popular tales. His letters and newspaper articles contain many narratives and anecdotes, direct addresses, and expositions of an idea that sketch out a whole "literature for the people." The forms are short and simple, the style is clear and unpretentious, the range of effect is from a modest gay inventiveness to a severity of logic and a mood of *memento mori*. It is a religio-pastoral literature, very reminiscent of that of the Christian Middle Ages.

One example is Gandhi's letter to the ashram children, written from Yeravda jail soon after his arrest in 1930.

Little Birds,

Ordinary birds cannot fly without wings. With wings, of course, all can fly. But if you, without wings, will learn how to fly, then all your troubles will be at an end. And I will teach you.

See, I have no wings, yet I come flying to you every day in thought. Look, here is little Vimala, here is Hari, and here Dharmakumar. And you also can come flying to me in thought.

There is no need for a teacher for those who know how to think. The teacher may guide us, but he cannot give us the power of thinking. That is latent in us. Those who are wise get wise thoughts.

Tell me who, amongst you, are not praying properly in Prabhubhai's evening prayer.

Send me a letter signed by all, and those who do not know how to sign may make a cross.

Bapu's Blessing.[34]

This is the side of Gandhi that can aptly be compared with St. Francis of Assisi, the side most often turned toward the general public, especially by his Anglo-Catholic admirers. He told Kasturba to recite the Ramanama, which was

familiar to the very animals and birds, the very trees and stones of Hindustan through many thousand years ... You must learn to repeat the name of Rama with such sweetness and such devotion that the birds will pause in their singing to listen to you—the very trees will bend their leaves towards you, stirred by the divine melody of that name.[35]

Another example, slightly more complex, is a joint effort by him and Mirabehn, published in *Young India* for December 5, 1929, called "Our Brethren the Trees." Mirabehn tells of asking a volunteer to pick her some babul leaves for hers and how he brought her a great bundle. She went to Gandhi to show him how the leaves were all "asleep" (tightly folded) because it was dark. Gandhi was indignant; leaves were living creatures, not to be torn off at night, and why so many?

... deeply it pains me that people pluck those masses of delicate blossoms to fling in my face and hang around my neck.... Yes, Bapu, I know—I understand, said I, hanging my head in shame.... Often have I put my arms around the trunk of an old mighty tree and listened to his hushed words of wisdom and peace.... How could I have been so heartless?[36]

(When Gandhi's disciples wrote about their dealings with him, they usually presented themselves as children standing before an adult, being scolded or being consoled.)

Then Gandhi's brisker and drier commentary begins. "Let not the reader call this sentimental twaddle. . . . India has cultivated no small respect for trees and other sentient beings. . . ." He goes on to cite figures of legend, like Damayanti and Shakuntala.

This literature was spread by other Gandhians, for instance in their narratives of the Gandhi campaigns. Mirabehn made the story of his midnight arrests (in 1930 and 1932) sound like the Gospel story of Jesus' arrest before the Crucifixion. Rajendra Prasad wrote about Champaran, Mahadev Desai about Bardoli, in *The Story of Bardoli*; about which Rabindranath Tagore said that it had the spirit of the Epic Age in its narrative of the triumph of moral right over arbitrary power. In fact, of course, such writing is epic only by a paradoxical transvaluation of the term; it is epic transformed into pastoral. That is clear in Pyarelal's title for his pamphlet about the 1932 fast, "The Epic Fast." The story of the fast can only paradoxically be compared with, say, *The Iliad*. The real significance of such terms is to testify to our sense that time has been turned back, and that we are escaping from the sordid empiricism and complexity of the modern into an earlier, naiver, nobler age.

Perhaps the most gifted of the Gandhians for literature was Rajagopalachari, and he continued and extended this work after Gandhi's death by his retelling of the great epics, *Ramayana* and *Mahabharata*. But there were many gifted writers among them; for instance, Vinoba Bhave, whose special field was the philosophical and religious *pensée*, and J.C. Kumarappa, who wrote about village economy and about history. Kumarappa's tone is sharp enough at times to be called Orwellian, but he is also Gandhian in the pastoral picturesqueness of his intellectual schemes.

Kumarappa was temperamentally fiery and intellectually proud. Vinoba's criticism could be very biting and Rajaji's cynicism is sometimes all engulfing. But they were all Gandhian writers, and all this Gandhian writing can be described as a soothing idyll, by modern standards. It transforms the ashram, the campaigns, the jail-going, the moments of anguish, and even the political dealings with other leaders, British and Indian, all into something simple, gentle, colorful, idyllic. When Gandhi got a disappointing reply from the viceroy, he told the world. "On bended knees I asked for bread, and was given a stone instead." He usually presents his allies and himself as "in love with" each other, able to deny each other nothing, making each other a gift of a favorite disciple. They plead with each other, they yield, tears of joy spring to their eyes, and so on. It all rings very oddly in the modern ear, Indian as well as Western. Nehru wrote to Dr. Ansari on October 10, 1931, about the negotiations at the Round Table Conference:

There seems to me too much sugariness in its proceedings, at least so far as our side is concerned. That of course is Gandhiji's way, and we must not complain. But a little pepper would add to the taste.[37]

As usual, one can find an answer to this complaint in another place in Gandhi. In 1925 a correspondent protested against Gandhi's editing of his letter (in publishing it) and said he always followed W. L. Garrison's motto; "I will be as harsh as truth, and as uncompromising as justice." Gandhi replied; "I do not mind harsh truth, but I do object to spiced truth. Spicy language is as foreign to truth as hot chilies to a healthy stomach . . . truth suffers when it is harshly put."[38]

Gandhi did not use such terms as pastoral, epic, or idyll, but he did use the Hindu terms for "qualities"—terms that can be applied to anything from food through art to temperaments—*tamas* (dark, gloomy, inert, or chaotic) *rajas* (fiery, passionate, energetic, or enthusiastic) and *sattva* (marked by peace and reason, and what I have called "pastoral"). Touring the United Provinces in 1924, Gandhi had a sheet of paper thrown into his car by a peasant, which he found to be covered with couplets and quatrains from Tulsidas. Gandhi talked about this incident some time after, for he found it significant and moving.

Historians have testified that nowhere in the world are the peasants as civilized as in India. This sheet of paper is proof of it. . . . I firmly believe that in our country it is not tamas which rules supreme but sattva . . . people who have such ideas [as that peasant] have a sattvic civilization.[39]

Tolstoy 1894–1910, Renunciation of Art and Intellect

Events and Ideas

During this period, Tolstoy's relations worsened with both his family and the authorities. His philosophic-religious belief, which

She—as I now see—was the very wife I needed. [Long before Fet had told him that Sonia was the perfect wife for a man of letters.] She was an ideal wife in the pagan sense of loyalty, devotion to family life, self-sacrifice, family affection, yet, heathen as she is, she has in her the possibilities of a Christian friend.[4]

On the 24th he wrote:

I'm the only one she holds by, and in the depths of her soul she fears I don't love her, because she hasn't followed me. Don't believe that. I love you even more. I know you couldn't. You're not alone. I'm with you.[5]

On December 7, he noted that she was going through the change of life. She had begun to suffer "periodic madness every autumn, and felt as if a stone were pressed to her breast."[6]

The children were growing up, but the spectacle they presented was distressing, to both Tolstoy and his wife. Sonia declared she wanted to write "The History of a Mother," and that she could no longer bear the weight of bringing up a lot of weaklings and wastrels. But this did not mean she was in harmony with Tolstoy. She wrote in her diary for June 6, 1897: "He is indifferent to everyone around him, and lives only for himself"; and on September 22: "I do not believe in his goodness and love of humanity. I know the source of all his actions; glory and glory, insatiable, unlimited, feverish . . . he has no love for his own children and grandchildren."[7] She was aware of the dangerousness of her own anger. "Oh, if only I could choke the volcano of my uncontrollable nature!"[8]

The great family scandal among the Tolstoys in this period was Sonia's infatuation with the pianist Taneev, who was forty years old (twelve years younger than she) when the infatuation developed in 1896. It was like Sonia's suicide attempts in being such a reprise of a fictional situation Tolstoy had invented (in *The Kreutzer Sonata*) but it was a prolonged piece of behavior, or misbehavior, on Sonia's part, lasting nearly ten years.

It was intimately related to another piece of Tolstoy's writing, *What Is Art?* Sonia was protesting, by her misbehavior, her husband's argument against the religion of art. Taneev's music was charged with erotic power, for herself and for others, even though he himself was, by general agreement, a cold, stiff personality decidedly uninterested in women, who relied on an old nurse to look after him. Sonia later described him as "extremely uninteresting, always equable, extremely secretive, and wholly incomprehensible." The Tolstoy family called him "that sack with sounds"—a music box.[9] His effect on her was completely outside reason. She associated him mystically with the dead child Vanya.

However, the effect was not limited to Sonia. Her daughter Tania's diary gives evidence of the erotic mood of which Taneev was the involuntary progenitor. On February 16, 1889, she wrote, about his performance of the *Appassionata*:

From the first sounds, we were all carried far away, and I saw nothing, forgot myself, and everything that had been, and only felt that tremendous thing, and my face was so drawn by spasms that I could not keep it still, and pressed my forehead against the back of a chair. When he had finished, Papa came forward from his corner, his face wet with tears. . . . Besides being a brilliant musician, Taneev is a very charming person, and I have a very reprehensible longing to be more to him than other people. I know that is bad.[10]

Sonia herself wrote. "Oh what a terrible violent hopeless desire to hear that man play again! Will I *never* hear him?"[11] Her emotion was partly associated with Mendelssohn's *Song Without Words*. She declared that her heart turned over when he played it to her. She played it to him, and she wrote a story with that title. But she assembled other kinds of art around her feeling too. For instance, Tiuchev's poems about the rebirth of passionate love in an old man. Only in 1904, after Sonia had sent him an "absurd letter," which he destroyed, did Taneev break off the affair by pointedly leaving Sonia's box during a concert.

In the same years as this was going on, Tolstoy was leading the agitation about the Dukhobors, and the contrast between the two preoccupations represents the general split between the public and the private halves of his life. (Sonia called the Dukhobors "arrogant revolutionaries," and said her children would soon be unable to buy white bread to eat, as a result of their father's activities.) The Dukhobors were a long established Christian sect with some communist and pacifist principles, who refused to do military service for the Russian state when the latter introduced general conscription in 1887. Strictly speaking, they at first submitted to the order, prosperity having relaxed the severity of their principles, only telling their young men not to actually fire a weapon. But when they were penalized, suffering reradicalized them, and in 1893–1894 they renounced tobacco, meat, and wine, redivided their property, and refused military service. In the summer of 1895, they burned their arms and their conscripted young men refused further obedience. The Cossacks were sent against them, and charged through their village twice and raped the Dukhobor women while the Dukhobors sang hymns. Three hundred men were imprisoned, four hundred families forced to sell up their farms.

Tolstoy had long seen in the anarchism (resistance to the state) of some of the sects the main hope of his times; in them and *not* in the liberal parliamentarians or the terrorist revolutionaries. On November 27, 1903 he wrote to Biriukov that the sectarians sapped the foundations of the regime worse than the revolutionaries or the political anarchists because their resistance was not calculated but commanded and absolute.[12] He now called the behavior of the Dukhobors a rebirth of Christ.

There were other sects beside the Dukhobors who resisted military service. The Mennonites did other work for the state in place of it, and the Nazarenes went to jail. The Molokans sought Tolstoy's help in emigrating also. (In England the Quakers especially responded to Tolstoy's appeal on the Dukhobors' behalf.) Tolstoy took a great interest in all such cases, and Chertkov and the other Tolstoyans collected an archive of material about the sectarians in general.

In connection with this, Tolstoy became in this period the first great patron of war resistance. In 1898, one of his followers, Popov, wrote *The Life and Death of Drozhin*, a young man who had died in the disciplinary battalion he was sent to for refusing military service. (Drozhin had met Prince Khilkhov in 1889, and through his influence moved from a belief in revolution to Tolstoyism.) Tolstoy wrote a postscript to this book, urging everyone else to refuse to obey such cruel laws. And he drew attention to other such cases in other countries, as in "The Beginning of the End," a story about a young Dutchman who was refusing to serve. In this way Tolstoy created a legend of heroes and martyrs for his case, as Gandhi did for his case in South Africa and later in India.

In the winter of 1901, Tolstoy was very ill and his family was lent a villa in the Crimea, which had a Mediterranean climate, for him to recuperate in. For their train journey down they were given a special coach and they found the villa (it belonged to a Countess Panin) a pseudo-Scottish castle full of gilded furniture and marble statuary. (Other villas nearby were owned by members of the Tsar's family). Five doctors consulted about Tolstoy's case when he had a relapse.

All these things were reminders—welcome to Sonia, unwelcome to Tolstoy—of his fame, and his character as a valuable national property. He thought there was a moral limit to the effort that should be put into keeping him alive; he asked that he should be allowed to die naturally, but that was not permitted.

For Sonia, illnesses were important ceremonies, and, particularly in his case, accessions of power to her. In March 1902 she wrote to Goldenveizer. "In any case, if there are a few more years of life for Lev Nikolaevich, . . . his life will be that of a decrepit old man, who will have to be looked after, to whom every excitement, movement, unnecessary interviews, will be forbidden. He will have to go to bed like a little boy, eat gruel and milk. . . . "[13] Even when she was the one sick, illness brought her the same accession of power. On September 2, 1906, she was to undergo an operation and there was a deathbed scene between her and Tolstoy, with him in the role of Karenin. In his diary the day before, he had written that the house was full of doctors, which meant that instead of submission to the will of God in the presence of death, the atmosphere was egocentric and disturbed.

Also in 1901, Tolstoy was finally excommunicated by the Holy Synod. This drew more public attention to him, both favorable and unfavorable. On the day the decree was published, he was recognized out on the street by someone who shouted: "There goes the devil in human form"; but for others in the crowd that gathered, he might have been beaten to death, he says. The police had to extricate him from the crowd and send him home. He also got threatening and accusing letters. For instance, one from "A Russian Mother" which accompanied a length of rope with which he was invited to hang himself.

In 1904–1905 came the Russo-Japanese War, in which Andrei Tolstoy served. And in 1905 the Russian Revolution had its first climax on the Bloody Sunday of February, when troops in front of the Winter Palace fired on the huge procession led by Father Gapon, who had come to appeal to the Tsar. Tolstoy was in sympathy with neither the authorities nor the revolutionaries, whom he described in March 1906 as showing all the corruptive effects of power: conceit, pride, ambition, and disrespect for other men. But he saw the revolution itself as "a violent spring," an unjudgable event, which might do more than the French Revolution for mankind's benefit.[14]

During the revolution there were disturbances in the country around Yasnaya Polyana. Ilya Tolstoy left his estate, judging the situation dangerous, and came back to his parents. The Cossacks were out in the streets of Tula, and there were rumors that they had been asked to defend Yasnaya Polyana. The governor did in fact supply some guards, at Sonya's request, who continued for some time after 1905; and when they were removed, at Sasha's request— for they were a source of shame to Tolstoy and her—Sonia hired a Circassian guard who, among other things, caught peasants who tried to steal wood from the estate. It is worth noting the recurrence of both Cossacks and Circassians in Tolstoy's life, and now not as embodiments of freedom, as he had seen them in the days when he wrote "The Cossacks," but as agents of oppression, enforcers of order and preservers of property, on whom he was dependent. In 1906, a story again got into the papers of the Tolstoys sending for the Cossacks to defend Yasnaya Polyana.

Perhaps the major event in all this period was the solidifying of his ideas and sympathies into a final religious form, which was so like that which Gandhi's ideas were even then assuming.

Tolstoy's philosophy, like Gandhi's, was extremely personal. On January 13, 1898 he wrote in his journal: "Organization, every kind of organization, freeing us from any kind of human, moral duties . . . All the evil in the world comes from that."[15] "We must always ask not "What is to be done?" but "What must I do?" We must ask, not "Can this be a general law?" but "How must each man act to fulfil his allotted task and save his soul?" This is what we might call the contracted consciousness, the opposite of the expanded consciousness Tolstoy was interested in as a young writer. There is something analogous in Gandhi's slogan: "One step enough for me." Tolstoy wrote:

In Political Economy and Sociology there is only one question to solve; 'Why do some people work and others do nothing?' This is the question, and not the nature of value, of capital, or profit.[16]

Both Tolstoy and Gandhi felt there was very little to be known about the world, very little to be felt, very little to be done—only one's duty. Socially they felt that most men lived in a world that was largely unreal because it was made up of imagined constructs that imposed unreal obligations. Thus when his daughter Masha died in November 1906, Tolstoy declared that he did not feel unhappy. He met the village fool Kinya, and asked: "You have heard of our grief?" Kinya answered "I heard," but then immediately said:

"Give me a kopek." Tolstoy commented: "How much better and lighter that is."[17] Lighter is perhaps the key word; so many things, like emotional obligations, became insubstantial and temporary to him. A month later, Tolstoy recorded in his diary Masha's last minutes. He had held her hand and felt her life cease, and it was one of the most important moments of his life; but much of the time he felt no grief and was glad to feel none.

He tried to feel the same way about his own guilt and shame. On July 8, 1908 he wrote in his diary:

If I had heard of myself as an outsider—of a man living in luxury, wringing all he can out of the peasants, locking them up in prison, while preaching and professing Christianity and giving away coppers, and for all his loathsome actions sheltering himself behind his dear wife, I should not hesitate to call him a black-guard! And that is just what I need that I may be set free from the praises of men and live for my soul. When I ask what I need, it is to get away from everyone—to where? To God. To die. I have a criminal desire for death.[18]

There was indeed much public mockery of Tolstoy for his divestment of his property—he was referred to as the Great Bankrupt—and he sought to embrace that mockery and turn it to his advantage. The most important things in the world were personal relations, but on June 20, 1898 he wrote in his journal: "Throw off personality from life, renounce it, and then there will remain that which makes the essence of life—love."[19]

Culture too was something Tolstoy simply struck out of life, to lighten its substance and open its texture. This lightness accounts for the curious optimism with which he declares that we have only to want no more war, and we shall have no more war. We find the same optimism in Gandhi—the moment Indians want *swaraj*, they will have it. This partly expresses the personalism mentioned before—everything depends on the individual act of will—but partly this lightness—a sense that the world exists only because we wish it to, or better, because God wishes it to. Much of what we call its substance—"human nature" and "what history teaches"—is quite unreal. It could perfectly well all be absolutely different tomorrow. This idea is something we find in Thoreau and the Transcendentalists generally, but in Tolstoy and Gandhi the lightness is validated by being rooted in strenuous heroism—a heroism of action and of death.

His Writing

During this period, Tolstoy devoted as much energy as in the past to writing, and most of his writing energies to polemic, even though he believed that writing was not good for him, and that polemic in particular was destructive and hateful. The explanation no doubt is that he was bound by long established habit—"*Qui a bu boira*" as he said—and that he enjoyed writing. On June 1, 1908, he wrote in his diary of his joy in beginning to write again, even such an angry piece as "I Cannot Be Silent." He could scarcely restrain tears of joy as he wrote. He was bound by his karma as a writer, at least as long as he stayed within the charmed circle of Yasnaya Polyana, to which he was bound by his karma as a husband. Within that situation, the best thing he could do was write. We must also take into account a sense of responsibility. He was a great and famous writer, and there were causes he could serve by his writing.

One theme of that polemic, as we have seen, was imperialism, and there he was at one with Gandhi. But another theme was patriotism, and about this he disagreed with Gandhi, more significantly than about anything else. One of his most Voltairean essays of this period is "On Patriotism" (1895), which begins by describing satirically the visit of the French fleet to Kronstadt and that of the Russian fleet to Toulon to celebrate the Franco-Russian alliance in 1894. Tolstoy simply denied the reality of nations and nationality. Citizenship, he said, was at that time too mixed for "being French" or "being Russian" to mean anything.[20] Patriotism he considered an ideology of slavery, imposed by governments to justify their own existence; and newspapers facilitated such lies.[21] But public opinion, which supported governments, could also destroy them. Let one man begin to speak, said Tolstoy, and all the opposition will melt away.

A notable feature of these polemical essays is the rhetoric of death that Tolstoy used to introduce and end several of them. Thus, in his preface to "The Christian Teaching" (1898), he wrote:

By my age and the state of my health I am standing with one foot in the grave, and so human considerations for me have no importance. Even if they had, I am well aware that this [what he is writing] could only disturb and grieve both unbelievers who demand from me works of art and not discussions of faith, and also the believers who are perturbed by everything I write about religion and scold me for it.[22]

The rhetoric of death, it will be seen, blends into a rhetoric of *dharma*, of duty, and on other occasions into a rhetoric of guilt and shame.

"There are no Guilty People" (1909) begins: "Mine is a strange and wonderful lot!" He has long felt keenly the oppression of the rich, but:

> I still live on amid the depravity and sins of rich society; and I cannot leave it, because I have neither the knowledge nor the strength to do so. I cannot. I do not know how to change my life so that my physical needs— food, sleep, clothing, my going to and fro—may be satisfied without a sense of shame and wrongdoing in the position which I fill. Now that I am over 80 and have become feeble, I have given up trying to free myself; and, strange to say, as my feebleness increases, I realize more and more strongly the wrongfulness of my position. . . . It has occurred to me that I do not occupy this position for nothing; that Providence intended that I should lay bare the truth of my feelings so that I might atone for all that causes my suffering, and might perhaps open the eyes of. . . ."[20]

He will use his guilt and shame for the benefit of others.

But the central discourse is of death. "The Law of Love and the Law of Violence" (1908) begins: "The only reason I am writing this is because, knowing the one means of escape for Christian humanity, from its physical suffering as well as from the moral suffering in which it is sunk, I, who am on the edge of the grave, cannot be silent."[24] He wanted to reintroduce death into our consciousness— into our awareness of everything. A little later in that essay he says, "Throughout the centuries the best, that is the real people, always thought about *it*." Which is "How it will all end." Tolstoy concludes the essay: "This is what I have wanted to say to you, my brothers, before I died."

He employed a similar rhetoric in his fiction. "Master and Man" (1895) ends with: "Whether he is better off, or worse off, there in the place where he awoke after that real death [Nikita seemed to die but recovered within the story; this confusion of seeming and real deaths has already made the reader uneasy.] whether he was disappointed or found things there just as he expected, is what we shall all of us soon learn."

In this sort of writing, Tolstoy performed something similar to Gandhi's political fasting. Both men "forwarded," as the formalist critics say, brought to the front of their contemporaries' minds, the facts of individual dying. Each made his own death, and that of his reader, relevant to issues of public policy. The message was: "Death, death, death awaits you every instant," as Tolstoy said in *The Pathway of Life*. The meaning of your death is what you have to seek for, seek relentlessly all the time.[25]

What has been said so far makes it clear that Tolstoy's eyes were on political events in this period, but they were also on religion—both Russian Church policy and the teaching of eastern sages and sects. Yet it seems possible to say that, at least in the first part of this period, he was occupied above all with the question of art.

He wrote a "Letter to N. A. Aleksandrov" (the editor of the *Aesthetic Journal*) in 1882, an essay entitled "About Art" and another on the same theme in 1889, one on "Science and Art" in 1889–1891, "On What They Call Art" in 1896, and the book *What is Art?* in 1897–1898. After that there is less to record, but a very significant essay, "Shakespeare and the Drama," appeared in 1906.

Tolstoy was responding to the new movement in the arts in Europe, which we can call symbolism or modernism, especially insofar as it reached Russia. In 1892 D. S. Merezhkovski brought out his volume, *Symbols*, and in 1893 his essay, "On What Is New in Literature and the Reasons for the Decline of Russian Literature." He had just returned from Paris, and he drew a contrast between Zola—politically a protestor but culturally respectable, and already practically a member of the French Academy—and Verlaine, a disreputable writer of obscure and decadent verses who lived in cafés. It was of course the latter who represented "the New in Literature" to Merezhkovski, and it was the former who was the French Tolstoy.

Perhaps the distinguishing feature of this aestheticism was its combination of religious and political pretensions with a defiant insistence on the aesthetic principle against all others. But the aesthetic turned out to be closely allied to the erotic and the feminine. Merezhkovski and his wife Zinaida Hippius hoped for a third testament, a testament of the Holy Ghost that would also be feminine. It was a ritualist religion. Briusov, writing about Balmont's volume of verse, *Sun*, in 1903, said: "Our days are exceptional—some of the most remarkable in history. . . . Unexpected and marvelous possibilities are being revealed to mankind. . . . Balmont is first of all a 'new man,' there is a new soul in him, new passions, ideals, expectations—different from those of earlier generations. . . . To freely submit to the succession of all desires is the idea. To place the full excitement in every moment is the goal."[26]

This kind of New Life was of course unsympathetic to Tolstoy's radical religion, and it detected far too much moralism in his great novels, but it reacted most sharply against his old enemies, the social-democratic critics in the line begun by Chernyshevski. Merezhkovski and his friends much admired *War and Peace* and *Anna Karenina*.

Tolstoy's objections to the new movement were naturally manifold, but they can be summed up in a single moralism; on November 2, 1896, he wrote in his diary: "Art is play, and good when it is the play of normal, hard-working men, bad when it is the play of corrupt parasites."[27] Clearly, symbolism and decadence seemed to him the latter; but he was not ready to call his own art, in the style of *Anna Karenina*, the former. All post-Renaissance art seemed to him the play of parasites. A. V. Zhirkevich records a conversation with Tolstoy in 1890 in which Zhirkevich praised Fet's poems as distracting men from the depressing conditions of contemporary actuality. Tolstoy replied angrily that that was a bad thing, not a good thing. First because nothing *ought* to distract men from life, they have to live, and to live strenuously. Second because verses distract no one for long.[28] He denied the importance of art. "The principal thing which I wanted to say about art is that it does not exist, in the sense of some great manifestation of the human spirit."[29] His advice to someone beginning to write was don't, or write only when you have something to say that is so important that you can't bear not to say it.

He disliked Ibsen as a typical modern artist, both because he "wrote in riddles," and because he taught that without carnal love a man's heart will never feel anything more spiritual—man will freeze to death; Tolstoy said just the opposite was true.[30] The two objections went hand in hand because both the eroticism and the complexity of form testified to the "idleness" of writer and reader—their desire to build up something elaborate to take the place of real problems, real work, real duties.

In reaction against the new literature and its theory, Tolstoy made a critical value out of sincerity. In his introduction to S. T. Semyonov's *Peasant Stories*, he contrasted Semyonov with Flaubert, saying that the latter was very insincere in his story "Julien l'Hôpitalier." "I feel that the author himself would not have done and would not even have wished to do what his hero does [lie with lepers] and therefore I myself do not wish to do it and do not experience any agitation at reading of this amazing exploit."[31] How different Semyonov's story is: ". . . everytime I read it I feel that the author would not only have wished to have, but certainly would have, acted in that way under similar circumstances; his feelings infect me and I feel pleased, and it seems to me that I too should have done, or been ready to do, something good."[32]

Chertkov recorded in his diary for May 20, 1894 that Tolstoy said the most important thing in a work of art is always the reader's relation to the writer's life and what is said about that relation. And in Tolstoy's own diary for October 20, 1896, we find: "When an author writes, we the readers place our ears to his breast and we listen and say, 'Breathe. If you have any rumblings, we shall hear them.'"[33]

In *What Is Art?* Tolstoy directly challenged the new literature by criticising contemporary work by the criterion of its usefulness and pleasurableness to peasants. The people, he said, have always had art of their own and know what art is for.[34] He talked of art often in terms of food and compared the new kinds to cayenne pepper, limburger cheese, and alcohol. (These are of course *rajasic* foods, to use the Indian classification Gandhi employed, and Tolstoy was implicitly asking for a *sattvic* art.) Good art, he said in Chapter 6, of *What Is Art?*, is that kind which promotes the religious perception of its time, which in our case is the brotherhood of all men. But our art, since the Renaissance, has been a military caste's art,[35] which means that it has served to distract an idle class of aristocrats. (On February 4, 1897, he wrote in his diary: "The harm of art is principally this, that it takes up time, hiding people's idleness from them.")[36] According to Tolstoy, deprived of its proper (religious) subject matter, art becomes affected and obscure, artificial and insincere, and manifests erotic mania.

Some of these thoughts were developed further in his letter to Romain Rolland, October 4, 1887. Rolland had written to Tolstoy as a student, conscious of a vocation to become an intellectual, and troubled by Tolstoy's demand that everyone do bread labor. Tolstoy wrote to him: "All the evil of the day comes from the fact that so-called civilized people, together with the scientists and artists, form a privileged caste, like so many priests; and this caste has the fault of all castes. It degrades and lowers the principle in virtue of which it was organized. We are born and we clamber upon the rungs of the ladder, and we find among the privileged the priests of civilization, of *Kultur*, as the Germans have it."[37] This letter was mostly about the need for everyone to do physical work and to dispose of his own physical wastes. A prophet must *prove* his sincerity by sacrifice. We must distrust these "castes of the mind, which after having destroyed or subjugated the ancient ruling castes, the Church, the State, the Army, have installed themselves in the same place, and without wishing or being able to do anything useful for men, claim admiration and blind service from everyone."

It is worth remembering that two of Tolstoy's children, two he was especially close to, were semiprofessionally involved with the arts. His daughter Tanya went to the school of painting and sculpture in Moscow and was taught by Leonid Pasternak and went to Paris in 1899. His son Lev was sent to Paris in 1894, and in 1908 studied with Rodin. Yasnaya Polyana itself was a center of artistic activity and appreciation, where, quite apart from Tolstoy's writing, there were often other writers reading their work, painters and sculptors doing portraits, and concerts with singing and piano.

This too was on Tolstoy's mind in writing *What is Art?* On July 19, 1896 he wrote in his diary:

Yesterday I looked through the romances, novels and poems of Fet. I recalled our incessant music on the piano at Yasnaya Polyana . . . romances, novels, about how people fall nastily in love, poetry about that or about how they languish from boredom. And music about the same theme. But life, all life, seethes with its own problems of food, distribution, labour, about faith, about the relations of men. . . . It is shameful, nasty. Help me, Father, to serve Thee by showing up this life.[38]

As so often, however, it is Sonia who embodied most vividly the world of art for Tolstoy. In her diary for June 21, 1897, she says she must go and order the soup but doesn't want to hear anything more about soup and such matters.

I want to hear the most difficult fugue or symphony; I want to hear the most complicated harmonies every single day, so that my soul can struggle in its endeavor to understand what the composer is trying to express in his difficult musical language . . . a simple melody is like simple words—a sonata or symphony—is like a philosophical argument and can only be understood by a highly cultured person.[39]

Here as so often we see Sonia taking up Tolstoy's ideas and reversing their values so as to become his denier, the anti-Tolstoy.

The music she is thinking of we can identify with Taneev, as we see from her entry of October 11, saying she found Taneev's quartet wonderful: "It is the last word in modern music—so earnest, so complicated, so full of the most unexpected harmonic changes, so skillful and rich in ideas. It gave me the most exquisite pleasure."[40] (Sergei Tolstoy tells us that Taneev's music was like César Franck's.) On July 30 she wrote: "I played for four hours today; music seems to lift me from the earth, and it makes all these painful and annoying things less painful, and easier to bear."[41] On September 15 she had spent the evening with Taneev in Moscow and they had talked of the infinite. "May God help me to develop this longing for the spiritual, religious, posthumous infinity."[42] And four days later: "All I long for is music, music, and music."[43]

It is not surprising to discover that she did not like *What is Art?*, which she was copying and recopying during this period. On June 25 she found its tone "so angry and aggressive." She picked on the personal reference: "It just makes me feel as though he were attacking an invisible enemy (Taneev, for example, about whom he used to be so jealous) with the sole object of destroying him."[44] She goes on to record having read *Aphrodite*—"what a title—how corrupt the French are—but it gives you a good standard for judging the beauty of a woman's body."[45] (*Aphrodite* appeared in 1897, as did another novel with a significant title, *Demi-Vierge*; it is well to remember, when considering *What is Art?*, that the Tolstoys were then reading such novels—and *Physiologie de l'Amour Moderne*, and *Un Coeur de Femme*. The last of these appealed to Sonia as a subject, a woman in love with two men at the same time, which she herself could have written about: "Why should one love exclude another? And why can one not love and remain pure at the same time?")[46]

Gandhi 1931–1948, Leadership Lost and Retrieved

In this period of his life, Gandhi had a good deal to say about modern art, especially erotic literature, which was in line with what Tolstoy had said in his equivalent phase, and in which indeed he cited Tolstoy. We may also see a similarity between the ways history challenged both men, the 1905 Revolution in Russia paralleling the 1939 war which involved the British Empire. And it is an interesting coincidence that both men clashed most publicly with the representatives of orthodox religion in these equivalent phases. Tolstoy's being excommunicated was paralleled by Gandhi's being denounced by Brahmin pandits—with a good deal of black flag demonstration and even mob violence.

All of these similarities are, however, external and trivial compared with certain others. Of these, perhaps the most striking is the way both men were finally defeated by opponents who repeatedly raised the stakes of conflict, the scale of violence, and were ready to sacrifice self-respect (to sell their souls, in the old-fashioned phrase) to win the fight. In Tolstoy's case I have in mind his wife's voluntary descent into hysteria and madness, and something comparable or collusive in other members of his family; in Gandhi's case, I have in mind Jinnah's insistence on dividing India, at the cost of communal violence, and something comparable in other anti-Gandhian leaders like Savarkar and Ambedkar.

These opponents not only got their ways in the short run, they proved the prophets of peace and reason *wrong*. Gandhi had often said that if he were what he claimed to be, no violence or untruth could persist in his presence. Both he and Tolstoy had said confidently that nonresistance would triumph when offered even by one man against the greatest odds, but their deaths showed they were wrong. Of course it was not really that Tolstoy and Gandhi were stupid or failed in understanding; who was more clear-eyed than they about human weaknesses? Their confidence did not derive from a calculation of the probabilities, but from a faith in a possibility. "When challenged," they said, "men will always follow their better promptings, because otherwise they would debase themselves. When faced with a clear option, when subjected to loving pressure, men will have to rise above themselves, because otherwise they would not even stay where they are, but would fall back into obvious evil." But that second option was always available, though Tolstoy and Gandhi did not dwell upon it (because to do so would not be *sattvic* rhetoric, but *tamasic*). Sonia and Jinnah chose that second option. Her hysteria and his frigidity, and the chaos and darkness and suffering both spread around them, are a good illustration of *"tamas."* To that option, to such behavior, Tolstoy and Gandhi had no resistance to offer except their deaths.

It is also striking that in this period Harilal Gandhi completed his descent into the villain's role of naysayer to his father, like Sonia's to her husband. Harilal came back to his father in 1934, and was welcomed back to the ashram very much a prodigal son. But it was

not long before Gandhi had reason to believe that he had not
changed his ways, and soon after Harilal disappeared again. Once
again his relations with Gandhi are bound to remind us of Sheikh
Mehtab's, this time of the final episode in South Africa. Soon after,
Harilal announced his "conversion to Islam," much to the jubilation
of the Muslim press. Then he reconverted to Hinduism. Meanwhile
his addiction to drink continued and caused great distress to his
children as well as to his parents.

The pressure put upon an uneasy nature by contact with a powerful spirit like Gandhi (and Tolstoy) could provoke convulsive reactions. Both men felt that they had not been wise in their dealings
with wife and son, had been harsh and abrupt, especially early.
And it is not surprising that the world, ever hot on the track of feet
of clay, should have by and large espoused the deniers' cause and
condemned the saints. We of the twentieth century are in love with
antiheroes and think saints inhuman or inhumane. But it is a pitiful
way to be human that makes Sonia Tolstoy or Harilal Gandhi represent humanity while Tolstoy and Gandhi do not. We are drenched
with the spray from a fountain of false compassion, as Gandhi said.

We may also draw a parallel between Gandhi's alternating retirement from the return to political leadership, and Tolstoy's retirement from and return to literature. In the first five or six years of
this period, Gandhi turned to what we might call cultural politics,
taking up the cause of the Untouchables and then that of village
industries, to the neglect of state political issues like independence.
He even formally severed all connections with Congress as he had
done some years before. But when the issue came up of Congressmen participating in the new provincial legislatures constituted by
the 1935 Government of India Act, Gandhi supported their doing so
and gradually returned to the leadership of the party. He effectively
deprived Subhas Chandra Bose of the presidency of Congress in
1939, and in the first years of the war he conducted negotiations
with the government about the kind of support Congress should
give to the war effort.

In 1941 he formally withdrew from leadership and only returned
to anything like political prominence at the very end of his life,
after partition had been agreed on and independence granted. His
final fast of January, 1948, persuaded the Indian government to give
up its claims on money at dispute between it and Pakistan: he was
again active in politics. But on the very day of his death he was

drafting a proposal that his followers should leave the new Parliament and politics, to devote themselves to "constructive work."

What makes this pattern significant for us is the way it expresses an ambivalence in Gandhi about politics which may be compared with Tolstoy's ambivalence about literature. On the one hand, these two men had wonderful gifts for those two modes of action; they had great successes behind them and many solicitations to turn back to do more of the same. And both pleasure and responsibility came with those gifts. On the other hand, both had decided that this was not the heart of their responsibility, their calling, their *dharma*. Indeed, Gandhi partly hated politics, as Tolstoy hated literature. Those modes of action were morally acceptable to them only when accompanied by severe limitations and demanding conditions. So they were forever renouncing them with relief, and forever returning to them—often with some feeling of guilt. (That guilt is demonstrable in Tolstoy; in Gandhi the truth may be more subtle, but he did sometimes accuse himself of an "infatuation" with politics.)

Finally, there is an interesting likeness between the way Russian men of letters turned away from Tolstoy toward symbolism and modernism in the last years of his life, and the way Indian politicians turned away from Gandhi toward statesmanship—toward all the excitement of being the leaders of a powerful new state—in the last years of Gandhi's life. In both cases there was a profusion of personal tributes. Gandhi was the father of the Indian nation, as Tolstoy was the father of Russian literature—and there was sincere grief and even alarm at the thought of losing Gandhi and facing the world without his guidance. But the basic pattern of neglect and repudiation is clear. When he reminded Nehru of the creed he had formulated in *Hind Swaraj* and still held by, Nehru declared that he had always thought it utter nonsense. Nehru's biographer says that "while deriving his power from the Mahatma and the people, [he] used it continuously to protect India not only from communism and fascism, but also from Gandhism itself."[1] On receiving birthday wishes in 1947, the year of independence, Gandhi said: "Where do congratulations come in? It will be more appropriate to say condolences. There is nothing but anguish in my heart."[2] He had refused to attend the independence celebrations on August 15. And the reason was not just the communal violence but the eager turning of Indian ministers to industrialization and militarization. He was, as he said, a "back number." Like Tolstoy, he was "out of date." In both cases, the downward curve of their biological existence was coinciding with that of their moral influence.

The Main Events

Gandhi arrived back from Europe on the 28th of December 1931 to find his followers Nehru and Abdul Ghaffar Khan already in jail, and the viceroy unwilling to negotiate with him. On New Year's Eve, therefore, on his advice, Congress resumed civil disobedience. On January 4 Gandhi himself and Vallabhai Patel were arrested. Congress committees were declared unlawful, as were national schools, *kisan sabhas*, and so on. Thousands of Congress workers were interned or detained, and there were no-tax campaigns in Gujarat, Karnatak, and Bengal.

On August 17, 1932 Ramsay MacDonald, the prime minister, announced the British Government's Communal Awards, which gave the Scheduled Classes (the Untouchables) separate electorates for the legislatures. Gandhi said this would vivisect Hinduism and that he would fast to death if it were enforced. He acknowledged the mistreatment of Untouchables by caste Hindus, but insisted that this was a sin which the *latter* must expiate; if they did not, Hinduism would die. And first Dr. Ambedkar and then the British Government yielded to the pressure of his fast.

Having defeated the government's scheme, Gandhi was left with the responsibility of serving the Untouchables in his own way. He engaged in dialogue with the leaders of orthodoxy about the fundamental teachings of Hinduism and the status and meaning of the *Shastras*, the holy law books. He turned away from party politics toward this social work and so gave a new turn to the national movement which led ultimately to the suspension of civil disobedience.

In October, 1934, he decided to leave congress because he was "obstructing its growth" and because his leaving it would "rid it of hypocrisy." Congressmen apparently had to pretend to Gandhian attitudes and motives which they didn't feel. He felt sure that in their minds progress toward independence was all important, at the cost of even the spinning wheel, which was to him the "emblem of human dignity and equality" as well as "the nation's second lung."[3] Congressmen still objected to his raising the issue of untouchability, and did not share his concern about the means by which their aims

were achieved. So he "chose the path of surrender," as he had before in 1925.[4]

In place of politics he devoted himself to the All-India Village
Industry Association, which he set up to work for the "economic,
moral and hygienic uplift" of the rural population. This concern in
effect displaced the Harijan cause as the primary focus of his attention, although of course work continued on that cause. The cities
had grown up only out of the ruin of the villages and the A.I.V.I.A.
was to return to the villagers what had been cruelly and thought-
lessly snatched from them.[5]

It was in the last quarter of 1934 that Harilal returned and promised to turn over a new leaf. He had been out of his father's sight
for a long time, but not out of mind, inasmuch as so much of Harilal's behavior (drunkenness, embezzling, debauchery) was reported
in the newspapers and a good deal of it was directed at Gandhi or at
other members of the family. He had quarreled with his brothers,
calling them charlatans for emulating their father. He wrote long
letters of denunciation to Gandhi and threatened to send copies to
the press; he did send copies to Gandhi's friends.

Gandhi had toughened his mind, or at least his tone of reference,
against the distress his son caused him. Reporting on his family to a
friend, he said: "Harilal remains drowned in casks of liquor, or say
rather that his belly is always full of them. Thanks to their weight,
how can he shoulder any other burden?"[6]

In September and October 1934 we find letters to Harilal, wel-
coming him back but when, in the spring of 1935, Harilal disappeared again, Gandhi said to Narandas Gandhi: "Leave him to his
fate."[7]

But by one of those curious coincidences of public with private
life, in October 1935 Gandhi's other enemy, Dr. Ambedkar, declared that Untouchables should abandon Hinduism and convert to
some other religion. As soon as he had "thrown his bombshell,"
Gandhi says, Christian missionaries, Muslims, and Sikhs all came
forward to compete for the new converts.[8] Soon Gandhi heard that
Harilal had gotten a job with the municipality at Nagpur by threatening to convert to Islam unless they gave him one. And in May
1936, at a great mosque, the Jamma Masjid in Bombay, he was received as a Muslim and took a new name, Abdullah, in front of a
large congregation, to whom he made a wildly applauded speech.
(A Muslim Brotherhood wired Gandhi, affecting to expect his own

conversion to follow.) Harilal had apparently told his father only three weeks before that he would do anything "to satisfy his greed." And during the winter of 1936 he reconverted to Hinduism. His son Kantilal went to see him but found him such a distressing spectable that he wept and left. Gandhi wrote to Kantilal that these things must not be kept from him: "I must learn to endure unhappiness and get used to it." This was, he said, his punishment for his share in Harilal's sins.[9]

Harilal was seen in many parts of India traveling by train from one big city to another, his hair long enough to brush his shoulders, his face gaunt, toothless, ravaged by drink and tuberculosis. Gandhi and Kasturba one day at a station heard the familiar cries of "Mahatma Gandhi ki-jai" interrupted by "Mata Kasturba ki-jai," and there was Harilal, dressed in rags and carrying an orange which he had just begged from a passer-by and which he presented to his mother, ignoring his father. When the latter spoke to him, he replied: "I have only one thing to say to you—If you are so great, you owe it all to Ba." And yet his brother Devdas says that though self-willed and obstinate, people could not help loving him.[10]

At the time of Kasturba's last sickness, she and Gandhi were imprisoned in the Aga Khan's palace. The sons assembled in nearby Poona. On January 26, 1944, Harilal asked to see her but was refused permission because he was drunk. On February 17 he was admitted and given permission to come again, but he disappeared. On February 21, he reappeared and saw her but was drunk again. Kasturba beat her brow in anguish to see him, and the following day she died. At the time of Gandhi's death, Harilal appeared unannounced at the cremation ground after the ceremony and was taken home by Devdas, but disappeared soon after and died on June 15, less than five months later, in a Bombay hospital.

To return to public affairs, a Government of India Act was passed in July 1935 that set up dyarchy in the center, and legislatures with—apparently—more independence than before, in the provinces (including princely India as well as British). Both Congress and the Muslim League at first decided not to accept these terms, but controversy developed, and Gandhi was called in as an advisor by congress leaders, especially Nehru.

At this time Gandhi read Nehru's autobiography, and claimed to feel closer to him in feelings than ever before, though further away from him in opinions. In the early 1930s, Nehru's letters to Gandhi strike a plaintive note. In May 1934, hearing that he was fasting again, Nehru said: "Religion is not familiar ground to me, and as I have grown older I have definitely drifted away from it."[11] Above all, Gandhi's fasting was something he could not like. "It is hard to be so far from you, and yet it would be harder to be near you. This crowded world is a very lonely place, and you want to make it still lonelier. Life and death matter little, or should matter little. . . . I have loved life—the mountains and the sea, the sun and rain and storm and snow, and animals, and books and art, and even human beings—and life has been good to me. . . ."[12]

In August 1934, he wrote of the shock he had received when he heard of the reasons Gandhi advanced for withdrawing from civil disobedience: "I had a sudden and intense feeling, that something broke inside me, a bond that I had valued very greatly had snapped. I felt terribly lonely in this wide world. I have always felt a little lonely even from childhood up. But a few bonds strengthened me, a few strong supports held me up. That loneliness never went, but it was lessened. But now I felt absolutely alone, left high and dry on a desert island. . . ." He felt that reactionaries dominated congress and that: "Inside or outside the legislature I function as a revolutionary."[13]

Gandhi was not plaintive towards Nehru—that was a crucial difference between them—but he did use a considerable variety of tones with him, all within the general intention of warmth and gaiety. Without falsifying himself, Gandhi found a dozen ways to charm and attach Nehru. In September 1933, for instance, when the Hathising family made an offer for Nehru's sister, Gandhi acted as broker. About the same time, his old friend Saraladevi Chaudhrani asked him to arrange for her son to marry Nehru's daughter.

On December 3 and 4, Margaret Sanger had conversations with Gandhi as part of her world propaganda for birth control. He talked frankly with her and gave her "an intimate glimpse of his private life," according to Mahadev Desai. He told her, for instance, that he had often challenged his wife to lead her own life and that on one occasion he had been tempted to leave her for a woman "of broad cultural education"—that is, Saraladevi Chaudhrani.

Their talks left him exhausted, and only three days later he suffered a breakdown in his health that lasted two months and was very painful to him because it involved an involuntary episode of sexual excitement. He attributed it to the rest from work and pampering with food that doctors had forced on him because of his exhaustion. He was disturbed and disgusted because he had thought that he had, to use his own phrase: "become a 'eunuch' for the sake of this work." It seems impossible not to link this event with the talks that just preceded it.

In the summer of 1936, Gandhi settled in the village of Segaon, near Wardha, at the geographical center of India. This was a very poor community of six-hundred people, mostly Untouchables, with no post office, no medical care, no food supplies beyond the most primitive, and difficult to reach in rainy weather. He tried to improve their lives—with no great success—by methods which we can recognize as very modern though also Gandhian. Of the four hundred adults, he said: "They could put R100,000 into their pockets if only they would work as I ask them. But they won't. They lack cooperation; they do not know the art of intelligent labor. They refuse to learn anything new."[14] One hears there the voice of the modern Gandhi.

At the end of 1936 and beginning of 1937, politics began to intrude upon his attention. Though Congress was agreed about wrecking the new constitution (only divided about whether to do so from inside or outside the legislatures) the party had campaigned hard in the general elections and had got majorities in six out of eleven provinces. Nehru was still against Congressmen taking office, but Gandhi supported Rajagopalachari, Patel, and Prasad, who were for it.

Gandhi acted as mediator between the two parties in Congress—and between Congress and the government—so he returned, in mid-1937, to political leadership. (Many workers in the Gandhi Seva Sangh were bewildered by this turn back to politics and by the recommendation of entry into the councils, which he had so opposed in the past.)

This period of conflict and cooperation with Nehru seems to have introduced a yet warmer phase in their feelings for each other. Nehru, he explained, "mistrusts the human race a little. . . . He therefore places his faith in class struggle."[15] One hears the echo of Gandhi's curious tenderness for Nehru, answering perhaps the latter's plaintiveness. One might object that Gandhi mistrusted the human race much more than a little, and ask why he should feel himself to be so much more serene than Nehru. The explanation seems to be that paradoxical lightness of heart, that "faith," we have before remarked in Gandhi and Tolstoy. They did not "place their faith in the class struggle," because they trusted human nature. They refused to take seriously half the facts of life, by remaining convinced that half of the latter were temporary and mistaken, that the only substance to past, present, and future is the will of God. People like Nehru and Sonia Tolstoy seemed pathetically self-oppressed.

In February 1938, Congress had met at Haripura, under Subhas Chandra Bose, and he was reelected for the Tripuri session in 1939. Gandhi said Bose should choose a new working committee (the old one being Gandhian and therefore antiBosian in its views) and that if the All-India Congress Committee did not approve it, Bose should resign. This is what happened on April 29, 1939, and on May 3 Bose founded a new political party called the Forward Bloc.

Gandhi was enmeshed in a network of hostilities that were getting sharper. Bose was declared ineligible for Congress office for three years, because he had infringed Congress discipline. Jinnah said that Hindu-Muslim unity was foundering on the rock of Congress Fascism—meaning Gandhism—and Savarkar said. "Henceforth our politics will be Hindu politics," and exhorted Hindus to repudiate Congress leadership and reclaim their power. Gandhi sensed the anger in the air. "Each is arming for the fight with the other. The violence that we had harboured in our hearts during the non-cooperation days is now recoiling upon ourselves."[16]

In the summer of 1940—the summer of Germany's conquest of Northwest Europe—there were strikes and demonstrations in Indian cities, marches and trainstoppings in the countryside. The league claimed to have organized 10,000 meetings of Muslims on April 19 alone, and in the Punjab, armed bands of Khaksars, who hid out in mosques, roamed the countryside threatening Hindus. On June 29 Congress finally said it could not agree a hundred percent with Gandhi about nonviolent resistance. Even Rajagopalachari, perhaps his closest supporter in such matters, declared for armed resistance and brought over Patel. But Gandhi persuaded the A.I.C.C. to declare its faith in the principle of nonviolence as a method for India after independence.

The A.I.C.C. asked Gandhi to lead individual civil disobedience and in September he gave the word; one leader at a time was to be arrested; the only issue raised was to be freedom of speech—freedom to speak against the war. On October 1, 1941, Vinoba Bhave made the first such demonstration and was arrested. Nehru, who was to have been the second, was arrested before he could speak. By May 1942, 14,000 were in jail. The restriction of the issues to free speech, and the small scale and dignity of the proceedings, made it less spectacular than other campaigns. Gandhi refused to let Bose's Forward Bloc participate in the action because they were not non-violent, and he expected prospective *satyagrahis* to keep a log book of the constructive work they were were doing.

Japan's entry into the war in December 1941 put India into much more immediate jeopardy. Gandhi wanted India to offer only passive resistance to any invaders, and Mirabehn went to the areas that would be first affected, to make plans. But Nehru persuaded him to agree to accept both defense by the British and even support by the Indians (as free allies) for help to Russia and China. The civil disobedience campaign was suspended after a year's operation, and the Working Committee accepted Gandhi's resignation from leadership.

In 1942, he demanded that the British "Quit India," because "This unnatural prostration of a great nation—it is neither 'nations' nor 'peoples'—must cease if the victory of the Allies is to be ensured." He foresaw unwillingly but unflinchingly that a free India would be militarist itself. "I expect that with the existence of so many martial races in a free India, national policy will incline towards a militarism of a modified character."[17]

In August 1942, he was arrested and confined in the Aga Khan's palace together with Kasturba, Sarojini Naidu, Mahadev Desai, and others. (Six days later Desai died and in 1944, Kasturba died.) He was allowed no access to the press and was in general exiled much more completely than in his other imprisonments. His health also suffered more. After his release in 1944, he was found to be suffering from malaria, amoebic dysentery, and acute anaemia.

In 1946, partition was agreed to, and the Congress leaders began preparing themselves for office. In *Hind Swaraj*, Gandhi reminded Nehru of the plans *he* had made for a free India. "We can realize truth and nonviolence only in the simplicity of village life, and this simplicity can best be found in the charkha and all that the charkha connotes."[18] But Nehru firmly refused to consider them. "I do not understand why a village should necessarily embody truth and nonviolence . . . [men need] comfortable up-to-date houses where they can lead a cultured existence."[19] In 1947, there was both communal violence and enormous migrations of Hindus from territory that would be ruled by Muslims, and vice versa.

In England, Churchill said, on September 8, 1947: "The fearful massacres which are occurring in India are no surprise to me. We are, of course, only at the beginning of the horrors and butcheries, perpetrated upon one another with the ferocity of cannibals by

races gifted with the capacities for the highest culture, and who had
for generations lived side by side in general peace under the broad,
tolerant and impartial rule of the British Crown and Parliament."[20]
From his point of view, Gandhi was to blame, along with those
Englishmen who had listened to him.

The Great Campaigns

In this sixteen-year period we can see three substantial and mutually independent campaigns: Gandhi's fight against untouchability,
launched in 1932; his revival of village culture via village industries, launched two years later; and his Noakhali campaign of peace
and forgiveness after the communal rioting of 1946. (We can treat
his 1947 fast in Calcutta as a pendant to the last.) That classification
draws attention to a gap of at least ten years, 1936–1947, to which
no campaign is attributed. Of course the work begun earlier continued, and of course Gandhi continued to invent new strategies and
respond to new situations. The late 1930s saw his return to party
politics, when he persuaded congressmen to take part in the new
provincial legislatures and guided them in that work rather than
conducting satyagraha. Then the outbreak of war brought the prophet of nonviolence a number of problems other politicians did not
have to face, and to know that he could not carry most of his followers with him had a semiparalyzing effect upon Gandhi, however much he might protest that he spoke and acted for himself alone.

His campaign of individual satyagraha in 1941 was striking in its
style. One after another, congress leaders "offered satyagraha" individually, by delivering speeches attacking Britain's part in the war
and they were arrested. Gandhi himself did not provoke arrest and
maintained friendly relations with the viceroy so as not to embar-
rass the British Government in its hour of crisis. This could be
called "classical" satyagraha, marked as it was by restraint, decorum,
and gravity. It was an epitome of much that had been done elsewhere, but this time in a purer style and better taste. "This is to be
an example of unadulterated nonviolence," Gandhi said.[21] Because
of that classical quality it might be compared with "The Death of
Ivan Ilych" among Tolstoy's works in the equivalent sixteen-year
period. But a better comparison might be with Resurrection because
of a certain dullness of effect compared with the great novels or the
great campaigns. There is something as it were theoretical, and only
theoretically superior, about both. The one was dull politically, the

other aesthetically, because the politics and the aesthetics had been subdued, subjected to moral-spiritual controls.

There followed the "Quit India" campaign of 1942, and its weaknesses were opposite in character to those of individual *satyagraha*. This was a mass movement, it was not under Gandhi's control, and it soon ceased to be peaceful. Gandhi was arrested as soon as he had launched it on August 8, and was thrust into seclusion in the Aga Khan's Palace, while the other leaders went elsewhere. He felt more effectively isolated there than he had in other jails.

And when he came out of jail in 1944, he found everyone's attention concentrated first on the question of partition, where there was nothing for him to do but accept defeat—that is, to accept the Muslims' demand for some kind of separation; and then on that of the "transfer of power"; which was of no interest to him except insofar as this too involved his defeat—that is, it demonstrated his disciples' eagerness to modernize, industrialize, and militarize India. These questions of course brought him many claims on his attention but no attractive courses of action.

He was isolated and impotent, and knew it. After a meeting with Congress leaders about partition (on May 1, 1947, at the Sweepers' Colony in Delhi) he said: "They call me a Mahatma, but I tell you I am not even treated by them as a sweeper." And to the doctor who operated on Manu's appendix and who had said he must rest because the people needed his services: "Neither the people nor those in power have any use for me."[22] Mountbatten said later the Congress leaders egged him on to override or overpersuade Gandhi about partition. "I had the most curious feeling that they were all behind me, in a way, against Gandhi. They were encouraging me to challenge him, in a sense, on their behalf."[23] Finding no support, Gandhi doubted his own judgment and said nothing at the crucial moment when the plan for partition was publicly announced.

It was not until the terrible intercommunal violence broke out in 1946 that there was a job for Gandhi to do. On August 16 of that year, the Muslims of Calcutta undertook direct action in response to Jinnah's appeal; Jinnah said that month, in Bombay: "We shall have India divided or we shall have India destroyed." This was the signal for that intensification of violence that both offered Gandhi his opportunity and caused his death.[24] Thus the complexities of the political situation—and the animus of his rivals—often frustrated Gandhi's efforts and reduced him to little more than a bystander as far as the issues being debated went.

Let us then describe the three main campaigns, when he did find a way to act. Gandhi showed himself deeply concerned about the problem of untouchability all through his life in India, from 1915 on. And at the Round Table Conference in 1931 it became clear that the problem was a major and pressing one, when the British, and many Indians, proposed to give minorities separate electorates, to save them from being overborne by the Hindu majority and from getting no representation. Gandhi was willing to have seats in legislatures reserved for Muslims and for Sikhs, but not for Untouchables. They were, he insisted, Hindus.

As soon as he returned to India and before the Communal Award was announced, he wrote a series of directions for "Temple-Entry Satyagraha," in which he defined the problem as essentially religious. First of all, Untouchables must be welcomed in Hindu places of worship. Belief in temples and temple worship were necessary preconditions for *satyagrahis* engaging in such campaigns, although their belief must of course be enlightened. *Satyagrahis* were not to force actual barricades, and formal legislation was, as usual, to follow, not precede, the conversion of public opinion. Thus the changes were to be a religious reform coming from inside Hinduism; touchable reformers should lead such *satyagraha*.

In August the prime minister announced the award which gave Untouchables separate electorates, and in September Gandhi began his fast in protest. He got support from Dr. Bhagwan Das and from Acharya A. B. Dhruva for his contention that the Shastras did not enjoin untouchability. But he did not proceed by scholarly argument about the holy texts of Hinduism, which he always admitted he did not know. (Tolstoy *did* argue about the equivalent texts of Christianity.) His argument was that truly sanatana Hinduism must have always been dynamic, growing and changing to meet new social conditions, must have been a lived faith which was at root a lived morality. The *shastras* must have been ancillary; compiled to sustain and regulate the already accepted, intuitively known, first principles of morality.[25] When Hinduism became rigid and rule-defined and book-derived, it lost its natural health. (This was Tolstoy's theory of religion and his justification for preferring the sects' heresy—just as heresy—over the Church's static orthodoxy.)

But this was also the time when he began his second great campaign, on behalf of village industries. In the last quarter of 1934 he retired from Congress and set up the All-India Village Industries Association (the A.I.V.I.A.) for "the economic, moral and hygienic uplift of the rural population.[26] Soon it was serving 5,300 villages and supporting, for instance, 200,000 spinners. Gandhi said that the villages had become untouchable and invisible to the cities, so that just by fixing city Indians' gaze upon the villages the campaign did a great deal. Nai Talim, Gandhi's basic education, which excluded the teaching of English (and so could offer matriculation in seven instead of eleven years) and included manual work along with academic studies, became an integral part of the village program.

This was a very direct form of resistance to technocracy and industrialization, which he, like Tolstoy, thought always exploitative. "They say that the control over these hidden forces of nature enables every American to have thirty three slaves. Repeat the process in India and every Indian will be thirty-three times a slave."[27] Of a Congress meeting he said: "We sit here under the blaze of electric lights, at the expense of the poor." In the first months of the war he said that Europe's cities, monster factories, and huge armaments were so intimately related one could not exist without the other. The erstwhile village republics of India were the nearest approach to a civilization based on nonviolence.

Besides spinning and weaving, tanning, oil pressing, soap making, beekeeping, hand husking of rice and hand grinding of wheat, the making of paper and of gur (like molasses) were recommended. Gandhi, as always, went into great detail, both technological and economic. He did not expect townsmen to buy these things, but other villagers, who amounted after all, to 90 percent of the population. Local industries, supplying local markets, were what he wanted: "Large-scale, centralized industries in India . . . must mean starvation of millions."[28] He had scientific tests performed to prove that rice when polished lost Vitamin B along with its pericarp, that cow's milk was more nutritious than buffalo's milk, and that gur was 33 percent more nutritious than sugar. He recommended adding raw green leaves to the villager's diet, and said that everyone must become a scavenger, offering detailed prescriptions for digging lavatory trenches, six inches wide by one foot deep. He and his disciples cleaned up the village of Sindi, near Wardha.

The A.I.V.I.A., he said, could become a living link between the intelligentsia and the illiterate masses. It could turn city dwellers into real helpers and servants of the villagers. If it was the students he thought should work with Harijans, it was the middle class he invited to carry the message of the wheel to the villages—because it was they who had bartered away the economic independence of

India for a mess of pottage. He himself now wrote with a reed pen and *swadeshi* ink on *swadeshi* paper.

Of all Gandhi's campaigns, that which began on January 1, 1947 in Noakhali may be the most beautiful and the most purely spiritual, inasmuch as it was directed primarily against the violence the Hindu villagers there had suffered and against the threat of more violence on their part. Noakhali is a jigsaw of islands in the water-logged delta of the Ganges and the Brahmaputra, forty miles square and inhabited by 2.5 million people, 80 percent of whom were Muslim. They had rioted against their Hindu neighbors. The villages were separated by canals and streams, which were crossed by hand-poled ferries or by rope or bamboo bridges. Single-file paths, often jagged with pebbles and roots, led through mango orchards and palm groves, by scum-slicked ponds with geese and ducks, and through jungle to the next village.

On January 1, 1947, Gandhi, who had been staying in the village of Srirampur for a few days, announced that for the next seven weeks he would walk barefoot from village to village living on charity, with four companions. This would be his "last and greatest experiment" to "rekindle the lamp of neighbourliness."[29] He would visit forty-seven villages and cover 116 miles.

As they set out each day, his little group, going single file, sang Tagore's song: "If they answer not your call, walk alone, walk alone." In each village he begged for food and shelter, preferably from a Muslim, and went from door to door till he found it. He persuaded two village leaders, one Hindu, one Muslim, to live together and both to vow to fast to death if the other condoned communal violence. He inspected latrines and wells and suggested improvements: "The lessons which I propose to give you during my tour are how you can keep the village water and yourselves clean," he would tell the villagers, "what use you can make of the earth, of which your bodies are made; how you can obtain the life-force from the infinite sky over your heads; how you can reinforce your vital energy from the air which surrounds you; how you can make proper use of sunlight."[30]

At first he was met with courtesy and indeed reverence, by Muslims as well as Hindus. But later Muslim children were driven indoors away from Gandhi, a Muslim spat in his face, the bridges he was to cross were sabotaged, the trees bore slogans like "Go for your own good," and some paths had glass and shards and human turds placed on them for his bare feet. Whole villages had been

burned down, women raped, many forcibly converted or forcibly
fed beef. There was bitter hatred, legends of vendetta and communal violence. In many places all he could do was listen to the tales
of horror, see the ruined buildings and lives, and then, rather than
console, exhort them to courage and forgiveness: "I have come to
Bengal not to give consolation but to bring courage."[31] But he did
console, by the closeness of his attention and the gentleness of his
presence. One feels the difference between him and Nehru when
one reads Nehru writing to him: "In quality or lack of it there is
little to choose, to my mind . . . [between Hindu and Muslim riot-
ers]. They all represent utter degradation and depravity."[32] These
things drove Nehru to anger (and of course to horror); one hears of
him seizing a *lathi* and attacking Hindu rioters in Delhi.

Gandhi had some ineffective police protection but he eluded it.
He was accompanied by his two young grand nieces, Manu and
Abha, and his Bengali-speaking secretary, Nirmal Kumar Bose. Bose
was a young academic anthropologist, living with Gandhi for the
first time, who had come to Gandhi via Tolstoy and Kropotkin. The
girls massaged Gandhi's feet with a stone, prepared his food, looked
after his clothes, and so on. And other people often came to see
him, including journalists and photographers. There are many pictures of the white-clad party going in single file along narrow village paths, and in yet another village looking at ruined houses and
mutilated corpses.

Perhaps because it was so immediately picturesque and unequivocally spiritual (lacking the aggressive political element of the Dandi
March), the feeling of the Noakhali Pilgrimage is closer to sentimental piety than some other of the campaigns. And yet there was
another component to it; but that has undermined its effect for
many people and done more than anything else to make Gandhi
seem a whited sepulchre. That was the sexual scandal which attached to Gandhi there for the first time. It was publicly suppressed
but of course a circle of people in the Gandhian movement knew
about it at the time, and that circle spread out rapidly.

The scandal was that Gandhi would ask the young girls with him
to share his bed. He suffered from shivering fits at night, and he
wanted them to warm him; but it was also a test of his and their
purity. Abha in fact kept her clothes on when she did so, so the
scandal attached particularly to Manu. She had told Gandhi just before they came to Naokhali that she had never felt sexual impulses,
and he felt purely motherly feelings toward her. He therefore felt

that they could practice mutual chastity even in naked contact and both would be strengthened. But his friends thought he was simply infatuated with her.

The matter came to a head partly because the young secretary, Bose, protested to Gandhi against what he was doing. He had found (not that they were hiding, but he was apparently unprepared for what he saw) Gandhi and Manu in bed together on December 12. But it is important to realize that his objection was not that Gandhi was indulging his sensual appetites. No one suggested that in print, and I would guess that no one who knew and understood Gandhi has even thought it. What Bose objected to was the strain imposed upon the girls by so complete a flouting of ordinary propriety, plus—a related matter—the emotional hysteria of mutual jealousy, competitiveness, and possessiveness about Gandhi.

It is, I think, possible that Bose himself was speaking out of his own involvement in that group hysteria (between him and Sushila Nayar, who had herself on occasion slept with Gandhi, there developed a sharp irritation) but on the other hand common sense would certainly endorse him. Any hesitation to agree must base itself finally upon the feeling that this was not a common sense matter; that these girls, quite apart from Gandhi himself, were most uncommon creatures in their relation to him.

From Noakhali Gandhi went on to Bihar briefly, and then Calcutta. Gandhi had intended to be in Noakhali for August 15, 1947, Independence Day, but the authorities were very nervous about what would happen in Calcutta, the greatest trouble spot for communal rioting after the Punjab. First Mountbatten and then Shaheed Suhrawardy, the Muslim mayor of the city, asked him to be there to stop riots. He at first agreed to be there for two extra days on his way to Noakhali at the prompting of Mohammad Usman, a former mayor. But then Suhrawardy flew in from Karachi and begged him to stay longer. Suhrawardy was a prime example of the corrupt politician; forty-seven years old and a pillar of the Muslim League, he was a gourmand and womanizer who had made a fortune selling on the black market grain intended for the starving. He had a private army of *goondas* who clubbed his rivals into silence, and he had licenced the riots of Direct Action Day by telling his followers that the police would not interfere.

Gandhi agreed to come, on two conditions: that the Muslims of Noakhali pledge safety to the Hindus there, and that Suhrawardy come to live with him day and night, unprotected, in a Calcutta slum. He arrived on August 13 at 151 Beliaghata Road (according to *Freedom at Midnight* a decayed Tennessee Williams-style mansion). It stood in a Hindu district but on the border of a Muslim slum (Miabagan) which had just been the scene of raids and a massacre. People were awaiting him with cries of traitor and a shower of bottles and stones as he stepped out of the car. The Hindus accused him of being interested in the Muslims. "You wish to do me ill and so I am coming to you," he said.[33] And when Suhrawardy joined him there, there was a barrage of rocks against the house. Meanwhile in Lahore, in the Punjab, Hindus and Sikhs were isolated in the Old City and water supplies were cut off; women and children coming out with pails were butchered; geysers of sparks arose from blazes in six places. And in Amritsar, nearby, the Number Ten Down Express came in on Independence Day with nothing aboard but murdered bodies and the sign: "This is our Independence gift to Nehru and Patel." Calcutta should, by every calculation, have been worse, but by the 15th it was peaceful.

A band of girls, both Muslim and Hindu, had walked through the city at night to come to Gandhi in the morning, and that afternoon thirty-thousand people attended his prayer meeting. When Suhrawardy admitted to an angry crowd his responsibility for the Muslim Direct Action, their mood reversed itself and they cheered him. He and Gandhi toured the city by car, and there were cries of "Gandhiji, you have saved us." Later there were crowds of up to a million for his prayer meeting. But on August 31, Hindus brought him a bandaged man whom they claimed had been attacked by Muslims and demanded from Gandhi the lives of all the Muslims in his house. Gandhi tried to throw himself among them and be killed. On September 1 there were more riots. Hindus led by RSS men (of the Rashtra Swayamsevak Sangh) attacked the Muslim slums, and there was a murder with grenades on Beliaghata Road which Gandhi went to inspect minutes after it occurred. That night he decided to fast to death unless the communal leaders swore to prevent any more violence. He lived on water and bicarbonate of soda. The next morning he was missing one heartbeat in four and his voice was a whisper. Almost immediately there was an effect. A band of twenty-seven *goondas* came to beg his forgiveness; then those responsible for the grenade murder brought him their weapons and asked for punishment—he sent them to a Muslim quarter, to take up its defense.

The leaders worked out a joint declaration and on September 4 he broke his fast. Suhrawardy knelt at his feet weeping, to offer him the first drink of lemon juice. And in fact there was no more violence in Calcutta. Rajagopalachari said: "Gandhi has achieved many things, but there has been nothing, not even independence, which is so truly wonderful as his victory over evil in Calcutta."[34] And Mountbatten wrote: "In the Punjab we have 55,000 soldiers and large-scale rioting on our hands. In Bengal, our force consists of one man and there is no rioting . . . [I] pay tribute to my One Man Boundary Force."[35] This is an example of history making a pun with the idea of force.

CLIMAX

The Two Deaths

What is most important to us is the manner or the design of the two deaths and first of all the agency of other people in them. Who killed Tolstoy? Who killed Gandhi? Although we cannot call Tolstoy's death a murder, and although, in Gandhi's case, we cannot treat the actual murderer's responsibility as final—we cannot but look behind his arm to another man's brain—yet we must be struck by the sense in which each one died by the will of other people, people deeply involved with him, long beholden to him, and once his close comrades or in love with him. The deaths were the result of convulsive reactions, in people of unstable virtues, to the contact with powerful spirits.

G. B. Shaw said, when he heard that Gandhi had been assassinated, that it showed how dangerous it is to be good; and Tolstoy and Gandhi were indeed good men, holy men, saints, if these words have any meaning today. But they were saints of somewhat different kinds. Tolstoy was a saint of sacrifice, yielding, and weakness— of passive resistance or nonresistance to evil; Gandhi was a saint of strength and severity—of *satyagraha* or firmness in truth. Within Tolstoy's domestic life, which was the main arena of spiritual struggle for him, for thirty years he kept yielding to his wife until the basis of his honor, his personality, and his relations with others was undermined. When, in 1890, some Yasnaya Polyana peasants were persecuted for tree felling because Sonia had Tolstoy's power of attorney, his feelings were outraged, but instead of fighting her he gave her total control of the property henceforth. He lived the life of a hypocrite and left undone the work to which he felt called. In the last year of his life, for instance, he gave up his plan to go to Stockholm to deliver a speech against militarism because she threatened to poison herself if he went—she finally said she would go with him but such a trip would mean either his death or hers. Within Gandhi's last year, he too yielded whenever he was not sure of himself, of his political truth; he let Nehru set India on the track that led to industrialization and militarism. But he was not compromised by Nehru's policy and was taking countermeasures when he died. While within the field of his personal relations, which assumes special importance when one estimates his spirituality, he was often hard on those nearest to him.

To distinguish them, we may use the terms of Tolstoy's late tale, "Father Sergei," in which the brilliant and ambitious man who sets out to become a saint, to achieve perfect humility as the finest flower of spirituality, is contrasted with the meanly gifted, life-defeated, and self-ashamed woman, Pashenka, who never dreamed of being a saint any more than of being anything else great or famous. Both became saints by going their opposite routes, but Pashenka, having no life plan or purpose, merely through loving and yielding to her husband, her children, her neighbors—to everyone with whom chance brought her in contact. Both Tolstoy and Gandhi were like Sergei, and of the two, Tolstoy was originally the more so, but he became, in his relations with his wife, a Pashenka.

Secondly we must be interested in the source of each death in the comparatively early experience and self-determination of the two men—to be specific, in each one's choice of a life activity other than religion. In Tolstoy's case, this was his marriage and what went with that, his art; in Gandhi's case, it was his politics, and the direction of a national-liberation movement. Tolstoy's death was a domestic tragedy, Gandhi's was a political one.

Of course there was something quasireligious in the intense significance attributed both to Tolstoy's marriage, which was the climactic act of his cult of erotic and life values, and to Gandhi's kind of nationalist politics, which brought with it a nineteenth-century hagiography of saints and martyrs like Pym and Hampden, Lincoln and Gladstone, Mazzini and Garibaldi, and a great creed of freedom and patriotism, independence and honor. Both eroticism and nationalism were, moreover, allied to the two men's religion proper. That is, they were alternate forms of resistance to the spread of the modern-world system and its capitalist ideology. Tolstoy's marriage was allied to art, education, agriculture, and Gandhi's politics was allied to handicrafts, education, cultural revival. But both marriage and politics were also, at crucial points, the enemies of spiritual religion. In Tolstoy's case, this enmity became very obvious in the domestic melodrama of his last years—especially in his wife's behavior. In Gandhi's case there was a series of occasions when he said that if he had to choose between truth and India, he would always choose the former, and in 1947 he showed a dismay, an agony comparable with Tolstoy's, over what was happening politically. But "India" was a more multiform reality to him than marriage was to Tolstoy, and Gandhi could always find some form of it which was not in conflict with truth, so the warfare in his life was muffled.

Looking at the matter from their own point of view, one is bound to conclude that both erotic marriage and nationalist politics were distracting illusions for Tolstoy and Gandhi—illusions shimmering over the marshlands to the right or left of their straight and narrow path. And not only for them; these were two of the great maya-forms of nineteenth-century culture. But much truth was involved with those illusions, and the word must certainly not be taken to imply that there were other cultural ideas available which were true by contrast. The Tolstoy-Gandhi point of view was in one sense anticultural, and so irreconcilable with all social values, and so could not but be betrayed by an alliance with any of them. This adds another strand of meaning to the two deaths, which in a sense resulted from pursuing those illusions.

This is not to say that they died tragically only because they strayed from the path of pure religion. One could more plausibly argue the opposite—that it was the religion which caused the tragedy; but in the manner and design of the deaths one strand of connection, if not causation, leads us to that duality, that irreconcilability, as a source. Nor is it to say that they would have done better to concentrate upon purely religious truths, like the contemplative saints among their contemporaries, like Ramana Maharishi in India. They are perhaps the great saints they are because of the variety of their interests and ambitions. Gandhi could hardly have taught us so much if he had not tried to implement his religion in terms of politics. Finally, we must beware of treating Gandhi and Tolstoy as absolutely similar figures from this point of view; for Tolstoy did *not* try to implement his spirituality in terms of marriage. In his case the marriage came before the religious conversion, and he felt the two to be in mutual opposition. (If anything in Tolstoy's case could be compared with Gandhi's politics it would be not his marriage but his late experiments in new kinds of art and thought.)

The Death Lines

The point to establish is that their deaths issued from a long sequence of events which was rooted originally in their clovenness. We have then a problem in choosing the point to call the origin of each death-line. It would be logical to name 1862, when Tolstoy married, or 1906, when Gandhi first clashed with Savarkar and entered into competition for the exiles' leadership. But it would not be feasible to review the events of forty or fifty years in this conclusion.

It would also make sense to choose 1897 for Tolstoy because of the letter he wrote to his wife on June 8 of that year in which he said he finally must leave her. He acknowledged his inconsistency in now blaming her for being what he himself had made her; this guilt was the reason why he had for so long not left her. "To make you change your life, your habits in which I have trained you, I could not. . . ."[1] But he was now determined to leave: "the chief thing is that just as the Hindus, when close on 60 [as he was] go away into the forest, so every religious old man longs to devote the final years of his life to . . . [God]."[2]

And it would make sense to choose 1941 as an equivalent date for Gandhi, when the last act of his tragedy opened, because of the ominous communal riots in the spring of that year, in Dacca, Ahmedabad, Bombay, and Bihar, that Gandhi describes as something new, as a rehearsal for civil war[3] and as a miniature civil war.[4]

But it seems best, finally, to concentrate on the last year in each life—1909–1910 in Tolstoy's case and 1947–1948 in Gandhi's—looking backward from the events of those years to some degree. We look backward for an explanation, not of each man's death by itself but of each tragic scene as a whole, looking for the development of the complex tragic event. For these were not literal murders, they were deaths, each of which issued from and happened to a group of people. Death was in the air between them—there was an exacerbation of feeling, a sense of the intolerable, a desire to kill or be killed—and the literal event could have happened to another individual. But it was natural that the most eminent among them attracted the lightning.

Tolstoy and Gandhi had begun early to speak of death. In Tolstoy's case, at least since the time of the Arzamas episode, in Gandhi's case, at least since the beginning of *satyagraha*. In their last years they often wanted to die. "I am a spent bullet," said Gandhi, "I may last a year or two more"; and Tolstoy said: "I have a criminal desire for death."[5] They had indeed begun to practice death in their living as well as to desire it as an end to living. It was the energy with which they dived down toward self-extinction, pressing into imaginative depths of dissolution most men never enter, that lifted them up again over other people's stature. They practiced the death of appetite and ego in their physical asceticism and in a dozen disciplines of mind and imagination. They died daily and eagerly; it was in consequence that they lived another kind of resurrected life. This both soothed and irritated other people in alternating and escalating waves of impulse. One sees that clearly in the group reactions to Gandhi's fasts. In Calcutta in 1947 he was pelted with stones when he arrived, with rose petals a few days later; in Delhi groups publicly chanted "Let Gandhi die," and then knelt at his bier sobbing and groaning.

And in Sonia Tolstoy's diary for July 4, 1910,[6] amid the most insane outbursts of anger against her husband, we find her agreeing with Lev (the most murderous of Tolstoy's sons) that there was an unearthly beauty to Tolstoy's face now, and wishing that she too could see the vanity of all earthly things. Lev himself, even on his best behavior in his book about Tolstoy long after 1910, creates death images of his father full of ambivalent pathos. He says he had dreamed of Tolstoy lying on the ground, his beard in the mud, being trampled by a murderous crowd.[7] This comes only a few pages after he describes finding his mother, his champion, lying at the foot of one of the lime trees in the Yasnaya Polyana avenue, feeling herself spurned by Tolstoy.[8] And of course these images blend with others—Lev finding his father alone in an empty room prostrating himelf before an icon, while the life of the family proceeded a few feet away. And with more political anger and violence:

How many times, even some years before the death of my father, did the muzhiks of Yasnaya itself say to me, in a tone that was not only envious but was also tinged with hatred: 'Yes, your father talks a good deal, but just look round you for a moment! All the land round us belongs to him or to one or another of his children which is the same thing! We are shut in on every side.'[9]

Such violence was indeed in the air at Yasnaya Polyana. The youngest daughter, Sasha Tolstoy, told Dr. Makovitski that their birches would be used one day to hang the Tolstoys from. And when Chertkov found that a society lady had come calling with a gun which she left in the hall, he jokingly hid it in her pocket wrapped up in the pamphlet "Thou Shalt Not Kill." In the summer of 1909 Tolstoy heard a peasant woman call out: "Look at the devils eating," as the Tolstoys sat at breakfast outdoors.[10]

But there was also a personal struggle between him and his sons. In 1907 Lev wrote an article attacking his father as "a baneful influence largely responsible for the present revolutionary spirit in Russia."[11] And in 1905, Andrei had said. "If I were not his son, I would hang him." On April 25, 1906, Tolstoy recorded a dream of a son figure he was trying to drive away. Tolstoy was conscious both that he was using violence and that he was not succeeding. In the dream, the son started pushing Tolstoy off his chair with his backside; Tolstoy at first ignored this and then jumped up and swung the chair at him so that the son ran away. Tolstoy was then overcome with shame and sure he had not done it on purpose. It was a shame dream, for other people could see what was happening.

But above all it was his and Gandhi's embracing of death which provoked those who were dedicated to life. It is not surprising that those who were in contact with them tried to turn their own weapon against them—they spoke of dying and of killing themselves. When Gandhi fasted, his opponents often fasted against him; when he campaigned against untouchability, the Brahmins lay down in front of his car, halting his self-sacrifice with their own. And even in the first months of their marriage, Sonia said she would like to kill Tolstoy and replace him with someone exactly similar; and some faint echo of that high-spirited conceit lingers around her grotesque behavior in 1909-1910. There is even a sense in which the same could be said of Godse, Gandhi's assassin. Gandhi had been his hero; he had worked for the reform of caste and the elimination of untouchability. "My respect for the Mahatma was deep and deathless"[12] he said in the dock; he had gone to jail with other Gandhians before he met Savarkar. He claimed to have studied Gandhi as much as Savarkar.

And the killing in the air was not aimed exclusively at Tolstoy and Gandhi. Sonia often threatened to kill Chertkov. On July 24, 1910, she wrote in her diary: "I want to drive a knife into his fat body in order to free Lev Nikolaevich's soul from his harmful influence. . . . We shall see which of us conquers if he begins war on me. My weapon is death."[13] In the latter quotation, the "he" is Tolstoy, and the death is unspecified because it didn't matter who, so long as someone died. Godse and his friends planned to assassinate Jinnah, and then the Nizam of Hyderabad, before they turned to Gandhi.

Sonia wrote in her diary for June 20, 1910: 'I have become unnecessary to him. He puts the Chertkovs first. I must create *my own* personal life, or my own *personal* death."[14] And six days later: "Yes, if there is a devil, he is certainly incarnate in Chertkov who has ruined our life. My children, and you people who worship Lev Nikolaevich, know all of you that he has *killed* me."[15] And she was determined to evoke an answering violence in the others. When anger flashed in Tolstoy's eyes at one of her provocations, she said: "Ah, that is what you really are," and she noted "he was immediately silent."[16] Her greatest triumph was to draw Chertkov into the system of anger. On June 30 she says he has threatened to expose her in a book after Tolstoy's death, as Froude exposed Carlyle's wife. On July 27, Tolstoy writes that Chertkov has said Sonia will get him certified insane or incapable by bringing in politically reactionary (Black Hundred) doctors. Tolstoy refused to believe this and wrote to Biriukov three days later that Chertkov was drawing him into more quarrels.

The Assassins

Let us first consider Gandhi's assassins. Nathuram Godse was thirty-eight and his main coconspirator, Narayan Apte, was thirty-four, in 1948. Both were Chitpavan Brahmins (like Savarkar himself) and members of the Hindu Rashtra Dal, founded by Savarkar in 1942 as the secret society at the heart of the Rashtra Swayamsevak Sangh, which was the paramilitary arm of the Hindu Mahasabha. All the members of the Hindu Rashtra Dal had to be Chitpavan Brahmins and took an oath of loyalty to Savarkar as dictator.

The two men were quite different superficially. Apte dressed in smart British clothes, drank whisky, ate luxuriously, and was a womanizer. While Godse was puritanical, hypersensitive, afraid of women. He was, according to Manohar Malgonkar, brought up as a girl, to ward off evil fate, because his older brothers had all died. "Born in a devotional Brahmin family," he said in the dock, "I instinctively came to revere Hindu religion, Hindu history, and Hindu culture."[17] He was the theoretician among the conspirators, the intellectual. He was taught tailoring by American missionaries but long found no practical career for himself.

In 1929, however, his family moved to Ratnagiri, which was Savarkar's place of exile within India, once he returned from the Andamans. In 1929 the latter was forty-six, and, according to Malgonkar, "a soft, bald man, with the face of a family priest."[18] Collins and Lapierre speak of his drawn and sunken cheeks and cruel and sensual lips. Godse made acquaintance with him and soon became his secretary. In 1937 the new Bombay government of Congressmen (installed, to some degree, by Gandhi) released Savarkar from his sentence and he returned to Poona, with Godse still his secretary. Poona, 120 miles from Bombay, was the ancestral city of the Chitpavan Brahmins, the city of Tilak and his tradition of Maharashtran nationalism. Poona was where a bomb had been thrown at Gandhi in 1934. Savarkar became twice president of the Hindu Mahasabha, membership one million, whose doctrine was explicit Hindu imperialism. He taught that all but Hindus should leave India, that Gandhi had usurped Tilak's position and perverted his mission, that nonviolence was a coward's philosophy.

In 1944 a new newspaper, *Agrani* (the Forerunner), appeared in Poona. Its first issue contained a portrait of Savarkar, with Godse as editor and Apte as manager. In 1946, when communal hatred became widespread and respectable, this paper began to prosper. Suppressed in 1947 for calling for a Black Day of protest, it reopened under a different title immediately. (The Black Day was one of Savarkar's Hindu-nationalist demonstrations against the partition of India, against Muslims and their friends—a Hindu equivalent for Jinnah's Day of Direct Action.) Its last issue would carry the news of the assassination perpetrated by its editor.

Why did Godse kill Gandhi? In the name of "sound nation building." He decided it was a dangerous error "to imagine that the bulk of mankind is, or ever can become, capable of scrupulous adherence to these lofty principles . . ." of Gandhism. He saw that Gandhi had "developed a subjective mentality" and showed "childish insanities and obstinacies," and so his existence "should be brought to an end immediately."[19] Putting it another way, he said that Gandhism meant Muslim rule over all India.

Apte had had plans to blow up Jinnah and his assembly in Delhi, to blow up a Pakistan ammunition train, and to lead a commando raid into Hyderabad. His violence was more multidirectional. In 1946 he already knew one of the other conspirators-to-be, Vishnu Karkare, an illiterate but political Brahmin who ran a boarding house in Ahmednaggar. Karkare and six other Hindu Mahasabha workers had gone to Noakhali at the same time as Gandhi did. They too were rallying the Hindus there, with their own message of militant Hinduism, opening Vir Savarkar relief centers, and wearing chain mail under their shirts for protection. Karkare had returned humiliated by the failure of their efforts, which were counteracted by Gandhi's, and talking of revenge.

He went to see Godse and Apte, who already also knew Digambar Badge, who was to become the State's witness in the trial after taking part in the conspiracy. Badge ran a storehouse of weapons (he sold chain mail and tiger claws as well as pistols and knives) and supplied the conspirators with the means of assassination. He and his servant Shankar Kistayya had little of the political idealism of Godse and Apte. Shankar, who was supposed in an early plan actually to shoot Gandhi, never knew who Gandhi was.

The last of the conspirators we need name was Madanlal Pahwa, whose home was in territory taken over by Muslims and whose father had been a victim of violence. He had made money and amassed arms in Ahmednaggar and organized a gang in a Bombay refugee camp, blackmailing store owners. He was essentially a thug, though one with political convictions. In Poona in January, he and Karkare agreed with the plan to assassinate Gandhi.

The leaders of the group were clearly Godse and Apte. But it was in Savarkar that the idea of Hindu nationalism had been embodied and became infectious. He had hated Gandhi and fought Gandhism for forty years. The conspirators themselves were in one sense or another his agents; perhaps carrying out his orders or advice, probably carrying his blessing, certainly inspired by the hatred he had generated. But that hatred was a vortex swirling around Gandhi, and sustained by cross currents from Jinnah and Ambedkar and many other sources. For instance, Godse and Apte sought arms and got advice from Dada Maharaj, the head of an affluent Vaishnava sect in Bombay, the Pushtimarg Vaishnavites. But above all they visited Savarkar in his Bombay home, Savarkar Sadan (guarded by armed men day and night) immediately before the assassination.

Who is there in Tolstoy's case to compare with these men? As we are passing from the political to the domestic, and from actual assassination to psychic poisoning, we might consider Tolstoy's five sons, who were part of the domestic conspiracy against him, but its agents rather than its sources.

In a diary entry for March 18, 1905, Tolstoy divided up humanity between two great types, whom he labeled as the Horatios and the Quixotes, and said that his daughters belonged to the former type, his sons to the latter, except that they had no capacity for self-sacrifice.[20] The Horatios, presumably, are the steady and reliable companions and comrades; and certainly Masha, Sasha, and even Tania were that, in their different ways, to him. "Quixotes without self-sacrifice" presumably points to spiritual ambition combined with moral feebleness, to uneasy spirits, full of discontent and plotting to be great, but easily distracted and not really believing in their own plans. Taken individually, only Lev answers to that image strikingly, but taken as a group the sons fit the label well enough for us to see what Tolstoy meant.

After Tolstoy had left home in 1910, his children wrote messages to put into a joint letter to him for Sasha to take when she went to join him. In his message, Sergei said Tolstoy had done the right thing and that his parents probably should have parted long before. Ilya said that since his father had always regarded Sonia as a cross he had to bear, it was a pity that he had not been able to bear it to the end, and would he please write to her. Andrei said something similar, and Misha, who was playing bravura waltzes while the letter was being composed, said over his shoulder: "Everyone knows that I don't like to write! Tell him that I agree with Tania and Ilya."[21] Had Lev sent a message, it would probably have been the bitterest of all.

Sergei was the least hostile to his father, at least when he was writing about him and perhaps to him; and yet their relations were always difficult. Sergei's was a spoiled life, and the spoiling could not but be to some degree his father's fault. Tolstoy had clearly failed with his eldest son—and indeed with the others. Ilya, the second, led a self-indulgent life, always short of money and appealing to his mother for help. He worked as a journalist after trying the civil service. Without sharing his father's ideas, he remained within his gravitational field, and when the Dukhobors were emigrating asked to be found a job related to that. He wanted a paid job, which his father refused him (Sergei, a liberal idealist, did sail with the Dukhobors). Ilya's relation to his father seems to have been less incisive, less important, than his brothers; but, as his letter of 1910 indicates, it was malicious or plaintive rather than supportive. In his book about Tolstoy, he says he never received any marks of affection from him.

The third son, Lev, (born the same year as Tolstoy's spiritual son, Gandhi) was the most destructive, though the most imitative and in his youth the most doctrinally discipular. He was an amateur writer and also sculptor, and his ego was clearly poisoned and swollen with jealousy. As a writer he produced a transvalued version of *The Kreutzer Sonata*—he was trapped equally within his father's field— but he was not gifted enough to compete in that kind of activity.

Lev was nervous and sickly from birth and especially close to his mother, who rejoiced in the prospect of his becoming an artist, which would give her a role in promoting yet another creative career. He was to be what she had always wanted, the new version— her version—of his father. She could close her eyes to the difference in quality between their work. (His father, on the other hand, told him, on June 22, 1898, that what he was writing was stupid, vulgar, and untalented.) Lev was the bitterest of them all toward Tolstoy. When the latter was so ill in the Crimea in 1902 and the whole family was gathered round his sick bed, Lev read aloud to the others a letter in accusation of his father. And when Tolstoy wrote him a conciliatory reply, Lev tore it up publicly. Lev was at home in July, 1910, modeling his mother. On the 10th, when Sonia made a terrible scene and ran out into the garden saying she would kill Chertkov, Lev turned on his father and swore at him (scolded him like a child, as Tolstoy wrote in his diary) and ordered him to go and find her and bring her back. The next month Tolstoy noted that Lev was proposing to settle in Yasnaya Polyana, a prospect Tolstoy found unbearable.[22]

In 1909 Lev and his brother Andrei had wanted to have Tolstoy declared feebleminded. (This was a scheme Sonia pursued intermittently, reviving it after each of his illnesses; it was her main strategy for defeating whatever he might be putting into his will.) Like Misha, Andrei led an openly dissolute life, but Tolstoy said he would be good, "but for that Bers self-confidence." He more than once noted his own fondness for Andrei, seemingly because of a certain open-heartedness; moreover, "of all the sons, he is the only one who loves me."[23] Andrei married a serious-minded girl, the sister of Chertkov's wife, but fairly soon left her and then eloped with another man's wife. Indeed, in terms of actual behavior, Andrei became one of his father's worst enemies. In the June 23, 1910 entry in Sonia's diary, full of jealous rage, fantasizing her suicide, she added: "And you, Andrei, avenge your mother's death! You loved her and understood who was her enemy. . . . "[24]

Misha seems to have been the most simply dissipated and unintellectual, the least touched by Tolstoy's ideas. He married splendidly, with a famous choir and a grand duke at the ceremony, and like Andrei became a member of one of the Black Hundreds, a group that one can compare with Savarkar's Rashtra Swayamsevak Sangh, a paramilitary organization to promote reaction. Indeed, just the fact that he, like Andrei, chose the army for his career, was a profound defiance of his father's ideas. Sergei explains, in his book of reminiscenses, that he saw little of his parents in the last twelve months of his father's life because Misha had involved him in a quarrel over hunting rights in Sergei's forest, that led to Sergei being challenged to a duel. The suit took two months to settle, and the incident as a whole represents the kind of issues which absorbed the sons' interest and distracted them from their parents' final tragedy.

All five of these men produce a muffled impression, of muddled or wasted lives, of failed or unfocused aspirations, on anyone who contemplates Tolstoy's life. Of course the lens appropriate for looking at Tolstoy is inappropriate for looking at most other people. But even by comparison with their mother, the sons seem muted, confused, reduced to merely phenomenal status. Indeed, by 1890, Tolstoy and Sonia were united in grief by the dismal and painful spectacle of their children (though not by the practical problems of what to do about them) even when other spectacles divided them emotionally. They both knew their children did not measure up to them.

This was particularly true of the sons. There are photographs of the family in which they stand stolidly at the back of the group like uninvited visitors, strangers. But it was only their sympathies that were alienated; their interests remained attached, often channelled through a demand for their share of the property, but involving much more than greed. Thus they were, as Godse and Apte were for

Gandhi, the agents of the ugly resentment that surrounded Tolstoy from so many sources and poisoned the air he breathed. When Tolstoy wanted to die it was because of that sullen and sometimes violent anger and reproach always assailing him.

But of course none of them were as wholly engaged in this struggle as their mother. She too may be said to have been possessed by forces (passions) outside herself—the passions of her calling as priestess of home life—and she was palpably destroyed as well as destroying. But it was her struggle, and she acted in it as they did not, in the same way Jinnah and Savarkar may be said to have acted in their struggle against Gandhi, while Godse and Apte were acted upon.

As the beginning of their last year's struggle, we might take Sonia's extraction from Tolstoy of a promise that he would make it clear that the deletions in his diary (made to preserve her image) were his own work. He noted this in his diary for April 30, 1909. On May 10/11 he wrote a final letter, to be given her after his death, confided to Sasha's care. On the 13th she made a scene of jealousy because she had been reading *The Devil* and "the old yeast began rising in her."[25] This sequence proceeded up to one sort of climax in late September 1910. He had been away, and she had rearranged the photographs of him, notably one taken by Chertkov, which hung over his chair. Tolstoy left them as she had put them; Sasha reproached him for yielding to her mother, and he wept. On the 23rd Sonia had Bulgakov take a photograph of him and her together. On the 24th, Tolstoy got a reproachful letter from Chertkov, and noted: "They tear me in pieces."[26] The Chertkov photograph was again hung over his chair. On the 26th Sonia tore it up and threw it down the toilet and then fired a toy pistol at Tolstoy.

Her love was thus largely possessiveness and partly hatred, as Tolstoy said, but not entirely. One cannot refuse all sympathy to the entry of July 7, 1910: "He kissed me; Mine! Mine! cried my heart, and now I shall be calmer and come to myself."[27] And on October 3, after Tolstoy's attack she said to Sasha, (with whom she was on very bad terms), "My suffering is greater than yours; you lose a father, but I lose a husband of whose death I am guilty."[28] Such remarks announce both the corruption of love by egotism and the persistence of love within the egotism.

But her behavior made Tolstoy say: "My illness is Sonia Andreevna"; and write in his diary for August 28, 1909: "It is not love, but a demand for love, which is close to hatred. Yes, egoism is madness. She was saved by having children—that love is animal but still it is self-sacrificing." After his illness she told all and sundry that she could now contest his will, on the grounds that he was an imbecile.[29]

Besides imbecility, she accused him of homosexuality and of demoniac possession, because of his fondness for Chertkov, whom she called his "handsome idol." On September 2, 1910, while he was away, she had his room exorcised by the local priest, to whom she told her suspicions about the sexual relations between her husband and Chertkov. She read to all sorts of people Tolstoy's early diary confession of his love for men. She told Chertkov's aged mother of her suspicions, and the young Bulgakov. Her jealousies and suspicions were entangled together. Aksinia was still alive (at least she was in 1908) and her son by Tolstoy, Timofei, and they figured in Sonia's fantasies. On June 30, 1910 she wrote in her diary: "Peasant women are 'the people' he loved and still loves. Gentle-women he never loved and does not. Now it is a *man*."[30] And on August 1, she says Tolstoy had three candidates in the village for some free seed rye and because he hasn't named one of them she suspects it must be Timofei.

She followed him and Chertkov everywhere in an ecstasy of jealousy, sometimes using opera glasses and hiding in a ditch to watch them. When he went for a ride, she followed in the cabriolet. On July 7, 1910, she recorded: "I always ask him where he's going, so I can send a coat or a carriage, but he doesn't like to tell me."[31] On July 10, he and Chertkov went riding. "For some reason they dismounted in the wood, and Chertkov pointed his camera at Lev Nikolaevich and photographed him in a gully."[32] This was the night of the bad scene in which Lev intervened; she demanded Tolstoy's diaries to check his reference to their conflicts. She lay down outside the door of Tolstoy's room, groaning, and then ran out and lay down in the garden. She described the scene in her diary and pointed out its moral: "If any foreigners had seen in what a condition the wife of Lev Niolaevich was brought in . . ."[33] On July 25 she left home, but meeting Andrei by chance at the station in Tula, she came home with him. On the 26th, she says she is leaving, and prepares a press release (which was never published): *The Facts Can Be Verified on the Spot:* In peaceful Yasnaya Polyana an extraordinary event has occurred. The Countess Sofia Andreevna has abandoned her home . . . because Lev Nikolaevich, enfeebled by age, has fallen under the influence of Mr. Chertkov."[34] On August 6 she says she got up early to see if Tolstoy was meeting Chertkov in the wood; on the 18th she wrote to the minister, Stolypin, asking him to exile Chertkov, when she heard that the latter again had government permission to live near Yasnaya Polyana. "I will kill him!" she exclaimed; and so on.[35]

On October 3 when Tolstoy fell ill, Sonia took the blame on herself but at the same time seized his portfolio; Tania got it back from her, while Sergei took care that his father's notebook and bureau key did not fall into her hands. On the 16th, when he went to see Chertkov at Teliatinki, she followed him secretly and hid in a ditch with opera glasses to spy on what they were doing. Accosted by Chertkov's secretary, she made light conversation; and then, as soon as he was gone, whipped out her glasses again.

In these terms of personal and domestic drama—sexual jealousy, personal property, suicidal complaint, medical diagnosis—Sonia kept raising the emotional temperature and psychological costs of their struggle, raising them toward the ultimate, death; just as, by his public rhetoric and private conspiracy, Jinnah raised the communal temperature and the political costs for Gandhi. ("We will have India divided or we will have India destroyed.")[36] And in both cases the climax of this escalation was the act of killing.

The Victims

As for the two men themselves, subjected to these pressures of hatred they reacted with similar mixtures of exhaustion and activity, death wish and hopeful enterprise. On the one hand, Tolstoy wanted to die and said his readiness for death was the one good thing in him. On the other, as late as October, 1910, he recorded in his diary a "wonderful" idea for a story; and proposed, to a man who wanted to give money to a good cause, that he should fund a new kind of book, an encyclopedic dictionary designed for barely literate readers. Only the year before, he had planned a series of short books on world religions. And Gandhi, brokenhearted by the first actions of the new India and by the slaughterhouse slop already staining his new creation, spoke often of dying. On the day before he died he told Manu that only if he died from a bullet and with "He Ram" on his lips would he have been a true Mahatma. But at the same time he had planned another major campaign—a pilgrimage to Pakistan—and was on the last day of his life drawing up a new constitution for Congress.

The energy at Yasnaya Polyana never failed. On New Year's Day, 1910, to entertain the children, Sonia played a witch in a masquerade, and Tolstoy led a last charge of the Numidian Cavalry. But it was Sonia's energy—it was her life they were living, together; his projects were tangential to the household; hers were all-pervasive. On May 19, she noted: "Ill-health and weariness prevented my doing anything of importance. I made leather-cloth covers for the tables, and covered the sofa in the living room with Andrei's help."[37] But Tolstoy felt bitterly ashamed of the way he lived. On January 7, 1910, he wrote in his diary that he suffered most not from his actual suffering on his own behalf, but from his ceaseless shame before the people: "Can this be how I end my life, in this condition of shame?"[38] And on April 12: "The horrible shame of this life." He had just walked by some men who were breaking stones on the road, "and it was as though I was running the gauntlet."[39] (He had written some vivid descriptions of the Russian army punishment of running the gauntlet," in which a convicted man ran between a double file of men with sticks and got a blow from each.) He was accused of hypocrisy by revolutionaries, peasants, students, as well as his own family. On February 7, he recorded a letter from a Kiev student advising him to leave home and become poor; on April 19, another young man had demanded that he should join the revolutionary struggle and use bombs and not prayers against the oppressors.

Being a saint of strength, Gandhi did not have to feel shame, but he felt bitter doubt ("What to do? What to do?") and crushing responsibility for all that got done. And he too met constant reproach and accusation from young men, like Bose in Noakhali, and J. P. Narayan and Rammanohar Lohia, in political matters. Above all, both he and Tolstoy managed to absent themselves from the scenes of their ostensible triumphs in politics and literature respectively; Gandhi absented himself from the Independence Day celebrations, Tolstoy canceled the plans for a literary celebration of his eightieth birthday and finally, of course, absented himself from Yasnaya Polyana itself.

On Tolstoy's side, we can distinguish three phases of response to Sonia's campaign. He made plans to leave, he made accusations, and he yielded himself to her. In July, 1909, he is seriously discussing with friends ways and means of running away, and on October 21, 1910 he wrote to Novikov:

I have never concealed from you that in this house I am boiling as if in hell, and I have always dreamed of going away, and longed to go somewhere into the forest to a keeper's hut, or to a village to some lonely peasant's hut, where we could help one another. But God has not given me the strength to break away from my family. My weakness is perhaps a sin, but I could not for the sake of my personal satisfaction make others suffer, even though they are members of my family. . . .[40]

To Sonia he wrote in 1909:

But just because you were what your mother made you, and stayed like that and didn't want to change, didn't want to work on yourself, to progress towards goodness and truth, but on the contrary clung with such obstinacy to all that was most evil and the opposite of all that was dear to me, you did a lot of evil to other people and sank lower and lower yourself, and reached the pathetic condition you are now in.[41]

That is the accusing style that we also find in his letter to Sasha of October 29, 1910, the day after leaving:

For me, with this spying, eavesdropping, everlasting disposing of one according to caprice, everlasting control, pretence of hatred for the man who is nearest and most necessary to me, with this obvious hatred of me and affectation of love . . . such a life is not merely unpleasant for me, but utterly impossible. If anyone is to drown himself, it is not she but I [Sonia had thrown herself into the Middle Pond at Yasnaya Polyana when she found out he had left] . . . I desire only one thing, freedom from her, from the falsity, hypocrisy, and malice with which her whole being is saturated. . . . All her behavior to me not only shows a lack of love, but seems to have been unmistakably aimed at killing me. . . . You see, dear, how bad I am. I do not conceal myself from you.[42]

And in a letter of the same time to Sonia, he said that for him to return home would be suicide; another sign of the dominance of death and killing in their thoughts.

But if one looks at the main outlines of his behavior, what becomes clear is that these were outbursts, protestations of resistance, and that by and large he yielded. This was not merely a matter of his staying at Yasnaya Polyana, but of his trying to make the relationship work, trying to reach her, reclaim her from violence and malice. He told her that he loved her, that he could not live without her, and he dwelt as much as he could upon the sense in which that was true and as little as he could upon the opposite ones among his feelings. (This was not erotic love, of course, but it was emotionally warm.) The yielding was graceless because it was interrupted by other more spontaneous outbursts, but by yielding yet again after each of the latter he accepted his loss of grace as part of his personality.

On July 13, 1910, he wrote Chertkov a letter of apology (he had had to turn his friend away at the door because of Sonia) and handed it to him. Sonia immediately asked to see the letter and then burned it. The next day he promised to give his current diary to no one (she was afraid Chertkov would get it and copy out things unflattering to her), to get the old ones back from Chertkov, and, if he ever did leave Yasnaya Polyana, not to go to his friend. Sasha brought the diaries back from Chertkov's home at Teliatinki, and the next day Sukhotin, Tania's husband, deposited them in a bank in Tula. Nevertheless, that day again she pretended to take poison in despair. (On the 19th, Professor Rossolino, a psychiatrist, examined her and diagnosed hysteria and paranoia.) And yet Tolstoy stayed on, in that atmosphere of anger and violence which was a fluid presence like electricity, able to seize and possess almost anyone.

When Gandhi got to Delhi in 1947, he found the Muslim population in terror for their lives and taking refuge in the courtyard of the Jamma Masjid and in the grounds of Humayun's Tomb. At the Purana Qila Fort, 75,000 people awaited evacuation, but had hidden stores of arms and ammunition. The curfew was lifted for only a few hours each day, and Jinnah and Liaquat Ali Khan had no control over the situation, while Nehru and Patel had very little. Patel had decided he had to treat all Muslims as traitors to the new state of India. Gandhi went to the fort with three of his young girls, and though he was greeted with cries of "Death to Gandhi," "Gandhi Mordabad," he was able to abate the fever somewhat. But on October 2 he said to Patel: "What sin have I committed that He should have kept me alive to witness all these horrors?"[43] And the question was not entirely rhetorical, for there were plenty who felt that Gandhi was indeed responsible.

A somewhat comparable situation occurred to Tolstoy in September 1909. When he and Chertkov and Sonia were leaving Moscow for Yasnaya Polyana, the time of their departure somehow became known and a huge crowd assembled at Moscow station. The crowd was good-humored and shouted: "Keep on helping us! Live to be a hundred!" And Sonia was delighted, and kept saying: "They are seeing us off like Tsars." (Tolstoy replied: "Yes, it means we have done something very bad.")[44] Chertkov, who took charge of the task

of getting them through the mob to the railway platform, thought
there were government agents among them who intended to have
Tolstoy crushed or maimed. (His secretary, Sergeenko, says Chertkov had a "sick suspiciousness" of such an event occurring sooner
or later.)[45] The scale of this crowd was much smaller than the equivalent—so much more frequent, also—for Gandhi. But Tolstoy was
greatly exhausted by the excitement, in part because he was unused
to it, no doubt. He was used to only domestic hysterics.

There were many extensions and elaborations of the primary situation for both men. For instance, the competitive jealousies between
Chertkov and Sonia, between Sasha and her mother, and between
Sasha and the young secretaries, Gusev and Bulgakov—who had to
go live at Teliatinki because of her jealousy. These bear an obvious
similarity to the relationship between Bose and Sushila and the other girls with Gandhi in Noakhali. But if we are to look for something political to compare with Sonia's jealousy of Chertkov, something comparable in cooperative malevolence, we should turn to
Jinnah's and Savarkar's mutual jealousy. It was these two men
whose interests were most completely opposed, who were formally
each other's worst enemies. Both men seem to have fought with
their eyes on Gandhi rather than on each other, and the arrows of
hate they discharged made their way towards him.

There were moments when all these enemies of Gandhi did join
forces. In October, 1939, Savarkar and Ambedkar and some liberals
jointly protested that Congress could not speak for all Hindus,
while Jinnah had long advanced the same protest on behalf of Indian Muslims. Soon after, a correspondent said Gandhi should make
Jinnah negotiate directly with Savarkar and the Mahasabha since
these were the ultimate opponents; and Gandhi admitted the logic
of the proposal.[46] But of course the logic was superficial because
they were really concerned more with Gandhi—what they wanted
from each other was alliance against him. Gandhi encouraged them
to make alliance, he congratulated Jinnah on giving his opposition
to Congress a national character (making it an opposition in the
parliamentary sense) by joining forces with Ambedkar and the Justice Party and by going to see Savarkar.[47] (But Jinnah replied that
there could be no national opposition because India was not a nation but a continent containing many nations.)

As Ved Mehta says: "Gandhi had had many previous adversaries
in his life, but none of then had ever aroused his passion or made

him despair as Jinnah did."[48] And despite Jinnah's august imper-
sonality, when he speaks to or about Gandhi the note of malevolence makes itself heard. Gandhi appealed to him in February 1938
not to make civil war between the League and the Congress, re-
minding him of the nationalist hopes which had inspired both men
in 1915, and asking him why he had changed. Jinnah replied:

Evidently, you are not acquainted with what is going on in the Congress
press—the amount of vilification, misrepresentation, and falsehood that is
daily spread about me—otherwise, I am sure, you would not blame me. . . .
I would not like to say what people spoke of you in 1915 and think of you
today. . . . I think you might have spared your appeal and need not have
preached to me on your bended knees to be what you had thought I was.[49]

What he and Savarkar said in private is not recorded, and from
Ambedkar we have only a few phrases, though those of a startling
venomousness.

I've a feeling I know him better than most other people, because he had
opened his fangs to me, you see, and I could see the inside of the man.[50]

The raising of the stake of violence, clearly, was the responsibility
of Jinnah on the Muslim side and of men like the other two on the
Hindu side. To what extent their political actions may be linked to
their personal hatred of Gandhi is not easy to say, but some connection there was. Of necessity, they did hate Gandhi's populism, pacifism, internationalism, and antipoliticism, and the result of their
behavior was to disable those policies and finally to eliminate
Gandhi.

They hated peace worse than their opponents in war. Tolstoy declared that Sonia's hatred of Chertkov was a pretence, to license
extremes of aggression really aimed at her husband. Something similar seems to be true of Jinah and Savarkar.

Tragedies of Concealment

The fact that Tolstoy's was a domestic, and in that sense bourgeois, tragedy meant also that it was suppressed or concealed as far
as the outside world was concerned. The writer Leonid Andreev
visited Yasnaya Polyana on April 21, 1910, and in a memoir of 1911
wrote that he had seen nothing of the anger between husband and

wife—to the contrary. There must have been two truths in their lives; to his eye, he said, Tolstoy "had attained an extraordinary softness and quite childlike purity and freedom from ill-will."[51]

Thus this was also one of the great tragedies of domestic hypocrisy. Charles Salomon was sleeping at Yasnaya Polyana the night of the scene between Tolstoy, Sonia, and Lev in July, 1910. He heard it all but left the next morning protesting that he had heard nothing. The Tolstoy story must have done much to discredit marriage at the end of the nineteenth century and to prepare for the antimarital mood of the twentieth. (For our purposes, the nineteenth century ended in 1914, and the twentieth began in 1918.) That story can be put together with the Max Weber story in Germany, and many other great legends of the whited sepulchre of marriage; people chained to each other by the institution and depriving each other of the happiness of free union—which is what the various youth movements promised, from the artistic bohemias to youth hostels. Tolstoy's marriage was a particularly graphic case because of that relationship's beautiful beginnings, so lyrically described in the great novels. Young parents as well as young lovers had been celebrated there, and they were all icons of marriage desecrated by the events of 1909–1910.

There is a hypocrisy proper to politics too, and Gandhi did not entirely escape it, as his party's suppression of the rumors about his sexual life showed, and—to take a more political example—his public silence about the Kashmir invasion and the other signs of India's entry into power politics. That insincerity did not react so immediately and poisonously upon Gandhi's honor as it did upon Tolstoy's: Gandhi was not married to Nehru, even politically. But he had to suffer in concealment not to spoil the triumph of nation building, as Tolstoy had to suffer in concealment not to spoil the legend of domestic happiness.

Once India was divided, the communal hatreds became uncontrollable. Forty-million Muslims were left living in Hindu India. Altogether twelve-million people migrated from there to Pakistan or vice versa. Ultimately there were seven-million homeless in India, one million of whom were in Delhi, doubling the city's size. It was one of the great migrations of history; one column was eight-hundred thousand strong. But the worst of it was that these were all manifestations of violence. There were columns of women, five hundred at a time, who had been stripped naked; there were hundreds of thousands of mutilated and murdered bodies.

Gandhi had passed Independence Day in Calcutta with Shaheed
Suhrawardy and was asleep at the midnight at which India became
a free nation. He refused to celebrate the event. He told the students who came to him for a message for the occasion: "This is a
sorry affair." From Calcutta he had set off for the Punjab where the
killings were worst. He had to go back to Bihar first, and then coming to Delhi en route he found the situation there so serious that he
could not leave it. He arrived on September 9, and on the 6th Nehru and Patel had in effect handed power back to Mountbatten, because the situation was beyond their control. Communal violence
seemed inevitable, and, with a million refugees in the city, which
doubled its population, seemed also limitless.

Gandhi wanted to send the refugees back to their native villages
and to get the Muslim houses of Delhi, taken over by Hindus, vacat-
ed so that their owners could return. He also wanted India to send
to Pakistan £40,000,000 of the Reserve Bank's holdings; this had
been agreed to be Pakistan's share of British India's capital, but
Nehru and Patel had decided they could not send such a sum of
money to a country which would spend it on arms to use against
themselves. On January 12, 1948, Gandhi saw Mountbatten, then
Governor General, to announce his intention to fast until Nehru
and Patel changed their minds. He began his fast the next day, and
it was then that Godse and Apte decided to kill him. On January 14
they and Badge (disguised as a *saddhu*) went to Bombay to see
Savarkar.

The event had already been rehearsed. An ominous anecdote of
1944, after Gandhi had met Jinnah and accepted the principle of a
Pakistan, was a prediction of, or overture to, the assassination. The
Hindu Mahasabha picketed the ashram at Sevagram in protest and
threatened to use force. The policeman who arrested the leader of
the pickets called him a martyr—presumbably in jest—but the latter
answered that that was a title which would belong to the man who
actually killed Gandhi. "Why not leave that to the leaders to settle
among themselves—to Savarkar?" the policeman said. "That will be
too great an honour for Gandhiji. The jammadar [N.C.O.] will be
quite enough for the purpose."[52] The *jammadar* was Nathuram
Godse.

This incident was in some sense a rehearsal for the catastrophe to
come. So were Sonia Tolstoy's suicide attempts, even though the
death fantasized was not the one that actually occurred. Take for
instance the events of June 23, 1910. Tolstoy had gone to visit

Chertkov and when Sonia sent a wire asking him to return immediately because she was sick, he replied that the 24th would be more convenient than the 23rd.

She was furious with resentment and anger and planned an accusing suicide with a document to explain just what she was doing and why. This was entitled: "Yet Another Suicide (a sick woman's ravings)" and subtitled "Memorandum before Death." In it she wrote: "What is the matter with me; Hysteria, a nervous stroke, angina, the beginning of insanity? I do not know. I have spasms in the throat and cry all the time—cry day and night. Where do so many tears come from?"[53]

But the mood of the document shifts from pathos to accusation and malevolence:

> He has a repulsive, senile love for Chertkov (in his youth he used to fall in love with men) and is completely subject to his will . . . [unprintable expression]. I thought of going to Stoltsov and lying down there under the train in which Lev Nikolaevich would be travelling *more conveniently*. I thought of going to Tula to ask the Governor's permission to buy a pistol as if for the servants and then shooting myself right in the temple, like Masha Kolokotseva. . . .[54]

The mood changes with the minutes, plainly excited by the feeling that she is transcribing all this into sentences, creating literature:

> I was sad and wept in solitude . . . while he wrote me falsely affectionate letters and continued to live at Meshcherskoe with his handsome idol. . . . The painters have come asking whether they are to paint the roof. And immediately I see a vivid picture of a rounded coffin-lid covered with rose-coloured or white brocade, and under it—myself. How enormous my nose will seem as it sticks up . . . another hour has passed. It will be soon! I shall take poison a few minutes before his arrival. I shall watch his fright with angry joy—my revenge on him for deserting me *for a man*—and I shall fall asleep for ever.[55]

She did take poison, but ineffectively, and later added to her diary that she had not succeeded, and "above all I must live in order not to yield up Levochka to his idol, Chertkov."[56]

The Two Fates

Each of the men suffered in accordance with the form of *maya* which he had pursued. Tolstoy's peace was destroyed by conflicts

over property of all kinds; in Gandhi's tragedy the destructive role
was played by power. The slogan "domestic happiness" announced
Tolstoy's cult of erotic values, implying the material possession of
embodied truths, and his punishment was to see the materialization
of all his imaginative truths, the turning of all his art into property
over which his family and disciples fought. In 1910, Sonia began to
bring out the twelfth edition of his complete works, in twenty volumes. On October 24th, just four days before he ran away, the Enlightenment Publishing Company sent its representative to Yasnaya
Polyana with an offer of a million rubles for the complete rights.

Perhaps even more upsetting was the reification of his living consciousness itself in the form of his (and other people's) diaries.
Aylmer Maude tells us that during Tolstoy's last year seven people
were keeping diaries about the events at Yasnaya Polyana, not
counting Tolstoy and Sonia, who were keeping two each. (He kept a
secret one because his ordinary diary had become such public property, and she kept a day book as well as her diary.) His were a major
object of desire (and focus of fear and resentment—Eros and Thana-
tos at once of that little world) for their publishing and therefore
financial potential, for the field they offered to a future editor and
censor to shape the image of Tolstoy (and Sonia), and for the authority they would confer on their possessor, even without publication, to speak in his name. The other people's diaries were comparatively private, being non-numinous, nonerotic, but they too were
usable property, being reified. Sasha's friend, Varvara Feokritova,
wrote in her diary some stories Sonia told against Tolstoy, and his
friend Goldenveizer the pianist copied them out and sent them to
him.[57]

It is no mere coincidence that all this reading of others' diaries
and stealing and preserving of diaries, censoring and rewriting,
copying out of extracts, and mailing of them off to other people
should remind us of Richardson's *Pamela* and of other domestic
novels in the great tradition which leads to Doris Lessing's *The
Golden Notebook*. That is not a coincidence because the domestic novel has been an exercise in consciousness (an exercise *of* consciousness, its muscularization, and usually its reification) which raised its
various modes, among which the diary is central, to high levels of
potency. And Tolstoy was not only a great novelist in that tradition,
and not only a great personality by virtue of his consciousness, he
was also the center of a group life that lived by the manifestation
and reflection of consciousness. For instance, Sonia's diaries all "an-

swered to" his, in a variety of ways, were shadows and caricatures of his. (It is typical that in June, 1910, she claimed she needed to consult the volumes he had consigned to Chertkov's keeping to help her in writing her own memoirs.)[58] Thus it was not only the idea of erotic marriage which ground to a creaking halt and broke apart in Yasnaya Polyana in 1910, but the idea of novelistic consciousness too. (Of course people went on writing novels, some of them with genius, just as people went on marrying, some of them with enthusiasm; but the writing was on the wall for those who looked to see it.)

Tolstoy had been so eager to produce, to create works of art, to turn his experience into acts of imagination, and then later to grow apples, and keep bees, and generate children, and build up a family life, a center of the arts, a house of hospitality, at Yasnaya Polyana; and at the end everything in his life had reified, had turned to solid gold about him. He had found the Philosopher's Stone, he had given himself the Midas' touch and everyone around him was fighting for the proceeds. (On October 21, 1909, he recorded that Sasha had told him that the other children were greedily in need of money and therefore of his royalties, and—consequently—of his death.) For him, and for Sonia in the beginning, the point had always been not the proceeds but the process, the magic by which one brought values and things into existence. When his children concentrated upon the things themselves, their distribution and ownership, they had the effect upon him (not unintentionally) of cruel satire.

One of the issues was the copyright of his books, another was the land at Yasnaya Polyana and at Samara. On February 4, 1909, Tolstoy had written in his diary that all the copyrights should be given up, and the Yasnaya Polyana land should be given to the peasants. (Sasha carried out this wish in 1912, and in 1917 the peasants defended the Tolstoy mansion against revolutionary attack.) All that had to do with his manuscripts had to be disposed of in his will, which therefore became the focus of as intense concern, vicious intrigue, secrecy, and suspicion as did his diaries. And one might note again that the domestic novel very often made a will one of its focal centers. Tolstoy had given away all his property except his writings, his reified consciousness, but that was enough to cause bitter battles. Gandhi's will was empty and innocent, though there were battles over how much truth he should tell about his sexual practices.

Tolstoy's first will was drawn up on September 18, 1909, at Krekshino, and it appointed Chertkov to edit and publish at his discretion all that Tolstoy had written after 1880. This will was found not to be binding legally, and so another one was drawn up on November 1, with F. A. Strakhov's help, naming Sasha as heir to all his works; and a last one on July 22, 1910 (signed at a secret rendezvous in a field, while Tolstoy was supposedly taking his afternoon ride), made Sasha and Chertkov (though hostile to each other) coheirs and editors. This had to be kept secret from Sonia, who nevertheless discovered that something was going on, and trouble of all kinds ensued, even among the Tolstoyans. For instance, Biriukov, when he heard of the existence of the will, persuaded Tolstoy that he should tell his family about it, but then Chertkov overpersuaded him by writing him a very long letter.

On August 24, Sonia wrote in her diary that the "apparition" of Chertkov haunted Yasnaya Polyana. "That huge and hateful figure with the immense sack he always brings with him and in which he cunningly and carefully collects all Lev Nikolaevich's manuscripts will always appear everywhere."[59] This image is reminiscent of the dream figure that haunts Anna Karenina, but in this case what is at stake is not an imaginative moral truth, but the manuscripts in which it was inscribed. There seems no doubt that Chertkov was obsessive too. Bulgakov reports a conversation with him on July 12, 1910, about Sonia's demand for the diaries. " 'Do you mean to say,' he broke in, raising his large, light-coloured, restless eyes upon me, 'that you came right out and told where the diaries were?' And with these words, to my utter amazement, Vladimir Grigorevich made a hideous grimace and stuck out his tongue at me."[60]

Another aspect of materialization, less metaphorical but no less imaginative, was Akhmet, the mounted Cherkess, guard to the property, who had been hired by Sonia when Yasnaya Polyana's police protection was withdrawn at Sasha's request. The image of a mounted Cherkess had been intimately involved with all Tolstoy's youthful dreams of freedom in the Caucasus and with what he had written about that experience, but now it was associated with oppression of the most sordid kind and oppression inflicted in protection of him and his property. On October 20, 1909, he recorded having an unpleasant conversation with Sonia about Akhmet and about the thefts (which he found justified) perpetrated by peasants on Andrey's property at Taptikov. On June 4, 1910 he came back from an enjoyable ride to find Akhmet arresting a peasant called Prokov whom Tolstoy had known all his life—who had been one of the boys in Tolstoy's school. And on June 6, a boy came from the village to get Tolstoy's explicit permission to go into the Zakaz wood because now Akhmet was beating up anyone he found there without it.

Yet another aspect of this materialization was the issue of Tolstoy's photographs—the rivalry to shape and dispose of his image—"taking his picture" became an act fraught with power and evoking jealous violence at Yasnaya Polyana. With whom he stood on such photographs was, for instance, a matter of great importance, Sonia would not have him standing with his disciples, and there were many extensions and elaborations of the feelings involved—as when Sasha bitterly reproached her father for allowing her mother to have Bulgakov take a picture of them together on the last anniversary of their wedding, September 23, 1910. (This photograph is in itself a ghastly image of marital ownership, Sonia clutching Tolstoy by the arm and turning her gaze upon him into an act of possession, while he grimly endures both it and the camera.) And of course who took the photograph was even more important than who stood with him. On August 19 she had extracted from him a promise not to let Chertkov photograph him again. "It was repulsive to me that his idol should photograph Lev Nikolaevich, like an elderly coquette, in woods and ravines, and that he should despotically turn the old man all ways to take pictures of him."[61] Here again Gandhi's case was different, and his self-possession showed itself in his refusal to pose. He often told photographers—for instance, when he arrived in Marseilles in 1931—that he was "not at their disposal"; he had taken a vow against posing in South Africa.

And then there was the straightforward case of literary property. Tolstoy believed there should be no such thing. But yielding to his wife, he had resolved the issue for himself—as he hoped—by transferring such property to her, as far as his fiction, his financially significant pre-1880 manuscripts, went. But problems continually cropped up. On July 12, 1909, he recorded that Sonia wanted to sue a St. Petersburg publisher who had used Tolstoy's stories, *Three Deaths* and *Childhood*. She also wanted to sue Tolstoy's disciple, I. I. Gorbunov, for putting "A Prisoner in the Caucasus" into a Posrednik edition; on the ground that this was a story and so belonged to her even though it was a part of Tolstoy's school reader. She had deposited some of his manuscripts in a museum to keep them out of Chertkov's hands; in effect, she had stolen them. When I. V. Denisenko, a lawyer, reported that she was preparing to sue Sergeenko, Chertkov's secretary, for anthologizing something else, Tolstoy decided he had to make a will to control the situation after his death.[62]

But ultimately, it seems true to say, all these acts of materialization were forms of her possessing *him*. She turned *him* into property in order to own him—and to dispossess him of himself—of his spirit. According to Chertkov, when people told her she was killing Tolstoy, she replied that his soul had long been dead for her, and his body she didn't care about. (When they said, "Suppose he dies?," she replied: "I shall go to Italy at last," according to the same source.) Tolstoy himself certainly felt that to be the crucial issue. When he described finding her searching his bureau the night of October 28, he said:

On the evening before she begged and insisted that I should not lock the doors. Both her doors were opened so that she could hear my slightest movement. Both by day and by night all my movements and my words must be known to her and under her control. I don't know why this aroused in me unrestrained indignation and aversion.[63]

In Gandhi's case the problems of property had been effectively solved by his self-dispossession of property but also by his self-possession—no one else was in a position to control him. But his slogan of "nation building" announced a cult of political militancy, and he had grave problems to do with power. It was not so much (as far as we know) that he doubted his own use of it, as that he aroused his followers' appetite for it. So much of his early effort had been directed at winning self-respect for them and teaching them to win it; teaching them to demand freedom, to defy oppression, to follow a steady resolve through years of disappointment, to fight—even in the simple sense of learning to shoot a gun, wield a bayonet, and maneuver as a military unit. (One of the demands he made in 1930 for his countrymen was the right to bear arms.) Indians had to cease to be a depoliticized and demilitarized race incapable of self-government; they must become a free nation like the English.

But at the end of his life he found that his teaching was realized in the form of communal riots, the Indian National Army, the R.S.S.S., and the military academies of Nehru and Patel. If Tolstoy had Midas' touch, Gandhi had Mars' touch, Shiva's, which turned everyone militant.

Before going to Calcutta, in August, Gandhi's home in Delhi had been the Valmiki Temple in Reading Road, a sweeper's colony. On the open space there, where Gandhi held his prayer meetings, the

R.S.S.S. also held its drills and parades, at which its men saluted the flag of Mother India the Terrible, Kali. And the man of the hour, as far as the newspapers went, was Lord Mountbatten, the last viceroy, a modernized Kipling hero who always appeared in uniform and loved to wear his medals. Nehru and he became great friends. Gandhi had created a state, a great country, and its greatness consisted in military power, which Mountbatten symbolized better than he.

And if Nehru was turning away from Gandhi personally, there were hundreds of signs in state policy and practice of the same tendency politically. Gandhi was distressed at the prompt establishment of military academies in India. He was distressed at the invasion of Kashmir, a classic result of the power conflict between Jinnah and Nehru. Kashmir was a territory of 84,000 square miles with a population of four and a half million, of whom 77 percent were Muslim; but the Maharajah was Hindu. Nehru wanted the ruler to bring his state over to India, while of course Pakistan had a (better) claim to any state so predominantly Muslim. The ruler himself wanted to keep his independence, but when Jinnah sent armed Pathan raiders across the border (ostensibly nothing to do with Pakistan) the Maharajah appealed to India for help, and Nehru flew in an army which added the territory to India.

In 1947 the leaders of India rejected the flag with the spinning wheel design which had been Congress's emblem. Gandhi's charkha was replaced with the Dharma Charkha of the ancient Indian King Asoka. It was the sign carried by Asoka's conquering soldiers signifying his law, and it was flanked by two lions signifying force and courage. Gandhi observed that the new leaders were saying Swaraj did not belong to old women but to warriors; he also observed that the new flag was not made of khadi cloth, but of a beautiful new material made from glass. Nehru assured him that it was the same wheel, only modified by the "exigencies of art." Gandhi had of course thought a good deal about those exigencies. "However artistic the design may be," he said, "I shall refuse to salute a flag which carries such a message."[64]

Pyarelal says that in December 1947, Gandhi was "the saddest man one could picture." "If India has no further use for nonviolence," he said, "Can she have any for me?" He said Nehru and Patel were "hypotized by the glamor of the scientific progress and expanding economies of the West."[65] He kept letting Nehru and Patel know of incidents of corruption and extravagance in the new state. He distrusted the elite who were going to rule India and proposed that they should be sent "with their town-bred bodies" to live in a village, to drink from the pool where the villagers bathe and water their cattle, and to "bend their backs under the hot sun as they do."[66] He abhorred Westernization as much as ever.

He was as grieved at India's industrialization as at her militarization and bureaucratization:

God forbid that India should ever take to industrialism after the manner of the West. The economic impact of one single tiny island kingdom is today keeping the world in chains. If an entire nation of three hundred million took to similar economic exploitation, it would strip the world bare like locusts.[67]

He wrote to Nehru that the hope of peace and justice rested on the organization of India as a society of villages as he had declared in *Hind Swaraj* nearly forty years before.

Nehru replied: "I do not understand why a village should necessarily embody truth and nonviolence. A village, normally speaking, is backward intellectually and culturally, and no progress can be made from a backward environment. Narrow-minded people are much more likely to be untruthful and violent."[68] Pandey adds: "Nehru ignored Gandhi, wondering, perhaps for the first time, whether the Mahatma had outlived his usefulness,"[69] and says that during Gandhi's tours, from October 1946 to March 1947: "He was not missed in Delhi, where Nehru and Patel had taken upon themselves the sole responsibility for making policy decisions and planning strategy."[70]

And yet below their enthusiasm lay something close to despair. In the very letter in which Nehru rejected Gandhi's call for simplification and declared his own faith in the modern world if it would just follow the dictates of common sense and common decency, he ended, "but the world seems bent on committing suicide."[71] This was of course Gandhi's starting point, but Nehru could reach it only as an ending, a giving up. This was Gandhi's bitterest disappointment.

The Final Scenes

To put the two deaths in sharpest focus, we must concentrate upon the events that followed from Tolstoy's arousal on the night of October 28, 1910, and those that followed from Gandhi beginning to fast on January 13, 1948, each about two weeks before the climactic moment. When Tolstoy saw his wife going through his papers looking for his diaries, he was seized with disgust. He stayed silent, pretending to be still asleep. Only after she had left the room did he light his lamp. She returned immediately to see if anything was the matter, but he took that to be hypocrisy. He now remembered having heard something the night before, which must have been similar activities on her part. It was in the pattern of her behavior: she would pour meat stock into his mushroom soup before it left the kitchen in order to "look after him" by circumventing his vegetarianism.

Down below, Sasha and her friend had lain awake listening to the voices and movements above. It was 3 A.M. when Sonia went to bed. Tolstoy stayed awake, feeling out of breath from agitation and counting his pulse. Finally he decided that he must after all, despite so many decisions and revisions, leave. He went downstairs to Sasha and Varvara, now asleep. Sasha describes his standing in their doorway with a candle in his hand and "a bright face resolute and beautiful."[72] As companion he took only Dr. Makovitski, his physician, friend, and disciple.

Describing the night, Tolstoy said: "I tremble at the thought that she will hear and will come out—a scene, hysterics, and no getting away in the future without a scene."[73] He went to the stables to order horses to take them to the station:

It is night, pitch-dark. I get off the path to the lodge, fall into the bushes, get scratched, knock against trees, fall down, lose my cap, cannot find it; with difficulty make my way out, go home, take a cap, and with a lantern make my way to the stable and order the horses to be harnessed.[74]

On the way to the station, they saw some lights in the village houses where the peasants were lighting their stoves. Still full of doubts about what he ought to be doing, Tolstoy remarked sadly that he had not been able to endure to the end. "At Shchekino we wait an hour, and every minute I expect her to appear."[75]

He went first to Shamardino (the convent where his sister was living) and Sasha joined him. But he decided he would be found there, and they set off again by train. Tolstoy however, fell sick, and had to be taken off at a small station called Astapovo, where the station master, Ozolin, moved out of his station house to accommodate the sick man. His whereabouts were soon known to the press, who wired it to his family. Chertkov wired his congratulations when he heard what happened, and hastened to join Tolstoy when he learned how ill he was. Sonia hired a special train and followed with the other children. But she was refused entrance to the sick room, because of the agitation she was likely to cause the patient.

Tolstoy wrote his last words in his diary on November 3. "Fais ce que dois, advienne. . . . And it is all for the best, for the others and for me."[76] On November 5, he began to fumble with his sheets, perhaps trying to write, to inscribe, to compose, one last time. Sasha tells us that he hiccoughed a lot and could not be helped by milk, sugar-and-water, or anything else. When she and Tania asked if they should rearrange his pillows, he replied, obviously in irritation: "No, I only ask you to remember that there are many people besides Lev Tolstoy in the world, and you are thinking only of me."[77] On the sixth Sergei wrote to his wife that his mother was talking incessantly, and the journalists were listening to her avidly; that was the source of all the filthy gossip in the papers. (She was on veronal.) One of the things she told them was that Tolstoy had run away from home to advertise himself. On the seventh he died. Sonia was let into the room at 2 A.M., and he died at 5:45. The day after his funeral, she herself fell badly ill.

There were journalists at Astapovo from all over Russia and beyond. There was even a movie camera from Pathé News which took pictures of Sonia peering through the windows at the death bed she was denied entry to. Those inside had drawn the blinds when she looked in, for fear Tolstoy should open his eyes and see her face there. At her request, the cameras photographed her when she stood on the steps, posed to seem to be emerging from it.

Just so there were journalists and photographers at Birla House in Delhi where Gandhi spent his last days, although no one was there to record the actual assassination. He began his final fast on January 13. The first day cost him two pounds of his weight, reducing him to 109 pounds. The next day his doctor found acetic acid in his urine, which meant that his reserves of carbohydrates were used up and his body protein was being consumed. His kidneys were also failing to eliminate the water he drank. On that day Patel yielded over the money, but Gandhi demanded an agreement between all the communal leaders in Delhi (similar to the one he had got in Calcutta) promising that they would cooperate to prevent the outbreak of any more violence. In Pakistan people began to be anxious for Gandhi's life. But in Delhi the public response was sluggish and resentful. In the bazaars people said: "When will that old man stop bothering us?" and on the first evening Gandhi could hear a procession chanting hostile slogans. The communal leaders' signatures were finally secured on the morning of the eighteenth, and he took his first sip of orange juice.

From the point of view of rival politicians this fast was, like the others, a performance. And from the point of view of a people whose bloodlust had been aroused by Black Days and Direct Action Days and the riots and killings they produced, it was an inhibition. Gandhi and his peace making were both resented. As he lay on his cot on the first day of his fast, he could hear hostile slogans chanted: "We want blood for blood," and "If he wants to die, let him die." When Nehru heard the last, he stopped his car and jumped out to tell the chanters they would have to kill him before they said that again in his presence. His indignation and horror were no doubt sincere, but every politician must have felt, about one or another of Gandhi's fasts: "If he wants to die, let him die." Some sense of unwelcome complicity with the demonstrators may have fueled Nehru's anger.

In Bombay on the fifteenth, having seen Savarkar, the conspirators examined the weapons Badge had brought them and found that the pistols were unreliable, home-made weapons. On the nineteenth, in Delhi, they attempted some target practice and found that one would not fire at all and the other would not aim. Godse and Apte then made another trip, went to Gwalior, and got a decent pistol from the leader of the R.S.S.S. And on the twentieth they made their first attempt to kill Gandhi, which failed because various small things went wrong and Badge lost his nerve and failed to fire. Madanlal Pahwa was arrested for setting the time bomb which was to have been the others' signal. The details are as sad and ludicrous as those of Sonia's suicide attempts.

Recovering from his fast, Gandhi planned a pilgrimage on foot to Pakistan, for which he had received Jinnah's permission. He dispatched Sushila Nayar there to make plans. His idea was to lead as many Hindu refugees in India as he could back to the homes they had been driven from in Pakistan, to guarantee their safety with his life, and then perhaps to lead back Muslim refugees to India. He had fixed February 13 as the date of his departure from Wardha. Meanwhile of course he was busy with other things, like the new constitution for Congress, to redirect activity to village work again; and on the afternoon of January 30 he was arguing with Patel to withdraw the resignation from the cabinet which he had just made because of a quarrel with Nehru.

Because of this argument Gandhi was, most unusually, a few minutes late for his prayer meeting. As he approached the dais, along a corridor through the crowd, Godse stepped forward to meet him with the pistol concealed within his two clasped hands, bowing and saying: "Namaste, Mahatma." Then he pushed Manu aside with his left hand and fired point blank three times. It was 5:07 P.M. Gandhi sank to the ground with "He Ram" on his lips, according to Gurbadu Singh, a Gandhian businessman who was there. Karkare said it was just the guttural rasp, "Aagh."

Both deaths had profound immediate reverberations. Korolenko was in Poltava when Tolstoy died. He tells us that he stopped to buy a newspaper in the street, and the paperman said: "He's dead," and two passers-by halted, knowing who "he" must be. Despite the government's efforts to prevent them, five thousand students came from Moscow to Yasnaya Polyana to the funeral, and many more attended demonstrations for causes associated with his name on that day. Thus in the public sphere, Tolstoy's funeral marked, in Lenin's view, the end of Russia's period of reaction (1908–1910) and the beginning of a new period of radical protest.

On the private level, it caused a great change in Sonia's personality, seeming to free her from domination by an evil spirit, but subjecting her to grief and guilt. On November 29 she wrote in her diary: "Unendurable anguish, gnawing of conscience, weakness, and pity for my late husband that amounts to suffering. How he suffered latterly. . . . I cannot live." And on December 7: "Profound and unendurable despair all day." On the sixteenth she recorded a painful discussion of the inheritance with her sons. "Andrey pitiable with his nervous instability. We are all like that."[78] On the seventh, Goldenveizer had visited Yasnaya Polyana, and he reports that Sonia said to him, "in a broken and trembling voice, 'What happened to me? What overcame me? How could I have done it? I myself don't know what it was. . . . If you only knew what I am enduring, Alexei Borisovich! These terrible nights. How could I have been so blind: You know I killed him.'" She was reconciled to Sasha and died in 1919.

Gandhi's death was a uniquely national event. He was given an enormous state funeral that a million people attended and that removed him from his ashram and family connections. It was military in style because Mountbatten persuaded Nehru that only the military could handle the crowds, the processions, and the dangerous emotions involved. But of course his family members were there, including Harilal, soon to die and already a ghost. And personal grief was intense all over India and beyond. Vincent Sheean, like so many American journalists in love with Gandhi, suffered literal stigmata; many people felt a hope of personal and political salvation had been destroyed. On the public level the most striking short-term effect of the assassination was the discrediting of the R.S.S.S. and the Hindu Mahasabha. An angry crowd besieged Savarkar Sadan in Bombay and Godse's newspaper office in Poona, and all the leaders of right-wing nationalism had to disappear for a year. Savarkar was put on trial, though nothing could be proved against him. And with the paralysis of the right wing, India was able to follow a more conciliatory policy towards Pakistan.

Thus for all the ignominy and ignobility surrounding them, these were two great deaths, worthy of, fit conclusion and crown to, two great lives.

Russian and Indian Words Used in the Book

ahimsa (Indian) harming no one and nothing
anjuman (Indian) association
bania (Indian) of the commercial caste
brahmacharya (Indian) renunciation of sexual activity
charkha (Indian) spinning wheel
chela (Indian) disciple
desyatina (Russian) about 2.7 acres
dharma (Indian) duty or law
dhoti (Indian) cloth tied around the waist
diwan (Indian) chief administrator
duragraha (Indian) mute reproach
goonda (Indian) rowdy or thug
harijan (Indian) Gandhi's word for Untouchable
hartal (Indian) general strike
karma (Indian) action, in its moral character
khadi (Indian) homespun cloth
ki-jai (Indian) hail to!
kisan (Indian) peasant
kshattriya (Indian) of the warrior caste
maya (Indian) what seems real but is not
moksha (Indian) freedom, in the vision of God
nai talim (Indian) Gandhi's new education theory
narodnik (Russian) populist

raznochintsy (Russian) of mixed caste
sabha (Indian) association
sadhana (Indian) method
saddhu (Indian) ascetic
sanatana (Indian) orthodox
sanyasi (Indian) religious wanderer
shastra (Indian) holy book
shakti (Indian) female power
shudra (Indian) of the agricultural caste
shuba (Russian) fur coat
swadeshi (Indian) locally made
swaraj (Indian) self-rule
vakil (Indian) attorney
vanaprastha (Indian) giving up domestic life
varna (Indian) caste
varnashrama (Indian) division of life into developmental stages
yurodivi (Russian) God's fool

In sums of money relating to Tolstoy, "R" stands for rubles; in sums of money relating to Gandhi, "R" stands for rupees.

Note on the Endnotes and Bibliography

The edition of Gandhi used most often is the Navajivan *Collected Works of Mahatma Gandhi*, of which seventy-seven volumes have so far appeared. They are referred to in the footnotes in the following way: Gandhi, the Roman number of the volume, and the Arabic number of the page. I have also referred to some of his works from other editions.

In the case of Tolstoy, I have used mainly the *Sobranie Sochinenii*, which appeared in Moscow in 1960 in twenty volumes. It is referred to in the following way: Tolstoy, the Roman number of the volume, followed by the Arabic number of the page. Sometimes I have referred to the fuller "Jubilee" edition of ninety volumes, which is called the *Polnoe Sobranie*; in those cases I put "Jubilee" in parentheses. I first read Tolstoy in English (I have gone back from the English to the Russian, most often), and the fullest edition available to me was that published in Boston in 1904, edited by Leo Wiener. I have identified it by putting Wiener in parentheses.

In other cases, the author's name and the page reference alone are given in the footnote and fuller detail is to be found in the bibliography. When two books by the same author are in the bibliography, a brief form of the title in question is included in the footnote.

When I have quoted from the *Sobranie Sochinenii* edition of Tolstoy's diaries, I have let the date take the place of a page number for reference purposes because it is usually more precise. The diary is to be found in volumes XIX and XX of that edition.

In the case of Tolstoy's major fiction, I have trusted to the modern translations, because translating Tolstoy has been a consistent and in some sense collaborative venture for nearly a century now, and the new versions have the benefit of considerable critical scrutiny. The nonfiction, however, has been translated more rarely and with less scholarly scruple, since it was meant for immediate social effect. And a lot of letters, journals, and some essays have never been translated. In these cases I have tried to go back to the Russian originals and translate, with the help—which I much appreciate—of Dina Birman. However, this was not possible in all cases, because some of the major sources gave no clue of their sources. This is true of Paul Biriukov, of Cynthia Asquith, and in many places of Leo Wiener. While the translators of Tolstoy's anthologies of devotional readings rearranged his work quite radically. In these cases, I have not gone behind the English-language sources.

While this approach appears to give a half-scholarly character to my dealings with Tolstoy's texts, the whole work is only half-scholarly if we use scholarship in the sense—which is obviously a valid sense—in which it is used by those who have devoted their lives to the study of Tolstoy or of Gandhi. I am not a specialist in these subjects, but a generalist. I obviously know more about the two men than the average reader, but I have learned more just in order to give me the authority to generalize about them. I hope this will justify my half-way position.

Notes

INTRODUCTION

1. Tolstoy, XVI:439, 450 (Wiener).
2. Tolstoy, *Letters*, II:341.
3. Ibid., p. 343.
4. Tolstoy, XIX:388.
5. Gandhi, XLVII:368–369.
6. Payne, *Mahatma Gandhi*, p.410.
7. Gandhi, XXIV:551.
8. Gandhi, LVIII:248.

SECTION I: THE FIRST NINETEEN YEARS, Tolstoy 1828–1847, Gandhi 1869–1888

A. The Beginnings

1. Devanesan, p. 143.
2. Biriukov, I:18.
3. Troyat, p. 17.
4. Ilya Tolstoy, p. 132.
5. Prabhudas Gandhi, p. 17.
6. Gandhi, *Autobiography* (Washington ed.), p. 12.
7. Ibid., p. 33.
8. Ibid., p. 32.
9. Ibid., p. 34.
10. Payne, *Mahatma Gandhi*, p. 24.

B. Tolstoy's Boyhood

1. Tolstoy, XXIII:7 (Wiener).
2. Simmons, *Tolstoy* (1973), p. 20.
3. Sukhotina-Tolstoy, *Tolstoy Remembered*, p. 156.
4. Troyat, p. 31.
5. Biriukov, I:25.

C. Gandhi's Boyhood

1. Gandhi, XXIV:170.
2. Ibid.
3. Prabhudas Gandhi, p. 28.
4. Ibid.
5. Gandhi, *Autobiography* (Ahmedabad ed.), p. 6.
6. Shahani, p. 6.
7. Gandhi, *Autobiography* (Ahmedabad ed.), p. 6.
8. Watson and Brown, p. 26.
9. Gandhi, *Autobiography* (Boston ed.), p. 21.

D. Tolstoy's Adolescence

1. Troyat, p. 31.
2. Simmons (1946), p. 51.
3. Ibid.
4. Tolstoy, XIX:39.
5. Tolstoy, *Childhood, Boyhood, Youth*, p. 179.
6. Troyat, p. 48.
7. Ibid.
8. J.J. Rousseau, p. 107.
9. Ibid. pp. 94, 96, 97.
10. Ibid. p. 154.

E. Gandhi's Adolescence

1. Gandhi, *Asia* (November, 1936), p. 699.
2. Ibid., p. 700.
3. Gandhi, *Autobiography* (Washington ed.), p. 38.
4. Ibid.
5. Ved Mehta, p. 78.
6. Upadhyaya, p. 44.
7. Hay, in *Encounter with Erikson*, p. 82.
8. Doke, p. 33.
9. Gandhi, I:53.
10. Ibid.
11. Gandhi, *Autobiography* (Boston ed.), p. 40.
12. Payne, p. 52.
13. Gandhi, I:61.
14. Gandhi, I:7.

SECTION II: YOUTH,
Tolstoy 1847–1862, Gandhi 1888–1906

A. Tolstoy 1847–1855, Moscow and Dandyism

1. Biriukov, I:101.
2. Tolstoy, *Diary*, p. 37.
3. Biriukov, I:110.
4. Troyat, p. 62.
5. Tolstoy, *Childhood, Boyhood, Youth*, p. 170.
6. Tolstoy, *The Cossacks*, Afterword by F.D. Reeve, p. 214.
7. A. Tolstoy, *My Father*, p. 165.
8. Biriukov, I:127.
9. Ibid., p. 142.
10. Ibid., p. 147.
11. Tolstoy, *Childhood, Boyhood, Youth*, p. 184.
12. Tolstoy, *Diary*, p. 17.
13. Ibid., p. 18.
14. Ibid., p. 37.
15. Biriukov, I:169.
16. Simmons (1946), p. 111.
17. Simmons (1973), p. 43.

B. Gandhi 1888–1894, London and Vegetarianism

1. Gandhi, I:37.
2. Gandhi, *Autobiography* (Washington ed.), p. 86.
3. Ibid.
4. Gandhi, XXVII:108.
5. Gandhi, XXVII:111.
6. Gandhi, XXXIX:74.
7. Gandhi XXXIX:80.
8. Gandhi, *Autobiography* (Boston ed.), p. 97.
9. Ibid.
10. Gandhi, *Autobiography* (Boston ed.), p. 112.
11. Gandhi, *Autobiography* (Washington ed.), p. 157.
12. Gandhi, I:74.
13. Ibid., p. 76.
14. Mehta, p. 103.
15. Gandhi, *Autobiography* (Washington ed.), p. 173.

C. Tolstoy 1855–1862, St. Petersburg and Literature

1. Troyat, p. 128.
2. Vucinich, *Social Thought*, p. 1.
3. Tolstoy, XX:192.
4. Biriukov, I:243.
5. Tolstoy, XIX:201.
6. Ibid., p. 199.
7. A. Tolstoy, "Memoirs," in *Tolstoy in the Memory of his Contemporaries*, p. 64.
8. Tolstoy, *Tolstoy's Letters*, p. 122.
9. Tolstoy, XIX:230.
10. N.I. Peterson, in *Tolstoy in the Memory of his Contemporaries*, p. 101.

11. Shklovsky, p. 263.
12. Tolstoy, *Tolstoy's Letters*, p. 190.
13. S. Tolstoy, *Autobiography*, p. 27.
14. S. Tolstoy, *Diary*, p. 13.
15. Tolstoy, XIX:249.

D. *Gandhi 1894–1906, Johannesburg and Politics*

1. Gandhi, *Autobiography* (Washington ed.), p. 203.
2. Gandhi, XXXIX:133.
3. Huttenback, *Gandhi in South Africa*, p. 159.
4. Gandhi, II:12.
5. Ibid., p. 224.
6. Ibid., p. 282.
7. Carstairs, p. 107.
8. Gandhi, III:110.
9. Gandhi, *Satyagraha in South Africa* (Stanford ed.), p. 72.
10. Gandhi, III:168.
11. Ibid., p. 261.
12. Ibid.
13. Gandhi, *Satyagraha in South Africa* (Ahmedabad 1928 ed.), p. 77.
14. Ibid., p. 151.
15. Gandhi, III:330.
16. Gandhi, IV:1.
17. Ibid., p. 6.
18. Ibid., p. 69.
19. Gandhi, *Autobiography* (Boston ed.), p. 247.
20. Gandhi, LI:101.

INTERLUDE: THE NEW LIFE, 1894–1910

1. Tolstoy, *The Kingdom of God is Within You*, p. 9.
2. Ibid., p. 140.
3. Phelps, p. 11.
4. Gandhi, IX:388.
5. Ibid., p. 480.
6. Nag, p. 82.
7. Ibid., p. 96.
8. Gandhi, X:7.
9. Ibid., X:35.
10. Ibid., p. 54.
11. Ibid., p. 14.
12. Ibid., p. 40.
13. Ibid., p. 47.
14. Ibid., pp. 51, 42.
15. Ibid., p. 41.
16. Nag, p. 71.
17. Ibid.
18. Gifford, p. 167.
19. Tolstoy, X:369.
20. Carpenter, p. 203.

21. Gandhi, IX:302.
22. Payne, p. 202.
23. Ibid., p. 617.
24. Ibid., pp. 204–205.
25. Pandey, *Indian National Movement,* pp. 26–27.
26. Ulam, p. 249.
27. Emily Brown, *Har Dayal,* p. 148.
28. Koestler, p. 153.

SECTION III: MANHOOD, Tolstoy 1862–1881, Gandhi 1906–1921

A. *Tolstoy 1862–1870,* War and Peace

1. S. Tolstoy, *Diary,* p. 90.
2. Ibid., p. 89.
3. Ibid., p. 227.
4. Ibid., p. 246.
5. Ibid., p. 109.
6. Ibid., p. 97.
7. Ibid., p. 93.
8. Ibid., p. 88.
9. Ibid., p. 127.
10. Ibid., p. 132.
11. Ibid., p. 144.
12. Ibid., p. 48.
13. Ibid., p. 28.
14. A. Tolstoy, *My Father,* p. 240.
15. Maude, ed., *Family Views,* p. 111.
16. Tolstoy, *Tolstoy's Letters,* p. 182.
17. Tolstoy, XIX:264.
18. S. Tolstoy, *Diary,* p. 156.
19. S. Tolstoy, *Autobiography,* p. 27.
20. Ibid., p. 32.
21. Tolstoy, XIX:266.
22. A. Tolstoy, *The Tragedy of Tolstoy,* p. 316.
23. Asquith (London ed.), p. 36.
24. Kuzminskaya, p. 124.
25. Ibid., p. 164.
26. Asquith, (London ed.), p. 68.
27. Tolstoy, *Tolstoy's Letters,* p. 182.
28. Ibid., p. 201–202.
29. Troyat, pp. 282–283.
30. K.B. Feuer, p. 316.
31. Tolstoy, *War and Peace,* p. 1,364.
32. Ibid., p. 264.
33. Ibid., p. 1,049.
34. Eikhenbaum, *Tolstoy in the Sixties,* p. 150.
35. Tolstoy, *War and Peace,* p. 457.
36. Ibid., p. 459.
37. Ibid., p. 461.
38. Ibid., p. 462.

39. Ibid.
40. Ibid., p. 357.
41. Ibid., p. 950.
42. Ibid., p. 797.
43. Ibid., p. 1,122.
44. Ibid., p. 1,226.
45. Ibid., p. 67.
46. Ibid., p. 599.
47. Ibid., p. 356.
48. Ibid., p. 1,147

B. *Gandhi 1906–1915,* Satyagraha *in South Africa*

1. Gandhi, VII:529.
2. Gandhi XI:133.
3. Payne, p. 243.
4. Gandhi, XXXIX:491.
5. Gandhi, VIII:232.
6. Gandhi, X:429.
7. Gandhi, XI:68.
8. Ibid., p. 237.
9. Gandhi, XII:410.
10. Ibid., p. 177.
11. Elwin and Winslow, p. 45.
12. Ibid., pp. 43–44.
13. Gandhi, XII:46.
14. Ibid., p. 47.
15. Ibid., p. 52.
16. Ibid., p. 48.
17. Huttenback, *Racism and Empire*, p. 14.
18. Gandhi, XI:66.
19. Gandhi, X:312.
20. Gandhi, *Satyagraha in South Africa* (Stanford ed.), p. 107.
21. Ibid.
22. Rajendra, Prasad, *At the Feet of Mahatma Gandhi*, p. 113.
23. Gandhi, *Indian Opinion*, Jan. 4, 1908.
24. Gandhi, VIII:4.
25. Gandhi, VII:118.
26. Yule and Burnett, p. 44.
27. Gandhi, *Satyagraha in South Africa* (Stanford ed.), p. 287.

C. *Tolstoy 1870–1881,* Anna Karenina

1. Tolstoy, *Tolstoy's Letters*, p. 243.
2. Ibid.
3. Ibid., p. 244.
4. August 26, 1875.
5. Tolstoy, *Letters*, p. 247.
6. Sergei Tolstoy, p. 33.
7. Tolstoy, *Socialisme et Christianisme*, p. 344.
8. Troyat, p. 346.
9. Ilya Tolstoy, pp. 199–201.
10. Simmons (1946), p. 338.

11. Tolstoy, XIX:292.
12. Leon L. Tolstoy, p. 36.
13. Tolstoy, *Anna Karenina*, p. 37.
14. Ibid., p. 109.
15. Ibid., p. 69.
16. Ibid., p. 76.
17. Ibid., p. 225.
18. Ibid., p. 560.
19. Ibid., pp. 154–155.
20. Ibid., pp. 566–567.
21. Ibid., pp. 300–301.
22. Ibid., p. 244.
23. Ibid., p. 275.
24. Ibid., p. 265.
25. Ibid., p. 37.
26. Ibid., p. 57.
27. Ibid., p. 425.
28. Ibid., p. 430.
29. Ibid., p. 157.
30. Ibid., pp. 486–487.
31. Ibid., p. 351.
32. Tolstoy, *Portable Tolstoy*, p. 681.
33. Ibid., p. 679.

D. Gandhi 1915–1921, The Mahatma of India

1. Gandhi, XX:526.
2. Gandhi, XIV:95.
3. Gandhi, XIII:301.
4. Gandhi, XIV:367.
5. Ibid., p. 190.
6. Ibid., p. 385.
7. Ibid., p. 53.
8. Ibid., 474.
9. Gandhi, XV:264.
10. Ibid., p. 88.
11. Gandhi, XVII:118.
12. Ibid., p. 119.
13. Ibid., p. 124.
14. Ibid., p. 127.
15. Ibid., p. 122.
16. Ibid., p. 121.
17. Ibid. XVIII:191.
18. Gandhi, XVII:376.
19. Ibid., p. 130.
20. Ibid., p. 193.
21. Gandhi, XIX:80.
22. Ibid., p. 137.
23. Gandhi, XIX:138.
24. Ibid.
25. Ibid.
26. Sanger (*Asia*), p. 701.
27. Gandhi, XVII:358.

28. Gandhi, XIV:468.
29. Ibid., p. 434.
30. Ibid., p. 65.
31. Ibid., p. 437.
32. Ibid.
33. Gandhi, XVI:78.
34. Gandhi, XIV:444.
35. Gandhi, XXI:319.
36. Gandhi, XIV:476.
37. Ibid., p. 485.
38. Ibid., pp. 515–516.
39. Ibid., p. 509.
40. Rajendra Prasad, *Autobiography*, p. 104.
41. Gandhi, XIV:505.
42. Gandhi, XIX:13.
43. Ibid., p. 213.
44. Ibid., p. 105.

SECTION IV: OLD AGE,
Tolstoy 1881–1910, Gandhi 1921–1948

A. Introductory

1. Tolstoy, XIX:523 (Wiener).
2. Tolstoy, *The Pathway of Life*, II:181.
3. Tolstoy, *The Circle of Reading*.
4. Ibid.
5. Gandhi, XLVII:317.
6. Tolstoy, *Portable Tolstoy*, p. 655.
7. Tendulkar, II, p. 131.
8. Prabhu, p. 25.
9. Gandhi, XLVII:398.
10. Tendulkar, II:58.
11. Gandhi, XLVII:71.
12. Reynolds, *Gandhi Marg* IV:283.
13. Shklovsky, p. 547.
14. Sergeenko, p. 62.
15. Fischer, p. 141.
16. Mehta, p. 3.
17. Watson, p. 13.
18. Ibid., p. 33.
19. Muratov, p. 128.
20. Tolstoy, XIX:477.
21. Tolstoy, XVIII:109.
22. Elwin, p. 52.
23. Sukhotina-Tolstoy, *Tolstoy Remembered*, p. 25.
24. Ibid., p. 191.
25. Dwarkadas, p. 22.
26. Shukla, *Reminiscences of Gandhiji*, p. 178.
27. Tendulkar, I, Foreword by Nehru.
28. Moon, p. 12.

29. Bhave, *The Third Power*, p. 103.
30. Bhave, *The Steadfast Wisdom*, p. 30.
31. A. Tolstoy, *My Father*, p. 437.
32. Goldenveizer, p. 36.
33. Tolstoy, XX:260.
34. Tolstoy, *Tolstoy's Letters*, p. 356.
35. Asquith, p. 90.
36. Sergeenko, p. 62.
37. Gandhi, LXI:26.
38. Tolstoy, XX: July 12, 1900.

B. Tolstoy 1881–1894, Renunciation of Rank and Wealth

1. Sergei Tolstoy, p. 35.
2. Gandhi, XLIII:361.
3. Behrs, pp. 134–135.
4. Asquith, (London ed.), p. 161.
5. Tolstoy, *Walk in the Light* (Wiener) XIX:237.
6. Troyat, pp. 384–385.
7. Troyat, p. 427.
8. S. Tolstoy, *Countess Tolstoy's Later Diary*, p. 50.
9. Ibid., p. 20.
10. Ibid., p. 60.
11. Ibid., p. 65.
12. Ibid.
13. Tolstoy, *Tolstoy's Letters*, p. 391.
14. Ibid.
15. Ibid.
16. Tania Tolstoy, *Tolstoy Remembered* (New York ed.), p. 202.
17. S. Tolstoy, *Countess Tolstoy's Later Diary*, p. 13.
18. Ibid., p. 16.
19. Ibid., p. 14.
20. S. Tolstoy, *Diary of Tolstoy's Wife*, pp. 225–227.
21. Chertkov, p. 97.
22. Tolstoy, XIX:326.
23. Tolstoy XIX:327.
24. Tolstoy, XIX:334.
25. Troyat, p. 430.
26. Simmons (1946), p. 375.
27. Asquith (Boston ed.), p. 112.
28. Shklovsky, p. 600.
29. Ibid., p. 595.
30. S. Tolstoy, *Diary of Tolstoy's Wife*, p. 238.
31. S. Tolstoy, *Countess Tolstoy's Later Diary*, p. 20.
32. Tolstoy, XXII:180 (Wiener).
33. Tolstoy, XVI:4 (Wiener).
34. Ibid., p. 17.
35. Tolstoy, XVII:63 (Wiener).
36. Tolstoy, XV:38–39.
37. Simmons (1946), p. 372.
38. Tolstoy, *Tolstoy on Art*, p. 62.
39. Ibid.
40. Ibid.

C. *Gandhi 1921-1931, Politics Left and Returned To*

1. Gandhi, XXXIX:291.
2. Gandhi, XXIII:339.
3. Moon, p. 292.
4. Tendulkar, II:91.
5. Gandhi, XXII:10.
6. Ibid., p. 271.
7. Ibid., p. 377.
8. J. Nehru, *A Bunch of Old Letters*, p. 24.
9. Gandhi XXII:501.
10. Ibid., p. 435.
11. Ibid., p. 437.
12. Gandhi, XXIII:114–115.
13. Gandhi, XXVI:137.
14. Ibid., p. 138.
15. Ibid., p. 140.
16. Ibid., p. 486.
17. Ibid., p. 488.
18. Ibid., p. 490.
19. Ibid.
20. Gandhi, XXVI:491.
21. Ibid.
22. Rao and Sardasai, p. 109.
23. Ibid., p. 114.
24. Ibid.
25. Gandhi, XXXIV:285.
26. Gandhi, XXXVII:212.
27. Ibid., p. 200.
28. Gandhi, XLII:424–425.
29. Ibid.
30. Gandhi, XLII:426.
31. Gandhi, XLI:499.
32. Gandhi, XLVIII:434.
33. Gandhi, *Satyagraha In South Africa* (Stanford ed.), p. 93.
34. Gandhi, LXIII:406.
35. Gandhi, LVII:446.
36. Gandhi, XLII:238.
37. Judith Brown, *Gandhi and Civil Disobedience*, p. 246.
38. Gandhi, XXVII:183.
39. Gandhi, XLI:356–357.

D. *Tolstoy 1894–1910, Renunciation of Art and Intellect*

1. Simmons (1946), p. 511.
2. Tolstoy, XX:12.
3. Ibid., p. 39.
4. Ibid.
5. Ibid.
6. Asquith (Boston ed.), p. 166.
7. S. Tolstoy, *Later Diary*, p. 216.
8. Asquith, p. 195.
9. Tolstoy, XVIII:187.
10. Sukhotina-Tolstoy, *The Tolstoy Home*, p. 134.

11. Asquith, (Boston ed.), p. 183.
12. Tolstoy, *Socialisme et Christianisme*.
13. Muratov, p. 301.
14. Tolstoy, XVIII:363 (June 7, 1905).
15. Tolstoy, XX:182.
16. Tolstoy, *On Life*, pp. 257–262.
17. Tolstoy, XX:256.
18. Chertkov, p. 6.
19. Ibid., p. 242.
20. Tolstoy, *Civil Disobedience*, p. 76.
21. Ibid., p. 312.
22. Tolstoy, *On Life*, p. 212.
23. Tolstoy, *Father Sergius, etc.*, pp. 287–288.
24. Tolstoy, *The Law of Love and the Law of Violence*, Preface.
25. Tolstoy, *The Pathway of Life*, p. 95.
26. Proffer, ed., *The Silver Age of Russian Culture*, p. 20.
27. Tolstoy, XX:59.
28. *Tolstoy in the Memory of his Contemporaries*, p. 406.
29. Tolstoy, XX:57.
30. Tolstoy, XX:26.
31. Tolstoy, XVIII:157.
32. Tolstoy, *On Art*, p. 43.
33. Tolstoy, *Journal*, p. 78.
34. Tolstoy, *What is Art?* pp. 67, 70, 127.
35. Ibid., p. 74.
36. Tolstoy, XX:72.
37. Rolland, *Tolstoy*, p. 188.
38. Tolstoy, *Journal*, p. 64.
39. S. Tolstoy, *Later Diary*, p. 155.
40. Ibid., p. 225.
41. Ibid., p. 183.
42. Ibid., p. 213.
43. Ibid., p. 215.
44. Ibid., p. 158.
45. Ibid.
46. Ibid., p. 88.

E. Gandhi 1931–1948, Leadership Lost and Retrieved

1. Pandey, *Nehru*, p. 12.
2. Radhakrishnan, *Mahatma Gandhi*, p. 10.
3. Gandhi, LIX:4–5.
4. Ibid., p. 57.
5. Ibid., p. 355.
6. Gandhi, LV:240.
7. Gandhi, LXI:242.
8. Gandhi, LXIV:35.
9. Ibid., p. 52.
10. Payne, pp. 474, 469.
11. Gandhi, LV:438.
12. Ibid., p. 439.
13. Gandhi, LVIII:460–461
14. B.R. Nanda, "The Legacy of Gandhi and Nehru," *Gandhi Marg*, January 1980, p. 621.

15. Gandhi, LXV:419.
16. Gandhi, LXVII:132.
17. *Harijan*, June 21, 1942.
18. Tendulkar, VII:15.
19. Tendulkar, VIII:16.
20. Ibid., p. 138.
21. Gandhi, LXXIII:103.
22. Collins and LaPierre, p. 129.
23. Ibid., p. 156.
24. Ibid., p. 29.
25. Gandhi, LII:9.
26. Gandhi, LVIII:459.
27. Tendulkar, IV:3.
28. Gandhi, LX:104.
29. Collins and LaPierre, p. 22.
30. Ibid., p. 38.
31. Watson and Brown, p. 103.
32. Pyarelal, *Mahatma Gandhi, The Last Phase*, II:15.
33. Collins and LaPierre, p. 233.
34. Ibid., p. 310.
35. Ibid., p. 302.

CLIMAX: THE TWO DEATHS

A. The Death Lines

1. Chertkov, *The Last Days of Tolstoy*, p. 71.
2. Ibid.
3. Gandhi, LXXIV:132.
4. Gandhi, LXXIV:113.
5. Tolstoy, XX:310.
6. S. Tolstoy, *The Final Struggle*, p. 129.
7. Leon L. Tolstoy, p. 218.
8. Ibid., p. 210.
9. Ibid., p. 54.
10. Asquith, p. 233 (1961).
11. Ibid., p. 228.
12. Payne, p. 469.
13. S. Tolstoy, *The Final Struggle*, p. 178.
14. Ibid., p. 99.
15. Ibid., p. 109.
16. Ibid., p. 111.
17. Payne, p. 637.
18. Malgonkar, p. 29.
19. Payne, p. 638.
20. Tolstoy, XX:212.
21. Ibid., p. 218.
22. S. Tolstoy, *The Final Struggle*, p. 198.
23. Tolstoy, XVIII:363.
24. S. Tolstoy, *The Final Struggle*, p. 104.
25. Tolstoy, XX:331.

26. S. Tolstoy, *The Final Struggle*, p. 281
27. Ibid., p. 136.
28. Ibid., p. 296.
29. A. Tolstoy, *My Father*, p. 500.
30. S. Tolstoy, *The Final Struggle*, p. 121.
31. Ibid., p. 139.
32. Ibid., p. 141.
33. Ibid., p. 142.
34. Ibid., p. 185.
35. Ibid., p. 233.
36. Collins and LaPierre, p. 29.
37. S. Tolstoy, *The Final Struggle*, p. 86.
38. Tolstoy, XX:387.
39. Ibid., p. 552.
40. Chertkov, p. 24.
41. Tolstoy, *Tolstoy's Letters*, p. 687.
42. Chertkov, p. 67.
43. Payne, p. 547.
44. Sergeenko, p. 271.
45. Ibid.
46. Gandhi, LXVIII:382.
47. Gandhi, LXXVI:109.
48. Mehta, p. 168.
49. Gandhi, LXVI:182.
50. Watson and Brown, p. 10.
51. S. Tolstoy, *The Final Struggle*, p. 78.
52. Pyarelal, *Mahatma Gandhi: The Last Phase*, I:86.
53. S. Tolstoy, *The Final Struggle*, p. 104.
54. Ibid.
55. Ibid., p. 105.
56. Ibid., p. 106.
57. Tolstoy, XVIII:495.
58. S. Tolstoy, *The Final Struggle*, p. 113.
59. Ibid., p. 242.
60. Bulgakov, p. 158.
61. S. Tolstoy, *The Final Struggle*, p. 234.
62. Chertkov, p. 35 ff.
63. Ibid., p. 64.
64. Collins and LaPierre, p. 196.
65. Ibid., p. 369.
66. Ibid.
67. Pyarelal, *Mahatma Gandhi, The Last Phase*, II:589.
68. Pandey, *Nehru*, p. 252.
69. Ibid.
70. Pandey, *Nehru*, p. 276.
71. Pyarelal, *Mahatma Gandhi, The Last Phase*, II:546.
72. Chertkov., p. 65.
73. Ibid., p. 66.
74. Ibid.
75. Ibid.
76. Chertkov, p. 131.
77. A. Tolstoy, *Tolstoy*, p. 316.
78. S. Tolstoy, *The Final Struggle*, p. 431.

Bibliography

Aksakov, Sergei. *Chronicles of a Russian Family.* Translated by M. C. Beverley. London, 1924.

———. *A Russian Gentleman.* Translated by J. D. Duff. London, 1917.

———. *Years of Childhood.* Translated by J. D. Duff. New York, 1960.

Ambedkar, B. R. *Gandhi and Gandhism.* Introduction by Bhagwan Das. Jullundur, 1970.

Anand, M. R. *The Humanism of M. K. Gandhi.* Bombay, 1967.

Armytage, W.H.R. *Heavens Below.* London, 1961.

Ashe, Geoffrey. *Gandhi.* New York, 1968.

Asquith, Cynthia. *Married to Tolstoy.* Boston, 1961 (London, 1964).

Baddeley, John F. *The Russian Conquest of the Caucasus.* London, 1908.

———. *Russia, Mongolia, China.* New York, 1967.

Baig, Tara Ali. *Sarojini Naidu.* New Delhi, 1974.

Baker, James H. *St. Petersburg: Industrialism and Change.* Montreal, 1976.

Balvantsimha. *Under the Shelter of Bapu.* Ahmedabad, 1962.

Bandhyopadhyaya, J. *Mao Tse Tung and Gandhi.* Bombay, 1973.

Barr, Mary. *Bapu.* Bombay, 1949.

Basham, A.L. *The Wonder That Was India.* New York, 1954.

Bataille, Georges. *Eroticism.* London, 1962.

Bearce, George D. *British Attitudes Towards India 1784–1858.* New York, 1961.

Bedford, C. H. *The Seeker: D. S. Merezhkovsky.* Lawrence, Kansas, 1975.

Behrs, C. A. *Recollections of Count Tolstoy.* London, 1893.

Benson, Ruth Crego. *Women in Tolstoy.* Urbana, Illinois, 1973.

Berlin, Isaiah. *Karl Marx: His Life and Environment.* New York, 1978.

Bernal, J. D. *The World, the Flesh, and the Devil.* Bloomington, Indiana, 1967.

Bhattacharya, J. N. *Hindu Castes and Sects.* Calcutta, 1968.

Bhave, Vinoba. *The Steadfast Wisdom.* n.p., 1966.

———. *Talks on the Gita.* n.p., 1970.

———. *The Third Power.* n.p., 1972.

Bill, Valentine T. *The Forgotten Class.* New York, 1959.

Billington, James H. *Fires in the Minds of Men*. New York, 1980.
―――――. *The Icon and the Axe*. New York, 1966.
―――――. *Mikhailkovsky and Russian Populism*. London, 1958.
Biriukov, P. *Leo Tolstoy: His Life and Work*. New York, 1906. See also Tolstoy, *Socialisme et Christianisme*.
Birla, G. D. *In the Shadow of the Mahatma*. Bombay, 1953.
Bodelsen, C. A. *Studies in Mid-Victorian Imperialism*. London, 1968.
Bolitho, Hector. *Jinnah*. London, 1954.
Bondarev, Timothy (and Tolstoy). *On Toil*. Chicago, 1891.
Bose, N. K. *Lectures on Gandhism*. Ahmedabad, 1971.
―――――. *My Days With Gandhi*. Calcutta, 1953.
―――――. *Selections From Gandhi*. Ahmedabad, 1947.
Bowle, John. *The Imperial Achievement*. Boston, 1975.
Boyer, Paul. *Chez Tolstoi*. Paris, 1950.
Brogan, Denis. *Proudhon*. London, 1934.
Broido, Vera. *Apostles into Terrorists*. New York, 1977.
Brontë, Charlotte. *Jane Eyre*. New York, 1950.
Broomfield, J. II. *Elite Conflict in a Plural Society*. Berkeley, California, 1968
Brower, Daniel R. *Training the Nihilists*. Ithaca, New York, 1975.
Brown, Emily C. *Har Dayal*. Tucson, Arizona, 1975.
Brown, Judith M. *Gandhi and Civil Disobedience*. Cambridge, 1977.
―――――. *Gandhi's Rise to Power*. Cambridge, 1972.
Bulgakov, V. G. *The Last Year of Leo Tolstoi*. Translated by Ann Dunnigan. New York, 1971.
Bunin, I. *Memoirs and Portraits*. Translated by Traill and Chancellor. New York, 1951.
Byrnes, Robert. *Pobedonostsev*. Bloomington, Indiana, 1968.
Carpenter, Edward. *My Days and Dreams*. London, 1921.
Carstairs, G. Morris. *The Twice Born*. Bloomington, Indiana, 1961.
Chertkov, Vladimir. *The Last Days of Tolstoy*. London, 1922.
Clarke, Arthur C. *Prelude to Space*. London, 1951.
Collins, Larry, and LaPierre, Dominique. *Freedom at Midnight*. New York, 1975.
Confino, Michael. *Daughter of a Revolutionary*. LaSalle, 1974.
Cook, Nilla Cram. *My Road to India*. New York, 1939.
Coomaraswamy, A. K. *Selected Works*. Edited by Roger Lipsey. Princeton, New Jersey, 1977
Curtiss, John S. *Russian Army Under Nicholas I*. North Carolina, 1965.
de Custine, M. *Journey for Our Time*. Translated by P. P. Kohler. New York, 1951.
De Kiewiet, C. W. *A History of South Africa*. New York, 1940.
De Lubac, H. *The Unmarxian Socialist*. Translated by R. E. Scantlebury. London, 1948.
Desai, Mahadev. *Day to Day with Gandhi*. Ahmedabad, 1968.
―――――. *The Diary of Mahadev Desai*. Volume I. Ahmedabad, 1953.
―――――. *Gandhiji in Indian Villages*. Madras, 1927.
―――――. *The Story of Bardoli*. Ahmadabad, 1929.
Detienne, M. *Dionysos Slain*. Baltimore, Maryland, 1979.
Devanesen, C. D. S. *The Making of the Mahatma*. Madras, 1969.
Dillon, E. J. *Count Leo Tolstoy*. London, 1972.
Dimock, Edward C. *The Thief of Love*. Chicago, 1963.
Doke, Josephy J. *M. K. Gandhi: An Indian Patriot in South Africa*. London, 1909.
Dolgoff, Sam. *Bakunin on Anarchy*. New York, 1972.
Donnelly, Alton S. *The Russian Conquest of Bashkiria*. New Haven, Connecticut, 1968.
Dostoevsky, F. *Crime and Punishment*. New York, 1968.
Dudley, Donald R. *History of Cynicism From Diogenes to the Sixth Century A.D.* London, 1937.

Dumas, Alexandre. *Impressions de Voyage*. Volume I. Paris, 1900.

Durga Das. *India From Curzon to Nehru and After*. London, 1969.

Dwarkadas, Kanji. *Gandhiji Through My Diary Leaves*. Bombay, 1950.

Eikhenbaum, B. *Tolstoy in the Seventies*. Ann Arbor, Michigan, 1981.

————. *Tolstoy in the Sixties*. Ann Arbor, Michigan, 1981.

————. *The Young Tolstoy*. Ann Arbor, Michigan, 1972.

Elwin, Verrier. *The Tribal World of Verrier Elwin*. Bombay, 1966.

Elwin, V. and Winslow, J. *Gandhi: The Dawn of Indian Freedom*. New York, 1930.

Erikson, Erik. *Gandhi's Truth: On the Origin of Militant Non-Violence*. New York, 1969.

Fanger, Donald. *Dostoevsky and Romantic Realism*. Cambridge, Mass., 1967.

Fedotov, G. P. *The Russian Religious Mind*. Cambridge, Mass., 1960.

Feuer, K.B. "The Genesis of War and Peace." Unpublished Dissertation. Columbia University, 1965.

Field, Daniel. *The End of Serfdom*. Cambridge, Mass., 1976.

————. *Rebels in the Name of the Tsar*. Boston, Mass., 1976.

Figner, Vera. *Memoirs of a Revolutionist*. New York, 1922.

Fischer, Louis. *Life of Mahatma Gandhi*. New York, 1950. (Only when signaled).

————. *Life of Mahatma Gandhi*. New York, 1954.

Florovsky, George. *Christianity and Culture*. Belmont, Mass., 1978.

Forster, R. and Green, Jack P. *Preconditions of Revolution in Early Modern Europe*. Baltimore, Maryland, 1970.

Frank, J. *Dostoevsky*. Princeton, New Jersey, 1976.

Freeze, Gregory L. *Russian Levites*. Cambridge, Mass., 1977.

Fülop-Miller, R. *Lenin and Gandhi*. London, 1927.

————. *Tolstoy: New Light on His Life and Genius*. New York, 1931.

Gallie, W. B. *Philosophers of Peace and War*. Cambridge, 1978.

Gandhi Marg. Volume I. Bombay, 1957. A quarterly journal of Gandhian thought.

Gandhi, M. K. *Collected Works*. Volume I. Ahmedabad, 1958.

————. *An Autobiography*. Washington, D.C., 1948 (Boston, 1960).

————. *My Dear Child*. Ahmedabad, 1956.

————. *Satyagraha in South Africa*. Stanford, California, 1954.

Gandhi, Madan C. *Gandhian Aesthetics*. New Delhi, 1969.

Gandhi, Prabhudas. *My Childhood With Gandhiji*. Ahmedabad, 1957.

Gandy, D. Ross. *Marx and History*. Austin, Texas, 1979.

Ganguly, B. N. *Gandhi's Social Philosophy*. New Delhi, 1973.

Gerstein, Linda. *Nikolai Strakhov*. Cambridge, Mass., 1971.

Gifford, Henry., ed. *Leo Tolstoy: Penguin Critical Anthology*. London, 1971.

Gillard, David. *The Struggle for Asia*. London, 1977.

Glaspell, Susan. *The Road to the Temple*. New York, 1927.

Gleason, Abbott. *European and Muscovite*. Cambridge, Mass., 1972.

————. *Young Russia*. New York, 1980.

Gogol, N. *Taras Bulba*. Translated by John Cournos. London, 1954.

Goldenveizer, A. B. *Talks with Tolstoi*. Translated by S. S. Koteliansky and V. Woolf. London, 1923.

Goncharov, I. *Oblomov*. Translated by D. Magarshack. London, 1954.

Gopal, Ram. *How India Struggled For Freedom*. Bombay, 1967.

Gorky, M. *Reminiscences of Tolstoy, Chekhov and Andreev*. New York, 1946.

Gudzy, N. K. *History of Early Russian Literature*. New York, 1970.

Gupta, A., ed. *Studies in the Bengal Renaissance*. Calcutta, 1958.

Guser, N. N., and Mishin, V. S., eds. *Tolstoy in the Memory of his Contemporaries*. Leningrad, 1955.

Haimsun, Leopold H. *The Russian Marxists and the Origins of Bolshevism*. Cambridge, Mass., 1967.

Haithcox, J. G. *Communism and Nationalism in India*. Princeton, New Jersey, 1971.

Hammond, Dorothy and Jablow, Alta. *The Africa That Never Was*. New York, 1970.

Hay, S. N. *Asian Ideas of East and West*. Cambridge, Mass., 1970.

————. "Gandhi's First Five Years," in *Encounter With Erikson*. Edited by D. Capps, etc. Missoula, Montana, 1977.

Herzen, A. *My Past and Thoughts*. New York, 1968.

Hingley, R. *A New Life of Anton Chekhov*. New York, 1976.

————. *Russian Writers and Society*. New York, 1969.

Hobson, J. A. *Imperialism*. London, 1902.

Hutchins, F. *The Illusion of Permanence*. Princeton, N.J., 1967.

Hunt, J. D. *Gandhi in London*. New Delhi, 1978.

Hutton, J. M. *Caste in India*. New York, 1963.

Huttenback, R. A. *The British Imperial Achievement*. New York, 1966.

————. *Gandhi in South Africa*. Ithaca, N.Y., 1971.

————. *Racism and Empire*. Ithaca, N.Y., 1976.

Huxley, Aldous. *Jesting Pilate*. London, 1948.

James, William. *The Writings of William James*. Edited by John J. McDermott. New York, 1967.

Jules-Verne, J. *Jules Verne*. New York, 1976.

Kalelkar, D. *Stray Glimpses of Bapu*. Ahmedabad, 1950.

Karlinsky, Simon. *Anton Chekhov's Life and Thought*. New York, 1973.

Kelly, Laurence. *Lermontov*. New York, 1978.

Kenworthy, John C. *A Pilgrimage to Tolstoy*. 1896.

Kipling, R. *The Light That Failed*. New York, 1969.

Klyuchevsky, V. O. *Peter the Great*. London, 1958.

Koestler, A. *Darkness at Noon*. London, 1941.

Korolenko, V. G. *History of My Contemporary*. London, 1972.

Kravchinsky, Serge. *Underground Russia*. New York, 1883.

Krishnadas. *Seven Months With Mahatma Gandhi*. Ahmedabad, 1959.

Kropotkin, P. *Selected Writings on Anarchism and Revolution*. Cambridge, Mass., 1970.

Kumar, R., ed. *Essays on Gandhian Politics*. New York, 1971.

Kuzminskaya, T. S. *Tolstoy As I Knew Him*. New York, 1948.

Lenin, V. O. L. N. *Tolstom*. Edited by S. M. Breitburg. Moscow, 1969.

Lensen, G. A. *Russia's Eastward Expansion*. Englewood Cliffs, New Jersey, 1964.

Lester, Muriel. *Entertaining Gandhi*. London, 1932.

Lipsey, Roger. *Coomaraswamy: His Life and Work*. Princeton, New Jersey, 1977.

Lyons, John D. *The Invention of the Self*. Carbondale, Illinois, 1978.

McLean, Hugh. *Nikolai Leskov*. Cambridge, Mass., 1977.

McLellan, David. *Karl Marx: His Life and Thought*. London, 1973.

The Mahabharata. 18th ed. Translated by C. Rajagopalachari. Bombay, 1976.

Maitland, Edward. *Life of Anna Kingsford*. London, 1895.

————. *The Perfect Way*. London, 1890. (With Anna Kingsford).

Malgonkar, Manohar. *The Men Who Killed Gandhi*. New Delhi, 1978.

Malia, Martin. *Alexander Herzen and the Birth of Russian Socialism*. Cambridge, Mass., 1961.

Markovitch, Milan I. *Tolstoi et Gandhi*. Paris, 1928.

Marx, K. *Capital*. London, 1974.

————. *On Colonialism*. New York, 1972. (With Friedrich Engels).

Masaryk, T. G. *The Spirit of Russia*. London, 1919.

Mashruwala, K. *Gandhi and Marx*. Ahmedabad, 1951.

Matlaw, R. E., ed. *Belinsky, Chernyshevsky, and Dobrolyubov*. Bloomington, Indiana, 1976.

Maude, Aylmer. *Family Views of Tolstoy*. Boston, 1926.

————. *Life of Tolstoy*. London, 1908.

————. *Tolstoy and His Problems*. London, 1901.

Mehta, Ved. *Mahatma Gandhi and His Apostles*. New York, 1977.

Melotti, U. *Marx and the Third World*. Translated by P. Ransford. New Jersey, 1972.

Mendel, Arthur P. *Dilemmas of Progress in Tsarist Russia*. Cambridge, Mass., 1961.

Merezhkovski, D. S. *Peter and Alexis*. London, 1905.

————. *Tolstoy as Man and Artist*. London, 1902.

Miliukov, Paul. *Outlines of Russian Culture*. Translated by Vignet and Davis. Philadelphia, 1948.

————. *Russia and Its Crisis*. New York, 1962.

————. *Russian Culture: Origins of Ideology*. Translated by J. L. Wieczynski. Florida, 1974.

Miller, Wright. *Russians As People*. New York, 1961.

Moon, Penderel. *Gandhi and Modern India*. New York, 1969.

Morris, James. *Heaven's Command*. New York, 1973.

————. *Pax Britannica*. New York, 1978.

Morton, Eleanor. *The Women In Gandhi's Life*. New York, 1953.

Mukherjee, H. U. *Bipin Chandra Pal and India's Struggle for Swaraj*. Berkeley, Calif., 1958.

Munshi, K. M. *I Follow the Mahatma*. Bombay, 1940.

Muratov, M. V. *Tolstoi i Chertkov*. Moscow, 1934.

Nag, Kalidas. *Tolstoy and Gandhi*. Calcutta, 1950.

Nanda, B. R. *Gokhale, Gandhi, and the Nehrus*. London, 1974.

————. *The Nehrus*. New York, 1963.

Nehru, Jawarhalal. *A Bunch of Old Letters*. New York, 1960.

————. *The Discovery of India*. New York, 1960.

————. *Glimpses of World History*. New York, 1962.

————. *Towards Freedom*. Boston, Mass., 1958.

Nikitenko, A. L. *Diary of a Russian Censor*. Amherst, Mass., 1975.

Norman, Dorothy. *Nehru: The First Sixty Years*. New York, 1965.

O'Flaherty, W. D. *Hindu Myths*. London, 1975.

Orme, Robert. *History of the Military Transactions of the British Nation in Indostan*. London, 1780.

Pal, Bipin Chandra. *My Life and Times*. Calcutta, 1932.

Pandey, B. N. *Indian National Movement*. New York, 1979.

————. *Nehru*. New York, 1976.

Parikh, Narahari D. *Mahadev Desai's Early Life*. Ahmedabad, 1953.

Parker, W. H. *An Historical Geography of Russia*. Chicago, 1968.

Payne, R. *The Life and Death of Mahatma Gandhi*. New York, 1969.

Phelps, G. *The Russian Novel in English Fiction*. London, 1955.

Philipp, F. H. *Tolstoj Und Der Protestantismus*. Giessen, 1959.

Philipson, M. *The Count Who Wished He Were a Peasant*. New York, 1967.

Pomper, Philip. *Peter Lavrov and the Russian Revolutionary Movement*. Chicago, 1972.

————. *Sergei Nechaev*. Brunswick, New Jersey, 1977.

Prabhu, R. K. *This Was Bapu*. Ahmedabad, 1954.

Prasad, Madho. *A Gandhian Patriarch*. New Delhi, 1965.

Prasad, Rajendra. *At the Feet of Mahatma Gandhi*. New York, 1961.

————. *Autobiography*. Bombay, 1957.

Presniakov, A. E. *Emperor Nicholas I of Russia*. Florida, 1974.

Proffer, C. and E. *The Silver Age of Russian Culture*. Ann Arbor, Michigan, 1975.

Purves, J. G. and West, D. A. *War and Society in 19th Century Russia*. Toronto, 1972.

Pushkin, A. *Pushkin on Literature*. Edited by Tatiana Wolff. London, 1971.

————. *Works of Pushkin*. Edited by Yamolinsky. New York, 1936.

Putnam, A. G. *Russian Alternatives to Marxism.* Knoxville, Tennessee, 1977.

Pyarelal. *Mahatma Gandhi. Volume I: The Early Phase.* Ahmedabad, 1965.

————. *Mahatma Gandhi. Volume II: The Last Phase.* Ahmedabad, 1956.

Raddatz, Fritz J. *Karl Marx: A Political Biography.* Boston, 1978.

Radhakrishnan, S., ed. *Mahatma Gandhi.* London, 1949.

————. *One Hundred Years.* New Delhi, 1968.

Radhakrishnan, S. R. S. *Vinoba and His Mission.* Wardha, 1948.

Raeff, M. *The Decembrist Movement.* New Jersey, 1966.

————. *Michael Speransky.* The Hague, 1969.

————. *Origins of the Russian Intelligentsia.* New York, 1966.

————., ed. *Peter the Great.* Boston, 1963.

Rai, Lala Lajpat. *Autobiographical Writings.* New Delhi, 1965.

Rai, Lala Danpat. *Life Story of Lala Lajpat Rai.* New Delhi, 1976.

Ramachandran, G. *Gandhigram Thoughts and Talks.* Bombay, 1964.

————., ed. *Gandhi: His Relevance For Our Times,* Bombay, 1964.

————. *A Sheaf of Gandhi Anecdotes.* Bombay, 1945.

The Ramayana. Translated by C. Rajagopalachari. Bombay, 1975.

Rao, G. Ramachandra. *An Atheist With Gandhi.* Ahmedabad, 1951.

Rao, M. B. and Sardasai, S. G., eds. *The Mahatma.* New Delhi, 1969.

Ray, S., ed. *Gandhi, India, and the World.* Bombay, 1970.

Reynolds, R. *A Quest for Gandhi.* New York, 1952.

Riasanovsky, N. "Nicholas I and the Course of Russian History," in A. E. Presniakov, *Emperor Nicholas I of Russia.* Gulf Breeze, Fla., 1974.

————. *History of Russia.* New York, 1977.

————. *Nicholas I and Official Nationality in Russia.* Berkeley, 1969.

————. *A Parting of the Ways.* New York, 1976.

————. *Russia and the West in the Teaching of the Slavophiles.* Cambridge, Mass., 1952.

Rice, Martin F. *Valery Briusov and the Rise of Russian Symbolism.* Ann Arbor, 1975.

Riha, Thomas. *Readings in Russian Civilization.* Chicago, 1964.

Rolland, R. *Prophets of The New India.* New York, 1936.

————. *Inde: Journal 1915–43.* Paris, 1951.

————. *Rolland-Gandhi Correspondence.* New Delhi, 1976.

————. *Tolstoy.* New York, 1911.

Rousseau, J. J. *Reveries of a Solitary Walker.* Translated by Peter France. London, 1979.

Roy, D. K. *Among the Great.* Bombay, 1945.

Roy, M. N. and Spratt, P. *Beyond Communism.* Bombay, 1947.

Roy, Samoyen. *The Restless Brahmin.* Bombay, 1970.

Rudolph, L. and S. *The Modernity of Tradition.* Chicago, 1967.

Saksena, M. *Motilal Nehru.* New Delhi, 1961.

Schwartz, B. *In Search of Wealth and Power.* Cambridge, Mass., 1964.

Sergeenko, P. *Tolstoy and His Contemporaries.* Moscow, 1911.

Shahani, R. *Mr. Gandhi.* New York, 1961.

Shah, Kantilal, ed. *Vinoba on Gandhi.,* 1973.

Shaw, Nellie. *Whiteway: A Colony on the Cotswolds.* London, 1935.

Shklovsky, V. *Leo Tolstoy.* Translated by Olga Shartse. Moscow, 1978.

Shub, David. *Lenin.* New York, 1948.

Shukla, Chandrashankar. *Incidents of Gandhiji's Life.* New Delhi, 1949.

————. *Reminiscences of Gandhiji,* n.d.

Simmons, E. J. *Leo Tolstoy.* Boston, 1946.

————. *Leo Tolstoy.* Boston, 1973.

————. *Pushkin.* Cambridge, Mass., 1937.

Singam, S. D. R. *Anamda Coomaraswamy: Remembering and Remembering Again and Again.* Petading Jaya, 1974.

Sinha, M. P. *The Contemporary Relevance of Gandhi*. Bombay, 1970.
Slade, Madline. *Letters to a Disciple*. London, 1951.
————. *The Spirit's Pilgrimage*. London, 1978.
Smedley, Agnes. *Battle Hymn of China*. London, 1978.
Snyder, Louis. *The Imperialism Reader*. Princeton, N.J., 1962.
Soloviev, V. *A Solovyov Anthology*. Edited By S. L. Frank. Translated by N. Dudding-
    ton. New York, 1950.
Spear, P. *The History of India*. Volume II. London, 1973.
————. *The Nabobs*. Oxford, 1963.
Spector, I and M. *Readings in Russian History and Culture*. Boston, 1965.
Spratt, P. *Blowing Up India*. Calcutta, 1955.
Sprigge, C. J. S. *Karl Marx*. New York, 1962.
Starr, J. F. *Decentralization and Self-Government in Russia 1830-1870*. Princeton, New
    Jersey, 1972.
Sukhotina-Tolstoy, Tatiana. *The Tolstoy Home*. Translated by Alec Brown.
————. *Tolstoy Remembered*. Translated by Derek Coltman. London, 1977.
Sumner, B. H. *Survey of Russian History*. London, 1944.
————. *Tsardom and Imperialism*. New York, 1968.
Swinson, A. *Six Minutes to Sunset*. London, 1964.
Szamuely, T. *The Russian Tradition*. London, 1974.
Tagore, R. *Creative Unity*. Calcutta, 1971.
————. *A Tagore Reader*. Edited by A. Chakravarty. Boston, 1966.
Tandon, Prakash. *Beyond Punjab*. New Delhi, 1971.
Tendulkar, D. G. *The Mahatma*. Volume I. New Delhi, 1951.
Tennyson, Hallam. *India's Walking Saint*. New York, 1955.
Thaden, E. C. *Conservative Nationalism in 19th Century Russia*. University of Washing-
    ton, 1964.
Theen, Rolf H. W. *Lenin*. New York, 1973.
Thompson, Edward. *The Other Side of the Medal*. Connecticut, 1974.
Thompson, E. P. *William Morris*. New York, 1977.
Tinker, Hugh. *A New System of Slavery*. New York, 1974.
Tolf, R. W. *The Russian Rockefellers*. Stanford, Calif., 1976.
Tolstoy, Alexandra. *Tolstoy: A Life of My Father*. Translated by E. R. Hapgood. New
    York, 1953.
————. *The Tragedy of Tolstoy*. London, 1933.
Tolstoy, Ilya. *Reminiscences of Tolstoy*. London, 1914.
Tolstoy, Leon L. *The Truth About My Father*. London, 1924.
Tolstoy, L. N. *Anna Karenina*. Translated by D. Magarshack. New York, 1961.
————. *Childhood, Boyhood, Youth*. Translated by Rosemary Edmonds. New York,
    1972.
————. *Tolstoy's Writings on Civil Disobedience and Non-Violence*. New York, 1967.
————. *Complete Works of Tolstoy*. Edited by L. Wiener. Boston, 1904.
————. *The Cossacks*. Translated by A. R. McAndrew. New York, 1961.
————. *Circle of Reading*. New York, 1911.
————. *Diaries 1947-52*. Translated by C. J. Hogarth and A. Smith. London, 1917.
————. *Diary, 1953-7*. Translated by A. Maude. New York, 1927.
————. *Essays from Tula*. London, 1948.
————. *Father Sergius, etc.* Edited by Hagberg Wright. New York, 1911.
————. *Forged Coupon*. Edited by Hagberg Wright. New York, 1912.
————. *Journal of Leo Tolstoy 1895-9*. Translated by Rose Strunsky. New York, 1917.
————. *The Kingdom of God is Within You*. New York, 1961.
————. *Law of Love and the Law of Violence*. New York, 1970.
————. *Les Quatre Livres De La Lecture*. Paris, 1928.

————. *Letters of Tolstoy and Alexandra Tolstoy.* Translated by Leo Islavin. London, 1929.

————. *On Life.* Translated by A. Maude. London, 1934.

————. *The Pathway of Life.* Translated by Archibald Wolfe. New York, 1919.

————. *Tolstoy On Art.* Edited by Aylmer Maude. Boston 1924.

————. *Polnoe Sobranie Khudozhestvennykh Proizvedenii Lva Tolstovo.* Edited by I. I. Glivenko and M. A. Tsuavkivskii, beginning in Moscow, 1928. (The Jubilee Edition.)

————. *Portable Tolstoy.* Edited by Bayberg. New York, 1978.

————. *Recollections and Essays.* Translated by A. Maude. London, 1937.

————. *Rede gegen den Krieg.* Frankfurt, 1968.

————. *Resurrection.* London, 1916.

————. *Sebastopol.* Ann Arbor, Mich., 1961.

————. *Short Stories.* Introduction by L. Leonov. Moscow, 1960.

————. *Sobranie Sochinenii Lva Tolstovo.* Moscow, 1960.

————. *Socialisme et Christianisme: Correspondence Tolstoi-Birioukoff.* Paris, 1957.

————. *Tolstoy's Letters.* Translated by R. F. Christian. New York, 1978.

————. *Tolstoy's Love Letters.* Translated by S. S. Koteliansky and V. Woolf. London, 1923.

————. *War and Peace.* Edited by G. Gibian. New York, 1966.

Tolstoy, Sergei. *Tolstoy Remembered by His Son.* Translated by M. Budberg. London, 1961.

Tolstoy, Sonia. *Autobiography of Countess Sophie Tolstoy.* Translated by S. S. Koteliansky and L. Woolf. London, 1922.

————. *Countess Tolstoy's Later Diary.* Translated by A. Werth. New York, 1929.

————. *Diary of Tolstoy's Wife.* Translated by A. Werth. London, 1928.

————. *The Final Struggle.* Edited and translated by A. Maude. New York, 1936.

Tolstoy, Tania. *Tolstoy Remembered.* London, 1977.

————. *Tolstoy Remembered.* New York, 1977.

Troyat, H. *Tolstoy.* New York, 1967.

Tulsidas, *The Holy Lake of the Acts of Rama.* Translated by W. Douglas Hill. Cambridge, 1952.

Twain, M. *Roughing It.* New York, 1962.

Tyler, J. E. *The Struggle for Imperial Unity.* London, 1938.

Ulam, A. *In the Name of the People.* New York, 1977.

Upadhyaya, J. M. *Mahatma Gandhi—A Teacher's Discovery.* Ahmedabad, 1969.

Venturi, F. *The Roots of Revolution.* New York, 1960.

Vucinich, A. *Science in Russian Culture.* Stanford, Cal., 1963.

————. *Social Thought in Tsarist Russia.* Chicago, 1976.

Watson, F., and Brown, M. *The Trial of Mr. Gandhi.* London, 1969.

————. *Talking of Gandhiji.* London, 1957.

Weisbein, Nicholas. *L'Evolution Religieuse De Tolstoi.* Paris, 1960.

Wellock, W. *Off the Beaten Track.* Varanasi, 1963.

Winsten, Stephen. *Salt and His Circle.* London, 1951.

Wiser, W. W. and C. V. *Behind Mud Walls.* Los Angeles, 1963.

Wolfe, B. *Three Who Made A Revolution.* Boston, 1948.

Wolpert, S. A. *Tilak and Gokhale.* Berkeley, Calif., 1962.

Yajnik, I. K. *Gandhi As I Knew Him.* New Delhi, 1943.

Yule, H., and A. C. Burnett. *Hobson-Jobson: a Glossary of Anglo-Indian Words.* London, 1905.

Zenkovsky, V. V. *A History of Russian Philosophy.* Translated by G. L. Kline. New York, 1953.

Zernov, N. *Three Russian Prophets.* London, 1944.

Index